Settler Societies

University of the
West of England

BRISTOL

**ST. MATTHIAS
LIBRARY**

SAGE SERIES ON RACE AND ETHNIC RELATIONS

Series Editor:
JOHN H. STANFIELD II
College of William and Mary

This series is designed for scholars working in creative theoretical areas related to race and ethnic relations. The series will publish books and collections of original articles that critically assess and expand upon race and ethnic relations issues from American and comparative points of view.

Volumes in this series include

Unsettling Settler Societies

Articulations of Gender, Race, Ethnicity and Class

Daiva Stasiulis
Nira Yuval-Davis
editors

Sage Series on Race and Ethnic Relations

v o l u m e   1 1

SAGE Publications
London • Thousand Oaks • New Delhi

Editorial arrangement and Chapter 1 © Daiva Stasiulis and
Nira Yuval-Davis 1995
Chapter 2 © Wendy Larner and Paul Spoonley 1995
Chapter 3 © Jan Jindy Pettman 1995
Chapter 4 © Daiva Stasiulis and Radha Jhappan 1995
Chapter 5 © Dolores Janiewski 1995
Chapter 6 © Natividad Gutiérrez 1995
Chapter 7 © Sarah A. Radcliffe 1995
Chapter 8 © Elaine Unterhalter 1995
Chapter 9 © Susie Jacobs 1995
Chapter 10 © Anissa Hélie 1995
Chapter 11 Nahla Abdo and Nira Yuval-Davis 1995

First published 1995

SAGE Publications Ltd
6 Bonhill Street
London EC2A 4PU

SAGE Publications Inc
2455 Teller Road
Thousand Oaks, California 91320

SAGE Publications India Pvt Ltd
32, M-Block Market
Greater Kailash – I
New Delhi 110 048

British Library Cataloguing in Publication data

A catalogue record for this book is
available from the British Library

ISBN 0 8039 8693 9
ISBN 0 8039 8694 7 (pbk)

Library of Congress catalog card number 95-068149

Typeset by M Rules
Printed in Great Britain by Biddles Ltd, Guildford, Surrey

Contents

Foreword

During the past 30 years, scholars have become increasingly interested in comparative race and ethnic studies. Especially during the mid-1960s to mid-1970s, there was much debate about the comparative characteristics of societies created through European-descent domination and exploitation. Most of these attempts to define and study such 'settler societies' dead-ended with efforts in developing historically static topologies portraying idealized frozen states of such societies. The lack of sophisticated attention paid to the complexities and material dialectics of historical processes as well as imbalances in status analyses resulted in a comparative literature of plural and/or settler societies which was grossly inadequate.

The major consequence of the absence of material dialectical historical analysis in settler society research has been the neglect of or, better yet, the oversimplification of the roles of the consciousness, movements and political economic contributions of the racialized oppressed in the formation of such societies. The imbalance in status analyses has meant the focus on affluent male-centric issues regarding the roles of dominant and oppressed populations in the construction of European-descent settler societies.

This book fills an important gap in the comparative race and ethnicity field. It offers sophisticated case-by-case societal and regional level analyses of the historical materialistic dynamics behind the construction and transformation of settler societies. The roles of women, people of colour, indigenous people and the poor are centred in efforts to establish a more complex and accurate perspective on the histories, politics and social organization of settler societies around the world. The Introduction offers an inviting theoretical overview of issues which cannot help but begin to change the minds of many scholars who have assumed that the last word has been written on the sociological and political nature of settler societies.

John H. Stanfield II
Race and Ethnic Relations Editor

Acknowledgements

The vast historical and geographical scope of this book required feedback from many expert readers. The following friends and colleagues, each experts on the different case studies in the book, graciously agreed to read and comment on individual chapters, indicated in the parentheses. For their thorough, detailed and incisive comments on various drafts of the chapters, we would like to thank: Abigail Bakan (Canada); Jacky Cock (South Africa); Avishai Ehrlich (Palestine/Israel); Cynthia Enloe (United States); Marie de Lepervanche (Australia); Marie-Aimée Hélie-Lucas (Algeria); Rosemary du Plessis (New Zealand); Donna Pankhurst and Terence Ranger (Zimbabwe); Marilyn Thompson and Judith Moe (Mexico); Gina Vargas (Peru); and Radha Jhappan and Wendy Larner who read the Introduction. We also wish to thank Margaret Phillips for her research and assistance on the Introduction and the chapter on Canada. The responsibility for the contents of the text, however, is strictly that of the authors.

We also wish to acknowledge John H. Stanfield II and Stephen Barr, Karen Phillips and Rosemary Campbell from Sage for their sustained support and encouragement in getting on with this ambitious and difficult endeavour. We are grateful for the financial support of the British Council (Canada) and Carleton University (GR-6)

This book is dedicated to all those who are involved in progressive struggles to transform settler societies beyond dichotomies.

Biographical Notes

Nahla Abdo is a Palestinian living in Canada. She is an Assistant Professor of Sociology at Carleton University, Ottawa. She has published extensively on women, the political economy and politics in the Middle East. She is currently conducting research into women, law and democratization in the West Bank and Gaza Strip.

Natividad Gutiérrez is a sociologist who teaches theories and problems of nationalism at the London School of Economics. She is a founding member of the Association of Ethnicity and Nationalism (ASEN). She is currently undertaking research on the critical responses of ethnic groups to the nation-building project. Her other research interests include the rise of ethic intelligentsia, women and nationalism and the militarization of indigenous peoples.

Anissa Hélie was born in Algeria on February 24, 1964 – the day of nationalization of oil in Algeria. Her parents were involved in the national liberation struggle and she comes from a line of feminist women – mother, grandmother, great aunt and great grandmother. After completing secondary education in Algeria, an MA on Women's History in France and an MA in Women's Studies in Holland, she is currently finishing a PhD in Women's History on European women primary school teachers during colonization in Algeria. She is working within the international solidarity group, Women Living Under Muslim Laws, where she has been handling many solidarity campaigns.

Susie Jacobs was born in Houston, Texas. She studied at the London School of Economics and obtained her D.Phil. at the Institute of Development Studies, University of Sussex. She has worked in north-eastern areas of Zimbabwe and has published various articles on aspects of gender, land and the state in Zimbabwe and elsewhere. She currently teaches sociology at Manchester Metropolitan University.

Dolores Janiewski holds a Senior Lectureship in US History at Victoria University of Wellington, New Zealand. Among her previous publications are *Sisterhood Denied: Race, Gender and Class in a New South Community* (Temple University Press, 1985, 1993) and various articles dealing with labour history, women's history and race relations. She is currently working on *Passion, Power and Punishment: Citizenship and*

Criminality in North Carolina, 1866–1932 (University of North Carolina Press, forthcoming). Her other research interests include gender, colonization, Native Americans and settler societies from a comparative perspective. She received her PhD in History from Duke University in 1979.

Radha Jhappan is an Assistant Professor in Political Science at Carleton University, Ottawa. Born and raised in Guyana of Indian and Irish parents, and educated in England, she has published many papers on the politics of indigenous peoples and specializes in law and constitutional politics.

Wendy Larner was a Lecturer in Geography at the University of Waikato, New Zealand. She is currently a Commonwealth Scholar at Carleton University, Ottawa. Her research is on economic globalization, restructuring, and changing sexual and spatial divisions of labour.

Jan Jindy Pettman is a Senior Lecturer in Political Science at the Australian National University. She has recently published *Living in the Margins: Racism, Sexism and Feminism in Australia* and is currently writing a book on gender and international politics.

Sarah A. Radcliffe lectures in Geography at Royal Holloway, University of London. She is the co-editor of *Viva: Women and Popular Protest in Latin America* (Routledge, 1993).

Paul Spoonley is Associate Professor and Associate Dean of Social Sciences at Massey University's Auckland campus at Albany, as well as a member of the Department of Sociology. He is the author or editor of 16 books including *Racism and Ethnicity* (Oxford University Press, 1993) and *New Zealand Society* (Dunmore Press, 1994), as well as an editor of *New Zealand Sociology*. His current research is on the labour market participation of Maori, right-wing extremism and the politics of majority/dominant groups.

Daiva Stasiulis is Associate Professor of Sociology at Carleton University, Ottawa. Born in Canada of Lithuanian and Estonian parents, she has written extensively on racism, multiculturalism, and the responses of the state, the feminist and other social movements to ethnic diversity and racism. Her current research includes an investigation of domestic workers and nurses from the Philippines and West Indies which explores the racial and gender boundaries of citizenship. She is co-editor of *Not One of the Family: Foreign Domestic Workers in Canada* (University of Toronto Press, forthcoming).

Elaine Unterhalter is the Director of Research on Education in Southern Africa (RESA) based at the Institute of Education, University of London. She was born in South Africa and educated in South Africa and Britain. She has written on the experience of colonial rule in Zululand, South African women's organization and education in South Africa. She co-edited the writings of the Women in South African History (WISH) group and two collections on the transformation of South African education, *Apartheid Education and Popular Struggles* (Rauan, 1991) and *Education in a Future South Africa: Policy Issues for Transformation* (Heinemann, 1991).

Nira Yuval-Davis is an Israeli who lives in London where she is a Reader in Gender and Ethnic Studies at the University of Greenwich. She has written extensively on women, nationalism, racism and fundamentalism mainly in Israel and Britain. Among others, she co-edited *Woman-Nation-State* (Macmillan, 1989) and *Refusing Holy Orders: Women and Fundamentalism in Britain* (Virago, 1992) and has co-written *Racialized Boundaries: Race, Nation, Gender, Colour and Class and the Anti-Racist Struggle* (Routledge, 1992). She is currently finishing *Gender and Nation* (Sage, forthcoming).

1

Introduction: Beyond Dichotomies – Gender, Race, Ethnicity and Class in Settler Societies

Daiva Stasiulis and Nira Yuval-Davis

The complex articulations of race, ethnicity, nation, class and gender that form the subject of this book on 'settler societies' have only recently been explored within feminist literature. Analyses of societal development in mainstream social science have generally been inattentive to these multiple and intersecting social relations. When comparative models of ethnicity and race typologies have been attempted (see Schermerhorn, 1970; Rex, 1983; van den Berghe, 1979), they have tended to construct ethnic and racial collectivities as organic wholes and have failed to examine their inter-class, gender and other social relations. The chapters in this book join a small but growing body of work which has begun to tackle these issues (for example, Anthias and Yuval-Davis, 1983, 1992; Bottomley et al., 1991; Enloe, 1989; Kandiyoti, 1991; Pettman, 1992; Stasiulis, 1987, 1990). Moreover, the analyses in this book reflect a long-standing preoccupation among its editors and contributors with rendering a richer and more complex sense of political economy and social transformation – one that is inextricably bound up with gendered, racial/ethnic and class relations.

The impetus for this book arose from two observations on the part of its editors. First, whatever their variations in historical genesis and development, settler societies share certain common features and challenges pertaining to the coexistence of diverse indigenous and migrant collectivities. Furthermore, these commonalities stem from the foundational claims made by European migrant groups intent on settlement and on the building of self-sustaining states independent of metropolitan centres. Further similarities pertain to the settlers' political domination over the indigenous populations as well as other racialized minorities.

Secondly, while comparative analyses of settler societies have led to various insights into societies which have developed relatively advanced economies in conjunction with colonial and other hierarchies of privilege, most of this work has remained untouched by the growing body of feminist scholarship on the gendered constructions of colonization, nation, citizenship, the state, development and oppositional movements. Thus, while the concepts of class, colonialism, race and ethnicity figure prominently in studies of settler societies, gender and the distinctive hierarchical and interdependent relations of women from various national, ethnic and racial collectivities have for the most part been neglected. One major purpose of this book is to locate the shifting conditions and politics of women in settler societies within frameworks that provide a sense of the ways in which indigenous peoples, 'settlers' or superordinate migrants, and other migrants not regarded as 'settlers' have been constructed relative to one another.

The notion of 'settler societies' presented in this book is therefore, on one level, a concrete empirical phenomenon and historical reality and is analysed as such. Of course, in many settler societies the dominant groups have been forced to relinquish their dominance, sharing in the more general global decline in colonialism. In some classifications, however, they are considered to be just one of several sub-types of colonies (together with occupation colonies, mixed colonies and plantation colonies – see Fieldhouse, 1966; Fredrickson, 1988; Shafir, 1989). Nonetheless, as Weitzer (1990: 24–5) argues, because settler states represent 'home' to a dominant group, the intransigence of settlers regarding both indigenous resistance and metropolitan or other external pressures for change complicate the transformation of these states. Change in the form of accommodation of the claims of indigenous peoples and non-dominant migrants offers quite different challenges in 'settler societies' than those involved in the decolonization of 'conventional' colonies where the imperial power has not rooted itself through settlement.

On another level, the cleavages and conflicts that characterize 'settler societies' can be found in virtually all contemporary societies which have involved encounters between indigenous and migrant groups, and successive waves of free and coerced migration corresponding to different phases of capitalist development and political upheavals. Several authors have viewed settler societies as *extreme* examples of 'plural' societies, characterized by profound cleavages along racial, ethnic and religious lines (Kuper and Smith, 1969; Weitzer, 1990: xi). However, the current conflagrations in the former Yugoslavia and Rwanda, the fierce national and ethnic struggles in the former Soviet Union, and the racist violence perpetrated against 'foreigners' across Europe lend caution to such judgements. While the book concentrates on settler societies created primarily as a result of European settlement in non-European territories, it does not date the beginnings of these societies at the European invasion. Nor does it assume regional and ethnic conflicts resulting from conquest or other processes of settlement to be specific only to those countries. They exist and are far from being resolved in many areas of the third world and within Europe itself – including the countries from which the settlers originated. Indeed, the complex dynamics of gender, race, ethnicity and class analysed in the different case studies in this book exist, albeit in different combinations and intensities, in all societies. The case studies presented in this volume therefore invite comparisons with a variety of societies, including those not constructed as settler regimes.

If we define 'settler societies' as societies in which Europeans have settled, where their descendants have remained politically dominant over indigenous peoples, and where a heterogeneous society has developed in class, ethnic and racial terms, then it becomes clear that 'settler societies' must be seen as falling along a continuum rather than within clear and fixed boundaries. As elaborated below, our resistance to drawing an unambiguous line of demarcation between settler and other (colonial, post-colonial or metropolitan) societies is consistent with our understanding that the circuits of power are vastly more complicated both globally and in specific locations than any binary division allows. Moreover, the extent to which a society is a 'settler society' is contested by the de-colonizing movements of various ethno-national groups within. Settler colonization may play a more formative role in state formation and nation-building in some periods than in others. Different settler societies have ties to different colonial powers and forms of imperialism, as well as to diverse social movements; they have different demographic ratios of indigenous, European, non-European and mixed populations. Some (for example, Mexico and Algeria) are acknowledged more in the present-day as countries of emigration, rather than immigration.

'Settler societies' have complicated the neat dichotomy between Europe and the rest of the world insofar as they are distinct from 'colonies of exploitation' (Adam, 1972: 17). The latter typified a more common form of colonialism whereby the appropriation of land, natural resources and labour entailed indirect control by colonial powers through a 'thin white line', a relatively small, sojourning group of primarily male administrators, merchants, soldiers and missionaries. In contrast, settler societies were characterized by a much larger settler European population of both sexes for permanent settlement. Settler states developed much more elaborate political and economic infrastructures and 'achieved *de facto* or *de jure* political independence from the metropole' (Weitzer, 1990: 26).

Curiously, most of these societies maintained relations of dependency with their original 'sponsors', even as they achieved considerable political and economic autonomy from European colonial powers. In some instances, as in the case of the 'white dominions' (Canada, Australia and New Zealand), the dominant culture and institutions were fashioned directly on those of the 'mother' country (Britain).

Typically, settler societies featured extensive systems of exclusion and exploitation of both 'indigenous' and 'alien' peoples within, exercised through a variety of coercive, ideological, legal, administrative and cooptative mechanisms. One measure of the sense of broadly shared interests among settler societies has been the modelling and borrowing of systems of control over indigenous and migrant populations among settler states. Instances of this were the reserve and pass systems of control over indigenous peoples, which South African elites borrowed from Canada and Australia, and the 'Natal formula' used to restrict the entry of migrant people of colour throughout the British colonies of settlement.

The paradox of settler societies is that they simultaneously resisted and accommodated the authority of an imperialist Europe, where 'colonial rule was the foundry within which [non-European institutions and culture] were melted down and recast into new political alloys . . . compatible with European requirements' (Kennedy, 1987: 335). The relative prosperity, high material standards and liberal democratic governments of many settler societies have captured the attention of historians and political economists insofar as these were achieved in a context of dependence on European colonial powers for capital, transport and markets (Denoon, 1983; Ehrensaft and Armstrong, 1981; Panitch, 1981). But to the extent that the focus of these inquiries has been on the capitalist and liberal democratic achievements (and limitations) of settler societies, they often read as Eurocentric 'settler historiographies', categories in which indigenous peoples and others who are not considered to be settlers go missing (Abele and Stasiulis, 1989; Denoon, 1983: 207; McGrath, 1990: 191).

Historical accounts of settler colonies tend to focus on the transplanted habits, tastes and skills of a European capitalist culture among 'settlers' or more accurately among the racially and ethnically dominant settlers. This focus has had four consequences. First, by dating history or the 'formative period of history' in settler societies as coinciding with the beginnings of European colonization, it effaces and distorts the complex histories and societies of indigenous peoples which existed prior to and during prolonged periods of contact with Europeans. Where oral traditions rather than written records prevailed and historical periods were not clearly defined, the temptation has been for social scientists to construct for indigenous peoples 'a unitary and static "past" in which changing realities are reduced to the lowest common denominator' (Etienne and Leacock, 1980: 5). The 'prehistory' of (pre-contact) indigenous peoples is rendered irrelevant to the 'history' of settler societies, a dichotomy that exists in contemporary disciplinary boundaries between 'Native (or indigenous) studies' and 'history'. Secondly, the selective gaze on the institutions and values of British and other European migrants deflects attention from how diverse the 'settlers' and the settlement process in such societies have been. Hence, adventurers, merchants, homesteaders, convicts, slaves, indentured labourers, religious and political refugees and many other types of migrants – from many different European and non-European countries – have all shaped the settler societies to which they migrated.

Thirdly, analyses of settler societies have tended to concentrate on a relatively narrow range of societies – either those which have emerged as a result of British imperialism or those whose formative periods as settler societies took place during the nineteenth or early twentieth centuries. In spite of marked differences among the colonizing powers whose imperial projects included the transplanting of European communities, the settler communities established by, for example, the British, Spanish, French and Dutch had a number of characteristics and problems in common (Elliott, 1987; Pagden and Canny, 1987). Furthermore, as Weitzer (1990: 25) remarks, 'The period during which the foundations of settler domination were laid is . . . not the distinguishing feature; settler states were established in the seventeenth century in South Africa, the nineteenth century in Rhodesia and Liberia, the 1920s in Northern Ireland, and as late as the 1940s in Taiwan.'

Fourthly, analyses of settler states have tended to privilege one form of social relations and one form of domination – such as centre–periphery, class or race – and thus reduced the inherent complexity of the social relations in such societies (Wallerstein, 1979, 1980; Denoon, 1983; Huttenback, 1976). Moreover, the gendered character of nation-state building in settler colonies, recently problematized in feminist scholarship, has been almost entirely ignored in most (non-feminist) accounts of settler societies (Haggis, 1987; Yuval-Davis and Anthias, 1989). Moreover, few analyses of settler societies have examined how settler capitalism exacerbated and transformed relations based *simultaneously* on colonialism, capitalism, gender, class and race/ethnicity.

In this book we attempt to move beyond the dichotomies and compartmentalization which characterize the literature on settler societies, particularly those that separate the histories of indigenous peoples from those of (im)migrants, frameworks of colonialism versus migrant labour systems; race versus class; gender versus race; and so on. The different case studies – individually and in combination – reflect an understanding of settler societies which views the histories of indigenous and migrant peoples as interdependent, and which takes into account the gendered character of these histories. Each case study examines how the process of development of these settler societies, and the positions of indigenous and migrant peoples within them, reflects the place of these societies within a global economy, and internal dynamics based on articulations of race, gender, ethnicity and class. The ways in which these various social relations combine are explored in relation to state-building processes and ideologies, economic life and oppositional social movements.

While the historical period surveyed in the chapters varies, many of them are cognizant of the contemporary internationalization of production and the neo-liberal and neo-conservative cast of states, associated with the 'New World Order'. As Wendy Larner and Paul Spoonley suggest, the internationalization of the economies of countries such as New Zealand and many others with formative settler society histories profoundly challenges the regional economic orientation and identities of these societies; this problematizes the contemporary applicability of the concept 'settler society' to countries which had earlier been viewed by settlers as fragments of Britain (Spain, France or other metropolitan 'sponsors'). New Zealand and Australia view their future in the context of the Pacific Rim, not the British Commonwealth; Canada and Mexico in the context of North America, not Britain and Spain; and so forth. Several chapters, then, analyse the effects of contemporary globalization of production, the division of labour and the state, and concomitant New Right agendas on indigenous and migrant populations. They also explore the effects of these volatile and unsettling trends on the nationalist/ethnic/feminist projects and politics pursued by women in these diverse collectivities.

Beyond these commonalities, the individual case studies are diverse, reflecting the varied and distinctive histories of both the different countries and the contributors. Together, however, they represent a wider definition of the concept of 'settler societies' than the one currently dominating the literature. The latter generally only recognizes settler projects that have occurred during the nineteenth century onwards. We include studies of countries in which the foundations for European settlement occurred earlier, during the sixteenth and seventeenth centuries (Mexico, Peru, South Africa and the United States). Most settler societies analysed in this book were products of British colonial expansion. In addition to the so-called 'white dominions' of Australia, Canada and New Zealand, this volume includes South Africa and Zimbabwe, which similarly became part of the emerging British 'empire of free trade' but where, in contrast, the European settlers have always formed a numerical minority. The United States is also included; although it is usually taken to be either 'exceptional' or the ideal-typical case of a metropolitan society, Dolores Janiewski cogently makes the case that as the first settler society to gain independence, the US can usefully be compared to other settler colonies. Also included are cases of settler states which were sponsored by imperial powers other than

Britain (such as Spain for Mexico and Peru, and France for Algeria), those involving two European powers (France and Britain for Canada; Holland and Britain in South Africa) and one (Israel) which, although aided by Britain, was largely supported by international interests (western governments, especially the US, and diasporic Jewish communities). Interestingly, the Zionist settler model, it has been claimed, was the 'internal colonization' model developed by the Prussian government in its eastern frontiers during the second half of the nineteenth century (Shafir, 1993: 112).

In settler societies, European capitalist expansion saw movement not only of European capital, but also of European settlers and other types of migrants into non-European territories with pre-existing 'indigenous' societies. The process of establishing settler societies was accompanied by varying levels of physical and cultural genocide, alienation of indigenous land, disruption of indigenous societies, economies and governance, and movements of indigenous resistance. One of the main imperatives of settler rule, as identified by Weitzer (1990: 27), has been 'to consolidate control over the indigenous population . . . [in order to] prevent or contain natives' political mobilization, unrest, and threats to the system's stability and also to discourage metropolitan interference on their behalf.'

A second pillar of stable settler rule has been to maintain unity within the dominant or settler population, a cohesion which is never guaranteed given the prevalence of class, ethnic, religious and other divisions among settlers (Weitzer, 1990: 28). The historical development of settler regimes has been characterized by varying levels of privilege, protection, rights and oppression accorded to, as well as contested, by migrant populations. The evolution of these complex dynamics *vis-à-vis* both indigenous and migrant populations has occurred in very different ways in the different societies, as witnessed by such diverse outcomes as the collapse of settler rule in Rhodesia/Zimbabwe, the flight of almost the entire settler population on the eve of Algerian independence, the celebration of *mestizo* or race mixing in Mexico, and the extensive legitimation of Maori interests in New Zealand.

There were and are today important differences among the settler societies in demographic ratios of indigenous to non-indigenous populations, definitions of 'indigenousness', and claims to sovereignty and distinct status made by collectivities which are not historically part of 'first nations', yet have inhabited certain territories for long periods of time. There are also important variations in the official recognition and status accorded to the 'mixed race' populations. Embedded in almost all legal and popular discourses about mixed collectivities, however, are patriarchal and sexist as well as racist assumptions. A common pattern of sexual unions between settler and indigenous (as well as other subaltern) populations, at least at the early stages of settlement, was a 'double standard' – that of 'sexual apartheid' for indigenous men and settler women, but not for settler men and indigenous women (Weitzer, 1990: 30–1). Sarah Radcliffe's study of Peru in this volume illustrates, however, that the regulation and status outcomes of mixed sexual unions and miscegenation could be stunning in their complexity.

Finally, the extent to which various dominant settler groups have had control of the state to mould and control civil society according to their visions of settler societies has also varied (Greenberg, 1980: 49). The greater the degree of the settler state's political autonomy from the metropole, 'the greater the settlers' room for manoeuvre in moulding economic, social and political structures' (Weitzer, 1990: 26).

The concepts of '(white) settler society' and 'settler colony' are historical constructs, which often reveal as much about the hegemonic myths of colonial settlers as about historical patterns of societal development and state formation (Abele and Stasiulis, 1989). These hegemonic myths are gendered as well as racialized, consigning distinctive roles in production, reproduction and nation-building to indigenous and different groups of European and non-European women and men. Notwithstanding their primarily ideological nature, such concepts have continued relevance for these societies. They have been absorbed within the political and legal-juridical institutions, 'myths of origin' and national metaphors of these countries. They also have utility for multinational corporations who have profited immeasurably from the appropriation of indigenous lands and from the cheap and divided labour of racially, ethnically and gender-segmented labour markets. Hegemonic myths are both defended and contested in the competing claims of indigenous peoples, racially/ethnically dominant settlers and other migrants over such issues as land ownership and use, sovereignty, state representation, and institutional and cultural pluralism.

The political, economic, legal and symbolic ramifications of these competing claims are apparent in the current movements of indigenous peoples in different settler societies to reclaim lands and political rights usurped over centuries of European settlement. Land claims negotiations, litigation and constitutional struggles as well as forms of direct action such as blockades are being pursued to these ends (Jhappan, 1991; 1993). They are also evident in the anti-racist movements and politics of empowerment of racial and ethnic minorities who seek citizenship rights that are on a par with hegemonic settler groups, and policies that redress historical and contemporary forms of exclusion and oppression. As discussed below, women in indigenous and racial/ethnic minority communities have played particular roles in nationalist and oppositional movements which have simultaneously reflected their shared status and aspirations with men in their communities and their distinctive positions in colonial and capitalist configurations.

The Political Economy of 'Settler Societies'

The broad variations in settler societies render any generalizations about the particular forms of development pursued within these societies hazardous at best. Particular attempts have been made to find shared features of development, the best known of which is Donald Denoon's (1983) ambitious study of six settler societies in the southern hemisphere (Australia, New Zealand, South Africa, Argentina, Chile and Uruguay) from 1890 to 1914. In this book, Denoon attempts to answer the paradox of the 'rich dependency' (Panitch, 1981: 8), that is, why settler societies proved to be prosperous in comparison with conventional colonies, while following a course of development that was heavily reliant upon staples exports in a world market, and dependent upon Britain, the leading colonial power, for capital, markets and transport. In particular, Denoon challenges the notion that the foremost determinant in pursuing a path of dependent development was the direct intervention of the imperialist power, contending that 'unforced dependence' upon Britain came about through market forces rather than through direct imperial control (Denoon, 1983: 223). Denoon sees these societies as responding differently to world market conditions, with the specific forms of development varying in accordance with the particular alignment of social classes and the consequent policies pursued by settler states. Nonetheless, he identifies certain 'powerful strands of commonality among them', the most obvious ones being the 'absence (or the attenuated survival) of peasants' and of plantations whose existence would pose barriers to the penetration of capitalist relations of production (Denoon, 1983: 122–3). As revealed in the case studies of Zimbabwe, Palestine and Mexico, however, all of which had substantial peasant populations at the time of settler colonization, even such generalizations are problematic.

Denoon concedes important variations in the capacity of indigenous 'nomadic' peoples to withstand European invasion, with the Maoris of New Zealand surviving 'a generation of skirmishing and even a full-scale land war, to recover their numbers and sometimes to regain the initiative' (Denoon, 1983: 26–7). However, the absence of 'settled communities', particularly agricultural communities, which have denser populations than nomadic groups, was a major factor in facilitating a transition in these societies, not from feudalism to capitalism, but rather from 'frontier capitalism to more settled and intensive production', that is, settler capitalism (Denoon, 1983: 124). The opportunities for new forms of production, the development of transport, a world market in agrarian products, and a capitalist labour market formed through massive immigration presented themselves during the 'British century' from the Napoleonic wars until World War I. By and large, in spite of the anti-imperial sentiments of some settlers, specialized production of agricultural and mineral exports consonant with the needs of the British metropole were 'shown to be compatible with a wide autonomy and considerable prosperity' (Denoon, 1983: 222–3).

The tacit permission given to settlers by metropolitan elites to mould economic, social and political structures to suit settler interests has also been noted by other authors in the case of the Spanish- and French-sponsored, as well as the British, settler societies. While some settler societies (South Africa and Israel) enjoyed *de jure* independence, with the metropole relinquishing 'its juridical authority to interfere in issues such as native political rights, land expropriation and labour exploitation, and the fundamental constitutional status of the territory' (Weitzer, 1990: 26), others (Rhodesia) had *de facto* autonomy over political and coercive institutions.

While differing in specifics, separate analyses of Australia by McMichael (1984) and of Southern Rhodesia and Kenya by Mosley (1983) support Denoon's view that the exceptional prosperity of these settler societies was shaped by alignments of dominant class forces among the settlers. In those societies, the state actively intervened to protect settler interests. In the case of South Africa, deep contradictions within the ruling bloc were papered over by the drive for racial supremacy apparent in active state assistance for capitalization by whites which undermined the black rural economy (Keegan, 1989). The dispensing of material incentives and privileges to the lower echelons of the settler collectivity was evident in the emergence of 'labour aristocracies' of white workers in South Africa and Rhodesia, and of Protestant workers in Northern Ireland (Weitzer, 1990: 28).

Ehrensaft and Armstrong's (1981) account of 'dominion capitalism' yields a similar interpretation of the common features of Canada, Australia, New Zealand, Argentina and Uruguay. These authors argue that in contrast to colonies of military occupation, conquest and impoverishment in Asia, Africa and the Caribbean, the three dominions and (in some periods) Argentina and Uruguay enjoyed a privileged cultural, social and political linkage to British imperialism. Unlike tropical regions, these countries also had small, sparse indigenous populations who were 'eliminated, assimilated or pushed into distant corners of the hinterland', and a temperate climate that did not favour the importation of either African slaves or indentured workers (Ehrensaft and Armstrong, 1981: 100). These demographic and climatic conditions coincided with the availability of cheap transoceanic transport to encourage colonial ruling groups to construct a capitalist labour market of free-wage labourers by promoting large-scale European migration.

Several discourses and myths become woven into settler colonization practices to justify appropriation and exploitation of indigenous peoples. These include the racist discourses of *terra nullius* (or barren lands, sparsely populated), the myth of the disappearing indigene, manifest destiny and the doctrine of fatal impact (Richardson, 1993; Wetherell and Potter, 1992: 123–4). In contrast to these myths, the various studies in this volume illustrate the fundamental importance for European-led development of indigenous labour and indigenous lands, and in some cases for the survival of early European populations. They also highlight the significance of the coexistence of indigenous subsistence production with capitalist production, the ratios of indigenous peoples to Europeans, and the recognition and accommodation by colonial authorities and settler states of inherent indigenous rights to territory and self-governance. All of these factors vary significantly across time and space both within and across settler societies. Moreover, the recent developments in indigenous politics across the globe whereby indigenous peoples have insisted upon the actualization of their unsurrendered rights is a reminder that settler societies cannot easily disengage from these formative histories of indigenous–European 'encounters'.

In addition to the omission of the place and importance of indigenous peoples, another conceptual difficulty in prevailing models of settler societies pertains to the image of free-wage labour. Along with the private ownership of land and resources, free-wage labour is commonly taken to define both metropolitan and settler capitalism. In reality, various forms of unfree and coerced labour were characteristic not only of early phases of 'primitive accumulation' in settler societies, but also of later ones (Keegan, 1989: 113; Miles, 1987; Satzewich, 1991). Since European settlers could not entirely dispossess indigenous peoples from lands and subsistence forms of production, a vast array of coercive mechanisms were used to recruit unfree-wage labourers from abroad or to maintain indigenous peoples in various states of labour indenture or servitude. With the exception of Australia, where convict labour from Britain was used to build infrastructure in New South Wales as a means of achieving their 'moral regeneration' (Miles, 1987: 96), the major portion of unfree labour was imported from countries whose populations were constructed as racially and culturally inferior.

Restrictive immigration legislation formulas (such as the South African and Australian Natal Formula, the Israeli 'Law of Return' and the Canadian head taxes) were used to explicitly restrict the migration or settlement of undesirable migrants, often without making explicit mention of race or specific ethnicities. The exclusion/inclusion strategies incorporated into immigration, settlement and other state policies were frequently compromises reached by the state in reconciling the different interests of capitalists and ethnically dominant workers. While employers turned racial/ethnic divisions to their advantage in meeting labour market needs for cheap labour and diverse skills, ethnically dominant workers were intent on protecting wage standards by keeping out racial/ethnic minority workers. Such strategies were generally flexible enough to meet the needs of employers and the resource development strategies of state authorities, but restrictive enough to deny settlement and other citizenship rights to those who were deemed racially and ethnically undesirable.

Because of structural and historical similarities with the experiences of colonized populations in third world countries, several writers have adopted the term 'internal colonialism' to characterize the network of coercive legal, political and economic constraints imposed on racial/ethnic minorities and indigenous peoples in settler societies (see Wolpe, 1975 for South Africa; Zureik, 1979 for Israel; Hechter, 1975 who has applied the term to European regional minorities such as the Celts in Britain; and Dolores Janiewski, in this volume, on Mexican Americans in the US). As defined by Barrera (1979: 195), '[i]nternal colonialism is a variety of colonialism in that it shares with classic colonialism essential characteristics (ethnic/racial subordination, the serving of certain interests) even though there is no clear geographical distinction between metropolis and colony.' Key to internal colonialism is a set of features that facilitate the exploitation of minorities as workers – segmented labour markets, separate wage scales, and state and employer-imposed discriminatory practices.

The concept of 'internal colonialism' has been criticized for its failure to acknowledge significant class and racial/ethnic divisions and differential class benefits of internal colonialism within the non-colonized population. It does not, as Sarah Radcliffe points out in this volume, account for the 'varied positions of non-conquering immigrants, such as black slaves, Asian workers and other Europeans'. However, internal colonialism has served as an important metaphor to draw international parallels between conventional forms of colonialism and the forms of unfreedom and subordination imposed on minorities within settler societies whose founding myths and liberal democratic states emphasized principles of freedom, equality and non-discrimination (Barrera, 1979: 202; Geschwender, 1977; Zureik, 1979).

The Gendered and Racialized Character of Settler Colonization

Until recently, social scientists have paid little attention to the transformation of gender relations that resulted from colonization. This silence reflected the male domination of these disciplines. But in addition, social scientists of European origins have tended to view the gender division of labour in indigenous societies through Eurocentric and sexist lenses that refracted women's lack of power in the public sphere. Mistrustful of oral accounts by oral peoples (a mistrust that continues to beleaguer contemporary juridical forms of redress for indigenous peoples in Eurocentric courts), social scientists have relied on profoundly biased written documents by European men. They have tended to project certain European sexual and familial norms onto indigenous societies. The clear evidence of indigenous women's central roles in production and community governance has consequently been ignored. As the chapters in this book demonstrate, pre-colonial societies evince a wide variation in gender-based power relations and gendered rules of inheritance, division of labour and governance. These range from the patrilineal and patrifocal Shona and Ndebele societies of southern Africa to the matrilineal and matrifocal Huron societies of North America.

Imperialism created new sites for gender struggles and relations between and within communities of indigenous peoples and Europeans. 'The interchanges which ensued between men of each group, between women, and across the sexes, were governed by two sets of [indigenous and European] gender configurations, each novel to the other' (McGrath, 1990: 189). Within these, class, tribal, clan, religious and other affiliations 'caused further dramatic diversity' (ibid.).The effects of colonization on the position of both indigenous and European women cannot be dissociated from its effects on more general patterns of hierarchy and inequities involved in different modes of production. For example, Haggis (1990) critiques the tendency in some analyses of white women in colonial society to ignore the impact of legal and other restraints associated with unfree (indentured or slave) labour on the servant–mistress relationship (Callaway, 1987; Knapman, 1986). The impact of colonization on gender relations and subordination of indigenous women is most striking in societies organized on a relatively egalitarian basis. Here, women had joined men in the production of basic necessities, and 'relations between the sexes [were] based on the reciprocal exchange of goods and services' (Etienne and Leacock, 1980: 9; see also Jameson, 1988: 779).

The autonomy and influence of indigenous women were frequently undermined by the almost exclusive access of men to a money economy via wage labour while women remained the custodians of traditional economies. Ideologically they were also undermined by missionaries and their wives who imposed Christian European sexual, conjugal and nuclear familial norms through religious indoctrination and the teaching of European homemaking skills. The inculcation of European cultural values and familial patterns was seen as key 'to restructuring productive relations and attitudes toward colonial domination, bringing the Indians from "savagery" to "civilization"' (Etienne and Leacock, 1980: 18).

There appears to be a consensus that the combined effects of colonization, new trading relations, wage labour and individual property 'generally exacerbated preexisting [gender] stratification or promoted its emergence in previously unstratified societies' (Etienne and Leacock, 1980: 20–1; see also Bourgeault, 1989). However, it was the arrival of European women that was particularly significant in reinforcing class and racial distinctions, in part because of the emergence of new sanctions against intermarriage between indigenous women and European men (van Kirk, 1983). Nonetheless, it is difficult to disengage the effect of the arrival of large numbers of white women from the disruptive impact on indigenous societies of intensified white settlement, and emergent racial conflicts over land and labour, of which white female migration formed a part (Jolly, 1993: 109).)

Several feminist anthropologists have attempted to demonstrate that in spite of the brutal sexual exploitation that accompanied first the development of commercial trade relations and then capitalist wage labour relations, indigenous women have not been passive victims of colonization. Some indigenous women who had the opportunity to alleviate their own exploitation did so by entering into official and unofficial marriages with European men. They also performed the role of cultural intermediaries between the European merchants and traders and the indigenous societies, which proffered certain privileges until the arrival of European women (Dickason, 1992: 167–72; van Kirk, 1983). In other instances, indigenous women employed collective strategies to defend the cultural integrity and economic interests of their communities. Some accounts of contemporary indigenous societies document how female autonomy in the spheres of production, sexual and familial relations along with participation in community politics and ceremonies has withstood generations of profound change (Bell, 1980; Fiske, 1988).

For their part, settler women in the early phase of colonialization were burdened not only with involvement in various forms of agrarian and household production, the arduousness and specific forms of which varied by class, but also with the breeding and ideological tasks of reproducing 'the nation' (Yuval-Davis, 1993b). While in some cases the lives of settler women were less constrained by convention than their counterparts in Europe, these women were nonetheless increasingly subjected, as Dolores Janiewski argues in this volume, to the laws and regulations of a public patriarchy which at times reinforced, and at times mediated, the patriarchal power of individual men.

The racial/ethnic diversity of women migrants in settler societies has recently received much attention. Anti-racist feminist scholarship since the early 1980s has revealed the distinctive and asymmetrical, yet varied, positions of racial and ethnic minority migrant women in the nexus of relations among the state, labour market and family/household. While much of white feminist writing during the 1970s focused on the male-breadwinner/female-dependant household as the locus of oppression for 'women' (McIntosh, 1978), many third world, black and anti-racist feminists revealed that these formulations were rooted in the specific conditions of white, western and middle-class women (Anthias and Yuval-Davis, 1986; Carby, 1982, 1987; hooks, 1981, 1984, 1988; Jayawardena, 1986; Lord, 1984; Mullings, 1986; Sen and Grown, 1987; Stasiulis, 1987, 1990; WING, 1985).

These critiques underscored how unfree conditions of entry inscribed in restrictive immigration and citizenship laws imposed special liabilities on minority communities. Such policies explicitly or implicitly reproduced the (white) settler society assumption that only those who embodied or could be assimilated to the culture and values of the dominant racial/ethnic group were legitimate 'settlers' or citizens of settler societies. The outcome of these racially/ethnically exclusionary policies was the disintegration of minority families, through separation of husbands from wives, wives from husbands and parents from children, and the imposition of generations of hardships upon minority communities.

In contrast to the hegemonic image of female dependence on the earnings of male breadwinners, migrant women and women from racial and ethnic minorities have historically had greater rates of labour force participation than longer-established or ethnically dominant women. Moreover, within a labour market that is stratified by gender, women are further segmented by race, ethnicity, language and citizenship statuses. Minority women are overrepresented in occupational enclaves which are low-paying, insecure, hazardous and unprotected by legislation or strong unions. In both settler and other advanced industrial countries, minority and migrant women are prominent in sectors such as the garment trades, seasonal agriculture, private domestic service, and more recently, 'McJobs' performed in hospitals, nursing homes, restaurant kitchens, hotels and commercial cleaning. Aided by the new technologies and organized through networks of subcontracting, the global restructuring by large corporations reproduces sweatshop conditions of work for vulnerable (migrant, indigenous, racial/ethnic minority, and especially undocumented) women both in third world and industrialized western countries (Mitter, 1986).

As well as exploring the specificity of different racial/ethnic women's conditions, a fruitful direction taken in recent anti-racist feminist work is the exploration of the *relations between and among women* who are differently constituted by race/ethnicity and class. In settler societies, the advancement of racially/ethnically dominant women was predicated upon assumptions of the inferiority and backwardness of indigenous and minority women. 'Feminism was thus inherently imperialistic' (Lake, 1993: 378). Asymmetrical power and interdependence involved in relations among dominant and subordinate groups of women are also evident in domestic service within private households, a growth area for minority and migrant women globally in low-wage, unprotected occupational niches (Arat-Koc, 1989; Bakan and Stasiulis, 1994, 1995; Cock, 1980; Enloe, 1989; Colen, 1989; Glenn, 1992; Radcliffe, 1990) .

In private domestic service as well as other sectors of employment, racial and ethnocultural discourses of womanhood, sexuality and femininity not only play an important allocative role, but also establish employer expectations of employee attitudes and behaviour (Bakan and Stasiulis, 1995; Jewell, 1993: 67). These discourses reveal the simultaneous interdependence and hierarchy among different racial/ethnic groups of women (Glenn, 1992). In contemporary domestic service, the images that emerge of employers and employees respectively are of white professional yet feminine 'superwomen' in contrast with women of colour who are 'naturally' nurturing, docile and suited for degraded service work for racially/ethnically dominant families.

During an earlier phase of settlement and nation-building, the predominant images of racially/ethnically dominant women were those of virtuous and dependent wives, 'breeders' and mothers of children, as well as of courageous yet feminine 'frontier women', whereas those of minority women were likely to emphasize some form of sexual deviance – for example, unbridled sexuality and masculine or even brute-like strength (Carby, 1987; de Lepervanche, 1991; Jewell, 1993). Insofar as state policies such as immigration both fostered and reinforced these hegemonic images of dominant and minority women, such discourses were tied to the nation-building role played by the state in settler societies.

Nation and State

The nationalist agendas of both liberal and socialist movements have assumed an ideal type of a nation-state in which all citizens would be members of the same ethnic collectivity (Gellner, 1983). However, there is no such pure nation-state anywhere in the world. Most modern nation-states are, to a varying degree, multi-ethnic if not multi-racial. However, the contradictions between the ideal image of the nation-state and the reality of contemporary nation-states are especially striking in settler societies. The evaluation of these contradictions requires that we examine the processes of construction of the boundaries within settler societies between ethnic, national and other collectivities, as well as the relationships between these collectivities and the state.

Definitions of the 'state' variously focus on its legal-juridical and institutional composition, or its role with respect to capitalism, class, gender and race relations (Mahon, 1991). While the state is not uniform in either its practices or its effects, it is useful to retain the concept of the state to refer to a particular set of institutions and relations which are centrally organized around the intentionality of control and has a given apparatus of enforcement at its command (Yuval-Davis and Anthias, 1989: 5). This set of institutions and relations usually govern (at least formally) a specific territory and a given population. The concept of civil society is similarly contested, but generally refers to a social space, networks, institutions and social relations, including families, households, voluntary associations, the production of signs and symbols, and in some definitions, production relations (Cohen, 1982; Keane, 1988; Melucci, 1989). Civil society is thus distinct from the state, though its various components are acted upon by state institutions.

One of the central questions in analysing the development of settler societies pertains to the demarcation of the boundaries between the state and civil society and the respective role of each sphere in nation-building. This is important because while agents both of the state and from within civil society may engage in regulation, coercion and control of populations within (and entering) a given territory, it is usually the state which generally has legitimate authority to exercise control over such matters. However, in many societies, especially in settler and developing societies, the state cannot penetrate effectively certain social and ethnic enclaves, and other, customary systems of control have retained their legitimacy. Moreover, in many such states, customary laws and social hierarchies become incorporated into the state legislation and their traditional authority becomes reinforced by the state. As Elaine Unterhalter and Susie Jacobs point out in their respective analyses of South Africa and Zimbabwe, the codification of customary or traditional law for southern African peoples by settler colonial regimes was a major tool in defining women as 'minors' and increasing women's subordination.

This question of boundaries between state and civil society raises the question of the relationship between citizenship and the national collectivity. The prevailing assumption within a large corpus of work on citizenship, including the literature based on the path-breaking formulations of T.H. Marshall (1950, 1975, 1981), has been that the boundaries of the national collectivity and civil society are the same. Although not all members of the civil society are (as yet) full citizens, Marshall developed an evolutionary model to describe the uneven distribution of citizenship rights. Even those – like women and children – who lacked such rights were assumed to be part of the national community. The notion of 'the community' itself assumes an organic wholeness with given, 'natural' boundaries, which does not allow for the continuous ideological and material reconstructions of the boundaries themselves (Bhabha, 1990; Yuval-Davis, 1991). Contrary to this model of universal citizenship, in which all members of the society belong to 'the community', most states are characterized by those who lack many or most citizenship rights (such as migrant labourers, slaves or people under occupation) who exist within the boundaries of civil society but outside the boundaries of the national collectivity. Some indigenous people are also contesting individualistic western notions of citizenship and rights and proposing other definitions based on first nations' sets of collective principles and responsibilities. Deconstructing these different relationships is vital for the analysis of settler societies.

The ambiguity in definitions of the state and civil society also characterizes the definitions of the nation and its relationship with the state and civil society, as well as with other (for example, ethnic and racial) collectivities. What constitutes a nation and the extent to which it is a particularly modern or even western phenomenon are controversial questions. At one extreme there are 'the primordialists' (Shils, 1957; Geertz, 1963; van den Berghe, 1979) who claim that nations are natural and universal, an 'automatic' extension of kinship relationships. Their historical importance might rise or fall but they are always there, waiting to be discovered rather than to be historically constructed. At the other extreme are 'the modernists', those who see nationalism and nations as phenomena which are particular to capitalism (Althusser, 1969; Hobsbawm, 1990) or other modern developments – such as the invention of print (Anderson, 1983).

There are varying definitions of 'the nation'. Some definitions provide a 'shopping list' of properties which are essential for identifying 'nations', including a shared sense of language, territory, economic life and culture. Different constructions of 'the nation' are differentially organized around notions of common origin, culture and the state (Yuval-Davis, 1993a, b). Anthony Smith (1986) views nationalism as a modern phenomenon, but one which is intimately linked to 'the ethnic origins of the nation'. In contrast, Hobsbawm (1990: 22) argues that definitions of nations as based on shared ethnicity, language and history were not the decisive criteria of liberal nation-making. More decisive were three criteria: (1) the historic associations with a current state or one with a lengthy or recent past; (2) a long-established cultural elite possessing a written national literary and administrative vernacular; and (3) a capacity for conquest. The Eurocentric biases in such definitions are clear for indigenous peoples who have long histories of governance based on oral rather than written traditions. Nor do they pay sufficient attention to the articulations of gender and ethnic/racial divisions with those of class and nation.

Obviously, any analysis of 'nations' in the context of settler societies can only define them as constructed rather than as essential phenomena. Moreover, many of the settler colonies 'developed their identities over a period when their respective "mother countries" – with the possible exception of England – were in the process of acquiring *their* identities as nations' (Pagden and Canny, 1987: 274, original emphasis). Clearly, also, there were important distinctions between the self-images of colonial elites, and the multifarious senses of identity among less privileged groups. Pagden and Canny persuasively argue that 'when . . . the elites of these colonies came to create independent nations, they were, of necessity, imposing upon a large number of . . . people an identity and a political culture many of them did not share' (1987: 270). Nonetheless, the myth of 'ethnic origins' – or, rather, the tension between the hegemonic 'ethnic origins' myth of settler nation-states and the real, historical origins and experiences of the inhabitants which is much more heterogeneous – is at the heart of this book. Nations and nationalism are not unitary phenomena. Migration, conquest and settlement have played different roles in the histories of various nationalist projects. Particular nationalist ideologies and 'foundational fictions' (Bhabha, 1990: 5), rather than particular constituent elements of 'the nation', are vital for defining national collectivities. The myth of common ethnic origin is one important element for nationalist ideologies. However, nationalist ideologies cannot be understood satisfactorily, especially those in settler societies, without also considering what Otto Bauer has called (the myth of) 'common destiny' (Bauer, 1940; see also Nimni, 1991; Yuval-Davis, 1987).

This element of 'common destiny' is of crucial importance. Implicit in this concept is the notion of future, rather than just past, orientation. It accounts for the subjective sense of commitment of people to ethnic collectivities and nations, in settler societies or in post-colonial states, in which there is no one overriding shared myth of common origin. The myth of 'common destiny' can also explain the dynamic nature of any national collectivity and the perpetual reconstruction of boundaries which takes place within them via immigration, naturalization, conversion and other similar social and political processes.

It is important to emphasize that ethnic, national and indeed racial collectivities are *all* socially constructed or 'imagined communities' (Anderson, 1983) which are 'culturally fabricated' (Gellner, 1983). They all share in historically specific and differential ways myths of common origin and common destiny. In addition, each of these collectivities institute 'their imaginary unity *against* other possible unities' (Balibar, 1991: 49, original emphasis). Collectivities become labelled as ethnic, racial or national by different agents and/or different historical circumstances. What vary are the distinctive discourses and projects of ethnicity, racism and nationalism.

Ethnic discourse involves the construction of exclusionary and inclusionary boundaries which draws upon the myths of common origin and/or destiny, providing individuals with a mode of interpreting the world based on shared cultural resources and/or collective positioning *vis-à-vis* other groups. Racial discourse involves modes of exclusion, inferiorization, subordination and exploitation. It constructs signifiers of collectivity boundaries as immutable and hereditary. These signifiers are frequently arbitrary, though as in the case of skin colour, deeply rooted through association with slavery, colonialism and so on. Nationalist discourse involves an explicit political project, a claim for a separate political representation of the collectivity which often takes the form of a claim for a sovereign and autonomous 'nation-state'. All of these discourses are also gendered, assigning specified roles and images to women and men of different collectivities in ethnic, racist and nationalist projects.

The extent to which a political movement focuses on creating or claiming a separate state is related both to the relative political strength of the nationalist/ethnic movement and to the overall political project of the state(s) in which it is active. It is also related to the degree of correspondence between the collectivity's national/ethnocultural boundaries and specific territorial boundaries as well its demographic position within the population of a given territory. As mentioned above, there is virtually no contemporary state in which the boundaries of the civil society and the boundaries of the hegemonic ethnic collectivity in that state are identical.

In settler societies, this reality is often more visible than in other societies. Colonial settlers, the offspring of European imperialism, refused to integrate with the indigenous population. Moreover, they kept Europe as their myth of origin and as a signifier of superiority even when formal political ties and/or dependency with European colonial powers had been abandoned. This sense of identification with the 'mother country' has not, however, mitigated the unevenness and fragility of settler identities, which were often forged in defence against metropolitan contempt (Pagden and Canny, 1987: 269). Thus, as Natividad Guttiérez notes in her case study of Mexico, the antagonism held by Spanish Americans for Spaniards born in Europe was a strong impetus for the movement for Mexican political sovereignty.

Whether stressing the differences or the similarities with their mother countries, the settlers' ideologies involved in nation-building have a historical starting point, which occurs at the moment of colonial conquest and the beginning of settlement. As discussed earlier, the period prior to conquest and settlement is often constructed as pre-historical. The decline in the pre-historical society is accounted for by such racist discourses as the 'doctrine of the fatal impact' which renders natural and inevitable the supplanting of indigenous peoples by 'militarily and mentally superior' Europeans (Wetherell and Potter, 1992: 124–5). As in other societies, claims are made for legitimate dominance of the kind that, '"We" were here first.' In some settler societies, there may also be competition or accommodation of such claims among different collectivities claiming 'founding nation' status (as for the French and British in Canada). In some societies (South Africa and Israel), dominant groups claim that indigenous peoples have themselves moved to the contested territories only as a result of the European settlements. However, the claims for being the 'indigenous' or the 'true' or 'first' nations are backed by different precepts, interpretations of history and jurisprudence when they are voiced by the indigenous populations that peopled the land prior to the colonial encounter. In some contexts, these competing claims become exceedingly complex, when some of the pre-colonial population, such as Arabs in Algeria, are themselves descendants of earlier waves of conquest and settlement, and coexist with other collectivities, such as Algerian Berbers, who claim indigenous status.

The line drawn between the indigenous population and what Australian Aborigines call the 'Imposing Society', however, is by no means the only significant boundary between collectivities within settler societies. There are always those who become settlers who are not part of the dominant ethnic collectivity(ies) and have come to seek work and/or refuge from other countries. There are also those who by virtue of their race/ethnicity are deemed 'unassimilable' to the culture and values of the settler society and who face extraordinary legal-juridical and political obstacles in acquiring access to citizenship rights, including those of settlement.

The nation-building ideologies of 'the new nations' of settler societies always include notions of hegemony of 'old (European) ethnicities' which are transformed and enriched by their new context and other available myth–symbol complexes (Smith, 1986). In this sense there is a continuum, rather than a dichotomous break, between settler societies and the 'old' European nations which have also absorbed massive numbers and waves of immigrants. Many European countries constructed the migrant labourers as 'guest workers', while in settler societies a much larger proportion of immigrants were constructed (through immigration and citizenship policies) as settlers. In reality, there has been a similar process involved in the creation of the 'new minorities' both in Europe and in most settler societies as a result of the settlement of migrant labourers and refugees in all these countries (Castles, 1984; Castles and Miller, 1993). In addition, settler societies have also relied on migrant labour schemes in sectors such as seasonal agricultural work and private domestic service, which have restricted the settlement and citizenship rights of these groups.

While the practices among settler societies reveal certain similarities *vis-à-vis* indigenous populations and racial minorities, there have also been significant differences. There were differences among the various colonial powers (British, French, Dutch, Portuguese, Spanish and so on) in their attitudes toward indigenous peoples and 'subject races'. Thus, the French drew from the revolutionary decree of 1794 conferring French citizenship on 'all men, without distinction of colour' to base their famed policy of assimilation (Fyfe, 1992: 17). As Anissa Hélie points out in this volume, this assimilationist policy was applied in Algeria to non-French Europeans in order to bolster the numbers of 'French' *vis-à-vis* the indigenous population. For their part, the British colonizers eschewed assimilation, yet declared that they were 'respectful of cultures' (Balibar, 1991: 43). In formal terms at least, they viewed all subjects of the crown, regardless of race, colour or religion, as equal before the law (Huttenback, 1976). Clearly, in most cases of settler regimes, the law itself was an important means of differentiating and indeed constructing different deserving and dangerous peoples. Differences have also existed in the construction of and attitudes towards mixed populations as part of or separate from other racial/ethnic collectivities, including the valorization of *mestizaje* (race-mixing) as a nation-building ideology in Mexico, the recognition of a separate mixed *Métis* (aboriginal-European) population in Canada, and the development of complex and negotiable racialized and gendered statuses of mixed groups in Peru.

Regardless of national differences in colonial discourses, seeking to valorize specific European peoples, the various European powers collectively forged an 'imperialist superiority complex'. The idea of the 'White man's burden' was decisive in 'moulding the modern notion of a supranational European or Western identity' (Balibar, 1991: 43). How the various self-governing colonies chose to interpret these various precepts was largely based on the internally contradictory colonial discourses which were simultaneously universalistic and racist, and the expedience of meeting various class and nation-building interests within the settler societies.

When we examine the processes of nation-building in settler societies, we can usually distinguish four main sources for the myth–symbol complexes that can be found in them. First, there are the resources associated with the hegemonic collectivity. These include language and other cultural resources, systems of law, and economic and political links with a specific country of origin and/or sponsoring empire. Secondly, the history of nation-building of a settler society involves the process of distinguishing between national collectivities of the new and mother countries. Certain crucial moments invested with great symbolic significance form a vital part of the narration of the nation's construction. These moments vary depending on whether a revolutionary rupture with the 'mother country' occurred – from the 'Boston tea party' to the Australian 'ANZAC day'.

Thirdly, there is usually at least an attempt to appropriate some elements of the cultural resources of the indigenous population. While the indigenous populations are themselves usually excluded, appropriation of some of their cultural symbols is often used to signify the difference between the members of the 'old' and 'new' hegemonic ethnic collectivity. Examples range from the installation of Aboriginal artefacts in the Australian Parliament not far from the statue of Queen Victoria to the adoption of *falafel* or Palestinian embroidery as Israeli identity symbols.

Fourthly, there are cultural symbols of other ethnic collectivities who have immigrated to the settler societies. For immigrants who are perceived to be similar to the hegemonic ethnic collectivity, there are usually pressures for assimilation. Towards others, especially members of racialized migrants, there are pressures to construct their presence as temporary and/or external to the new national collectivity. What has happened in virtually all settler societies, however, is that neither policies of assimilation nor policies of exclusion have been wholly successful, and new ideologies of 'common destiny' and solidarity, such as biculturalism (New Zealand) or multiculturalism (Canada and Australia), have been sought.

A variety of exclusionary and inclusionary mechanisms – political, economic, social and legal – operate in settler societies for constructing and deconstructing boundaries between collectivities. Crucial mechanisms for exclusion/inclusion have been those of immigration control and citizenship policies. While different settler societies in different historical periods vary in their immigration policies, what seems to be common is the need to balance ideological pressures for encouraging 'desirable' immigrants – that is, those of the hegemonic ethnicity – to settle in the country and to block entry to the 'undesirable' ones, especially from racialized collectivities.

Because there is usually an insufficient supply of 'desirable' immigrants, the immigration policies of most settler societies can be described as a process of accommodation which involves gradually opening the gates to 'less desirable' immigrants. The gates are opened first to immigrants with ethnic origins perceived to be less 'foreign' or racially different than others – for example, from southern Europe or the Middle East in postwar Australia and Oriental Jews in Israel in the early 1950s. Later, immigration policy often comes to seek out those with capital or valued professional qualifications, from groups that have historically ranked low in racial/ethnic desirability.

In recent years, certain counter-ideologies have developed within the settler societies and internationally to aid in these changes. Bodies such as the United Nations have exerted pressure on different countries for less racist immigration legislation and more generous refugee policies. However, we are not aware of the existence of any country having a truly non-racist immigration policy, where meaningful equity exists in legislation, regulations and administration. Moreover, under conditions of global recession and the global aftermath of the collapse of the Soviet Union, citizens in settler and other more privileged societies are experiencing increased levels of unemployment and deteriorating living standards in the face of restructuring strategies of international capital. Hence, they are now susceptible to claims that their shrinking privileges must be protected from 'aliens', a category whose construction draws upon historical notions of racial and ethnic inferiority.

Obviously, means other than immigration control have been used to exclude and segregate the indigenous populations. The most devastating forms of control occurred through physical extermination as happened among the Beothuk in Newfoundland and Natives in Tasmania, armed conflict, compounded by chronic infectious disease (tuberculosis, influenza, venereal disease and so on), and the practice of eugenics through forced sterilization. Indigenous lands were either simply expropriated or were extracted through formal treaties. However, the framers of the treaties (the white colonial authorities) invariably recorded *their* preferred terms, and so ensured that interpretation of the treaties would favour them (legal imperialism). Alternatively, when it suited them, treaties were simply disregarded. Many indigenous populations were pushed to 'Reserves' in remote parts of the country or to 'Bantustans'. Travel from these reserves for the purpose of providing cheap migrant or commuting labour became regulated through travel permits and passes. Cultural imperialism occurred through a variety of means, including the outlawing of indigenous religions, customs and languages, forced removal of children from parents, and the imposition of European norms of gender roles, nuclear family institutions and forms of knowledge. These various means of social disruption of indigenous societies expressed ambivalent movements of assimilation and exclusion of indigenous peoples who were systematically painted as sub-human or as 'savages'.

Indigenous peoples might have been, at least partly, under the control of the state, but they did not enjoy citizenship, let alone identification as part of the national collectivity. Symbolic of such exclusion was the fact that, until recently, indigenous peoples in liberal democracies have not been part of the 'universal franchise', and have been counted in a haphazard and incomplete manner in population censuses. The segregation of indigenous people has had a contradictory effect. On the one hand, it has deprived them from access to state power and the possible benefits that such access might entail. Yet, on the other hand, segregation contributed to their survival as distinct groups and later facilitated political organization.

The political struggles of indigenous peoples are usually aimed at regaining control of territory and resources, for which a reproduction of their legitimate boundaries as separate, self-governing nations is vital. The nature of their engagement in these struggles, their degree of success and the variety of strategies employed vary in the different case studies discussed in this collection. These strategies have ranged from armed struggle to litigation and constitutional battles, and have resulted variously in permanent warfare, peace treaties, negotiated land claims and self-government, or other dramatic outcomes.

In Algeria, for instance, following the victory of the indigenous population in their national struggle, the political climate of the country resulted in the mass exodus of the settler community. In Zimbabwe, the settlers were allowed to become part of the new national collectivity under the hegemony of the victorious indigenous population (although white settlers remain a privileged minority). In South Africa, the end of apartheid has meant universal suffrage and a majority government for the first time in that country's history. The Maori in New Zealand have achieved considerable autonomy within the nation-state. In Canada, Aboriginal peoples have made significant strides in constitutional entitlements, litigation struggles to secure Aboriginal title to lands and resources improperly expropriated or over which Aboriginal rights have not been extinguished, as well as in different institutionalized forms of self-government. In other countries, such as Australia, Aboriginal peoples have achieved considerably less recognition of their claims. In Israel/Palestine, the negotiations for a political settlement or treaty based on some measure of recognition of the rights of the indigenous people have entered a crucial stage. The last few years have seen a raised level of activity among indigenous peoples globally, and the development of novel forms of regional and international linkages through organizations such as the World Council of Indigenous Peoples (Guttiérez, this volume; Jhappan, 1992). Correspondingly, there has been growing international legitimation of their rights, which tended to remain largely invisible in earlier decades when most colonized peoples received their independence.

As in the processes of construction of other national collectivities, the emergence of indigenous peoples as cohesive national collectivities is a continuous political process rather than a 'natural' one. Indigenous peoples are at least as linguistically, culturally and materially heterogeneous as European nations, if not more so. Depending on their access to territories, resources and legal rights, the extent to which strategies involve inclusion or separation from the institutions of the settler society also varies immensely. One critical factor here is whether indigenous peoples live in urban centres of the settler societies or at a remove from such centres, where the state has only partially penetrated. A great deal depends on whether or not they continue to rely on traditional 'bush production', subsistence economies or have integrated partially or fully into the capitalist economy of the settler state.

For both indigenous peoples and subaltern minorities, recognition and reproduction of difference, racialized boundaries and racist exclusion have relied on a variety of signifiers – from skin colour to accent to class location. A more liberal mode of retaining ethnic boundaries and, arguably, ethnic/racial stratification has been state policies of ethnic pluralism such as multiculturalism. Multiculturalism, either as a state policy or philosophical ideal, has taken distinctive forms in different settler societies. It generally means a symbolic recognition that the national collectivity or the nation-state is composed of more than one ethnicity and encompasses a variety of cultural traditions. However, of central importance in multiculturalist ideologies is the assumption that these different cultural traditions are complementary and reconcilable with each other (Yuval-Davis, 1992).

Multiculturalist policies can have varying effects on different ethnic collectivities and on their relations to the state. Multiculturalism often corresponds to the interests of immigrant minorities and especially their leaderships. This can entail a certain accessibility to the state, albeit usually to segments which are at a far remove from the centres of power. The concept usually entails limited and primarily symbolic recognition of ethno-specific needs by the state (Stasiulis, 1988, 1991). Hegemonic ethnic collectivities tend to see multiculturalism as irrelevant to their concerns insofar as the institutions of the settler society are largely structured on the basis of traditions associated with the hegemonic ethnicity. Similarly, indigenous peoples in countries with official multicultural policies, such as Canada and Australia, tend to resist any policies which treat them as simply one among several ethnic collectivities. Unlike the immigrant communities who gain from multiculturalism a recognition of their legitimate existence in the settler society, multiculturalism de-legitimizes the claims of indigenous peoples for ultimate, or at least prior, claim on the territory, state and resources as the 'First Nations'. Multiculturalism also constructs the various immigrant communities as internally homogeneous in terms of class, ideology and politics (Yeatman, 1992). State recognition is provided to a specific and usually male and conservative leadership within ethnic communities. As multiculturalism usually constructs difference in mutually exclusive terms, this can give rise to fundamentalist leaderships who are more easily perceived to be 'the authentic other' (Sahgal and Yuval-Davis, 1992).

Women, especially minority and indigenous women, often find themselves in a difficult position *vis-à-vis* community and nationalist politics. Perceiving their own oppression as vitally connected to the oppression of their national/racial/ethnic collectivities, many are inclined to participate in political struggles which empower their particular communities and identities. Often, however, ethnic and national projects and ideologies of nationalism have, as Enloe describes, 'typically sprung from masculinized memory, masculinized humiliation and masculinized hope' as well as the 'anger at being "emasculated"' (1989: 44). The 'tradition' and the modernizing elements that are defended in many nationalist projects, or in defence of 'multiculturalism', are selectively patriarchal (Rowbotham, 1992: 105). Thus, the cultural constructions of womanhood inscribed in many national and ethnic identities and ideologies of nationalism demand women's submission. This tendency, as Elaine Unterhalter points out with regard to South African politics, transcends left/right divisions. The raising of any questions of the relations between women and men inside the nationalist or ethnic rights movement, may be labelled by male leaders as divisive, or even traitorous. In indigenous as well as other, non-Christian (for example, Muslim) societies, the interests shown by colonial administrators and Christian missionaries in reforming the sexual mores and family traditions produced a close association between feminism and cultural imperialism (Kandiyoti, 1991: 7). The dilemma for many indigenous women or other women involved in nationalist or anti-racist movements is therefore speaking to feminist issues in a context where feminist ideology is defined as foreign or an ideology of the enemy.

Women's Politics

The rise of the feminist movement in the 1970s and 1980s has had profound effects on women's politics in settler societies. However, given the degree of ethnic and racial heterogeneity among indigenous and migrant women, some of the core issues within feminist politics have probably been confronted even more sharply within settler societies than in other types of societies. As discussed above, many of the analyses of women's oppression had assumed a homogeneity in the backgrounds and interests of women. Assumptions of shared oppression and sisterhood could not sustain the challenges by women who articulated 'differences' based on class, race, ethnicity and sexuality.

Critical interventions have been made by black feminists, third world feminists and other feminists of colour (see hooks, 1981, 1984; Lord, 1984; Mohanty, 1991) who have pointed out the racist and exclusionary nature of hegemonic feminism. Some black feminists (Walker, 1984) and third world feminists (Jayawardena, 1993) have even claimed that feminism is beyond redemption and inappropriate as a politics of liberation for black and third world women. The strength of such critiques has been to open up understanding of women's experiences and politics to the plurality of women and their embeddedness not simply in gender relations, but also in significant relations such as colonialism, race and class. The impact of such analyses on women's politics cannot be overestimated. For many indigenous and racial/ethnic minority women, the new critiques and forms of knowledge for the first time provided frameworks within which to voice and validate their experiences and autonomous forms of organizing. For the first time, analytical tools were made available to demonstrate that issues such as land claims and self-government, immigration, policing and citizenship policies could also be in the province of feminist concerns, alongside reproduction and other favoured issues of the white women's movement. A new sense of empowerment was also expressed within many ethnic/racial communities where women for the first time organized to deal with painful issues such as domestic violence, heretofore taboo subjects whose airing it was felt would further pathologize these communities (Pettman, 1988; Thakur, 1992). Within feminist organizations initiated or dominated by women of hegemonic race/ethnicity, however, the efforts to broaden and become more inclusive has involved a painful process described by hegemonic and minority women alike as traumatizing and silencing (Stasiulis, 1993).

Part of the difficulty in responding politically to the black and anti-racist critiques of feminism can be understood in terms of the limitations of the new feminist frameworks. Just as earlier feminist models had constructed a binary universe of men and women (which in socialist feminism was complicated by relations of class), the emergent black feminist frameworks constructed binary divisions between white/black women, as if the construction and interests of all black women are the same, as obversely and antagonistically are the interests of all white women. Such a binary framework has, on the one hand, worked through 'strategic essentialism' to advance certain educational and political goals of black and indigenous women (Fuss, 1989). On the other hand, the heterogeneity of women in settler societies has meant that dichotomous models impede an understanding of racisms experienced by different groups of racial and ethnic minority women. The racialization of women through multiple and overlapping, linguistic, cultural, religious and other forms of dominance is overlooked in frameworks employing binary constructs. Resort to dichotomous categories also blocks the understanding of how racism experienced by racial minority women is mediated by class in communities characterized by heterogeneous class structures. Further, while many of these analyses critiqued essentialist notions of 'woman', the suggested alternatives created new forms of essentialism that combined race and gender and new hierarchies of oppression (for critiques, see Anthias and Yuval-Davis, 1986, 1992; Glenn, 1992; Spelman 1988; Stasiulis, 1987, 1990).

Partly as a response to these contributions and partly as a result of the rise of postmodernist theory, many feminist theorists have explored alternative theoretical avenues based on the notion of 'difference' (Gunew and Yeatman, 1993; Larner, 1993; Nicholson, 1990; Young, 1990). However, postmodernist feminism's embrace of 'difference', 'post-colonial', 'contingent identities' and 'hyphenated feminisms' faces problems at the other extreme insofar as it virtually dispenses with notions of asymmetrical and systemic power relations (Barrett, 1989: 42; Fuss, 1989; Stasiulis, 1990: 294, forthcoming; Yuval-Davis, 1991, 1994). Bondi argues similarly that feminist deployments of post-structuralism have ignored the 'materiality of social relations . . . in favour of a domain of representations in which structures of power are treated as illusory' (1993: 94). The pre-eminence given to culture, symbols, discourse and 'texts' in postmodernist feminism and postmodernism more generally means that global and national restructuring projects of capital are either ignored or paid lip-service in a manner which 'typically takes the form of an ersatz and astonishingly crude political economy' (Rosenthal, 1992: 104).

As feminism continues to inform political movement(s) as well as academic scholarship, new models in inter-ethnic, inter-racial and transnational feminist encounters and collaborations have emerged which have attempted to redress the limitations of 'dualistic' and 'difference' politics. Emphasis is placed within these emergent models on the interplay between global dynamics and local, historically produced and community-based forces, on women's agency and on shared political contexts which aid in engendering transnational political alliances. Detailed case studies of particular women's conditions in particular sites (workplace, family household, state policies, trade unions and so on) have revealed the various global and local relations, institutional mechanisms and discourses that have constructed circumstances that are sometimes unique to particular groups of racial/ethnic women and are sometimes shared. Such histories also document the spirited and creative resistance of these women to male, capitalist, racist, colonial and bureaucratic forms of domination, and thus undercut the image of subaltern women as hapless victims of seamless webs of oppression.

The new technology has been instrumental in further degrading the working lives and employment and wage stability of women workers to the advantage of multinational corporations. However, it has also facilitated transnational communication and meetings of women, enhancing their capacity to exchange experiences regarding such issues as sweatshop working conditions and sexism on the shop floor, environmental degradation and collective consumption. New opportunities have been created in international conferences and meetings to develop alternative survival strategies and to organize among women who are in circumstances which make it difficult to organize (for example, scattered homeworkers, nannies and self-employed women) (Mitter, 1986: 144–63). Transnational links and alliances have been made among women's groups, as in the anti-free trade coalitions among Mexican, Canadian and American women, to confront issues which are seen to adversely affect the most vulnerable segments of women across countries as they are positioned within international capitalism (Nadeau, 1992). Common cause and shared analyses of women's oppression have also been forged among women internationally in fighting (Christian, Hindu, Islamic and Jewish) fundamentalism through groups such as Women Living Under Muslim Laws and Women Against Fundamentalism (Saghal and Yuval-Davis, 1992).

As we remarked at the beginning of this introduction, binary and dichotomous (for example, indigenous/settler) analyses dominate in studies of settler societies, obscuring the complexity and interdependence of their social, economic, political and ideological relations. Similar tendencies have existed in relation to women's politics. All too often women in settler societies from ethnic and racial minorities, indigenous and immigrant collectivities, have been put in the position of having to choose between being 'feminist' or showing loyalty to their national or ethnocultural community.

One of the ways which indigenous and migrant women have found to be publicly active as autonomous agents without rejecting their collective national/ethnic identity has been by claiming public space using the authority of, rather than rejecting, their traditional constructions as women. This can involve wearing traditional clothing (including the veil) and being active as wives and mothers rather than rejecting these roles (Vargas, 1991). There is currently a debate, however, concerning the extent to which these 'role-based' activities can lead to meaningful social transformation in women's position within their collectivities (Molyneux, 1993). Similar questions have been asked concerning the participation of women alongside men during times of national liberation struggles and wars. The question is whether the public spaces and widening of legitimate roles for women which open up in times of crisis can outlive the moment of crisis to advance women's lives in enduring ways (Yuval-Davis, 1985; Enloe, 1983; 1989: 52–4) Such heterogeneous women's politics that form a large segment of women's collective action, however, raises serious questions about the adequacy of feminist theoretical frameworks. New (albeit provisional) concepts such as 'transversality' and transnational feminist practices have developed as substitutes for relativistic notions of 'difference' and such exclusionary notions as 'universality' or the fictitious kinship of global sisterhood. Such concepts provide a more promising basis for coalitions and women's political solidarity across national, racial/ethnic, religious and other forms of boundaries (Grewal and Kaplan, 1994; Hill-Collins, 1990; Nesiah, 1993; Yuval-Davis, 1993c). More significant than the over-arching concepts emerging out of these new alliances is the growing knowledge and support given to women's resistance around the world against the destructive aspects of global restructuring, the debt and environmental crises, and violence.

Conclusion

The various movements for social transformation, for empowerment and resistance to colonial, racial and gender domination in settler societies reflect the complexities of these societies. The problems these movements face in establishing solidarity and mutual support with each other also reveal the limitations of binary notions of social oppression. As the following case studies demonstrate, any effective analysis of settler societies must move beyond simplistic and misleading dichotomies. A cautionary note, however, is warranted. The case studies, of necessity, have had to use shorthand in compressing the analyses of the complex interrelationships of gender, race, ethnicity and class in each country. Moreover, the focus in the case studies on articulations among these four axes of differentiation in no way implies that there are not other significant social relations and identities (pertaining to, for example, sexuality, religion and language through which power and resistance are constituted. There are, however, real limits to understanding the complexity of power that has multiple levels of determination: all efforts have been made to avoid mechanistic, additive and non-relational analyses of heterogeneity. In addition, distinct historical periods which frame the analyses in these chapters must be understood more as narrative devices, rather than 'objective' chronologies. The effects of major events which can be considered significant watersheds for the political centre can take time and space to ripple through to the periphery; by which time their effects can already be hugely modified.

In this introduction we have been critical of comparative models and typologies of inter-ethnic relations which construct collectivities and national and ethnic 'communities' as 'natural' or homogeneous entities. Our intention, and those of the authors of the chapters which follow, is not, however, to develop an alternative typology. Typologies tend to be ahistorical and evolve 'ideal types' which fail to take into account the continuous processes of struggles and negotiations within and between collectivities, and the dynamics of restructuring and change. Thus, the following case studies represent a variety of prisms through which to view the articulations of gender, ethnicity, race and class in 'settler societies' that are confronting major challenges. As this book goes into press, many of the societies examined are undergoing or are entering periods of tumultuous change which will undoubtedly reshape the boundaries of these societies and the complexity of their social dynamics. Hopefully this book will contribute to the reconsideration of the social relations within settler societies and provide support to progressive political struggles and negotiations in their efforts to move beyond dichotomies.

References

Abele, Frances and Stasiulis, Daiva (1989) 'Canada as a "white settler colony": what about natives and immigrants?', in W. Clement and G. Williams (eds), *The New Canadian Political Economy*. Kingston: McGill-Queen's University Press. pp. 240–77.

Adam, Heribert (1972) *Modernizing Racial Domination*. Berkeley: University of California Press.

Althusser, Louis (1969) *For Marx*. London: Allen Lane.

Anderson, Benedict (1983) *Imagined Communities: Reflections of the Origin and Spread of Nationalism*. London: Verso.

Anthias, Floya and Yuval-Davis, Nira (1983) 'Contextualizing feminism : gender, ethnic and class divisions', *Feminist Review*, 15: 62–75.

Anthias, Floya and Yuval-Davis, Nira, in association with Harriet Cain (1992) *Racialized Boundaries: Race, Nation, Gender, Colour and Class and the Anti-Racist Struggle*. London: Routledge.

Arat-Koc, Sedef (1989) 'In the privacy of our own home: foreign domestic workers as solution to the crisis in the domestic sphere in Canada', *Studies in Political Economy*, 28: 33–58.

Bakan, Abigail and Stasiulis, Daiva (1994) 'Foreign domestic worker policy in Canada and the social boundaries of citizenship', *Science and Society*. 58: 7–33.

Bakan, Abigail and Stasiulis, Daiva (1995) 'Making the match: domestic placement agencies and the racialization of women's household work', *Signs*, 20 (2): 1–33.

Balibar, Etienne (1991) 'Racism and Nationalism', in E. Balibar and E. Wallerstein (eds), *Race, Nation, Class: Ambiguous Identities*. London: Verso. pp. 37–68.

Barrera, Mario (1979) *Race and Class in the Southwest: a Theory of Racial Inequality*. Notre Dame: University of Notre Dame Press.

Barrett, Michele (1989) 'Some different meaning of the concept of "difference": feminist theory and the concept of ideology', in E. Meese and A. Parker (eds), *The Difference Within: Feminist and Critical Theory*. Amsterdam: John Benjamins.

Bauer, Otto (1940) *The National Question*. Rehavia: Hakibutz Ha'artzi. (Hebrew.)

Bell, Diane (1980) 'Desert politics: choices in the "marriage market"', in M. Etienne and E. Leacock (eds), *Women and Colonization: Anthropological Perspectives*. New York: Praeger.

Bhabha, Homi K. (ed.) (1990) *Nation and Narration*. London: Routledge.

Bondi, Liz (1993), 'Locating identity politics', in M. Keith and S. Pile (eds), *Place and the Politics of Identity*. London: Routledge.

Bottomley, Gil, de Lepervanche, Marie and Martin, Jeannie (eds) (1991) *Intersextions: Gender/class/culture/ethnicity*. Sydney: Allen & Unwin.

Bourgeault, Ron (1989) 'Race, class and gender: colonial domination of Indian women', *Socialist Studies*, 5: 87–115.

Callaway, Helen (1987) *Gender, Culture and Empire: European Women in Colonial Nigeria*. London: Macmillan.

Carby, Hazel (1982) 'White women listen! Black feminism and the boundaries of sister-hood', in Centre for Contemporary Cultural Studies (ed.), *The Empire Strikes Back*. London: Hutchinson. pp. 212–35.

Carby, Hazel (1987) *Reconstructing Womanhood: the Emergence of the Afro-American Woman Novelist*. New York: Oxford University Press.

Castles, Stephen, in association with Heather Booth and Tina Wallace (1984) *Here for Good: Western Europe's New Ethnic Minorities*. London: Pluto Press.

Castles, Stephen and Miller, Mark J. (1993) *The Age of Migration: International Population Movements in the Modern World*. Macmillan, London.

Cock, Jacklyn (1980) *Maids & Madames: a Study in the Politics of Exploitation*. Johannesburg: Ravan Press. (Also London: Women's Press, 1989.)

Cohen, Jean (1982) *Class and Civil Society: the Limits of Marxian Critical Theory*. Amherst: University of Massachusetts Press.

Colen, Shellee (1989) '"Just a Little Respect": West Indian domestic workers in New York City', in D. Chaney and M. Garcia Castro (eds), *Muchachas No More: Household Workers in Latin America and the Caribbean*. Philadelphia: Temple University Press.

de Lepervanche, Marie (1991) 'Holding it All Together: Multiculturalism, nationalism, women and the state in Australia', in S. Allen, F. Anthias and N. Yuval-Davis (eds), *Gender, Race and Class*, special issue of the *International Review of Sociology*, 2: 73–96.

Denoon, Donald (1983) *Settler Capitalism: the Dynamics of Dependent Development in the Southern Hemisphere*. Oxford: Clarendon Press.

Dickason, Olive Patricia (1992) *Canada's First Nations*. Toronto: McClelland & Stewart.

Ehrensaft, Philip and Armstrong, Warwick (1981) 'The formation of dominion capitalism: economic truncation and class structure', in A. Moscovitch and G. Drover (eds), *Inequality: Essays on the Political Economy of Social Welfare*. Toronto: University of Toronto Press.

Elliott, John H. (1987) 'Introduction: Colonial identity in the Atlantic world', in N. Canny and A. Pagden (eds), *Colonial Identity in the Atlantic World, 1500–1800*. Princeton: Princeton University Press.

Enloe, Cynthia (1983) *Does Khaki Become You?* London: Pluto Press.

Enloe, Cynthia (1989) *Bananas, Beaches and Bases: Making Feminist Sense of International Politics*. Berkeley: University of California Press.

Etienne, Mona and Eleanor Leacock (1980) 'Introduction', in M. Etienne and E. Leacock (eds), *Women and Colonization: Anthropological Perspectives*. New York, Praeger. pp. 1–24.

Fieldhouse, D.K. (1966) *The Colonial Empires from the Eighteenth Century*. New York: Weidenfeld & Nicolson.

Fiske, Jo-Anne (1988) 'Fishing is women's business: changing economic roles of carrier women and men', in B. Cox (ed.), *Native People, Native Lands: Canadian Indians, Inuit and Metis*. Ottawa: Carleton University Press.

Fredrickson, George (1988) 'Colonialism and racism: the United States and South Africa in comparative perspective', in his *The Arrogance of Race*. Middletown: Wesleyan University Press.

Fuss, Diana (1989) *Essentially Speaking: Feminism, Nature and Difference*. New York: Routledge.

Fyfe, Christopher (1992) 'Race, empire and the historians', *Race and Class*, 33 (4): 15–29.

Geertz, C. (ed.) (1963) *Old Societies and New States*. New York: Free Press.

Gellner, Ernest (1983) *Nations and Nationalism*. Oxford: Basil Blackwell.

Geschwender, James A. (1977) *Class, Race and Worker Insurgency*. Cambridge: Cambridge University Press.

Glenn, Evelyn Nakano (1992) 'From servitude to service work: historical continuities in the racial division of paid productive work', *Signs*, 18 (1): 1–43.

Greenberg, Stanley B. (1980) *Race and State in Capitalist Development: Comparative Perspectives*. New Haven: Yale University Press.

Grewel, Inderpal and Kaplan, Caren (1994) 'Introduction: transnational feminist practices and questions of postmodernity', in I. Grewel and C. Kaplan (eds), *Scattered Hegemonies: Postmodernity and Transnational Feminist Practices*. Minneapolis: University of Minnesota Press.

Gunew, Sneja and Yeatman, Anna (eds) (1993) *Feminism and the Politics of Difference*. St Leonards, New South Wales: Allen & Unwin.

Haggis, Jane (1990) 'Gendering colonialism or colonizing gender? recent women's studies approaches to white women and the history of British colonialism', *Women's Studies International Forum*, 13 (1–2): 105–15.

Hechter, Michael (1975) *Internal Colonialism: the Celtic Fringe in British National Development, 1536–1966*. London: Routledge & Kegan Paul.

Hill-Collins, Patricia (1990) *Black Feminist Thought: Knowledge, Consciousness and the Politics of Empowerment*. Boston: Unwin Hyman.

Hobsbawm, Eric (1990) *Nations and Nationalism since 1780*. Cambridge: Cambridge University Press.

hooks, bell (1981) *Ain't I a Woman: Black Women and Feminism*. Boston: South End Press.

hooks, bell (1984) *Feminist Theory: from the Margin to the Center*. Boston: South End Press.

hooks, bell (1988) *Talking Back: Thinking Feminist, Thinking Black*. Toronto: Between the Lines.

Huttenback, Robert A. (1976) *Racism and Empire: White Settlers and Coloured Immigrants in the British Self-Governing Colonies, 1830–1910*. Ithaca: Cornell University Press.

Jameson, Elizabeth (1988) 'Towards a multicultural history of women in the western United States', *Signs*, 13 (4): 761–91.

Jayawardena, Kumari (1986) *Feminism and Nationalism in the Third World*. London: Zed Press.

Jayawardena, Kumari (1993) *With a Different Voice: White Women and Colonialism in South Asia*. London: Zed Press.

Jewell, K. Sue (1993) *From Mammy to Miss America and Beyond*. London: Routledge.

Jhappan, Radha (1991) 'Natural rights vs. legal positivism: Indians, the courts and the new discourse of aboriginal rights in Canada', *British Journal of Canadian Studies*, 6 (1): 60–100.

Jhappan, Radha (1992) 'A global community? Supranational strategies of Canada's aboriginal peoples', *The Journal of Indigenous Studies*, 3 (1): 59–97.

Jhappan, Radha (1993) 'Inherency, three nations and collective rights: the evolution of aboriginal constitutional discourse from 1982 to the Charlottetown Accord', *International Journal of Canadian Studies*, 7–8 (Spring–Fall): 225–59.

Jolly, Margaret (1993) 'Colonizing women: the maternal body and empire', in S. Gunew and A. Yeatman (eds), *Feminism and the Politics of Difference*. Sydney: Allen & Unwin.

Kandiyoti, Deniz (1991) 'Introduction', in D. Kandiyoti (ed.), *Women, Islam and the State*. Philadelphia: Temple University Press.

Keane, John (ed.) (1988) *Civil Society and the State: New European Perspectives*. London: Verso.

Keegan, Timothy (1989) 'Race, class and economic development in South Africa: a review article', *Social Dynamics*, 15 (1): 111–21.

Kennedy, Dane (1987) 'The expansion of Europe', *Journal of Modern History*, 59: 331–43.

Knapman, Claudia (1986) *White Women in Fiji, 1835–1980: the Ruin for Empire?* Sydney: Allen & Unwin.

Kuper, L. and Smith, M.G. (1969) *Pluralism in Africa*. Los Angeles: University of California Press.

Lake, Marilyn (1993) 'Colonised and colonizing: the white Australian feminist subject', *Women's History Review*, 2 (3): 377–87.

Larner, Wendy (1993) 'Changing contexts: globalization, migration and feminism in New Zealand', in S. Gunew and A. Yeatman (eds) *Feminism and the Politics of Difference*. Sydney: Allen & Unwin.

Lord, Audre (1984) *Sister Outsider*. Trumansberg: Crossing Press.

McGrath, Ann (1990) 'The white man's looking glass: aboriginal colonial gender relations at Port Jackson', *Australian Historical Studies*, 24 (95): 189–207.

McIntosh, Mary (1978) 'The state and the oppression of women', in A. Kuhn and A. Wolpe (eds), *Feminism and Materialism*. London: Routledge & Kegan Paul.

McMichael, Philip (1984) *Settlers and the Agrarian Question: Foundations of Capitalism in Colonial Australia*. Cambridge: Cambridge University Press.

Mahon, Rianne (1991) 'From "bringing" to "putting": the state in late century social theory', *Canadian Journal of Sociology*, 16 (2): 119–44.

Marshall, T.H. (1950) *Citizenship and Social Class*. Cambridge: Cambridge University Press.

Marshall, T.H. (1975) *Social Policy in the Twentieth Century*. London: Hutchinson. (First edition, 1965.)

Marshall, T.H. (1981) *The Right to Welfare and Other Essays*. London: Heinemann Educational Books.

Melucci, Alberto (1989) *Nomads of the Present: Social Movements and Individual Needs in Contemporary Society*. London: Verso.

Miles, Robert (1987) *Capitalism and Unfree Labour: Anomaly or Necessity?* London: Tavistock.

Mitter, Swasti (1986) *Common Fate, Common Bond: Women in the Global Economy*. London: Pluto Press.

Mohanty, Chandra Tolpade (1991) 'Under western eyes: feminist scholarship and colonial discourses', in C.T. Mohanty, A. Russo and L. Torres (eds), *Third World Women and the Politics of Feminism*. Bloomington: Indiana University Press.

Molyneux, Maxine (1993) 'Female collective action in socialist states', paper, Women's Participation in Societies Experiencing Conflict Conference, Belfast, September.

Mosley, Paul (1983) *The Settler Economies: Studies in the Economic History of Kenya and Southern Rhodesia, 1900–1963*. Cambridge: Cambridge University Press.

Mullings, Leith (1986) 'Uneven development: class, race and gender in the United States before 1900', in L. Leacock and H. Safa (eds), *Women's Work: Development and the Division of Labor by Gender*. South Hadey: Bergin & Garvey. pp. 41–57.

Nadeau, Denise (1992) 'Women fight back', in J. Sinclair (ed.), *Crossing the Line*. Vancouver: New Star Books.

Nesiah, Vasuki (1993) 'Towards a feminist internationality: a critique of US feminist legal scholarship', *Harvard Women's Law Review*, 16.

Nicholson, Linda J. (ed.) (1990) *Feminism/Modernism*. New York: Routledge.

Nimni, Ephraim (1991) *Marxism and Nationalism*. London: Pluto Press.

Pagden, Anthony and Nicholas Canny (1987) 'Afterword: from identity to independence', in N. Canny and A. Pagden (eds) *Colonial Identity in the Atlantic World, 1500–1800*. Princeton: Princeton University Press.

Panitch, Leo (1981) 'Dependency and class in Canadian political economy', *Studies in Political Economy*, 6: 7–34.

Pettman, Jan (1988) '"All the women are white . . .": racism, sexism and the re-presentation of black women', paper, SAANZ Conference, Melbourne.

Pettman, Jan (1992) *Living in the Margins: Racism, Sexism and Feminism in Australia*. Sydney: Allen & Unwin.

Radcliffe, S.A. (1990) 'Ethnicity, patriarchy and incorporation into the nation: female migrants as domestic servants in Peru', *Society and Space*, 8: 379–93.

Rex, John (1983) *Race Relations in Sociological Theory*, 2nd edn. London: Routledge.

Richardson, Boyce (1993) *People of Terra Nullius*. Vancouver: Douglas & McIntyre.

Rosenthal, Michael (1992) 'What was postmodernism?' *Socialist Review*, February: 83–105.

Rowbotham, Sheila (1992) *Women in Movement: Feminism and Social Action*. London: Routledge.

Sahgal, Gita and Yuval-Davis, Nira (eds) (1992) *Refusing Holy Orders: Women and Fundamentalism in Britain*. London: Virago.

Satzewich, Vic (1991) *Racism and the Incorporation of Foreign Labour: Farm Labour Migration to Canada since 1945*. London and New York: Routledge.

Sen, Gita and Grown, Caren, (1987) *Development, Crises and Alternative Visions: Third World Women's Perspectives*. New York: Monthly Review Press.

Shafir, Gershon (1989) *Land, Labor and the Origins of the Israeli–Palestinian Conflict 1882–1914*. Cambridge: Cambridge University Press.

Shafir, Gershon (1993) 'Land, labour and population in the Zionist colonization: general and specific aspects', in Uri Ram (ed.), *The Israeli Society: Critical Perspectives*. Tel Aviv: Breirot. pp. 104–19.

Schermerhorn, R.A. (1970) *Comparative Ethnic Relations*. Chicago: University of Chicago Press.

Shils, E. (1957) 'Primordial, personal, sacred and civil ties', *British Journal of Sociology*, 7.

Smith, Anthony D. (1986) *The Ethnic Origins of Nations*. Oxford: Basil Blackwell.

Spelman, Elizabeth V. (1988) *Inessential Woman: Problems of Exclusion in Feminist Thought*. Boston: Beacon Press.

Stasiulis, Daiva K. (1987) 'Rainbow feminism: perspectives on minority women in Canada', *Resources in Feminist Research*, 16 (1): 5–9.

Stasiulis, Daiva K. (1988) 'The symbolic mosaic reaffirmed: multicultural policy' in K. Graham (ed.), *How Ottawa Spends, 1988–89*. Ottawa: Carleton University Press.

Stasiulis, Daiva K. (1990) 'Theorizing connections: race, ethnicity, gender and class', in P. Li (ed.), *Race and Ethnic Relations in Canada*. Toronto: Oxford University Press.

Stasiulis, Daiva (1991) 'Symbolic representation and the numbers game: Tory policies on "race" and visible minorities', in F. Abele (ed.), *How Ottawa Spends, 1990–91: The Politics of Fragmentation*. Ottawa: Carleton University Press.

Stasiulis, Daiva K. (1993) '"Authentic voice": anti-racist politics in Canadian feminist publishing and literary production', in S. Gunew and A. Yeatman (eds), *Feminism and the Politics of Difference*. Sydney: Allen & Unwin.

Stasiulis, Daiva K. (forthcoming) 'Diversity, power and voice: the antinomies of progressive education,' in S. Richer and L. Weir (eds), *Beyond Political Correctness: the Future of the Canadian Academy*. Toronto: University of Toronto Press.

Thakur, Usha (1992) 'Combatting Family Violence', *Resources in Feminist Research*, 13 (1): 30–2.

van den Berghe, P. (1979) *The Ethnic Phenomenon*. New York: Elsevier.

van Kirk, Sylvia (1983) *Many Tender Ties: Women in Fur Trade Society, 1670–1870* (2nd edn). Winnipeg: Watson & Dwyer Publishing.

Vargas, Gina (1991) 'Women's movements in Peru: streams, sparks and knots', *European Review of Latin American and Caribbean Studies*, June.

Walker, Alice (1984) *In Search of Our Mothers' Gardens: Womanist Prose*. San Diego: Harcourt Brace Jovanovich.

Wallerstein, Immanuel (1979) *The Capitalist World-Economy*. Cambridge: Cambridge University Press.

Wallerstein, Immanuel (1980) *The Modern World System II: Mercantilism and the Consolidation of the European World Economy, 1600–1750*. New York: Academic Press.

Weitzer, Ronald (1990) *Transforming Settler States: Communal Conflict and Internal Security in Northern Ireland and Zimbabwe*. Berkeley: University of California Press.

Wetherell, Margaret and Potter, Jonathan (1992) *Mapping the Language of Racism: Discourse and the Legitimation of Exploitation*. New York: Columbia University Press.

WING (Women Under Immigration and Nationality Law) (1985) *Worlds Apart: Women Under Immigration and Nationality Law*. London: Pluto

Wolpe, Harold (1975) 'The theory of internal colonialism: the South African case', in I. Oxaal, T. Barbet and D. Booth (eds), *Beyond the Sociology of Development*. London: Routledge & Kegan Paul.

Yeatman, Anna (1992) 'Minorities and the politics of difference', *Political Theory Newsletter*, Canberra, March.

Young, Iris Marion (1990) *Justice and the Politics of Difference*. Princeton: Princeton University Press.

Yuval-Davis, Nira (1985) 'Front and rear: sexual divisions of labour in the Israeli army', *Feminist Studies*, 11 (3): 649–76.

Yuval-Davis, Nira (1987) 'Marxism and Jewish nationalism', *History Workshop Journal*, no. 24: 82–110.

Yuval-Davis, Nira (1991) 'The citizenship debate: women, ethnic processes and the state', *Feminist Review*, 39: 58–68.

Yuval-Davis, Nira (1992) 'Fundamentalism, multi-culturalism and women in Britain', in J. Donald and A. Rattansi (eds), *Race, Culture and Difference*. London: Sage and Open University. pp. 278–92.

Yuval-Davis, Nira (1993a) 'Nationalism and Racism', *Cahiers de Recherche Sociale*, no. 20: 183–202.

Yuval-Davi Nira (1993b) 'Gender and Nation', *Ethnic and Racial Studies*, 16 (4): 621–32.

Yuval-Davis, Nira (1993c) 'Women and coalition politics', in Mary Kennedy, Cathy Lubelska and Valerie Walsh (eds), *Making Connections: Women's Studies, Women's Movements, Women's Lives*. London: Falmer Press. pp. 3–10.

Yuval-Davis, Nira (1994) 'Women, ethnicity and empowerment', *Feminism and Psychology*, no. 4, special issue on 'Shifting identities: shifting racism'.

Yuval-Davis, Nira and Floya Anthias (eds) (1989), *Woman–Nation–State*. London: Macmillan. pp. 1–15.

Zureik, Elia (1979) *The Palestinians in Israel: a Study of Internal Colonialism*. London: Routledge & Kegan Paul.

2

Post-Colonial Politics in Aotearoa/New Zealand

Wendy Larner and Paul Spoonley

The last decade has been a period of profound economic and political change in Aotearoa/New Zealand. As the result of government-initiated reforms involving the deregulation of the financial sector and reduced levels of protection and industry assistance, the New Zealand economy has moved from being one of the most highly regulated economies in the world to one of the least regulated. The conditions of domestic production are now dominated by the international money market, large corporations and international speculators, in particular from Australia, Japan and South-East Asia. The state sector has also been reorganized. Many government departments have been turned into corporations and are now required to operate on a commercial basis. The result has been a reduction in both the services offered and staffing levels. A programme of asset sales, introduced in an attempt to reduce New Zealand's overseas debt, has seen a number of these corporations fully privatized.

Ironically, deregulation and privatization were first introduced by a Labour government which held office from 1984 to 1990. Following the election of a National government in 1990, economic restructuring has been accompanied by further substantive steps towards the dismantling of the welfare state, and by the introduction of labour market legislation that individualizes the employment contract between employers and employees. The consequences are dramatic. As one commentator recently observed, 'New Zealand . . . serves as a case study of the economic and social damage that can be wrought by monetarism' (Jesson, 1992: 38).

Yet during the same period, after nearly a century and a half of political pressure by indigenous Maori tribal groups, the Treaty of Waitangi, signed in 1840 between the British Crown and Maori chiefs, was finally acknowledged by the New Zealand state. In 1985 the Waitangi Tribunal, initially established in 1975, was given the power to investigate Maori claims of injustice back to 1840. In the years subsequent to this decision the Treaty has become a focal point for new forms of ethnic politicization among both Maori and Pakeha (the descendants of European colonizing settlers).

For Maori longstanding grievances about land and culture resurfaced in the 1970s as young activists, influenced by international civil rights movements, combined traditional concerns with new political strategies. The new phase of ethnic politicization, in evidence by the early 1980s, was associated with arguments for 'Maori sovereignty'. Buoyed by sympathetic court decisions, and with a substantial degree of inter-tribal consensus, Maori used arguments about colonialism and the provisions of the Treaty to extract substantial concessions from the New Zealand state. This not only involved a reformulation of public policy, as the tenets of the Treaty were incorporated into all new Acts of Parliament, but also resulted in ethnic rights dominating debates about resource allocation and social justice.

In response Pakeha have also entered a new phase of ethnic politicization and are beginning to explore the implications of a locally focused identity. For some Pakeha this politicization involves the acknowledgement of the politics of Maori sovereignty, or *tino rangatiratanga* as it has come to be known, together with attempts to establish what is referred to as 'biculturalism' between Maori and Pakeha within the central institutions of Aotearoa/New Zealand. In an increasingly internationalized economic environment, and in the absence of alternatives, the Treaty of Waitangi is seen as the basis for some form of social contract between *tangata whenua*, or indigenous people, and the rest of the population. There is, however, considerable conflict between these new cultural and political forms, which stress notions of social justice and welfare based on the collective rights of ethnic groups, and the individualism underlying the New Right philosophies which sustain monetarist economic agendas.

The internationalization of the New Zealand economy, together with the ongoing political and economic struggles of Maori and more recent attempts by Pakeha to consider the specificity of their identity, all serve to problematize the notion that Aotearoa/New Zealand can be usefully classified as a 'white settler society' in the 1990s. The historical and cultural connections between 'white settler societies', reinscribed by contributors to this book, are precisely those that many Pakeha are being forced to reconsider. For Maori, for settlers from the Pacific and for the long-established but now rapidly expanding Asian communities in New Zealand, the racism and oppression embodied in such a label are more obvious.

While the importance of the colonial imperative in Aotearoa/New Zealand's development should not be underestimated, it is now widely accepted that historical connections with other 'white settler societies' should be balanced with those in the South Pacific. Not only do the micro-states of the Pacific share with New Zealand similar colonial histories, they also have similar post-colonial movements concerned with the rights of indigenous Polynesian groups, political independence and nuclear-free politics. Further, New Zealand has large Pacific Island communities, including Western Samoans, Tongans, Cook Islanders, Niueans and Tokelauans, which in some cases outnumber those remaining in the society of origin.

A second set of contemporary connections is also regionally based. In the last decade it has become apparent that, as a result of the internationalization of production and finance, New Zealand's economic future lies with Australia and the emergent Pacific Rim countries. The alliances necessary for effective political strategies within this context are in the process of being forged by both conservative and radical groups. While the outcomes of the interplay between post-colonial politics and internationalized production relations are as yet unknown, there can be no doubt that the country once described as the 'Britain of the South' (Fairburn, 1989: 24) is in the midst of an irrevocable transformation.

This chapter explores the way in which these contemporary political and economic changes have affected, and are affected by, the articulations between gender, ethnic and class identities in New Zealand. The gender divisions that exist within and across ethnic boundaries will be contextualized through a consideration of the processes of colonialism, including the incorporation or exclusion of distinct 'racial' or ethnic groups; the evolving nature of settler capitalism, especially labour market processes; and the new forms of politics that have mediated dominant, indigenous and migrant feminist interests. The starting point for the chapter, however, must be the reaffirmation of the integrity of a system that existed prior to European intrusion in 1769.

Imperial Sovereignty: the Realization of Capitalist and Colonial Intentions

Te tangata whenua, which can be translated as 'we who stand here' or 'people of the land', were well established in Aotearoa at the time of annexation. Although the country was not densely populated, it was actively occupied with established territorial demarcations between *iwi* (tribes) and *hapu* (sub-tribes), and well-known corridors of exchange. Land was not only an economic base, it was also of spiritual, cultural and symbolic importance. Tribal connections and individual identity were both integrally linked to the physical landscape. Localized social relations involved a complex lineage form of production which centred on *mana*, or status. *Mana* and the patterns of authority derived from lineage involved both men and women. As Pere (1987: 56) has explained,

With the exception of slaves (male and female), the women [in Maori society] were never regarded as chattels or possessions; they retained their own names on marriage. Retaining their own identity and whakapapa (genealogy) was of utmost importance and children could identify with the kinship group of either or both parents.

Following the arrival of Captain James Cook in 1769, European whalers and traders had dealings with many *iwi* and a number of these sojourners became settlers. More significant, however, was the arrival of British colonial administrators and the missionaries, recently described as 'the advance party of cultural invasion' (Walker, 1990: 85). Both the missionaries and administrators were imbued with the belief that their institutions and values were superior to *te tangata whenua*, or Maori as they insisted in calling them. Some commentators have emphasized the humanitarian aspirations of these early intruders (compare Pearson, 1990: 42). Certainly the Treaty of Waitangi, which was signed between some Maori and representatives of the British government in 1840, arose in part from the colonial administration's concern for Maori. But such an interpretation must be tempered with an understanding of the situation that existed.

At the time the Treaty was signed Maori still outnumbered Pakeha, as they called the newcomers, by forty to one. There was, however, genuine concern among *te tangata whenua* about the future of their relations with the growing number of incoming settlers. By this stage a considerable number of British migrants had arrived as part of the imperial process whereby entire families would 'recreate versions of the mother country' (Pearson, 1990: 30). Early attempts had been made by private interests to establish a British class society in New Zealand. This involved transplanting selected migrants to colonial settlements which were designed to replicate rural English communities. Although the numbers of migrants, and a degree of incompetence, overwhelmed such attempts at settlement, migrants did tend to come from most classes. And while migration was male dominated, significant numbers of complete families were involved.

In signing the Treaty, Maori chiefs did not believe that they were granting *mana whenua*, or control of the land, to the settlers. As Nopera Panakareao indicated at the time, 'the shadow of the land goes to the Queen but the substance remains with us' (Walker, 1990: 98). The colonial administrators, on the other hand, assumed that they had established sovereignty. The confusion arose not simply because of the existence of different versions of the Treaty (in both Maori and English) but, more fundamentally, as the result of different understandings of Maori and Pakeha. These were particularly manifest in the different conceptions of the ownership of land. The European view of land as being both privately owned and alienable, and as a commodity that could be voluntarily exchanged between individuals in a market place (O'Connor, 1991: 1), was not part of Maori understanding.

For a short period the Treaty appeared to provide a successful basis for both the establishment of a new order and the incorporation of Maori into it. In the two decades after 1840, local knowledge and navigational skills enabled Maori to dominate domestic production of foodstuffs. Not only did *iwi* provide an extensive array of produce for the New Zealand market, but they also supplied the east coast of Australia using their own ships. This partial incorporation, however, was soon challenged by the changing nature of colonial administrative sensitivities, initiated by the ever-increasing numbers of settlers from Britain.

By the 1870s the demographic dominance of Maori had been eclipsed and Pakeha settlers outnumbered Maori six to one. The issue of property rights grew as the incoming settlers made more vociferous demands for land. In the two decades following the signing of the Treaty, colonial administrators had used their institutions, in particular the judicial system, to extend the European conceptions of ownership (Kelsey, 1984). A series of Acts in the 1860s, including the Native Land Acts of 1862 and 1865, reinforced the notion of the private ownership of land, and gave the Native Land Court the mandate to transfer communal title to individual alienable title. The 1863 Settlements Act allowed land to be confiscated from those Maori who resisted colonization, although in practice even *iwi* who were in support of the colonists lost land through confiscation. As Pearson (1990) argues, Pakeha were the immigrants but the state they established acted as host.

'Legal imperialism' (Kelsey, 1984) was eventually replaced by outright armed conflict. The wars fought between the 1860s and the 1890s were not only about the access of Pakeha settlers to land, but also about whether Maori or Pakeha conceptions of land use and ownership would prevail. Given the demographic and political dominance of Pakeha, the outcome was not seriously in doubt, although Maori resistance was vigorous and varied in form. But it was undermined by the ongoing loss of land and therefore *mana* (understood in this context as cultural integrity derived from spiritual connections with, and economic control of, land), and by the effects of diseases introduced by Europeans.

From the 1770s, when venereal disease was introduced, through to the 1790s, when influenza appeared closely followed by chronic infectious diseases such as TB, Maori communities were devastated by diseases against which they had no resistance (Pool, 1991). In the 1880s and 1890s, 40 per cent of Maori girls would not have reached their first birthday, while only 30 per cent would have reached 35 years of age (Pool, 1991: 78). The loss of land, and consequently *mana*, and the

effects of diseases saw a rapid decline in the size of the Maori population and led some to conclude that Maori would disappear altogether
(Pool, 1991: 4). While this proved to be far from the truth, the disarray
of Maori society following the Land Wars enabled colonialism to give
way to settler capitalism.

An increasingly centralized state began to develop the infrastructure,
especially transportation systems, which enabled the replacement of
rudimentary forms of subsistence production with substantial pastoral
production, and a growing primary processing sector. Although some
Maori were proletarianized as the demand for labour grew, by this
time most were economically and geographically marginal to the new
forms of production. If the state was interested in Maori, it was only in
order to ensure that cultural imperialism proceeded. Institutions such
as schools were used not only to provide Maori with the skills to participate, if somewhat peripherally, in the labour market that served
capitalism, but also to convince Maori of the need to replace traditional cultural values and institutions with those of Pakeha (Spoonley,
1993).

These policies were not always successful. Geographic isolation protected some *iwi*, while others actively resisted the hegemonic policies of
Pakeha. In the latter half of the nineteenth century and the early parts
of the twentieth century there were a large number of political and
religious movements which aimed to retain and restore integrity for
Maori (see Walker, 1990). These movements ranged from strategic
attempts to participate in the institutions of the colonial state to seek
resources for Maori, through to the armed opposition of some
prophetic movements. These attempts, however, were increasingly overshadowed by the emerging conflict between the major economic actors
associated with settler capitalism. Elite rural interests, a growing working class and petty bourgeois concerns produced the major political
parties and, in turn, the 1890 Liberal government. Cultural imperialism
and land alienation had been largely achieved, and Maori were to all
intents and purposes a socially and geographically marginal group.

Relations between Pakeha and other migrants were also based on
racial exclusiveness. Initially Chinese and then Indian migrants were
targets in Pakeha attempts to define themselves and their new nation-
state. Chinese men came to New Zealand as itinerant workers following
the discovery of gold in the 1870s. They constituted a bachelor society,
not only because many planned to return to China, but also because of
the response to their arrival. While the number of migrants arriving
was small (between 1870 and 1881 6,000 people arrived while 3,100
left), a series of highly discriminatory policies and legislation ensued.
Chinese and, later, Indian migrants were seen by both Pakeha elite
and working class as an economic and moral/political threat. Twenty-

one bills were introduced into Parliament from 1879 to 1920 to limit or exclude the number of 'Asians' coming to New Zealand (Pearson, 1990). This legislation ensured that female migration and/or family reunification did not occur until well into the twentieth century.

European migrants from countries other than Britain were also few in number, although some Scandinavians arrived in the latter part of the nineteenth century, together with small groups of Italians, Greeks and Germans. The only other significant group of migrants, particularly in terms of New Zealand's racial politics, were Dalmatian migrants from the former Yugoslavia. They, like Chinese and Indian migrants, were seen as an economic threat by Pakeha, and confronted exclusionary attitudes and policies. This racism, prevalent in the last decades of the nineteenth century and the first decades of the twentieth, formed the basis of a 'white New Zealand' migration policy which prevailed until recently. It was also an important expression of the developing nationalism of the dominant Pakeha; a nationalism which at this stage was characterized by exclusivity and orientated towards Britain.

A Gendered Society?

The crisis over land which resulted in the Land Wars had its parallels in both class and gender relations within the Pakeha community. Although Pakeha as a whole benefited from the dispossession of Maori, there was considerable conflict between them as to who should gain access to land. As infrastructure improved and the significance of subsistence production declined, land ownership became more concentrated. Wealthy pastoralists were able to monopolize access to land, resulting in their increasing economic, political and social power.

An itinerant male labour force began to emerge as increasing numbers of Pakeha men opted for, or were forced into, wage-earning opportunities outside the household. As James and Saville-Smith (1989) have demonstrated, this development, in turn, had considerable impact on gender relations within the Pakeha community. Many Pakeha women found themselves dependent on transient men, whose lack of commitment to the financial and social well-being of the rest of the family (women, children and the elderly) often meant the impoverishment of the latter (James and Saville-Smith, 1989: 27). The participation of working-class Pakeha women in paid work also constituted a component of the crisis, in part because the nature of this work in the late nineteenth century was highly exploitative. Sweating, as a way of extracting labour from women and children, was a major concern, as were high levels of prostitution (James and Saville-Smith, 1989: 28).

Further, the breakdown of the subsistence household accompanied by the disintegration of networks of social control, meant that by the 1880s violence, drunkenness and crime were endemic.

Faced with increasing social instability the state was forced to take a more active role, notably in the promotion of a particular ideological position. The solution that emerged involved ensuring that Pakeha men took more responsibility for the social and economic welfare of their 'dependants'. On the one hand, this enabled the state to avoid having to take financial responsibility for welfare. On the other, the efficiency of production was seen as depending on a secure domestic situation whereby the male wage-earner took responsibility for those dependent upon him. Consequently the notion of the 'family man' and the cult of domesticity were both vigorously promoted. Employers, politicians and institutions of the state all had a vested interest in encouraging a particular conception of the public and private worlds and specific gender roles in these (Novitz, 1987: 26).

The increasing division of public and private sites of production with the corresponding distinction between male and female responsibilities that emerged in Pakeha communities in the early twentieth century had little overlap with the world of Maori. Despite the growing intrusion of state institutions, including the education system, public and private worlds were largely indivisible. Seasonal rural labouring was the major form of paid employment for Maori and involved both men and women, although some gender divisions were apparent. Further, concern about the exploitation of female labour did not extend to Maori women. The significant exception was the Ngata Commission in the 1920s which examined the relationship between Asian employers and Maori women and children employees. Generally the state was concerned with issues of a rather different nature. Following the election of the 1935 Labour government, the concern was with the hygiene and health of Maori communities, and women were targeted as those who were to be primarily responsible for improvements (Pool, 1991: 118).

Thus the social relations of the initial period of colonization, which were centred on Maori–Pakeha/*tangata whenua*–immigrant relations, gave way in the early part of the twentieth century to the relations of a developing capitalist economy in which the dominant issues were increasingly those of class and gender. The central state became a site of struggle over the nature of production and the welfare of labour. Class politics continued to dominate as the election of the first Labour government in the 1930s ushered in a period of Keynesian-inspired welfarism which remained in place until the election of another Labour government in 1984. But by this time, relations between Maori and Pakeha and the debates about the nature and effects of colonialism for these groups were firmly back as the dominant set of relations to be contested.

Postwar Labour Migrations

Contemporary forms of ethnic politicization have their origins in post-World War II developments. It was not until World War II, when the disruption in world trade necessitated an increase in domestic industrial production, that sustained industrial development was able to take place in New Zealand (Jesson, 1987). The dramatic growth in manufacturing generated a substantial increase in the demand for labour. This demand was not just the result of quantitative expansion, but also the move towards mass production techniques. The new jobs created were often dirty, monotonous, unhealthy and unpleasant. New Zealand manufacturers, like their counterparts in other developed countries, satisfied their need for unskilled and semi-skilled labour predominantly through migration, although at the same time increasing numbers of urban Pakeha women also entered the labour force as levels of part-time work increased and opportunities for employment in the service sector expanded.

Labour migration took a variety of forms. First, there were internal migrations. For Pakeha, economic expansion merely accentuated a rural drift to the cities that had started well before World War II, but for Maori the change was abrupt (Pearson, 1990). In 1945 three-quarters of the Maori population were living in rural areas. This figure was still two-thirds in 1956, yet by 1966 62 per cent of Maori people were urban (Pool, 1991: 153). By the 1970s three-quarters of Maori were resident in urban centres (Pool, 1991: 182), most of whom were living in non-tribal areas.

Secondly, there was international migration from various Pacific Islands that had been in colonial relationships with New Zealand earlier in the twentieth century. While in the early postwar era most migrants were men brought to New Zealand to do specific jobs, in the early 1960s the initial dominance of men in the migration flow was countered by the migration of large numbers of women. The reversal of the early pattern was due to a recognition of the demand for unskilled female labour in New Zealand, particularly in the textile and food processing industries. The majority were classic chain migrations in that intending migrants usually obtained their first jobs in New Zealand through friends or family who had already migrated. The result was that the Pacific communities established in New Zealand were concentrated in urban centres, in particular Auckland but also Wellington and Christchurch.

Finally, migration from Western Europe was also encouraged in order to expand the skilled work-force. The majority of these migrants were from the traditional British source, although labour shortages were such that other migrations were also encouraged. With the exception of a small number of Dutch migrants from the Netherlands and Indonesia, however, the numbers of non-British European migrants were relatively small. One study suggests that 85 per cent of all migrants who arrived in New Zealand between 1947 and 1958 were of British origin (Pearson, 1990: 114).

While the expansion of capitalism provided the catalyst for these labour migrations, outcomes were dependent on the ways in which economic relations articulated with other sets of social relations, including those of gender and ethnicity. Not only did new workers enter a labour market in which there was a clear distinction between the work of men and women, but they also performed specific tasks within these categories. Both Maori women and women from the Pacific, for example, were incorporated into a narrow range of manufacturing positions that were characterized by lower wages, poorer conditions, less security and fewer opportunities for advancement than those occupied by many Pakeha women (Ongley, 1991). British migrants, on the other hand, tended to take up skilled positions and were more occupationally dispersed.

New understandings of the composition of different ethnic groups and the relations between them were generated as a result of the interaction of once geographically and socially distinct groups of people. These understandings reflected the nature of previous and existing colonial relations as well as the views of dominant Pakeha about incoming migrants. The British, who were usually recruited as skilled and professional migrants, were regarded by Pakeha as the most acceptable, although there were periods when British migrants were disparagingly associated with trade union militancy. Maori, on the other hand, were treated warily by many Pakeha and there was a revival of racial beliefs about 'cultural behaviour'. Culturally and socially diverse migrants from the Pacific micro-states were not only homogenized as 'Pacific Islanders', but also viewed negatively by Pakeha. Pakeha racism focused on claims that migrants from the Pacific were 'taking the jobs of New Zealanders', despite the fact that many were New Zealand citizens by right. Maori, on the other hand, were more supportive of Pacific Island communities. This support was particularly manifest in the mid-1970s when, in response to growing 'law and order' problems in main centres, police and immigration officials tended to target anyone who was non-white. At the same time Maori were confronting their own social and economic marginalization as well as the continuing decline in their cultural practices and control of resources such as land. It was from this crucible that contestations over new political understandings emerged in the 1970s and 1980s.

The New Politics: Maori Sovereignty and Biculturalism

The critical transformation was centred around Maori politics. While the sovereignty guaranteed by the Treaty of Waitangi remained the primary issue, the ways in which the issues were articulated changed dramatically as new strategies were deployed to represent the message of Maori nationalism. Maori concerns for land and culture were recast in the late 1960s by protest strategies. These were first articulated by a relatively small group of urban-based, often tertiary-educated, Maori. Nga Tamatoa, a radical group which appeared in 1970, imported the language and strategies of the international civil rights and feminist movements into New Zealand.

The concerns of Nga Tamatoa were fuelled by the fact that many members had little contact with traditional tribal culture, and their knowledge of Maori language was often limited or non-existent. They were young, with a strong female leadership and with limited legitimacy in a traditional tribal sense. Soon, however, they formed alliances with tribal/non-urban groups, and in 1975 were influential in organizing a major land march to publicize the non-action of a Labour government on unresolved land issues. Protest actions continued throughout the late 1970s; the best-known example involved the occupation of Maori land in central Auckland for 507 days in protest at government plans to sell it to private interests.

These new forms of politics gained momentum following the 1981 tour of New Zealand by the South African rugby team. The tour, which took place despite United Nations sanctions and Commonwealth agreements about sporting boycotts, was the focus for massive civil disobedience. Maori issued strong challenges to Pakeha involved in anti-tour politics, and discussions about appropriate priorities served to focus attention on issues of 'race' and racism in New Zealand. By the mid-1980s widespread activism amongst Maori was often supported by a range of Pakeha political groups who were becoming increasingly conscious of both past and present injustices. During these years there was a move away from the early internationalized influences, and instead there emerged a set of political practices and beliefs that owed little to others and which privileged traditional concerns with land and culture. A new vocabulary was introduced to reflect changing subjectivities. The term '*tino rangatiratanga*' was widely used to refer to Maori sovereignty as defined in the Treaty of Waitangi. *Tino rangatiratanga* expresses the desire to gain control over those economic and social resources which would contribute to a form of Maori independence within the New Zealand nation-state.

Since 1867, when four Maori seats were established in the New Zealand Parliament, separate Maori institutions have existed within the state. The small number of seats, however, ensured that Maori interests were never influential in terms of parliamentary decision-making. The 1935 Labour government attempted to cater to the welfare of Maori in a more sympathetic way, principally through the Department of Maori Affairs, a government department which distributed substantial funds for the economic and social development of Maori. By the 1970s, however, this agency was coming under increasing attack for being out of touch with those it was designed to serve. In the late 1970s a new set of policies called *Tu Tangata* (Stand Tall) resulted in a community-orientated and decentralized department which was to be a model for other services aimed at Maori. The restructured department provided support for important initiatives, including pre-school language classes (*Kohanga Reo*) and new forms of community care.

By the mid-1980s 'biculturalism' between Maori and Pakeha had became the predominant theme, and concepts such as 'partnership' were widely used within the state itself and among sympathetic Pakeha institutions and groups. While there was considerable debate about what biculturalism actually meant, both in terms of the rhetoric of the period and the ways in which it should be translated into practice, the ambition to become 'bicultural' was central to most liberal and progressive agendas. The new mood was reflected in the actions of the Labour government which ruled from 1984 to 1990. The powers of the Waitangi Tribunal, a quasi-judicial body established in 1975 as a forum for the airing of concerns over Maori land, language and culture, were extended through the Treaty of Waitangi Amendment Act of 1985 (Ihimaera, 1993; Walker, 1990). This Act allowed *iwi* to pursue claims back to 1840. Subsequent court decisions, which found in favour of Maori claimants on a range of resource issues, in turn forced further changes in government policy and the reallocation of resources. Concessions extracted from the Labour government involved the recognition of land rights, the granting of fishing resources and the establishment of bodies such as the Maori Language Commission (Kelsey, 1993). New managerial strategies were used by *iwi* to consolidate control over both new and existing resources.

While the Pakeha reaction to such decisions was generally unsympathetic and often hostile, the impetus for attempts by Maori to establish *tino rangatiratanga* had developed to the point where they could not be deflected by a Pakeha backlash. There was a new confidence and major gains were evidenced by the appearance of new community-sponsored institutions and by a growing influence on government policies. Government departments, notably those in the social service area, were increasingly challenged to deliver appropriate 'bicultural' services. In a major review of the Department of Social Welfare, which appeared in 1986 as the report *Puao-Te-Atatu* (Ministerial

Advisory Committee, 1986), the concept of institutional racism was used to argue forcefully that the department was failing to serve its Maori clients. Further, it argued that Maori disadvantage was a direct result of land alienation and the effects of colonization. Similar sentiments were expressed in the Royal Commission on Social Policy report which appeared in 1988 (Royal Commission on Social Policy, 1988).

By the late 1980s there was a noticeable cooling in the sympathy of the government to Maori aspirations. While there had been a series of changes to government departments which delivered particular services to Maori, the new policy of devolving resources to Maori as a way of delivering on *tino rangatiratanga* proved to lack an adequate resource base. Growing concerns about state expenditure resulted in a move away from such targeted policies. The Department of Maori Affairs underwent major transformations in the late 1980s and early 1990s and progressively lost funding, personnel and its relatively innovative approach. The government also began to show an increasing reluctance to act on the advice given by tribal organizations and other agencies, including the Waitangi Tribunal. As Kelsey (1993: 243) notes, first a Labour government and then a conservative National government had to 'convince Maori of their goodwill . . . while reassuring an increasingly insecure Pakeha population and economic interests that their economic power was secure'. Consequently many of the important policy and legal precedents set during the 1980s were deflected in the 1990s for narrowly defined economic considerations. Further, deepening economic crises were generating severe hardship, and in a collapsing labour market Maori have been particularly marginalized. Unemployment rates for Maori are three times higher than those for Pakeha, and Maori, along with women, are most likely to be part of the casualized work-force (Spoonley et al., 1993). Yet, because of an ongoing commitment to notions of social justice based on the collective interests of ethnic groups, it is Maori who continue to present one of the most effective counters to monetarist policies premised on individualism and the 'free' market (Kelsey, 1993; Ihimaera, 1993).

As ethnic politicization of Maori proceeded, so too did an examination of what it meant to be Pakeha in the 1980s. Included within this category were not only the descendants of British settlers, but also those of other 'white' migrants who had made a commitment to New Zealand. While on the one hand there was an increasing awareness of the ethnic traditions of different migrant groups (including Jewish, Dutch and Dalmatian migrants), at the same time significant historical and cultural differences between groups were submerged as New Zealanders of European extraction began to explore the implications of a locally derived identity (see Spoonley, 1991). The label 'Pakeha' was increasingly used as a means of specifying the language, values and practices associated with such an identity. These explorations were prompted by the challenges of Maori and by the growing importance of a biculturalism premised on the understanding that both dominant cultures were based in Aotearoa/New Zealand.

In 1985 an 'ethnic autobiography', written by a Pakeha historian who had been extensively involved in researching and writing on Maori issues, was published (King, 1985). The book received considerable support from liberal and activist Pakeha. Among such people 'being Pakeha' came to invoke a particular form of politics; one which recognized Maori claims to sovereignty in some form, was built on a particular revisionist conception of New Zealand's colonial history, and was sensitive to claims of institutional racism within New Zealand society. Such claims mark a distinct shift in dominant group identity, most notably because the emergent form of ethnic politicization is inclusive in a way that other Pakeha nationalisms are not. It is not surprising, therefore, that the new form of ethnic politics has also generated extensive Pakeha opposition, manifest in the call by a Member of Parliament to ban the word.

In the 1990s the self-labelling of Pakeha has become an important marker in anti-racist and nationalist politics. Many of those who could be defined as Pakeha reject the label on the grounds that it involves a commitment to biculturalism within the institutions of New Zealand society. They opt instead for labels such as New Zealander. For some, multiculturalism is advocated as an option which bypasses the sensitive, and often difficult, issues of an effective biculturalism that privileges Maori/Pakeha relations and assumes the obligations of partnership. In this context multiculturalism is a soft option whose advocates might pay homage to diversity and tolerance, but do not seek any substantive redistribution of resources, nor an effective anti-racist, anti-colonialist politics. Biculturalism, in comparison, is identified with the issues of social justice, cultural integrity and the redistribution of resources. As a result, it is this form of politics that is understood to offer the best opportunities for a powerful and progressive social contract in Aotearoa/New Zealand. Thus, while even some sympathetic commentators remain ambivalent about whether a Pakeha ethnicity exists (Pearson, 1990), and others are clearly dismissive (Nash, 1990), such scepticism has not dampened the commitment to a label which marks the emergence of a new form of ethnic politics among those Pakeha who understand that the concerns of Maori must be addressed.

The New Politics: Feminism

The development of new cultural and political relations between Maori and Pakeha were paralleled by those between women and men as the second wave of feminism emerged in New Zealand in the 1960s. While initially involving women who were connected with existing progressive political organizations (Dann, 1985), by the early 1970s the first autonomous women's liberation groups had appeared. These groups were predominantly made up of middle-class Pakeha women. As was the case in many other countries, the early years were characterized by an emphasis on individual women understanding their own condition, mainly through consciousness-raising. The political explanation that emerged was that of a 'sisterhood of women, different from, oppressed by, and opposed to men' (Jones, 1991: 88). During the same period Maori women were also organizing, but around different issues and in different forums. As Te Awekotuku (1991) has explained, the reason why so few Maori women joined 'women's liberation' during this early period was because there were so many other struggles that were seen as having a higher priority.

It did not take long for challenges to the idea of women's universally shared experience to emerge. By the late 1970s ideological diversity and conflict had become manifest. While tensions had emerged in Pakeha groups around issues of class and sexuality, the most critical challenges came from Maori women who found themselves outside the dominant paradigms of Pakeha feminism. Maori feminists became increasingly vocal about racism within the women's movement specifically and New Zealand more generally. Moreover, the need for Maori women to be part of a unified struggle with Maori men challenged Pakeha women's understanding of the primacy of divisions on the basis of gender. Many Maori women regard traditional complementary gender roles on the *marae* (the speaking area in front of a meeting house) as a source of strength; 'Maori women work with all Maori people including men, a principle that stands Maori feminism apart from some other expressions of feminism' (Irwin, 1992: 12). Events at the United Women's Convention of 1979 (the last large-scale women's convention held in New Zealand), and the 1982 publication of an article on Maori sovereignty by Donna Awatere in a leading feminist magazine (Awatere, 1984), placed these issues firmly on Pakeha feminist agendas.

Although there were significant silences from some Pakeha feminists as they retreated in the face of a major critique of their practices, others were forced to confront issues of racism in feminist organizations and began to consider the political issues raised by Maori women (Jones, 1992: 295). One result was a widespread theoretical shift away from mono-causal explanations of women's oppression, usually based on patriarchy, towards analyses that considered how forms of oppression based on ethnicity, gender and class contributed to the specificity of different women's experiences. Initially these explanations were developed with reference to international bodies of work. During the early 1980s many Maori feminists were influenced by analyses developed from Black American writings (Te Awekotuku, 1991). Similarly Pakeha feminists were using theoretical categories derived from Anglo-American scholarship. Radical feminist analyses, in particular, were popular among activist Pakeha women. Thus, while socialist feminism had a major impact on feminist trade unionists and informed influential academic writings (James and Saville-Smith, 1989; Cox, 1987; Novitz, 1982), feminist debates in New Zealand during the 1980s tended to be characterized by complex articulations between Maori feminisms and radical feminisms.

The dominant formulation to emerge from these articulations was that of a binary framework consisting of opposing groups: men–women, Pakeha–Maori, heterosexual–lesbian, middle class–working class (Jones, 1991: 90). Parallels between Pakeha feminist critiques of patriarchy and the Maori sovereignty debate were identified, and the Treaty of Waitangi came to be seen as the basis for possible alliances between Maori and Pakeha feminists. Feminist organizations throughout the country, including the Ministry of Women's Affairs which was established in 1985, began to consider ways of implementing resource and power sharing (O'Regan and Varnham, 1992). While in too many cases this involved the co-option of Maori cultural symbols without any real devolution of power, there were also examples of significant change. The Women's Refuge Movement, for example, established a structure based on 'parallel development' in which the maintenance of Maori cultural values and beliefs is ensured through the development of separate, but complementary, services for Maori and non-Maori women (Alice, 1991; Lambourn, 1990).

The orientation of feminist thought changed again during the late 1980s, influenced by Pakeha support for Maori nationalism. While Maori women had long been critical of the notion that European norms could be used as the landmark of progress (Pere, 1987), Pakeha women also began to explore the differences between their experiences and a universalizing concept of 'white feminism' (Jones, 1992; Middleton, 1992). Today both Maori and Pakeha feminists are often critical of overseas models and theories, and there are increasing calls for indigenous feminisms. As one Maori academic recently argued, 'The development of Maori feminist theories, in which mana tane and mana wahine are equally powerful, is crucial if our culture is to retain its mana as Maori culture, and not a hybrid version of international patriarchy' (Irwin, 1992: 19). Pakeha feminist theorists have been challenged not only to support the development of Maori feminism, but also to consider the implications of their own positioning (Jones, 1992). The points of departure in these discussions are the common social experiences of Maori and Pakeha women respectively, even though differences within each group are recognized. Strong, politically grounded, bipolar variants of feminist scholarship are emerging (du Plessis et al., 1992), although, as Middleton (1992: 34) has noted, 'the result thus far is two sets of theoretical positions and, as yet, little analysis of relationships, conflicts and contradictions between them.'

These local versions of feminism, based on distinctive forms of identity politics, have many strengths. Maori feminists have forced the majority of Pakeha feminists to acknowledge, and understand, that there is more than one way of interpreting gender relations. There is a particular emphasis on the importance of grassroots organizations and those parts of the women's movement that have been institutionalized are widely understood to be accountable to the broad-based movement. Yet at the same time, as was recently observed, 'Local forms of feminism reflect wider cultural tendencies in New Zealand: of anti-intellectualism, a mistrust of "theory", and – ironically – a moralistic dislike of those who challenge accepted beliefs' (Jones and Guy, 1992: 301). There have been few attempts to move beyond the slogan that the 'personal is political', and implicit in many analyses is the assumption that identity guarantees the authenticity of accounts. Attempts to develop more complex political and theoretical understandings have met with considerable resistance.

The question remains, however, whether in the 1990s local feminisms will be sustainable in their present forms. Recently the increasingly diverse experiences of women in New Zealand have strengthened the demands for conceptualizations which examine difference in more complex ways (compare Jones, 1991; Jones and Guy, 1992; Larner, 1993; Ryan, 1989). While most immediately these demands are responses to contemporary economic and political shifts, they also reflect theoretical understandings which reject fixed notions of identity. In contrast ethnicity, gender and class are seen as identities that are being constantly renegotiated and transformed in relation to shifting contexts made up of economic and social conditions, cultural and political institutions, and ideologies (Alcoff, 1988: 433). The economic and political shifts discussed in the final sections of this chapter demonstrate why it may well prove necessary to consider the implications of such an approach in Aotearoa/New Zealand.

Post-Fordism, Ethnicity and Gender

The monetarist policies instituted in New Zealand during the 1980s were not original in that they were inspired by the New Right agendas of Chicago School economists, and were similar to those of Thatcher and Reagan. Strategies that took years to develop in Britain, however, were inflicted on New Zealand in a matter of months (Jesson, 1992: 38). In the economic and social turmoil that has resulted, the historical specificities of New Zealand's role in a global capitalist economy are once again apparent. The rapid exposure of the domestic economy to the vagaries of the global market can be understood as an attempt to create a 'post-Fordist' industrial base characterized by flexible forms of production based on new technologies and aimed at niche markets, in a context where the traditional primary commodities export base was no longer sufficient to sustain New Zealand capitalism. The result has been to confirm the declining influence of the traditional primary production sector, significant de-industrialization in the postwar manufacturing sector, and growth in a service sector dominated by overseas interests.

The changes date from the election of the 1984 Labour government, and reflect the decision to open the New Zealand economy to international competition. Economic liberalization and the emphasis on a market-driven economy led to dramatic changes in the patterns of capital flows in and out of the country (Britton, 1991: 7–15). The deregulation of financial markets not only allowed New Zealand-based capital to expand offshore in order to take advantage of new opportunities, it also enabled new competitors to enter once protected markets, particularly in the areas of business services and finance industries. International speculative investment has increased and the share holdings of major New Zealand companies are increasingly controlled by foreign interests. Government privatization of many functions, including telecommunications, banking and transport, has also encouraged increases in foreign ownership.

Significant changes have resulted from reductions in border protection. Plant closures and redundancies have affected companies unable to compete with increased levels of imported products. Those companies who have survived have had to make major changes to their operations, including technological innovation and organizational changes. Trade liberalization has also been integral to Closer Economic Relations – a free trade agreement between New Zealand and Australia designed to strengthen economic relations between the two countries. Second only to the European Union in the range of measures covered, the agreement has resulted in substantial capital movement and production reorganization. Between 1985 and 1989, for example, Australian companies invested $10 billion in New Zealand when the total share market capitalization was only $24.4 billion (New Zealand dollars). Moreover, by 1989 Australian interests controlled 10 per cent of New Zealand's GDP, 45 per cent of New Zealand's banking and 50 per cent of the stock exchange turnover (Spoonley, 1992: 169).

Nowhere are the results of the internationalization of the New

Zealand economy more apparent than in the labour market. Unemployment figures are now at their highest levels in fifty years. In 1986 Pakeha unemployment rates were 2.7 per cent and 3.9 per cent for men and women. The corresponding figures for Maori were 10.7 per cent and 12.4 per cent, and for Pacific Islanders 5.9 per cent and 7.3 per cent. By 1990 Pakeha rates had increased to 6.3 per cent and 5.7 per cent, but the figures for Maori were 22.2 per cent and 21.2 per cent. Pacific Islanders have also experienced very high rates; the corresponding figures are 24.3 per cent and 16.2 per cent (Brosnan and Rea, 1992).

Associated with the reduction of employment opportunities is an increased fragmentation of the labour market. Commentators have begun to speculate about the 'feminization' of the labour force, not only because women's job losses have been fewer than men's, but also because it seems likely that more workers, both men and women, will be employed in peripheral, part-time and insecure positions. The labour force is also being 'racialized' in significant ways as a result of the differential incorporation of the various ethnic groups (Spoonley, 1992). While there have been relative gains for Maori in some professional and skilled occupational categories, overall both Maori and Pacific Island workers have experienced a rapidly deteriorating labour market position with substantial job losses, together with significantly higher levels of lowly paid jobs and a greater incidence of casual and short-term work. Maori workers, in particular, have disproportionately suffered as a result of the declining number of full-time jobs in the manufacturing sector (Newell, 1992).

Trends towards fragmentation have been facilitated by the radical reform of labour relations legislation. The 1991 Employment Contracts Act, which shifts employment relations away from collective agreements towards individual contracts, is designed to 'free up' the labour market. It has allowed employers to push for more flexible work regimes and individual labour contracts (see Hargreaves, 1993). The result has often been a reduction in wages and conditions. The Act has been accompanied by significant cuts in welfare benefits, increases in the costs of health and education, and the introduction of market rents for state housing. These policies are not only explicit attempts to reduce government expenditure, they are also designed to reduce levels of dependency and force people into a collapsing labour market.

Supporters of the new policies, pointing to the substantial growth in export sales, argue that these changes have made the New Zealand economy internationally competitive. Much of this trade, however, is concentrated in the hands of a few globalized companies and producer organizations whose operations are unconstrained by regulatory frameworks (Britton, 1991: 27). Further, international competitiveness is being achieved on the basis of a low-wage economic strategy, rather than one emphasizing a high-wage, highly skilled labour force. The moves towards casualization, the feminization and racialization of labour markets, and the privatization of welfare functions, have all reinforced familiar patterns of marginalization. In the transformation of the New Zealand economy to a form of 'flawed post-Fordism' (Jessop, 1990), it is clear that the overall welfare of New Zealand society has been sacrificed for a narrow set of economic goals.

Labour migrations have also been affected by changes associated with internationalization. Overall, levels of international migration into New Zealand increased dramatically in the 1980s. Bedford (1990) has shown how the composition of migration flows changed during these years. In response to a contracting labour market, stricter control over immigration and settlement from the Pacific had, by the early 1990s, reversed a long-established trend, and migration to New Zealand from all Pacific Island countries except Fiji declined dramatically. Also significant has been the removal of the traditional source bias towards Europe and, as a result, relatively large increases in migrations from Asia. In the early 1980s migration from Europe comprised nearly one-third of total net migration; in the later half of the decade there was a substantial net loss of European citizens. Migration from Asian countries, on the other hand, increased from 21 per cent to 67 per cent of total net migration.

There are a number of aspects to the new migrations. Since 1986 significant attempts have been made to market New Zealand as a destination for wealthy entrepreneurs and their investment capital. Although there are some doubts about the future success of this scheme, increased levels of 'business migration', from Taiwan and Hong Kong in particular, have resulted (Trlin and Kang, 1992: 51). Further, a new migration policy, based on a points scheme, targets those people with the technical and professional skills that are in demand as the New Zealand economy is restructured. The migration of skilled non-manual workers will be an important aspect of labour migrations to New Zealand in the 1990s. While the source countries for these latter migrations are as yet unknown, they are likely to be more disparate than those traditionally associated with New Zealand.

A recent study of Hong Kong and Taiwanese migrants entering under the Business Immigration Programme shows that while the principal applicants have been predominantly male, in most cases they are accompanied by their spouses (Trlin and Kang, 1992). Migration research from a diverse range of countries confirms that a very high proportion of women who migrate as 'dependants' enter the labour market. The question of where and how remains to be explored in the New Zealand context, although the increasing importance of small businesses and self-employment may be significant given the declining opportunities in the core labour force. Already there are marked differences in the involvement of New Zealand-born and migrant populations in self-employment; Asian and Continental European groups in particular have long been over-represented in this labour force category (Haines, 1991: 23). Significantly, the basis for the organization of production in this form of employment is often clan and familial networks. Further, these networks are often characterized by marked gender differences in the tasks of responsibility.

Even if the proposed net annual gains of 20,000 migrants are not reached, it seems inevitable that the articulations between gender, economic and ethnic differences will be accentuated in New Zealand in the 1990s. Shameen (1992), in a discussion of the experiences of Indo-Fijian women in New Zealand, has illustrated the complexity of the issues. Solidarity between Pacific nationalisms meant that many Maori supported indigenous Fijians in their aspirations. Following the 1987 military coups in Fiji, which were an aspect of the Fijian nationalist struggle, many highly skilled Indo-Fijians took refuge in New Zealand. In common with Maori and other Pacific Islanders, however, they were confronted by Pakeha racism and often found it difficult to get satisfactory jobs. At the same time the establishment of tax-free zones in Fiji by the post-coup regime encouraged many New Zealand entrepreneurs, particularly those involved in the textile industry, to move their businesses to Fiji. While in Fiji local women have gained more opportunities for employment, women workers in New Zealand. including Maori and Pacific Island women, have lost jobs as a result. In this case not only are there complex mediations between indigenous nationalisms and internationalized production relations, but also each of these is cross-cut by the articulation of specific forms of gender, ethnic and class relations.

Conclusion

Post-colonial forms of politics in Aotearoa/New Zealand have involved a widespread critique of the hegemonic role of Pakeha. Even those Pakeha movements most sympathetic to Maori have been challenged for being racially exclusive, or overly centred on Pakeha or European political movements. For Maori the goal is the construction of a subjectivity which is relevant for people who are primarily urban based, but who want to retain cultural and spiritual connections with traditional tribal areas, and whose goal is the specific form of self-determination known as *tino rangatiratanga*. Autonomy within the nation-state is seen as the most effective way of protecting both economic and cultural resources; hence the redefinition of the relationship between Maori and Pakeha as that of 'two people within one nation' (Walker, 1990: 10), and the attempts to develop bicultural institutions within New Zealand society. The significance of these efforts is such that they play a prominent role in the articulation of all forms of politics. Class and gender concerns, in particular, are often subordinate to, or at least influenced by, the politics of Maori and attempts to establish *tino rangatiratana*.

Accordingly relationships between Maori women and Pakeha women are central to local versions of feminism. In the distinctive forms of identity politics that have evolved, women who identify as neither Maori nor Pakeha are largely ignored, or their experiences submerged within the Maori–Pakeha bifurcation (Jagose, 1988; Max, 1991). Increasing ethnic heterogeneity, therefore, may generate new tensions within the women's movement. Pacific Island women, for example, are increasing their involvement in local government and community organizations. The politicization of second-generation women, born in New Zealand to migrant parents, is also growing. For many second-generation women there are tensions between an ethnicity which is reproduced from the country of origin and which revolves around traditional conceptions of family, church and leadership, and a New Zealand-focused ethnicity which is less hierarchical, gerontocratic and gender divided (Larner, 1991; Pulotu-Endemann and Spoonley, 1992). Further, within Pacific Island communities opinions are divided about the respective merits of supporting Maori in their struggle for self-determination, or opting for strategies which will advance some form of multiculturalism.

More generally, as a result of the internationalization of the New Zealand economy, there will be a growing number of situations in which cross-sectoral forms of resistance based on a shared purpose, rather than a common identity, will be required. Kelsey (1991: 47), for example, has argued that the struggle for New Zealand's national and economic sovereignty could provide a source of common interest between Maori and Pakeha. There have also been calls for connections between women's organizations and other groups as a means of contesting the government's economic agenda (Du Plessis, 1991). At the national level, the Alliance, a coalition of minor political parties including New Labour, the Greens, the Democrats (a social credit party), and Mana Motuhake (an independent Maori nationalist party), may become a significant force in New Zealand politics (see Jesson, 1992). And while there have long been connections among nationalist groups in the Pacific, new links are being forged with other oppositional groups in the region. All of these forms of resistance involve the negotiation of significant political, social and cultural differences.

Moves towards dialogical forms of feminist politics, in which 'we should not assume consensus and we should not be afraid to disagree' (Du Plessis, 1991: 23), are essential in such a context. Such moves, however, will be mediated by bicultural forms of nationalism and feminism in which the particularism of localized cultural relations is stressed over the universalism of social and economic processes (Balibar, 1991: 6). The importance of these local understandings should not be underestimated; biculturalism in Aotearoa/New Zealand provides a powerful expression of progressive and inclusive forms of politics based on self-defined identities and reflecting local sensitivities. Moreover, biculturalism, even in its emergent and incomplete state, provides one of the most effective counters to New Right ideologies and the harsh realities of the monetarist experiment based on market competition and individualism. Finally, it is important to recognize that all negotiations over these issues will take place in a context dominated by conservative groups in which the arguments of anti-racists and feminists are inverted to suggest that it is they who are racist or sexist, giving rise to what Balibar (1991) has called neo-racism. Political discourses based on binary themes will continue to be the focus of major contestations in the years ahead.

Acknowledgements

Many thanks to Rosemary Du Plessis for her insightful and thorough review of this chapter. Margaret Phillips and Don Kerr also made useful comments, and David Bertram provided technical support.

References

Alcoff, L. (1988) 'Cultural feminism versus poststructuralism: the identity crisis in feminist theory', *Signs*, 13 (3): 405–36.

Alice, L. (1991) 'Whose interests? Decolonizing "Race" and "Gender"', *Race Gender Class* 11–12: 64–70.

Awatere, D. (1984) *Maori Sovereignty*. Auckland: Broadsheet Publications.

Balibar, E. (1991) 'Preface' and 'Is there a neo-racism?', in E. Balibar and I. Wallerstein, *Race, Nation, Class: Ambiguous Identities*. London: Verso.

Bedford, R. (1990) 'Ethnicity, birthplace and nationality dimensions of cultural diversity', *New Zealand Population Review*, 16 (2): 34–56.

Britton, S. (1991) 'Recent trends in the internationalization of the New Zealand economy', *Australian Geographical Studies*, 29 (1): 3–25.

Brosnan, P. and Rea, D. (1992) 'Rogernomics and the labour market', *New Zealand Sociology*, 7 (2): 188–221.

Cox, S. (ed.) (1987) *Public and Private Worlds: Women in Contemporary New Zealand*. Wellington: Allen & Unwin.

Dann, C. (1985) *Up from Under: Women and Liberation in New Zealand, 1970–1985*. Wellington: Allen & Unwin.

Du Plessis, R. (1991) 'Running backward over sand or getting somewhere else?', in

N. Armstrong, C. Briar and K. Brooking (eds), *Women and Work: Directions and Strategies for the 1990s*. Palmerston North: Massey University.

Du Plessis, R., with P. Bunkle, K. Irwin, A. Laurie and S. Middleton (eds) (1992) *Feminist Voices: Women's Studies Texts for Aotearoa/New Zealand*. Auckland: Oxford University Press.

Fairburn, M. (1989) *The Ideal Society and Its Enemies: the Foundations of Modern New Zealand Society, 1850–1990*. Auckland: Auckland University Press.

Haines, L. (1991) *Small Business is Big Business*. Wellington: New Zealand Planning Council.

Hargreaves, R. (1993) *Employment Contracts: New Zealand Experiences*. Wellington: Victoria University Press.

Ihimaera, W. (ed.) (1993) *Te Ao Marama 2. Regaining Aotearoa: Maori Writers Speak Out*. Auckland: Reed Publishing.

Irwin, K. (1992) 'Towards Theories of Maori Feminism', in R. du Plessis with P. Bunkle, K. Irwin, A. Laurie and S. Middleton (eds), *Feminist Voices: Women's Studies Texts for Aotearoa/New Zealand*. Auckland: Oxford University Press.

Jagose, A. (1988) 'The w(hole) story: lesbians of colour in Aotearoa', *Broadsheet*, September: 30–2.

James, B. and Saville-Smith, K. (1989) *Gender, Culture, Power*. Auckland: Oxford University Press.

Jesson, B. (1987) *Behind the Mirror Glass: the Growth of Wealth and Power in New Zealand in the Eighties*. Auckland: Penguin.

Jesson, B. (1992) 'The disintegration of a labour tradition: New Zealand politics in the 1980s', *New Left Review*, 192: 37–54.

Jessop, B. (1990) 'Regulation theories in retrospect and prospect', *Economy and Society*, 19 (2): 153–217.

Jones, A. (1991) 'Is Madonna a feminist folk-hero? Is Ruth Richardson a woman? Postmodern feminism and the dilemmas of difference', *Sites*, 23: 84–100.

Jones, A. and Guy, C. (1992) 'Radical feminism in New Zealand: from Piha to postfeminism', in R. du Plessis with P. Bunkle, K. Irwin, A. Laurie and S. Middleton (eds), *Feminist Voices: Women's Studies Texts for Aotearoa/New Zealand*. Auckland: Oxford University Press.

Jones, D. (1992) 'Looking in my own backyard: the search for white feminist theories of racism for Aotearoa', in R. du Plessis with P. Bunkle, K. Irwin, A. Laurie and S. Middleton (eds), *Feminist Voices: Women's Studies Texts for Aotearoa/New Zealand*. Auckland: Oxford University Press.

Kelsey, J. (1984) 'Legal imperialism and the colonization of Aotearoa', in P. Spoonley, C. Macpherson, D. Pearson and C. Sedgwick (eds), *Tauiwi: Racism and Ethnicity in New Zealand*. Palmerston North: Dunmore Press.

Kelsey, J. (1991) 'Tino Rangatiratanga in the 1990s', *Race, Gender, Class*, 11 (12): 42–7.

Kelsey, J. (1993) *Rolling Back the State: Privatization of Power in Aotearoa/New Zealand*. Wellington: Bridget Williams Books.

King, M. (1985) *Being Pakeha*. Auckland: Penguin.

King, M. (1991) *Pakeha: the Quest for Identity in New Zealand*. Auckland: Penguin.

Lambourn, B. (1990) 'Parallel development in women's refuge: the non-Maori women's perspective', *Proceedings of Mana Wahine Women's Studies Association Conference*, Rotorua.

Larner, W. (1991) 'Women and migration', in P. Spoonley, D. Pearson and C. MacPherson (eds), *Nga Take: Ethnic Relations and Racism in Aotearoa/New Zealand*. Palmerston North: Dunmore Press.

Larner, W. (1993) 'Changing contexts: globalization, migration and feminism in New Zealand', in S. Gunew and A. Yeatman (eds), *Feminism and the Politics of Difference*. Sydney: Allen Unwin.

Max, L. (1991) 'Having it all: the Kibbutznik and the Powhiri', in M. King (ed.), *Pakeha: the Quest for Identity in New Zealand*. Auckland: Penguin.

Middleton, S. (1992) 'Towards an indigenous university women's studies for Aotearoa: a Pakeha educationalist's perspective', in R. du Plessis with P. Bunkle, K. Irwin, A. Laurie and S. Middleton (eds), *Feminist Voices: Women's Studies Texts for Aotearoa/New Zealand*. Auckland: Oxford University Press.

Ministerial Advisory Committee (1986) *Puao-te-Atatu (Ministerial Advisory Committee on a Maori Perspective for the Department of Social Welfare)*. Wellington: Government Printer

Nash, R. (1990) 'Society and culture in New Zealand: an outburst for the end of 1990', *New Zealand Sociology*, 5 (2): 99–121.

Newell, J. (1992) *Recent Maori Employment Patterns and Trends*. Wellington: Te Puni Kokiri.

Novitz, R. (1982) 'Feminism', in P. Spoonley, D. Pearson and I. Shirley (eds), *New Zealand Sociological Perspectives*. Palmerston North: Dunmore Press

Novitz, R. (1987) 'Bridging the gap: paid and unpaid work' in S. Cox (ed.), *Public and Private Worlds: Women in Contemporary New Zealand*. Wellington: Allen & Unwin.

O'Connor, M. (1991) *Honour the Treaty? Property Rights and Symbolic Exchange*. Policy Discussion Paper, no. 11. Auckland: Department of Economics, University of Auckland.

Ongley, P. (1991) 'Pacific Islands migration and the New Zealand labour market', in P. Spoonley, D. Pearson and C. Macpherson (eds), *Nga Take: Ethnic Relations and Racism in Aotearoa/New Zealand*. Palmerston North: Dunmore Press.

O'Regan, M. and Varnham, M. (1992) 'Daring or deluded: a case study in feminist management', in R. du Plessis with P. Bunkle, K. Irwin, A. Laurie and S. Middleton (eds), *Feminist Voices: Women's Studies Texts for Aotearoa/New Zealand*. Auckland: Oxford University Press.

Pearson, D. (1990) *A Dream Deferred: the Origins of Ethnic Conflict in New Zealand*. Wellington: Allen & Unwin in association with Port Nicholson Press.

Pere, R. (1987) 'To us the dreamers are important', in S. Cox (ed.), *Public and Private Worlds: Women in Contemporary New Zealand*. Wellington: Allen & Unwin.

Pere, R. (1988) 'Te wheke: whaia te maramatanga me te aroha', in S. Middleton (ed.), *Women and Education in Aotearoa*. Wellington: Allen & Unwin in association with Port Nicholson Press.

Pool, I. (1991) *Te Iwi Maori: a New Zealand Population, Past, Present and Projected*. Auckland: Auckland University Press.

Pulotu-Endemann, K. and Spoonley, P. (1992) 'Being Samoan: Samoan ethnicity in New Zealand', in A. Trlin and P. Spoonley (eds), *New Zealand and International Migration: A Digest and Bibliography No. 2*. Palmerston North: Department of Sociology, Massey University.

Royal Commission on Social Policy (1988) *The April Report*. Wellington: Royal Commission on Social Policy.

Ryan A. (1989) '"New times": diversity, identity and feminist politics', *Proceedings of the Women's Studies Association Conference*, Christchurch.

Shameen, S. (1992) 'Post-coup exodus: Indo-Fijian women migrants in New Zealand', in R. du Plessis with P. Bunkle, K. Irwin, A. Laurie and S. Middleton (eds), *Feminist*

Voices: Women's Studies Texts for Aotearoa/New Zealand. Auckland: Oxford University Press.

Spoonley, P. (1991) 'Pakeha ethnicity: a response to Maori sovereignty', in P. Spoonley, C. Macpherson, D. Pearson and C. Sedgwick (eds), *Tauiwi: Racism and Ethnicity in New Zealand*. Palmerston North: Dunmore Press.

Spoonley, P. (1992) 'Economic transformation and the racialization of labour', *Australian and New Zealand Journal of Sociology*, 28 (2): 157–74.

Spoonley, P. (1993). *Racism and Ethnicity* (2nd edition). Auckland: Oxford University Press.

Spoonley, P., Teariki, Newell, J. and Taiwhenua o Heretaunga (1993) *Mahi Awatea*. Palmerston North: Department of Sociology, Massey University.

Te Awekotuku, N. (1991) *Mana Wahine Maori*. Auckland: New Women's Press.

Trlin, A. and Kang, J. (1992) 'The business immigration policy and the characteristics of approved Hong Kong and Taiwanese applicants, 1986–1988', in A. Trlin and P. Spoonley (eds), *New Zealand and International Migration: A Digest and Bibliography No. 2*. Palmerston North: Department of Sociology.

Walker, R. (1990) *Ka Whawhai Tonu Matou: Struggle without End*. Auckland: Penguin.

3

Race, Ethnicity and Gender in Australia

Jan Jindy Pettman

This chapter traces a brief history and critique of Australian national-ism, set as it is against both 'mother country' and the indigenous people, and now faced with increasing numbers and visibility of migrant 'others'. It explores the connections between collective politi-cal identities, the state and the globalized political economy. It locates women within these diverse identities and relations, and reveals the gendered construction of colonization, nation and citizenship in Australia. Tracing these complex articulations of race, ethnicity, nation, class and gender unsettles dominant understandings of Australian nationalism, and challenges the theory and politics of 'Australian' feminism.

Critiques of Australian nationalism are often uni-dimensional. Colonization models of Australia focus on indigenous people and their confrontation with the settler/invaders. Political economy of migration models focus on the international division of labour and the role of migrant labour. Multicultural models stress the diversity of migrant collectivities in Australia. Feminist models restore women and the dynamics of gender relations to central position, albeit in a manner that often focuses on 'white' women. There is little traffic between these different models, and it is unclear where and how the different dimensions are related to each other.

Academic representations, administrative practices and category pol-itics in Australia reflect and reinforce these boundary lines. 'Race' usually refers to Aboriginal people, 'ethnicity' to migrants from non-English-speaking backgrounds, and 'women' often turn out to be 'white'. These boundaries construct binary oppositions – Aborigines versus the rest; migrants versus the Australian-born; men versus women. These binaries limit our understanding of racism and sexism, and undermine alliances and strategies against them (Meekosha and Pettman, 1991). This chapter seeks to move beyond them, to analyse the complex ways in which the politics of difference relate to and reflect multiple and interrelated structures of power in Australian society.

Nation and State in Australia

The 1988 bicentenary of white settlement in Australia provided the occasion for much celebration and some speculation on the nature of Australian nationalism. The dominant history told a brave story of pioneers and settlers, soldiers and unionists, almost always white, English-speaking and male. The bicentenary also created a small space for other histories, some of them critically counter-hegemonic. This was especially the case for women's history and for Aboriginal history, often told and treated as if they were isolated from each other – as if some women are not Aboriginal, and as if Aborigines are all men.

By 1788 the indigenous peoples in Australia had a history of occupation for at least 60,000 years. They lived in small extended family and community groups, with particular association with their land and in complex kin relations within and across group boundaries. Aboriginal peoples were hunters and gatherers, pursuing diverse strategies in different geographic locations and environments, while the Melanesian people of the Torres Strait Islands were horticulturalists and fisher people.

In 1788 a British penal colony was established on the east coast at what is now Sydney. Only from the 1830s were there significant numbers of free migrants, overwhelmingly from Britain and Ireland. The construction of a white Anglo/Celtic Australia was confirmed in the federation of the colonies in 1901. The nationalist political project continued to be exclusivist – white, preferably British, and apparently male – until after World War II. Since 1947 there has been a remarkable increase in the numbers and diversity of sources of immigrants. Since the early 1970s, a range of state policies and political rhetorics have sought to manage Aboriginal nationalism and ethnic minority claims.

Political elites in the colonies and later in federated Australia were dominated by British and to a lesser extent Irish immigrants until World War I (Jupp, 1989). Settler nationalism grew through the late nineteenth century, with some competition between a conservative and empire loyalist tradition and a social democratic and occasionally republican one. The rise of the Australian Natives' Association (of Australian-born men) and 'Bulletin' nationalism in the 1890s declared 'Australia for the White Man', and strongly opposed Asian immigration (McQueen, 1970).

Nationalism was closely tied to British Imperialism, constructing Australia and defining Australia's security interests in terms of Mother Britain and Empire – the impulse for a series of 'foreign adventures' taking Australian troops into wars from the Sudan in 1885 through the Boer War and both World Wars (Alomes, 1989; Reynolds, 1991). World War I was particularly searing. Australia, with a population of

4 million, sent 300,000 young men to war, half of whom returned injured, and 60,000 of whom died in Europe and the Middle East.

The language of Australian nationalism was both masculinist and militarist (Lake, 1992). Nationalism was constructed in terms of patriotic commitment and defence against those who were different and therefore threatening, against whom the supreme sacrifice might be required. (A separate Australian citizenship was not invented until 1948.) Thus while the Australian state was established in 1901 and is celebrated on Australia Day (January 26), the birth of the nation is popularly celebrated on Anzac day (April 25), commemorating the killing fields of Gallipoli (Kapferer, 1989; Lerner, 1990). The close association between nationalism, patriotism and fighting in distant wars continues today, although since World War II Australian nationalism has been articulated as part of the West rather than the Empire, as illustrated by a string of sorties into the Korean, Vietnam and Gulf wars.

Despite tenacious historical attachment of Australian nationalism to British, and recently, Western allegiance, Australian identity has been constructed as in some ways unique. This nationalism calls up a fraternal contract – no longer rule of the fathers, including over the sons, but rule of the adult men (Pateman, 1988). Its public persona is a brotherhood summed up as mateship, an ideological representation of rough egalitarianism and 'innocent male virtue' (Lohrey, 1984) that disguises the class-ridden and homophobic nature of Australian society. It is a fraternity which excludes Aboriginal men and male migrants from non-English-speaking backgrounds, and women from all backgrounds. Even dominant group women are rarely visible within its representations, although historically they were at times attended and urged on as 'breeders of the white race' (de Lepervanche, 1989), while minority women were systematically excluded from the status of 'Australian women'. There was an active women's movement in support of women's suffrage and then of women's rights through the late nineteenth and early twentieth centuries (Spearitt in Saunders and Evans, 1992), though its supporters were more likely to look to the struggles of their sisters in England and America than to the condition of Aboriginal women. Some women were actively involved in the eugenicist movement, privileging concern for the health of the white race (Curthoys, 1989; Damousi in Saunders and Evans, 1992). Some feminists did articulate a concern about Aboriginal people's exclusion from the citizenship and social rights they claimed for themselves, and constructed notions of sisterhood with Aboriginal women (Lake, 1993).

Early Australian nationalism was personified in the struggling bush worker for whom solidarity meant survival, and modified from the 1890s and the rise of labourism to include blue-collar workers. Of late, national images include Crocodile Dundee and maybe the slobbish, beer-drinking, television-watching Norm, used extensively in government and media health education campaigns. Contemporary nationalism is also of the 'big blokes' of sporting and corporate success, an image which, since the 1970s, has been used robustly and commercially by political leaders as well (Lohrey, 1984; Alomes, 1989).

There is the possibility of an inclusive national project in Australia's rejection of guest-workers, as immigration has been geared as much to securing population to ensure effective occupation, defence and an expanding consumer market as to providing labour. The last two decades have witnessed the removal of racist selection criteria for immigration selection, the easing of conditions for acquiring citizenship, and eligibility for most welfare benefits and many rights for non-citizen permanent residents. At the same time, state policies such as multiculturalism, anti-discrimination and equal opportunity, while highly problematic, do open up spaces and recognize some differences.

Aboriginal people do now occupy a ritual place as the First Australians, although they are largely contained within the Past, or appropriated as magically spiritual, exotic and good for tourism (Lattas 1990). Both Aborigines and 'ethnic' Australians provide local colour at national celebrations. But the Nation is still routinely homogenized in ways that obscure differences along race, class and gender lines. The current discourse about citizenship and nationality remains largely exclusive. While Aboriginal people and non-white migrants are now legal citizens, their belonging is ambiguous, for they are still frequently constituted as outside the nation, and have difficulty securing their social rights (Pettman, 1992a).

Many migrants and some Australian-born people are thus relegated to the status of outsider by racialized and particular readings of Australianness. Racism is embedded in our language, social myths and day-to-day operations of our institutions (HREOC, 1991). Damage and despair still bedevil many Aboriginal communities. Australians have yet to resolve or dissolve colonialism. The inclusive national project is still fragile, and threatened by racism and by economic rationalism which denies 'special' claims and subverts social rights. The language of citizenship and nationality are dominated by the discourses of government-sponsored cultural pluralism within the frame of core institutions, and the New(ish) Right's politics of nationalist nostalgia. The recurring immigration debates speak of the ethnic mix, social cohesion and 'our culture', largely defined in terms of Anglo/Celtic whiteness. The arguments often claim to be about culture and difference rather than race and inferiority. But 'Asians' are presumed to be radically different and culturally incompatible with Anglo-Australians, despite the fact that many Asian migrants are

English-speaking and tertiary-educated, and often came to Australia precisely because they were attracted to its liberal democratic capitalism. They also become citizens at a very high and speedy rate, while migrants from Britain are often reluctant to do so.

There are clear connections between debates about immigration, which constantly call up issues of nation and race, and debates about foreign affairs, defence and Australia's place in the region. Each draws attention to national boundaries and ways of policing them. Many still see Australia as a white Anglo settler (rich underpopulated) country in the sea of Asia. Moral panics fly around Japanese investment and Asian immigration in the language of patriotism, invasion and the evocation of danger. Here colonization, empire and race resonate with concern about our rightful sphere of influence, and indeed about who we are and who threatens us (Pettman, 1992b). At the same time, revived support for a republic posits a conflict between our history and our geography, and urges a symbolic cutting of the monarchical umbilical cord, so Australia can approach its neighbours as a demonstrably free and adult country (Curthoys, 1993).

Making Australia

Australia is the product of two interlocking processes, colonization and immigration (Castles et al., 1988: 16). In both these processes, the state – first British colonial and then settler – has played the central role, determining status, treatment, access or exclusion for various groups of people defined in terms of 'race', colour and/or country of origin. It was, and continues to be, responsible for 'the Aboriginal problem' – a responsibility complicated by Australia's federal political structure in which the different state governments also play a role. Immigration has, since federation in 1901, been overwhelmingly a federal government responsibility, with close attention paid to who may or may not migrate to Australia. The federal government is now the strategic player in determining the status and rights of Aboriginal and ethnic minority people, though particular areas of policy or provision also lie with the states.

The Aboriginal population in 1788 is variously estimated to have been between 300,000 and 1 million. By 1851 it had fallen to 85,000 through a fatal combination of violence, disease and displacement. Today Aboriginal people at 277,645 in 1986, are much less than 2 per cent of the total population of 17 million.

'Australia' was founded on the legal fiction of *terra nullius* – unoccupied land – which effectively denied Aboriginal people any land rights or validated existence in the new settler state. No treaties were signed, and nineteenth-century social Darwinism and a declining

Aboriginal population encouraged settler perceptions of Aboriginal people as a dying race, a perception that lasted well into the 1930s.

For most of its 200+ years Australia's settler society nationalist political project was explicitly white, Anglo and capitalist. Colonization entailed the invasion, conquest and dispossession of Aboriginal people. Central to the conquest was conflict over land, involving acquisition of a land base for the development of a settler and capitalist society. Aboriginal people were 'outside the nation, inside the state' (Beckett 1988: 4). They were excluded psychologically and culturally in an extraordinary exercise in forgetfulness, so that Australian history could be taught in terms of 'discovery' by Captain Cook and heroic British explorers mapping a fierce and empty land.

Aboriginal people were excluded, too, from citizenship, and subject to an inferior and racialized legal status as wards of the state. This status varied over time and place, and often involved a complex racialized hierarchy of control, distinguishing between 'full bloods' and 'half-castes'. The former were largely neglected and expected to die out, the latter were increasingly subject to state intervention and control, and through the twentieth century until the 1960s liable to direct institutionalization (Tatz, 1979; Markus, 1990). In some states gradations of blood were used to name different categories of Aboriginal persons. McCorquodale (1986: 8) has distinguished some 67 different legal and administrative definitions of being Aboriginal. At times individuals would find their category arbitrarily changed, and their status along with it. Some Aborigines, for example ex-servicemen after World War II, did acquire a 'dog licence', an exemption certificate which allowed them to enjoy certain limited privileges of adulthood, but the price was that they lived a 'civilized' lifestyle, which required that they had nothing to do with other Aborigines, including their own relatives (McConnochie et al., 1988: 88–91).

Thus in the name of 'protection' of Aboriginal people, but often more as a means of clearing the land and protecting the settlers from contact, Aboriginal people were physically and socially excluded from emerging white society (Huggins and Blake in Saunders and Evans, 1992: 46). The forms of exclusion varied from place to place, dependent not only on different colonies' and later states' policies, but also on geographic location and the use to which the land was put (Broome, 1982). In the more settled south-east and south-west of Australia, Aboriginal people were almost always physically dispossessed, and often confined to government-administered reserves or missions. Some managed to eke out a precarious existence outside them in river camps and through transient and seasonal farm work, where women worked alongside men (Langford, 1988). In places with fewer settlers, large tracts of land were alienated to huge pastoral stations, where local Aborigines lived a marginal existence in stations camps, receiving rations and surveillance in return for local knowledge and labour. Early on women did station work, but as colonial relations became more settled they were increasingly confined to domestic labour and sexual relations with non-Aboriginal men. In these roles, Aboriginal women served as buffers and links between the camp and the homestead. Here, too, were government or mission reserves which functioned as labour reserves, providing men for the stations and women for domestic labour, including for white households in the cities. On these reserves young women were frequently confined to dormitory living, and their sexuality and social relations closely supervised (Huggins and Blake in Saunders and Evans, 1992).

Further still from settler populations and interest, some communities in the far north and centre continued to live on their own land, which was legally still unalienated crown land, pursuing aspects of their own political economy and social relations until recent decades. Ironically, it is these formerly least damaged communities which became the new frontier of the 1970s and 1980s, as they were suddenly confronted by the combined weight of huge multinational mining companies and development-orientated state and federal governments (Jennett 1987).

In this colonial history, Aboriginal women were affected primarily as Aboriginal, but also experienced colonial relations somewhat differently from Aboriginal men. In the horrific violence of the frontier, and in less blatant but still routinized brutality since, Aboriginal women have been vulnerable to various kinds of sexual danger, including rape (Evans, 1982; Pettman, 1992a: 126). There are fierce debates currently about their engagements in sexual relations with white men. Some relationships were apparently freely entered into, but always involved relations of domination and subordination of Aboriginal women. There is now some resistance to representing them as hapless and passive victims, asserting instead women's agency and their exploitation of a small space and a degree of protection in often threatening circumstances (Ryan 1986). Older Aboriginal women recalling earlier times tell of their own choices in sexual relations, against older Aboriginal men's representations of 'their' women stolen by white men. Yet violence and betrayal by white men form a part of the women's stories as well (McGrath, 1987).

These debates relate to wider disputes about the role and status of Aboriginal women traditionally, and the differential effects of colonization on Aboriginal men and women. Many Aboriginal women maintain that traditionally they enjoyed a degree of autonomy and independence that differed from the more dependent status of white women. Some also maintain that colonization and racism, rather than sexism, are their primary oppressions (Huggins, 1987; see also

Hamilton, 1986). The white women's position in these debates is problematic, in that the Australian nationalist project has been racist,
imperialist, capitalist – and fraternalist. White women's roles within the
wider project have involved them in complex power relationships which
may see them as simultaneously oppressed and oppressing, in some
cases having power over Aboriginal men and women. There is a silence
about Aboriginal and white women's friendships in historical writings,
and many Aboriginal women's auto/biographies relate conflicts and
hostilities (Huggins, 1987–88; Huggins and Blake in Saunders and
Evans, 1992; Ward, 1988). These relations challenge white women, and
especially white feminists who are politically committed to the liberation of all women; and raise complex issues about complicity, collusion
and the privileged status of white women in an unfinished colonial
project. Yet there is still a kind of myopia about 'race' in most
Australian feminist histories (Saunders, 1991).

White women in Australia were central if often subject to the construction of racialized sexual politics in familiar colonial terms
(Pettman 1988c). The simultaneous and interrelated construction of the
sexuality of white women, black women and black men allowed white
men access to and monopoly over white women's bodies and children,
and privileged their access to black women's bodies while blaming the
supposed immorality of black women. It also gave them control over
the movements and choices of black men. The purity of the white race
was further defended by legislation prohibiting miscegenation through
official control of Aboriginal women's sexual relations and marriages.
The possibility of relations between Aboriginal men and white women
was deemed unthinkable, so that any such suggestion was read into a
moral panic about the black rapist, familiar in other colonial situations
(Harris, 1982; compare Inglis, 1974; Carby, 1986). Further, all 'mixed
race' children were classified as Aboriginal, and therefore until recently
were wards of the state.

White women and Aboriginal women have engaged in numerous
'close encounters' (compare Davenport in Moraga and Anzaldua 1983)
over time and space, including through white women's employment of
Aboriginal domestic workers. In recent decades many Aboriginal
women – like migrant women – have experienced the state in the person
of a white woman, in such roles as health worker or teacher. Yet while
almost all Aboriginal women have some personal knowledge of white
women, many white women do not know any Aboriginal women, and
so draw heavily on commonly held views and stereotypes about them
and their communities.

In colonial politics the core opposition was that of Aborigines and
whites, and for many Aboriginal people this is still the salient
dichotomy. For most of settler history, 'white' was used interchangeably

with labels like English, British or occasionally European. This was a reflection of the demography of settlement for much of Australia's history, especially for the century following the 1860s. In more recent times, its use reflects the on-going structure of 'race' power in Australia, even while disguising the differences among those categorized as 'white', and leaving those who are neither Aboriginal nor white unaccounted for (compare Anthias and Yuval-Davis, 1983).

From 1788 to the 1840s 'Australia' was largely a penal colony, drawing most of its population from south-eastern England and Ireland. South Australia was established as a free colony in 1836. From the 1840s to 1890, there was increasing free migration, still overwhelmingly from Britain and Ireland, but with small settler minorities like German Lutherans and European Jews. In 1851 Australia's non-Aboriginal population was only 525,000, but this figure doubled in the next decade following the discovery of gold. This fuelled the momentum towards parliamentary democracy, and early steps against Asian immigration, which culminated in the White Australia Policy. Pastoralists were importing indentured labour from China and India in the 1830s and 1840s, and more Chinese men came as free immigrants in the gold rushes from the 1850s (de Lepervanche, 1989; Moore in Saunders and Evans, 1992). Fierce anti-Chinese sentiment and growing state restrictions against 'Asians', combined with return migration to China, meant that their numbers declined rapidly. While tiny communities existed through the twentieth century, the vast majority of Australian Chinese today are the product of recent immigration. Indentured, and almost exclusively male, Melanesian labourers were also imported from different Pacific islands from the 1860s. The rise of the Australian labour movement in the 1890s, and the emergence of a virulently racist nationalism, ensured that most of the islanders were deported by 1908. With federation in 1901, any suggestion of importing or allowing Asian labour was rejected. Here the move of the federal state to ensure rigorous exclusion of 'foreign' immigrants coincided with the development of official 'protection' policies which similarly excluded Aboriginal people from white society.

Australia maintained its highly restrictive immigration policy through federation and two world wars, so that in 1945 its leaders could proclaim it as white and 98 per cent British (Jupp, 1984). The federal Labour government embarked on a radical shift in immigration policy from 1947, seeking to increase the population for defence after the shock of Japanese expansionism, and to provide the labour and consumers for a massive industrialization programme (Collins, 1988). The subsequent policy reflected both the international division of labour within the long boom and current restructuring of capital, and dislocations and conflicts in other countries (Pettman, 1995).

A short-fall in traditional sources of immigrants led to a widening of the net. In the late 1940s displaced persons from Eastern Europe provided the construction industry with its main labour force. During the 1950s and 1960s, many came from Southern Europe and Turkey and served as 'factory fodder', especially in the newly growing manufacturing industries. In the 1970s immigration selection and citizenship rules became officially non-discriminatory on grounds of 'race', culture or country of origin. However, since then educational and occupational criteria for selection have favoured immigrants with English language and recognized trade or professional qualifications. Since the 1970s, increasing numbers of immigrants have come from the Asia-Pacific region. But ironically, this move coincided with the shift from a labour shortage to a labour surplus economy. Thus while immigrants from non-European countries experience racialization, defined as Other against an idealized white norm, their education and occupational backgrounds are frequently above the average for Australian-born residents. Their recent immigration and the selection criteria under which they have been admitted means that there is less of the bifucatory pattern of class among them than in some other settler states. The exception occurs in the case of refugees who have been admitted in significant numbers, some 420,000 since 1945, including about 100,000 Vietnamese refugees since 1975. Refugees, and those admitted under humanitarian programmes, for example from Lebanon, are strongly overrepresented in unemployment and unskilled labour statistics.

Most women migrated to Australia as dependants (de Lepervanche, 1989). Many, however, were pressured into the labour force, often at the time of their heaviest responsibility for children (Martin, 1986). These pressures arose from the excessive costs of migration and resettlement, from bringing out relatives or sending money back home, and from economic difficulties facing working-class migrant men. Many families remain dispersed, as rising economic and skills criteria kept relatives, including adult children and siblings, out. Loss of female kin support networks was keenly felt, though for some women having a paid job and working with other women was also liberating.

Australia's immigration programme since 1947 has been extraordinary in both its size and the diversity of its sources, second only to Israel (Castles, et al., 1988). In 1947 only 9.8 per cent of its population was born overseas; in 1988 21.8 per cent were. Thus more than one in five Australians were born overseas, and many more are the children of immigrants. In 1974 72.7 per cent of those born overseas were from Britain and Ireland; in 1988 only 33.2 per cent were. Other European countries accounted for 32.3 per cent, and 18.5 per cent were from Asia (including the 'Middle East'). In 1990/91, Britain and Ireland were still the largest countries source, but 51 per cent of the intake was from the Asia-Pacific area, especially from South-East and North-East Asia (Australian Bureau of Statistics, 1992). Thus ethnic diversity in Australia is relatively recent, stemming from post-war immigration. With a large proportion of the population born overseas, many ethnic minority Australians are first-generation migrants.

Constructing Identities – Aboriginality and Ethnicity

In the complex play of domination, subordination and resistance, of state and mobilized category politics, people with various migrant statuses and racialized or ethnic positions are differentially incorporated into Australia. The boundaries, the names, the criteria for inclusion and exclusion, and the consequences of belonging or not are contested and changing. In the process, Aboriginal people resist inclusion in a multi-cultural or minority model of Australian society. Their politics and relations with both the state and other Australians are routinely seen as separate, even though they hail the same state and are now embedded, albeit often in distinctive ways, in the same – increasingly globalized – political economy (Pettman, 1995).

Aborigines are a racialized category, where blood, colour and culture are used by outsiders as markers to exclude or entrap them, or at times to include them as beneficiaries of compensatory provision. The boundaries shift. People may be recognized as Aboriginal for the purpose of blame or discrimination, but their Aboriginality may be denied in other contexts as a way of undermining their political claims. Here too is the 'battle of the name' (Banton, 1987), as the politics of language is played out. Aboriginal people often refer to themselves as a nation, and stress the indigenous status that sets them apart from all other Australians. They also call up race and culture in ways that often conflate the two, and posit Aboriginality as an essence, an unbroken cultural continuity with those who occupied Australia for 60,000 years 'before the white man came' (Keeffe, 1988; Pettman, 1988).

Aboriginality is a highly contested terrain. For many Aboriginal people, and others, it refers to an essentialized cultural identity belonging to those of Aboriginal descent. So it can be claimed by those many Aboriginal people seized by the state as babies or young children and brought up in white institutions or families. Against a history which has seen degrees of 'blood' used to divide them, most Aboriginal people reject any notion of mixed or part-Aboriginal status. A child with one Aboriginal parent is defined as Aboriginal. Meanwhile, official definitions of who is Aboriginal specify anyone of Aboriginal descent, who identifies as such, and who is recognized as Aboriginal by others. The contingent nature of identity is demonstrated by the 1986 census figures, which recorded a 42 per cent increase in self-definition as Aboriginal since the 1981 census. This clearly reflects the growing self-confidence and political mobilization of Aboriginal people through the 1980s.

Aboriginality is often represented as a birth identity, but it is also mobilized as a political resource (Keeffe, 1988; Hollinsworth, 1992). It is a short-hand term for a celebration of survival through colonization and ongoing racism, and a retrieval and recovery cultural and community project. In this sense it is a strategic essentialism, a counter-hegemonic ideology which demands the right of Aboriginal people to say who is Aboriginal and what that should mean, after generations of 'being done unto' (Gilbert, 1973). At the same time, the diversity of Aboriginal economic and cultural circumstances and strong attachments to locality and kin undermine attempts to sustain national Aboriginal political organization and strategies (Rowse, 1991).

Ethnic minority Australians are also represented, and at times represent themselves, primarily in terms of culture, religion or place of birth. Where they look or sound different they are subject to racialization and defined in opposition to the dominant culture. They also experience 'migrantness', an ideology which locates them as coming from and still belonging to somewhere else, even when they are Australian-born (Morrissey, 1984; compare Green and Carter, 1988). A process of race-making has been directed at each 'wave' of newcomers, from the Irish and Jewish people in the late nineteenth century, through the Italians of the 1930s to each recent non-English group. Currently the least favoured and presumed least assimilable are Muslims, Lebanese, and 'Asians'.

'Ethnics' are commonly viewed as those who are neither Aboriginal, nor of the dominant group/s. The latter are variously called whites, Anglo-Australians, or simply Australian. 'Migrant' is often used interchangeably with 'ethnic', despite the fact that Britain continues to supply the largest numbers of migrants. Ethnic communities are often identified in terms of presumed country of origin as in Italian, or region as in Asia, or religion as in Muslim. These namings show little regard for the contested and shifting politics of identity. In the 1970s 'Asian' was a codeword for South-East Asians; or for Vietnamese or simply refugees. Nowadays it often refers to the growing numbers of Chinese migrants, but at times can be stretched to include people from Japan and south Asia. 'Muslim' is of more recent currency, apparently displacing 'Arab' in the fall-out of both reportings of the Rushdie affair and the Gulf War, including therefore many non-Arab Muslims and non-Muslim Arabs. At the same time, 'Asian' is sometimes constructed against 'ethnic', the latter then reserved to refer to earlier mass migration from southern Europe and the Middle East.

These large categories disguise the choices an individual might make among possible identities, for example as Muslim, Indian, Asian, migrant, Australian, feminist, and so on. They also ignore the reality of remarkably high levels of intermarriage in Australia. Over half of the Australian-born children born where one or both parents were immigrants from non-English-speaking backgrounds are of mixed origins (Price, 1990: 22). Some 7 million Australians have three or more ethnicities in terms of their origins (although this includes the Irish, Welsh, Scottish and Cornish as distinct ethnic groups in this calculation; Price, 1990).

'Ethnicity' is usually treated in culturalist and social problem or special needs terms, obscuring some earlier, more radical readings which analysed inequality within a political economy of labour migration model (Jakubowicz, 1989). 'Culture' is often viewed popularly and in official publications as fixed and ascribed, and so is depoliticized and commodified. Here, culture has to do with 'tradition', communities appear bounded, and identities are represented as unproblematic and unchanging. These static definitions exist despite the fact that 'the community' is in some cases called into existence by government funding and provision policy, and more often by particular experiences of racism, discrimination or exploitation in the 'new' country. Such a narrow understanding of ethnicity also denies the many migrants who came to Australia precisely to escape their communities, or the 'culture', including political culture, of their former country-of-origin, in which they may have had minority status, but to which they now find themselves labelled as belonging.

These essentialist and homogenized representations of culture and community disguise differences within 'the community' along divisions of class, gender, age, sexuality and ideology. Thus, they authorize spokespeople, usually older middle-class English-speaking men, to speak on behalf of the community. Their roles as brokers between the community and the state and as managers of difference and special needs are reinforced by their access to recognition, a hearing and to some funds.

'The community' as called up by community leaders and politicians is rarely gendered. Women are routinely absent, or occasionally represented as problems or victims, spoken for by 'their' men when they are spoken for at all (Eliadis, et al., 1989; Kalantzis, 1990). Debates about immigration and multiculturalism are usually ungendered or explicitly sexist, as when it is said that 'Australians' don't like Muslims because of the way 'they treat their women'. Where 'migrant women' are rendered visible it is primarily in terms of their presumed cultural identity, as ethnic first and gendered second, with social interests and experiences quite apart from those of white English-speaking background women.

Yet gender *is* experienced in racialized forms. Stereotypes of

Aboriginal women are remarkably similar to those of African-American women and of Afro-Carribean women in Britain. Indeed, it is possible to talk of Aboriginal women as 'black women' in terms of gendered and racialized stereotypes, including those of sexual temptress or black matriarch (Pettman, 1991).

Aboriginal men are stigmatized for their failure to perform according to dominant gender expectations, especially for not being effective heads of households and providers; while Aboriginal women are stigmatized precisely for being heads of households and providers, albeit often dependent on a form of public patriarchy through welfare. When women are blamed for doing what men are blamed for not doing, these representations are clearly sexist. Aboriginal children's poor educational outcomes and supposed behavioural problems are blamed on their 'damaged' families, their 'dominant' mothers, and their 'loss' of culture: a dreadful mockery of struggles to keep family and community together against the odds (Larbalestier, 1980). In these representations too, only 'traditional' Aborigines (often seen also as 'full-blood') are real Aborigines. Urban and/or 'mixed race' Aboriginal people, while still recognized as Aboriginal for the purposes of exclusion or control, have both their own Aboriginality and their right to speak as Aboriginal people denied them (Langton, 1981).

While urban Aboriginal people are seen as having 'lost' their culture, migrants from non-English-speaking backgrounds are seen as having 'too much' culture. Here women are represented as overly controlled by their husbands, brothers and sons. Asian women are presumed passive, oppressed, and privately or potentially sexually exotic. One manifestation of this representation is the Filipina bride trade (Cahill, 1990), where men who see 'Australian' women as loose, lazy, disrespectful and subverted by feminism seek wives who are constituted as the carriers of submissive femininity. Here Australian women are denied 'true womanhood', and the power relations inherent in sexual politics are again culturalized.

For anti-feminists and racists, patriarchy becomes something pertaining to 'tradition'. In terms of public rhetoric, Australian culture is valorized as secular, modern and equal, constituted in opposition to the supposedly repressive traditionalism of other cultures. At the same time strong anti-feminist discourse makes feminism somehow unpatriotic, attacking the fabric of the nation – family and culture – where it really hurts – in the bedroom and the kitchen.

The State's Role in Managing Difference

The state has come to play a key role in managing intergroup relations through policies of non-discrimination in immigration selection and citizenship rights, through the construction of 'ethnicity' as a part of politics, and through multicultural policy. Aboriginal people, too, are managed through limited difference policies.

In the late 1950s and early 1960s there were gradual and uneven moves towards assimilation of Aboriginal people. In 1958 a number of welfare and support groups came together to form the Federal Council for the Advancement of Aborigines and Torres Strait Islanders (Bandler, 1983), and during the 1960s, Aboriginal leadership and protest grew rapidly. In 1963, the Yirrkala people and in 1966 the Gurindji people initiated land and political claims that mark the beginnings of the land rights movement. In 1965 Charles Perkins and others, including white university students, began a series of freedom rides through New South Wales country towns to highlight segregation and discrimination against Aboriginal fringe dwellers (Perkins, 1975). The most dramatic symbolic protest was the establishment of the Aboriginal tent embassy outside federal Parliament House on Australia Day in 1972.

Aboriginal political protest from the 1960s grew alongside, but largely separate from other social movements, though with support from some non-Aboriginal student, church and union groups. These movements signalled an unsettling of the earlier class settlement and the politicization of new constituencies, often using the language of community. Early on, Aboriginal mobilization drew from the American civil rights movement, and for a brief time used the language of black power. However, the moral levers of indigenous claim and unceded sovereignty made the language of first nation more politically attractive, and helped mark the boundary between Aboriginal people and more populous and powerful ethnic organizations representing the immigrants of the 1950s and 1960s and their families (Jennett, 1987). In the face of anti-colonial pressure in the United Nations and among Australia's now independent neighbours, playing on white sensitivities to Australia's racist image made a space for Aboriginal claims. These pressures and Australia's growing trading and security interests in the region led to the official abandonment of racist criteria formerly used to exclude both Aboriginal people and 'foreign others' from the hegemonic nation.

Only in 1967 through a referendum supported by most Australians, did Aboriginal people finally come to be counted as Australians. They were briefly invited to join the assimilationalist project also offered to post-war eastern and southern European immigrants. However, by the late 1960s assimilation was under strong political attack from Aboriginal and ethnic minority protest movements. Federal governments of different political hues have since responded with attempts to manage the political claims through a combination of provision and incorporation of Aboriginal and ethnic leaders as brokers with and for the state. They have also responded by redefining the official Australian national political project, appropriating and domesticating some of the language and understandings of the different protest movements.

Until the late 1960s migrants, too, were expected to assimilate. By then it was clear that many were not so changing; and both a labour-based ethnic rights movement and a significant ethnic middle class among the more organized and older groups were mobilizing politically. Australia sought migrants who were expected to bring their families and to settle, for the Australian national project needed population and citizens as much as labour. Citizenship became progressively easier to gain. As increasing numbers of migrants became voters, politicians became convinced of an 'ethnic vote'. In the late 1960s with the re-emergence of concern over poverty, non-English-speaking background migrants were identified alongside Aboriginal people as especially socially vulnerable.

The short-lived Whitlam Labour federal government (1972–75) was elected with a reformist social democratic agenda. Some of its members saw disadvantage as related to the exploitation of a marginalized fraction of the working class. Others advocated new intergroup and migrant inclusion policies through multiculturalism. Australia was re-visioned by Minister of Immigration Al Grassby as a family of nations, in a model of cosy cultural pluralism.

The Whitlam government's election platform also included self-determination for Aboriginal people. While this, too, was compromised and contradictory in practice, it signalled increased federal government responsibility for managing 'the Aboriginal problem', and the equality issues involved. Subsequently, there has been some legislative recognition of separate status and limited land rights for Aboriginal people especially in the Northern Territory and South Australia. The Conservative Fraser government (1975–83) passed the Labour-initiated land rights legislation for the Northern Territory, and continued to use 'Aboriginal' as a category for administration and provision. The Hawke Labour government (1983–91) announced a commitment to national land rights legislation, but in 1986 abandoned its promises in the face of strong mining company and state government pressures, in addition to fears of a white backlash. These concerns signalled moves towards corporatist and consensus politics, away from the social justice rhetoric of the Whitlam era. The reversals continued with an apparently spontaneous Hawke promise to Aborigines of a treaty for 1988, suggesting possible recognition of Aboriginal claims of nationhood and of sovereignty never ceded. After some confusion there was a further retreat, and a different strategy emerged, in the announcement of a council which has until 2001, the centenary of federation, to effect a process of reconciliation between Aboriginal and non-Aboriginal Australians. This symbolized the federal government's tendency to 'make the running' on Aboriginal issues, and then to retreat in the face of big business and states' reactions (Mercer, 1993: 316).

With the declaration of a multicultural society in Australia, Aboriginal people's status remained in dispute. They now enjoy an official and rhetorical 'First Australians' status, and see Aboriginal art and design appropriated to mark public Australianness (Lattas, 1990). Aboriginal claims for self-determination are taken up by the state and reformulated as self-management, as a way to recognize difference in order to manage it (Rowse, 1984). Currently, there is a degree of structural pluralism with regard to 'Aboriginal Affairs', institutionalized initially through the Department of Aboriginal Affairs and now its successor the Aboriginal and Torres Strait Islander Commission (ATSIC), and in numerous Aboriginal desks and sections, especially in education and welfare departments (Rowse, 1991). This amounts to a racialized secondary welfare state, and is the occupational base for the recent growth of a small but strategic Aboriginal bureaucracy.

Aborigines are largely absent from more powerful 'economic' departments. In the current era, dominated by corporatism and economic rationalism, this reinforces Aboriginal incorporation and containment within 'culture' areas, and their administration as a special needs category. However, a recent landmark High Court judgment forms the basis for Aboriginal access to more resources, and effectively rewrites both Australian colonial history and common law (Mercer, 1993: 315). The 1992 High Court Mabo decision recognized native title for certain purposes, and so set aside the legal doctrine of *terra nullius*. This effected 'a paradigm shift in the underlying legal and moral assumptions of European colonisation' (Gregory 1992: 161).

While it appears that few Aboriginal communities will be able to present the exacting evidence of continuing occupation required to claim unextinguished native title, the decision has had dramatic, if still unclear, political consequences (Rowse, 1993). Aboriginal organizations and communities have rapidly mobilized to press the moment of opportunity in wider claims to self-government and compensation for those whose title has been obliterated by dispossession and displacement. With considerable Aboriginal input, the Federal government has enacted native title legislation which both recognizes and contains the judgment (Rowse, 1993; Whimp, 1994).

'Aboriginal Affairs' has long been kept separate from 'Multicultural Affairs', in terms of both grass-roots category politics and the state's attempts to manage the politics of difference, and Aboriginal distinctiveness is reinforced by the post-Mabo politicing. But there have been parallels over time in the kinds of attention and commitments to both areas. The 1975 Race Discrimination Act legislated against discrimination on the grounds of race, colour, ethnicity or country of origin. The Fraser Conservative government consolidated multiculturalism while redefining state management strategies. It reaffirmed non-discriminatory immigration policy and the declaration of Australia as a multicultural society, and laid the institutional base for multiculturalism through a series of enquiries and reports, including the 1977 Galbally Report. It shifted explanations of disadvantage to a focus on language problems and other cultural difference/cultural deficit notions, and sought to manage inequality and category claims through the construction of 'ethnic communities' seen as having special needs (Jakubowicz, 1989; Castles, et al., 1988).

The Hawke Labour government initially maintained multiculturalism as a management strategy. In 1986, the same year as its abandonment of national land rights, it announced a retreat which savaged language and multicultural education programmes and the Special Broadcasting Services. In the face of considerable opposition from the ethnic lobby and other supporters, it retracted somewhat. The Office of Multicultural Affairs was set up within the Department of Prime Minister and Cabinet, and a National Agenda for a Multicultural Australia announced in 1989. But multiculturalism is now often subsumed within the new nationalist and republican rhetoric, when another difference, between Australia and Asia, is privileged.

Multiculturalism as a policy has thus been reformulated over time (Foster and Stockley, 1989; Hampel, 1989). There are declared 'limits on multiculturalism', which assert the primacy of 'Australian' values and institutions, and the pre-eminent claim of the nation-state (Office of Multicultural Affairs, 1989). So multiculturalism can look like assimilation without tears, asserting the positive value of difference while relegating such difference to private and social spheres. The relations of domination and resistance of ethnic minorities are not available for scrutiny. On the ground, multiculturalism often translates as the acquisition of knowledge for the purpose of servicing or managing ethnic minorities. Multicultural programmes are often attached to education and 'troubled persons industry' courses (Gusfield, 1989). Even these are currently under threat from 'mainstreaming', supposedly incorporating ethnic and gender differences within each department and policy, but often 'losing' difference in the process.

Multiculturalism is also a community relations programme responding to fears that the 'ethnic mix' will inevitably lead to social conflict. The National Inquiry into Racist Violence reported that Aboriginal people in particular, and also those identified as Asian, Arab and/or Muslim, are regularly victims of racist violence and other forms of harassment and discrimination (HREOC, 1991). The federal government then released its Community Relations Strategy, which is largely a community education and cultural awareness training programme, about which little has been heard of late. This programme is ideologically far removed from a class analysis, and only occasionally takes note of gender. Ethnicity, culture and to a lesser extent Aboriginality, each inflected with depoliticized difference, are its organizing principles.

Women, Class and the International Political Economy

Aboriginal women and ethnic minority women, where they are noticed, are usually represented as being community members first and women second. Yet they are positioned also by other aspects of their identity, for example as workers or unionists. They are crucially treated as women through many exchanges with the welfare system, where dominant expectations about gender are enforced. Any understanding of the experiences and social interests of women thus requires analysis of the nexus between the family, the state and the labour market, in which race, ethnicity or/country of origin are constituting features among others (de Lepervanche, 1991; compare Stasiulis, 1990).

Colonization was part of the long process globalizing the developing capitalist political economy, into which Australia was incorporated primarily as a farm and mining resource-producing country. Only after World War II did a significant heavy manufacturing base develop, dependent on migrant labour. Since the 1970s older Australian manufacturing has declined drastically, and unemployment has grown along with financial deregulation and restructuring policies. The move offshore of Australian and transnational corporations is particularly affecting ethnic minority women working in the clothing, textiles and footware trades (Misztal, 1991). In the meantime, organized unionism and the centralized arbitration system guaranteeing a minimum wage system are under attack. Labour is becoming increasingly casualized, and outwork of various kinds, especially involving the exploitation of migrant and refugee women, is growing (Alcorso, 1987). In this process, large numbers of Australians of different backgrounds are entering the long-term unemployed, or else holding on to vulnerable and low-paid work.

Aboriginal people's position is distinct. Often seen as existing outside the Australian class structure and marginal to its economy, their work in the development of both the northern pastoral and more settled agricultural sectors has only recently become visible. This documentation also records the widespread exploitation of Aboriginal women, often from their early teens, as domestic servants in white households (Huggins, 1987–88; Ward, 1988).

Until 1968 many Aboriginal pastoral workers were poorly paid, or worked for rations and the right to camp on the land. Moves towards assimilation included the legal decision to pay Aborigines award wages in the Northern Territory. In response, many employers modernized their labour process, and sacked and rendered homeless Aboriginal people, thus increasing Aboriginal dependence on social security. Since the 1970s, 'Aboriginal Affairs' projects have generated a form of welfare colonialism. This term expresses the contradictions between Aboriginal people's official citizenship, their heavy welfare dependence and their continued constitution as a minority group largely outside the nation (Beckett, 1988: 11).

Governments have responded to Aboriginal political demands and to evidence of appalling Aboriginal poverty and social dislocation, which neither the market nor welfare is capable of ameliorating, by 'culturalizing' poverty and difference (Beckett, 1988: 12). This in part explains the apparent enigma of a colonial/capitalist state recognizing or creating non-capitalist forms of land holding (Peterson, 1985). 'Land rights' is a key demand, not only for those who have maintained links with their own land or 'country', but symbolically as a call for recognition of dispossession and for compensation. Such claims are also a potential material base for Aboriginal recovery from poverty and welfare dependence. Notwithstanding the significance for Aboriginal people of land rights, this particular form of rights is contained within the non-Aboriginal capitalist state. Moreover, in securing these claims, Aboriginal people in the Northern Territory must demonstrate their traditional affiliation with the land through a combination of western legal process and reconstructed anthropology (Bell, 1986).

Some 5 per cent of Aboriginal people currently live on outstations, in small, recently re-established communities on their own land (Fisk, 1985). Only some Aboriginal people have current or potential access to land rights or native title, though in the Northern Territory, where 22 per cent of the population is Aboriginal, 34 per cent of the land is now held by Aboriginal people, and in South Australia, where only 1 per cent is Aboriginal, 19 per cent of the land is now Aboriginal (Mercer, 1993: 312). These lands were largely unalienated crown land or ex-Aboriginal reserves. Most Aboriginal people now live in cities and towns, while some still live in fringe camps and small settlements on the edge of towns. Unemployment rates are extremely high – around 60 per cent.

Despite a strong Aboriginal political movement and many programmes and community organizations dedicated to improving Aboriginal life chances, Aboriginal people continue to experience appalling levels of poverty, health damage, imprisonment, and intra-family and community violence. Thus in Western Australia male Aboriginal imprisonment rates are 43 times those of non-Aborigines; Aboriginal women are imprisoned almost 50 times more than other Australian women, and everywhere Aboriginal children and young people are taken into 'care' and custody in large numbers (Gale and Wundersitz, 1986). The male Aboriginal life expectancy is only 55 years against the non-Aboriginal figure of 72 years. Aboriginal women's life expectancy is 63 years, against the Australian figure of 80 years. Maternal deaths among Aboriginal women are eight times those of other women; and Aborigines are 10 times more likely to be homicide victims than are other Australians. These profiles are typically fourth world, and in many ways quite unlike those of other poor and racialized minority groups in Australia, although they do experience the impact of some state policies and of racism in common.

Aboriginal families are often matrifocal, with women responsible for larger families within complex extended kin relations. The matrifocal nature of these families is now exaggerated by Aboriginal men's absence through seasonal work, imprisonment, and, finally, early death. In addition, restrictions on welfare entitlements favour female-headed, single-parent families (Langton, 1981).

Aboriginal women are on average better educated, and more likely to be employed than are Aboriginal men (Bradley, 1987). They often run community organizations, and provide most of the teachers and health workers. But Aboriginal men continue to dominate Aboriginal politics at state and federal level, and broker relations with the state (Aboriginal Women's Task Force, 1986; Moreton-Robinson, 1992). Those small numbers of Aboriginal people with tertiary qualifications are usually employed in Aboriginal Affairs or in servicing Aboriginal communities, with all of the difficulties in terms of the politics of representation (Hall, 1988) including serving a double constituency and coping with marginalized incorporation.

It is difficult to generalize about Aboriginal women's incorporation into the Australian state and political economy, especially given the local attachment and different socio-economic circumstances of many communities and of those women who do not live within or in contact with a community. It is even more difficult to generalize about migrant or ethnic minority women. These labels disguise differences within the categories and common interests as for example, workers, welfare users or single mothers across category boundaries. An additive model of oppression may seek to recognize multiple oppression, but ignores the constitutive and interactive relations involved. It can also suggest a mechanical accumulation of 'oppressions' whereby non-white non-English-speaking background women are assumed to be the most oppressed, always after Aboriginal women. Yet in Australia the lifting of racially discriminatory immigration selection criteria in the 1970s coincided with increasingly demanding skills selection and the encouragement of business migration. As a result non-refugee 'third world women' are better educated, more skilled and better paid than many white Australian-born women. Many of them are also first-language or fluent English speakers.

The class position of migrant women in their home country, and their time of arrival in Australia, have influenced their incorporation into the labour market, which is segmented along lines of ethnicity and gender (Misztal, 1991). Labour market studies often focus on gender or ethnicity. Putting the two together reveals that non-refugee third world women are over-represented in clerical, professional and technical occupations. White Australian-born women have profiles very similar to white migrant women from Britain and North America. Women from Vietnam and Turkey are drastically over-represented as production process workers and labourers. Women from a Spanish-speaking background are heavily engaged in office cleaning work; and nearly 25 per cent of employed Cypriot-born and Lebanese-born women work in wholesale and retail trade. The women who are worst off, second always to Aboriginal women, are older migrants from Turkey, older and more recent migrants from Lebanon, and recent refugee women, especially from Vietnam (Price, 1990).

Despite the segmentation of women's labour along ethnic lines, there are examples of women's cooperation across these lines, in union, workplace and women's health centres for example (Bottomley and de Lepervanche, 1984; Martin, 1986). There is some recognition of shared interests to do with 'family', although the particular household form or their own position within it may vary. These common concerns include child abuse and domestic violence; health and education; work, multiple tasking and child care; women's roles as unpaid or poorly paid community carers; and youth homelessness, unemployment and policing. These provide some opportunity for locality or interest-based alliances and solidarity.

Women's Politics

Feminism in Australia is represented by its critics as white, English-speaking and middle class. This representation denies the considerable feminist activism of many working-class women, and the traditions of feminism that some migrant women have brought with them to Australia. It also disguises the various feminisms currently operating in the political arena, with very different positions and practices regarding differences among women, and issues of colonization and racism.

Ethnic and Aboriginal category managers and state brokers are usually men, and the rhetoric employed in these dealings routinely subsumes women and obscures gender, while privileging notions of cultural difference as boundary markers. In this discourse, where women are made visible it may be as possessions of 'their' racialized or ethnic group, whose presumed differences in turn reinforce the boundaries. They are constructed as the bearers of authentic difference, charged with reproducing the group physically and culturally. Their 'difference' can be used politically to deny feminists within the group an authentic voice, and to deny feminists outside the category the right to speak for, or at times even about, 'women'.

Some Aboriginal women, too, are wary of 'white' feminism, and argue that their problems are to do with being Aboriginal, rather than women (Huggins, 1987). They are also critical of the continuing near-monopoly of academic knowledge-making about Aboriginal people of white, including feminist, academics (Huggins and Tarrago, 1990; Larbalestier, 1990; Pettman, 1992c). The few Aboriginal women employed within tertiary institutions have very demanding and usually marginalized positions within Aboriginal support programmes or in Aboriginal Studies; and they, like their sisters outside universities, are so pressured by community demands and survival issues that engaging with and educating white feminists is not their top priority (but see Huggins, 1987; Langton, 1989). But the politics of representation and the politics of voice are now audible, asking who can speak, how we authorize what we say, and how we are heard by differently positioned audiences (Huggins and Tarrago, 1990).

Aboriginal women have organized and campaigned mainly within Aboriginal and community organizations. They also struggled in central and northern areas for recognition of their separate knowledge and land rights in the face of trading between Aboriginal and white men, which often excludes them. In more populous areas, they are especially active in health and education campaigns against the state, and in attempts to combat police violence and racism at the community level. There are now separate women's councils in many areas, and networks and meetings of different Aboriginal women's groups are growing (Goodall and Huggins in Saunders and Evans, 1992). In 1989, Aboriginal women hosted the first International Indigenous Women's Conference in Adelaide, which coincidentally provided the occasion for Aboriginal women from very different situations and places to get together.

Danger comes in different forms to Aboriginal men and women. Thus almost all the Aboriginal victims of the highly publicized deaths in police custody are male, while more women die in family violence (Atkinson, 1990; Langton, 1989). Aboriginal women in many communities are engaged in campaigns against family violence and alcohol abuse. Their struggles are compounded by the politics of naming these dangers in a public domain where Aboriginal families and especially Aboriginal men are already stigmatized and criminalized; and where relations between Aboriginal people and the police – and other state agents, including welfare workers – are notoriously bad (Pettman, 1992a).

Ethnic women's organizations are also mobilizing around issues to do with family violence, again often in the face of pressures to remain silent rather than risk racist hearings of their community business. The existence of networks of women's health centres, refuges and rape crisis centres provide opportunities for cooperation and alliance across community lines, and a feminist politics around violence against women offers a language and the possibility for funding to different women's groups (Langton, 1989). However, some dominant group women within these politics have yet to address issues of racism and cultural difference.

Like other Australian women, ethnic minority women are primary workers, unpaid or underpaid, in community organizations and the delivery of category-defined government services. There are now many local or specific community networks and groups of women. In 1986 the Association of non-English-Speaking Background Women of Australia was formed, and is active in ethnic and feminist forums. There are now migrant women's desks in some government departments, and women's sections in ethnic community councils, mostly set up in the mid- to late 1980s. But ethnic minority women are still routinely absent or invisible in most forums to do with women's, ethnic and mainstream political and economic issues (Seitz, 1989). Despite considerable organization and political activity at the local level, they are rarely recognized as agents or players within either ethnic or feminist politics.

Many 'ethnic' background women are active as individuals in feminist politics, and some politic as feminists in their own community organizations or meet in ethnic women's networks or forums; though others do not see themselves as attached to any particular community. They, like Aboriginal women, frequently have cause to chide the women's movement or academic feminists for unthinkingly privileging white women's experiences. But there are also robust exchanges and alliances, for example between Asian feminists in Australia and in neighbouring countries, and other Australian feminists, against child prostitution, sex tourism in the Campaign Against Child Prostitution in Asia or against mail order brides (Marginson, 1992). There is also considerable union and women's and development non-government organizations' cooperation across state borders.

On occasion, Aboriginal and ethnic minority women constitute themselves separately as special claims groups addressing the state, concerned that they fall between the 'women' and ethnic or Aboriginal category cracks. The Aboriginal Women's Task Force 1986 report, *Women's Business*, was the first, and so far the only, national attempt at assessing Aboriginal women's needs and views, though it then languished in the Office of the Status of Women. A 1989 policy review paper on the needs of non-English-speaking background women is likewise rare (Eliadis et al., 1989), although there are now some reports and studies on particular groups of women or on a particular problem, like outwork or child care. The 1989 review paper noted in particular the difficulties of ethnic minority women of second and later generations to obtain a hearing, or have their needs and interests recognized by governments.

The Whitlam government had announced its intention to legislate against discrimination against women, but was toppled before it did so. The Fraser government did not move in this area. One of the first significant actions of the Hawke government was the 1984 Sex Discrimination Act, concerned especially with women's employment opportunities, but also with their access to some goods and services. An Affirmative Action Act was passed in 1986, and most federal government departments now have access and equity plans and programmes (Burton, 1991; Eisenstein, 1991). As a result, women now constitute 15 per cent of senior executives in the public service, though they occupy still only a tiny fraction of senior private-sector positions.

Some significantly placed women now work as femocrats in women's and equal opportunity sections and units in the public service, and more rarely in Aboriginal or ethnic sections and units. (In Australia equal opportunity is usually coded to mean women.) There is a lively debate about the relationship between femocrats, feminism as a political movement and women whose experience is outside both structures (Franzway et al., 1989; Sawer, 1990; Yeatman, 1990; Eisenstein, 1991). There is less scrutiny of women's roles in Aboriginal Affairs or Ethnic Affairs, both dominated by men, although again questions about class interests and about the conflicts inherent in serving two 'masters' – the bureaucracy and the community – are stirring.

Conclusion

Political, social and personal links and alliances exist between many different women of different backgrounds in Australia. But the domination of category politics, together with state policies which depoliticize class and gender and privilege communal politics, set special interest groups against each other in competition for scarce funds or for recognition as representatives. Differences are further mystified by dominant discourses which constitute us as members of an economy to be managed, rather than of a political community with social rights or a society composed of dominant and subordinate groups.

So the challenge is to move beyond the binaries: to analyse the particular claims and constructions of Aboriginal politics, and the implications for all Australians of ongoing colonial relations; and to analyse 'the migrant experience' and the significance of racialized difference and of whiteness in Australia. This analysis will include recognition that 'race' and ethnicity are mediated in and through class and access to dominant cultural capital, and that nation, 'race' and ethnicity are gendered collectivities. In all this the state reveals itself to be capitalist, racist and fraternal, but some aspects or functions of the state may also act or be activated in the interests of anti-racism or anti-sexism.

Currently the separation of the politics, study and management of Aboriginal, multicultural and women's issues from each other and their invisibility or marginality within the mainstream compound the difficulties. The task becomes one of recognizing difference and specificity, located within relations of domination and resistance that frame but do not determine people's identities and actions. It requires a repoliticization and problematization of 'community', including its sexual politics, and analysing the differences, conflicts and commonalities among women. It calls for a more inclusive feminism, which begins with differences among women but can develop ways of talking and working across the boundaries and binaries which so often contain them (Pettman, 1992a).

References

Aboriginal Women's Task Force (1986) *Women's Business*. Canberra: AGPS.

Alcorso, C. (1987) 'Outwork and migrant women', *Migrant Action*, 11 (3): 1–13.

Alomes, S. (1989) 'Australian nationalism and the eras of imperialism and internationalism', *Australian Journal of Politics and History*, 34 (3): 320–32.

Anthias, F. and Yuval-Davis, N. (1983) 'Contextualising feminism: gender, ethnic and class divisions', *Feminist Review*, 15: 62–75.

Atkinson, J. (1990) 'Violence in Aboriginal Australia: colonialism and its impact on gender', *Refractory Girl*, 36: 21–6.

Bandler, F. (1983) *The Time Was Ripe: the Story of Anglo-Australian Fellowship 1956–69.* Sydney: Alternative Publishing Company.

Banton, M. (1987) 'The battle of the name', *New Community*, 14 (1/2): 170–5.

Beckett, J. (1988) 'Aboriginality, citizenship and the nation-state', *Social Analysis*, 24: 1–15.

Bell, D. (1986) 'In the case of the lawyers and the anthropologists', *Journal of Intercultural Studies*, 7 (1): 20–9.

Bottomley, G. and de Lepervanche, M. (eds) (1984) *Ethnicity, Class and Gender in Australia*. Sydney: Allen & Unwin.

Bradley, C. (1987) 'Aboriginal women in the workforce', *Aboriginal History*, 11 (2): 143–55.

Broome, R. (1982) *Aboriginal Australians*. Sydney: Allen & Unwin.

Burton, C. (1991) *The Promise and the Price*. Sydney: Allen & Unwin.

Cahill, D. (1990) *Intermarriage in International Contexts*. Quezon City: Scalabrini Migration Centre.

Carby, H. (1986) 'Lynching, empire and sexuality in black feminist theory', in H. Gates (ed.), *Race, Writing and Difference*. Chicago: University of Chicago Press.

Castles S., Kalantzis, M., Cope, B. and Morrissey, M. (1988) *Mistaken Identity: Multiculturalism and the Demise of Nationalism in Australia*. Sydney: Pluto.

Collins, J. (1988) *Foreign Hands in a Distant Land*. Sydney: Pluto.

Curthoys, A. (1989) *For and Against Feminism*. Sydney: Allen & Unwin.

Curthoys, A. (1993) 'Feminism, citizenship and national identity', *Feminist Review*, 44: 19–38.

de Lepervanche, M. (1989) 'Breeders for Australia: a national identity for Australian Women?', *Australian Journal of Social Issues*, 24: 163–81.

de Lepervanche, M. (1991) 'The family: in the national interest?' in G. Bottomley, M. de Lepervanche and J. Martin (eds) *Intersexions: Gender/Class/Culture/Ethnicity*. Sydney: Allen & Unwin.

Eliadis, M., Colanero, R. and Roussos, P. (1989) *Issues for Non-English Speaking Background Women in Multicultural Australia*. Canberra: Office of Multicultural Affairs.

Eisenstein, H. (1991) *Gender Shock: Practising Feminism on Two Continents*. Sydney: Allen & Unwin.

Evans, R. (1982) 'Aboriginal women in Queensland's history', *Hecate*, viii (2): 7–21.

Fisk, E. (1985) *The Aboriginal Economy in Town and Country*. Sydney: Allen and Unwin.

Foster, L. and Stockley, D. (1989) 'The politics of ethnicity: multicultural policy in Australia', *Journal of Intercultural Studies*, 10 (2): 13–32.

Franzway, S., Connell, B. and Court, D. (1989) *Staking a Claim: Feminism. Bureaucracy and the State*. Sydney: Allen & Unwin.

Gale, F. and Wundersitz, J. (1986) 'Aboriginal visibility in the "system"', *Australian Social Work*, 29 (1): 21–6.

Gilbert, K. (1973) *Because a White Man'll Never Do It*. Sydney: Angus & Robertson.

Green, M. and Carter, B. (1988) 'Races and Race-Makers: the Politics of Racialisation'. Sage *Race Relations Abstracts*, 13 (2): 4–30.

Gregory, M. (1992) 'Rewriting History 1. Mabo v. Queensland: the decision', *Alternative Law Journal*, 17 (4): 157–61.

Gusfield, J. (1989) 'Constructing the ownership of social problems', *Social Problems*, 36 (5): 431–41.

Hall, S. (1988) 'New ethnicities', *Black Film/British Cinema*, ICA Documents, 7: 27–30.

Hamilton, A. (1986) 'Daughters of the imaginary', *Canberra Anthropologist*, 9 (2): 10–25.

Hampel, B. (1989) 'Themes, tensions and contradictions in government statements on multiculturalism', *Journal of Intercultural Studies*, 10 (1): 1–12.

Harris, C. (1982) 'The "terror of the law" as applied to black rapists in colonial Queensland', *Hecate*, viii (2): 22–48.

Hollinsworth, D. (1992) 'Discourses on Aboriginality and the politics of identity in urban Australia', *Oceania*, 63 (2): 137–55.

HREOC (1991) *Report of the National Inquiry into Racist Violence in Australia*. Sydney: Human Rights and Equal Opportunity Commission.

Huggins, J. (1987) 'Black women and women's liberation', *Hecate*, xiii (i): 77-82.

Huggins, J. (1987–88) 'Aboriginal women domestic servants in the interwar years', *Hecate*, xiii (ii): 5–23.

Huggins, J. and Tarrago, I. (1990) 'The politics of collaboration', *Hecate*, 16 (1–2): 140–7.

Hull, G., Scott, P.D. and Smith, B. (eds) (1982) *All the Women are White, all the Blacks are Men, but Some of us are Brave*. New York: Feminist Press.

Inglis, A. (1974) *Not a White Women Safe – Sexual Anxiety and Politics in Port Moresby, 1920–1934*. Canberra: ANU Press.

Jakubowicz, A. (1989) 'The state and the welfare of immigrants in Australia', *Ethnic and Racial Studies*, 12 (1): 1–35.

Jennett, C. (1987) 'Incorporation or independence? the struggle for Aboriginal equality' in C. Jennett and R. Stewart (eds), *The Three Worlds of Inequality*. Melbourne: Macmillan. pp. 57–93.

Jupp, J. (1984) 'Australian immigrations, 1788–1973' in F. Milne and P. Shergold (eds), *The Great Immigration Debate*. Sydney: Federation of Ethnic Communities Council. pp. 2–13.

Jupp, J. (ed.) (1989) *The Challenge of Diversity: Policy Options for a Multicultural Australia*. Canberra: Australian Government Publishing Service.

Kalantzis, M. (1990) 'Ethnicity meets gender meets class', in S. Watson (ed.), *Playing the State: Australian Feminist Interventions*. Sydney: Allen & Unwin.

Kapferer, B. (1989) 'Nationalist ideology and a comparative anthropology', *Ethnos*, 3–4: 161–99.

Keeffe, K. (1988) 'Aboriginality: resistance and persistance', *Australian Aboriginal Studies*, 1: 67–81.

Lake, M. (1992) 'Mission Impossible: how men gave birth to the Australian nation', *Gender and History*, 4 (3): 305–22.

Lake, M. (1993) 'Colonised and colonising: the white Australian feminist subject', *Women's History Review*, 2 (3): 377–86.

Langford, R. (1988) *Don't Take Your Love to Town*. Ringwood: Penguin.

Langton, M. (1981) 'Urbanising Aborigines: the social scientists' great deception', *Social Alternatives*, 2 (2):16–22.

Langton, M. (1989) 'Feminism – what do Aboriginal women gain?', *Broadside*, 2: 3.

Larbalestier, J. (1980) 'Feminism as myth: Aboriginal women and the feminist encounter', *Refractory Girl*, 20–21: 31–9.

Larbalestier, J. (1990) 'The politics of representation: Australian Aboriginal women and feminism', *Anthropological Forum*, 6a (2): 143–57.

Lattas, A. (1990) 'Aborigines and Australian nationalism', *Social Analysis*, 27: 50–69.

Lerner, A. (1990) 'Transcendence of the imagiNATION', IAS Conference Paper, Rio.

Lohrey, A. (1984) 'Australian nationalism as myth', *Arena*, 68: 107–23.

McConnochie, K., Hollinsworth, D. and Pettman, J. (1988) *Race and Racism in Australia*. Wentworth Falls: Social Science Press.

McCorquodale, J. (1986) 'The legal classification of race in Australia', *Aboriginal History*, 10 (1): 7–24.

McGrath, A. (1987) *Born in the Cattle*. Sydney: Allen & Unwin.

McQueen, H. (1970) *A New Britannia*. Ringwood: Penguin.

Marginson, M. (1992) 'Filipina migration and organization in Australia', *Lilith*, 7: 11–24.

Markus, A. (1990) *Governing Savages*. Sydney: Allen & Unwin.

Martin, J. (1986) 'Non-English speaking background women in Australia', in N. Grieve and A. Burns (eds), *Australian Women: New Feminist Perspectives*. Melbourne: Oxford University Press.

Meekosha, H. and Pettman, J. (1991) 'Beyond category politics', *Hecate*, 17 (2): 75–92 .

Mercer, D. (1993) 'Terra nullius, Aboriginal sovereignty and land rights in Australia', *Political Geography*, 12 (4): 299–318.

Misztal, B. (1991) 'Migrant women in Australia', *Journal of Intercultural Studies*, 12 (2): 15–34.

Moraga, C. and Anzaldua, G. (eds) (1983) *This Bridge Called My Back: Writings by Radical Women of Color*. New York: Kitchen Table Press.

Moreton-Robinson, A. (1992) 'Masking gender and exalting race: indigenous women and Commonwealth employment policies', *Australian Feminist Studies*, 15: 5–10.

Morrissey, M. (1984) 'Migrantness, culture and ideology' in G. Bottomley, M. de Lepervanche (eds), *Ethnicity, Class and Gender in Australia*. Sydney: Allen & Unwin.

Office of Multicultural Affairs (1989), *National Agenda for a Multicultural Australia*. Canberra: AGPS.

Pateman, C. (1988) *The Sexual Contract*. Oxford: Basil Blackwell.

Perkins, C. (1975) *A Bastard Like Me*. Sydney: Ure Smith.

Peterson, N. (1985) 'Capitalism, culture and land rights', *Social Analysis*, 18: 85–101 .

Pettman, J. (1988) 'Aborigines and white Australia's bicentenary', *Race and Class*, xxix (3): 69–86.

Pettman, J. (1991) 'Racism, sexism and sociology' in G. Bottomley, M. de Lepervanche and J. Martin (eds), *Intersexions: Gender/Class/Culture/Ethnicity*. Sydney: Allen & Unwin.

Pettman, J. (1992a) *Living in the Margins: Racism, Sexism and Feminism in Australia*. Sydney: Allen & Unwin.

Pettman, J. (1992b) 'National identity and security', in G. Smith and St John Kettle (eds), *Threats Without Enemies*. Sydney: Pluto.

Pettman, J. (1992c) 'Gendered knowledges: Aboriginal women and the politics of feminism', *Journal of Australian Studies*, 35: 1–12.

Pettman, J. (1995) 'Border crossings/shifting identities: minorities, gender and the state in international perspective', in H. Alker and M. Shapiro (eds), *Territorial Identities and Global Flows*. Minnesota: University of Minnesota Press.

Pettman, J. (forthcoming) *Worlding Women: Women and the International*. Sydney: Allen & Unwin.

Price, C. (1990) *Ethnic Groups in Australia*. Canberra: Australian Immigration Research Centre.

Reynolds, H. (1991) 'Catching up with our geography', *Australian Society*, April: 28–30.

Rowse, T. (1984) 'On the notion of Aboriginality', *Mankind*, 15 (1): 45–6.

Rowse, T. (1991) 'ATSIC's Heritage: The problems of leadership and unity in Aboriginal political culture', *Current Affairs Bulletin*, 67(8): 14–12.

Rowse, T. (1993) 'Mabo and moral anxiety', *Meanjin*, 52 (2): 229–52.

Ryan, L. (1986) 'Aboriginal women and agency in the process of conquest', *Australian Feminist Studies*, 2: 37–44.

Saunders, K. (1991) 'All the women were white? Analysing race, class and gender in Australian history', *Hecate*, 17 (1): 157–60.

Saunders, K. and Evans, R. (eds) (1992) *Gender Relations in Australia*. Sydney: Harcourt Brace Jovanovich.

Sawer, M. (1990) *Sisters in Suits*. Sydney: Allen & Unwin.

Seitz, A. (1989) 'Non-English speaking background immigrant women: some issues and concerns'. *Migration Action*, December: 3–5.

Spivak, G. with E. Rooney (1989) 'In a word. Interview', *Differences*, 1 (2): 124–56.

Stasiulis, D. (1990) 'Theorizing connections: race, ethnicity, gender and class' in Peter Li (ed.), *Race and Ethnic Relations in Canada*. Toronto: Oxford University Press.

Tatz, C. (1979) *Race Politics in Australia*. Armidale: University of New England.

Tucker, M. (1987) *If Everyone Cared: an Autobiography*. Melbourne: Grosvenor.

Ward, G. (1988) *Wandering Girl*. Broome: Magabala Books.
Whimp, K. (1994) 'Mabo: the inside story', *Arena Magazine*, 9: 16–19.
White, R. (1981) *Inventing Australia*. Sydney: Allen & Unwin.
Yeatman, A. (1990) *Bureaucrats. Technocrats and Femocrats*. Sydney: Allen & Unwin.
Yuval-Davis, N. and Anthias, F. (eds) (1989) *Woman Nation State*. London: Macmillan.

4

The Fractious Politics of a Settler Society: Canada

Daiva Stasiulis and Radha Jhappan

In 1992, coincidentally the five hundredth anniversary of the Columbian invasion of the Americas, Canada undertook a major political initiative in the rancorous terrain of constitutional reform. Had it not been defeated in Canada's first national referendum in fifty years, a wide-ranging package of constitutional amendments would have reshaped the symbolic order and political economy of Canadian society. The negotiations were prompted primarily by the fact that although Canada had formally severed the last colonial ties with Britain by repatriating the constitution in 1982, the new deal had failed to redistribute power from the federal to the provincial governments to the satisfaction of the province of Québec. Hence, the government of Québec did not then and has not since signed the constitution that was passed into law and applied with full force in Québec, despite the absence of the province's consent. Subsequent attempts by political elites to accommodate Québec's demands for enhanced autonomy had been foiled, partly because they activated long-suppressed hostilities from long-oppressed, marginalized groups, who now demanded that their identities receive constitutional acknowledgement and protection.

Two years of unprecedented campaigning by a wide array of interest groups eventually culminated in the Charlottetown Accord, a package of constitutional reforms far broader than the tidy bargains that political elites had hoped to negotiate quietly among themselves. The Accord was extraordinary, not just because it was Canada's first exercise in participatory democracy at the constitutional level, but also because it entailed a symbolic redefinition of Canadian identity. Indeed, it proposed to add a 'Canada Clause' to the constitution which was to express fundamental Canadian values, including Aboriginal rights, the distinct society of Québec, linguistic duality, racial and ethnic equality, and the equality of female and male persons. Further, beyond the rhetoric, substantive clauses provided for increased provincial autonomy (Québec's demand), and the creation of a new third level of government to accommodate Aboriginal self-government.

For various complex reasons, the Accord was rejected by 54 per cent of the electorate. However, the process which spawned it was remarkable in that for the first time in Canadian history, national Aboriginal and women's organizations played significant roles in negotiating and defeating constitutional proposals respectively (Jhappan, 1993; Vickers, 1993). Moreover, it was in this sphere of high constitutional politics that Canada's legacy of old oppressions and exclusions came back to haunt political elites. Here was a litany of the injustices stemming from the privileging of Canada's short history of European settler colonization: the suppression of the land, civil, political, cultural and religious rights of Aboriginal peoples whose ancestors have inhabited the land 'since time immemorial'; the subordination of the 'other' settler society (francophones in Québec, or Québecois) to the British-dominated federal state after the British won the imperialist war with New France in 1760; the patriarchal structures that repulse women's equality rights; and the continuing marginalization of racial and ethnocultural minorities who are defined outside the dominant discourses of 'two founding nations'. These themes have been recurrent throughout Canada's post-contact history, and have produced complex and diversified social movements dedicated to reversing historical marginalization.

This chapter explores the implications of Canada's development from the seventeenth to early twentieth centuries as a 'settler society' for its effects on the encounters among different peoples, and on the relative roles and autonomy of Aboriginal, immigrant/minority and ethnically dominant women. This account is not meant to be a chronology of historical events: rather it endeavours to highlight the types of articulations among gender, racial/ethnic and class relations that grew out of specific historical, material and ideological conditions associated with (dual) settler colonization of Canada. The chapter demonstrates how the British settler construct shaped Canadian development, relying on racial/ethnic and gender hierarchies expressed through laws, political institutions, immigration and settlement policies. After critically examining the 'white settler society' construct, the chapter explores the emergent patterns of gendered, racial/ethnocultural structures and relations during key eras in Canadian development: the pre-contact period, the fur trade, the French and British colonial periods, post-Confederation and post-World War II Canada. A brief examination of contemporary nationalist, racial and ethnic politics, and the mirroring of these politics in women's movements, will conclude the chapter.

The White Settler Society Construct

In puzzling over the paradox of Canada's development, much of the Canadian political economy tradition has absorbed the notion of

Canada's roots as a 'white settler society'. At its base, the white settler society construct refers to the intentions of colonial administrators to build in Canada an 'overseas extension' or replica of British society (Williams, 1976; see also Ehrensaft and Armstrong, 1981; Abele and Stasiulis, 1988). Hence, the dominant culture, values and institutions of the society mimic those of the 'mother' country; they must constantly be replenished via immigration and importation of British ideas, goods, fashions, institutions, and cultural and economic practices. The utility and the limitations of this characterization have not been sufficiently plumbed, however.

The white settler society construct does indeed illuminate our under-standing of Canada's unique developmental trajectory. In the first place, in contrast to other colonized parts of the world in Africa, Asia and the Caribbean, Britain privileged its white settler colonies in Canada, New Zealand and Australia by bestowing upon them the 'gifts' of liberal democratic government and relative political autonomy so that they might develop within a shared framework of civilization and moral and material standards. Hence, although Canada (and the other so-called 'white dominions') shared with the so-called 'dependent colonies' a peripheral position in the international political economy prior to the twentieth century, as a cultural, social and political entity, it was a chip off the metropolitan block.

'Nation-building' in Canada involved more than the construction of transcontinental railways, the development of successive staples for export, and industrialization through import substitution. Beyond recruiting and assembling the social/occupational classes necessary to provide the capital and/or labour for these industries, it also entailed facilitating the development of a morally and physically healthy settler population, and later a citizenry based on 'love and loyalty to Canada and the British Empire' (Roberts, 1979: 186; see also Valverde, 1991). This meant that those at the helm of the colonial, then dominion, states and those shaping civil society drew from British imperial and home-grown philosophies about the appropriate character, physical appearance, roles and behaviour of settler women and men.

The cloning of a British identity required more than the transplant of British bodies and British dispositions, however. It also meant the reproduction of British institutions. Indeed, even after Confederation when Canada formally became a self-governing dominion, Canadian political institutions were modelled directly after the British archetype. The 1867 British North America Act, the constitutional power map which established the framework for federalism and political institu-tions, created the Dominion 'with a Constitution similar in principle to that of the United Kingdom'. In fact, this British parliamentary statute baldly declared that the union of Canada, Nova Scotia and New

Brunswick would 'conduce to the Welfare of the Provinces and promote the Interests of the British Empire'.

Although the white settler society construct as applied to Canada is
useful, its explanatory potential is deficient in four major ways. First,
indigenous populations did not disappear in the face of white settler
colonization, but rather Aboriginal and Métis ('mixed-blood') peoples
have played a major role in shaping the history of specific regions. For
long periods, such as during the two hundred years when the fur trade
was the chief point of contact, indigenous peoples were essential to the
survival of the newcomers, and relations were built on a foundation of
cooperation and mutual benefit. As white settlement began in earnest,
however, the confiscation of indigenous peoples' lands and rights was
justified in terms of their failure to qualify as 'civilized' communities,
their different world-views, cultures, notions of property and 'pagan'
beliefs presented as evidence of their unfitness for ownership or governance of the land. Yet the indigenous peoples did not yield to
Euro-Canadian culture, despite legal and social policies designed for
forced assimilation. The continuing resistance of Aboriginal peoples in
Canada is evidenced most clearly in the many movements for cultural
revitalization and ongoing struggles for reclamation of rights to land
and self-government, particularly since the 1970s.

A second limitation of the white settler society construct is the fact
that immigration and settlement in Canada were considerably more
ethnically and racially diverse than the white British settler agenda
suggested. Indeed, it was this diversity which compelled the conscious
construction of a racial/ethnic hierarchy. The replication project meant
a 'white Canada' immigration policy that was designed aggressively to
recruit the 'best classes' of British men and women. Non-European
would-be immigrants would be excluded unless their cheap labour was
needed, in which case they would be granted lesser access to settlers'
and citizens' rights. In fact, the importation of ethnic/racial minorities,
often as unfree and super-exploited labour, was an intrinsic element in
sustaining the development of Canada's famed 'high wage' proletariat
(Panitch, 1981: 16–17), which in practice meant a minority of mostly
male, white and British skilled craft workers. Ethnic and racial fragmentation thus became a central feature of the settler society's labour
market from its onset, and overtly racist immigration policies were to
persist until the 1960s.

The white settler model is further complicated in the Canadian context by the inevitable conflicts engendered by the settler projects of
two competing colonizing powers – France until the mid-eighteenth
century, and Britain thereafter. Following the British military defeat of
the French in the Conquest of 1760, the French were treated not as
equal but as subordinate partners in nation-building, although as far as

Aboriginal peoples were concerned, they remained one of two settler societies which dispossessed them. Much to the chagrin of British elites, however, *les Canadiens* showed no sign of shedding their attachment to their language, culture, Catholicism or traditions. Efforts of British and Canadian elites demographically to swamp and assimilate the French-Canadian population with imported anglophones from the United States and Britain not only failed, but also fuelled a sense of national oppression among francophone Québeckers. Hence, the British could never claim full cultural hegemony over the country.

Finally, the assumptions of the white settler society construct are not only racist but also androcentric. They focus primarily on men's activities in the public sphere (in production and in government), and women are regarded as little more than breeders to reproduce 'the nation, the empire and the future of the race' (Roberts, 1979: 186). In reality, however, women played multiple, complex roles, depending on their own racial/ethnic, class and marital statuses. These factors not only determined the kind of work (domestic and otherwise) women performed, but also their role in controlling or oppressing other women. Anglo-Celtic women, for example, may have been restricted by male-ordered marriage, property and labour laws, but they joined Christian missionaries and state officials as key players in the 'moral reform', assimilationist and eugenics projects regulating working-class, single, Aboriginal and non-British immigrant women. Moreover, the white settler society construct ignores the differential impacts of specific institutions and policies on women and men in Aboriginal and immigrant communities. State policies (such as Native, immigration and employment policies) were inherently colonial, racist and sexist.

Pre-contact North American Societies

While the first enduring European settlement within the present-day borders of Canada dates from 1608, archaeological evidence shows human habitation of the length and breadth of the Americas by 11,000 BC, though populations tended to concentrate along the Pacific coasts of North and South America (Dickason, 1992: 34–5). For the most part, Euro-Canadian historians have ignored the dynamism and diverse accomplishments of Aboriginal peoples prior to the European migration, preferring to support the socio-legal myth that North America was 'a vacant territory, *terra nullius*, to which Europeans could freely take title' (Richardson, 1993: 29). The idea that indigenous peoples were only nomadic hunters lacking political or legal organization, and thus unencumbered by sovereignty over their territories, does not, however, hold up to anthropological scrutiny.

Long before European intrusion, indigenous societies manifested an impressive adaptability to local climatic, topographical and ecological conditions from the Arctic to the Great Plains, thus ensuring 'many variations on fundamentally similar ways of life' (Dickason, 1992: 63). From the sophisticated, socially stratified and economically diversified civilizations which thrived on the Pacific Coast (Tennant, 1990), to the migratory-hunting and more egalitarian Algonkian and the Iroquoian agriculturalist tribes of the Eastern Woodlands, to the Inuit who managed to subsist in the extremely harsh arctic climate, Aboriginal societies exhibited a rich kaleidoscope in cultural, linguistic and sociopolitical organization.

Although local conditions and subsistence bases generated great variety in social organization, languages, cultures and cosmologies, the majority of accounts of pre-contact societies describe a rudimentary division of labour based on age and sex (Prentice et al., 1988: 26; Valentine, 1980: 64). Women's work in indigenous societies varied according to resource base, however, as did their relative political authority and position *vis-à-vis* men within their cultures (Prentice et al., 1988: 26). Among the Huron, Montagnais-Nascapi and the Six Nations, women's labour produced the majority of staples and women were in control of the distribution of these subsistence goods (Anderson, 1991: 133–4; Prentice et al., 1988: 28; Brown, 1975). The crops that women cultivated also constituted important trade items among the Algonkian people further north (Brant Castellano, 1989: 46), although it was men who most frequently engaged in inter-tribal trade (a factor that would later condition the transformation in Native gender relations brought about by the fur trade with Europeans). Nevertheless, women were as likely as men to gain prestige as healers and foreseers of the future (Anderson, 1991: 119).

Female power in Iroquoian societies was linked to the longhouse, a social unit composed of three to six matrilineally related households or domestic groups (ibid.: 107). Here, men's access to the products of women's labour was regulated through their residency in the matrilocal longhouse, making men more dependent on their wives than vice versa (ibid.: 115). Such structuring of kin relations and residence gave women power in the longhouse, which later fuelled their resistance to the oppressive consequences for women of the activities of Christian missionaries. Although women did not hold political office, their substantial influence over public policy was derived from the fact that they controlled the appointment and removal of leaders.

In more highly stratified societies such as among west coast tribes which possessed slaves, the question of women's power is more complex. Thus, even though the west coast Haida, like the Iroquois and Huron, passed all property through the female line, women had a clearly subordinate status in marriage and limited access to formal political power. Yet even while the majority of women were relatively powerless, some high-status women could be chieftans. This practice increased with population decimation by European diseases in the late nineteenth century (Prentice et al., 1988: 34, 40).

In sum, women and men in pre-contact and especially hunting and gathering societies appeared to have influence in separate activities, with male influence predominating in hunting, trade and external (military and diplomatic) relations. However, in such societies, relations between male and female roles were often fluid. Women appeared to enjoy great power 'not only in their realms of production, distribution, and child care, but in the larger decision-making processes of the group' (Prentice et al., 1988: 40; see also Mitchell, 1992: 87). There is also little question that women in Aboriginal societies were considerably freer in matters of work, sexuality and political influence than their counterparts in seventeenth-century Europe. This female autonomy became a matter of considerable anxiety to European males and a prime target for the Christianizing drive of missionaries.

The Transformative Role of Contact, Trade and Christianity

The first recorded encounters between North American indigenous peoples and Europeans began with the Vikings and probably the (now disappeared) Dorset and Beothuk in about AD 1000 (Dickason, 1992: 86–7). The Norse were followed by Basque whalers in the sixteenth century, Portugese fishermen, Dutch traders who financed trading and whaling expeditions, and French missionaries (ibid.: 12). The success of European commercial and exploratory ventures depended upon the active cooperation of indigenous peoples. European explorers, vainly seeking a waterway through the North American land mass that would lead to the fabled riches of Asia, would not have been able to penetrate the interior without the guidance and provision of food, clothing and transportation facilities by Amerindians. European dependence on Micmac walrus-hunting expertise and on Inuit harpooning technology for the success of the Basque and French whale industries presaged the high level of cooperation required of Amerindians in the fur trade.

Indeed, it was the fur trade that came to structure and define Native–European relations for two centuries (1670–1870). The fur trade was based on a commodity exchange between Europeans and Native peoples, and it required much more extensive and sustained contact between these two racially/ethnically divergent groups of people (van Kirk, 1980). As such, it produced a complex outcome of bi-directional transformations in material conditions and world-views among both Amerindian and primarily French traders involved in a relationship of mutual dependence and benefit (Trigger, 1985; van Kirk, 1980; Coates, 1993).

While trade with Europeans afforded indigenous peoples access to European technology such as iron, Native 'adaptations were selective and within established cultural patterns' (Dickason, 1992: 104). The fact that beaver could be trapped and traded during two brief periods in spring and summer meant that trading with the French did not adversely affect subsistence production (Trigger, 1985: 204). Given that fur traders had little opportunity to hoard European goods, the fur trade also did not significantly disrupt property relations among peoples such as the Huron and Montagnais (Anderson, 1991: 152).

More devastating to Amerindians than changes wrought by trade were the scourges of disease against which Native peoples had little or no immunity (smallpox, influenza, bubonic plague, yellow fever and so on), and the intrusion of Christian missionaries. It is now estimated that through the Americas as a whole, 20 waves of pestilence killed as much as 90 per cent of the original population, although the extent of depopulation in regional populations clearly varied (Wright, 1992: 14, 123; Dickason, 1992: 111; Trigger, 1985: 242). The decimation of Aboriginal populations by disease alone had profound and devastating effects on their ability to resist the onslaught of white settlement and its attendant consequences. The decisive factor in New France, however, appears to have been the undermining of egalitarian values and collectivist structures zealously pursued by Jesuit missionaries (Anderson, 1991).

The Jesuits encountered the impossibility of instilling a hierarchical Christian order in egalitarian societies where women exercised considerable autonomy and power in sexual, political and economic matters. The key to Jesuit success was in securing female submission, chiefly to individual men, God and Church through Christian marriage, baptism and burial rites. This meant undermining the institutional basis for women's authority and autonomy in matrilocal and matrilineal kin corporate structures (Anderson, 1991; Trigger, 1985: 294–5). Women, who had much to lose from the Jesuit redefinition of men's and women's characters and roles, repeatedly resisted Jesuit domination, accepting baptism only during prolonged illness, and returning to traditional beliefs upon resumption of health.

Aboriginal women were clearly central to the success of the fur trade in ways that were deeply troubling for Protestant missionaries who arrived later. Native women were sexually exploited through 'prostitution with its attendant horror, venereal disease' (van Kirk, 1980: 27). Van Kirk argues, however, that marriage 'according to the custom of the country', rather than prostitution, was 'the usual pattern of sexual interaction between European traders and Indian women' (ibid.). Such unions were chiefly motivated by economic ends – to secure influence for traders through Aboriginal kinship networks, and to provide Natives with access to posts and provisions.

At fur-trade posts, women's (often unremunerated) labour was essential for key activities such as the dressing of furs, the provision and preservation of food, and the manufacture of bush footwear and birch-bark canoes. The success of inland voyages also depended on the presence and service of Native women in pitching camp, and as guides, interpreters and language teachers (ibid.: 63). On the north-west coast, the central role of women in the management and production of household goods extended to negotiations in a profitable maritime fur trade in sea otters such that women were frequently the chief negotiators (Littlefield, 1988).

The extensive intermarriage between Native women (followed by their Métis daughters) and European (chiefly French) traders complicated a social order that was stratified by class and ethnicity. The chief factors in the Hudson's Bay Company who governed the posts were principally Englishmen, while tradesmen and labourers were Scots (Orkneymen). The officer class of the North West Company was dominated by men of Highland Scots origin, while the labouring class were recruited from the French-Canadian voyageurs (van Kirk, 1980: 12).

The emergence of a sizeable Métis population with a distinctive identity in the Canadian prairies was the product of the mutual dependencies rooted in economic interests and daily intimacy between Natives and Europeans. Generally, the ethnicity and class of the fathers conditioned whether the Indian ancestry would be concealed or form the basis of identity. Scottish 'half-breeds' of the fur-trade elite were more likely to aspire to assimilate into the 'civilized' society of their fathers' world. In contrast, the more numerous Métis of Indian–French ancestry in the prairies were more likely to identify themselves as 'a "New Nation", neither Amerindian nor white but a distinctive blend of both, that incorporated farming, buffalo hunting and the fur trade' (Dickason, 1992: 263). The unique political consciousness of the Métis in the plains was mobilized to claim land rights and provincial status, and to resist the 'arrogant decision-making' of a distant and unsympathetic federal government (Redbird, 1980: 24), as well as the western advance of Canadian jurisdiction.

In fur-trade society, Amerindian women suffered a secular decline in their influence which coincided with the evolution in choice of marriage partners among traders: 'mixed-blood' wives replaced Native wives and were finally supplanted by white women in the early nineteenth century (van Kirk, 1980). In a familiar pattern within the British Empire, the appearance of white women was coterminous with white settlement and brought both a sharp rise in racist sentiment and heightened class-consciousness within fur-trade society.

By the late nineteenth century, the fur trade was in decline. The production of staples for export such as wheat in the new agrarian society and the burgeoning industries of central Canada dispensed with social and economic exchange between Europeans and Native peoples that had been the foundation of fur-trade society. No longer needing the labour and commerce of indigenous people, the European intruders enacted laws and engaged in a series of policies and practices which eroded the Amerindian peoples' fundamental place on the land, and even sought to legislate their cultures out of existence.

Mercantilism, New France and Settler Colonization

From the outset, the French pursued different settlement objectives from the British. As long as the fur trade remained the chief economic activity, and Amerindians provided all the labour it required, the French did not contemplate large-scale colonization. This was to change with the rise of seventeenth-century mercantilism in the states of north-western Europe, however. Colonies would provide the mother country with raw materials for her manufacturing industries, markets for her exports and protection of her territorial claims (Knowles, 1992: 8).

In France, a powerful commercial company (the Company of One Hundred Associates) was formed which provided title to all the lands claimed by France in North America and a monopoly on all commerce except fishing. In return, 'the company undertook to settle 4,000 French Catholics in its *domaine* between 1627 and . . . 1643' (ibid.: 5). It was during these years that a transition occurred from mere fur-trading post to settler colony, with population concentrating around Québec (Stadacona), Trois Rivières and Montréal (Hochelaga), and in the Atlantic seaboard colonies of Acadia and Louisbourg. The colony's economy was to be based on lumbering, mining, fishing, manufacturing and trade with the West Indies, all of which required the importation of capital, managerial talent and skilled labour (ibid.: 9).

A significant inducement in recruiting wealthy colonists was the seigneurial system – the granting of large tracts of land to organizations or private individuals who agreed to establish settlers on them. Notwithstanding this incentive, the French were 'half-hearted settlers' with only 27,000 migrants coming from the mother country in the roughly 150 years of French rule of Canada (Wright, 1992: 126), and with no more than 12,000 of these permanent settlers (Knowles, 1992: 13).

French colonial policy towards the more numerous Amerindians was ambiguous and also underwent change. The French regime was unsure as to whether Amerindians were to be treated as sovereign allies or as subjects of the French Crown (Dickason, 1992: 165). In practice, pragmatic considerations reigned. In order to ensure alliance with Natives in trade and war and in dealing with colonial rivals such as the English, French policy was to claim that Indians were allies and therefore sovereign peoples. Yet they were nonetheless increasingly subjected to the imposition of punitive French laws (ibid.: 166–7). Most importantly, French colonization proceeded on the basis of the European doctrines of discovery and occupation which held that North America was legally speaking *terra nullius* (uninhabited land), and that the presumed nomadic life of Amerindians disqualified them from being classified as inhabitants in the European sense. Through such mythologies, Europeans fancied they had legitimized both their 'discovery' – and hence title over land (as marked by symbolic acts such as flag-raising) – and their *de facto* occupation (via the creation of settlements). The French monarch 'never recognized aboriginal title' and freely disposed of Amerindian land to French subjects (ibid.: 176).

In the first years of settlement, intermixing of the predominantly male French population with the indigenous population, when sanctified by marriage, was official policy, the aim of which was to 'Frenchify' the Native population and produce a French population overseas. By early in the eighteenth century, however, alarmed that French–Native unions had produced a separate Métis sense of political identity in the north-west, the opinion of colonial elites shifted against intermarriage. A new racially endogamous policy also reflected the increased availability of white women as potential wives, the so-called *filles du roi* or 'daughters of the king', French women explicitly imported to marry male settlers (Brown, 1988: 137).

Non-Native women formed a minority of the population in New France. Following an initial effort to promote settlement in the 1660s and 1670s, for the next eighty years, fewer than one-fifth of the 50 migrants from France who arrived each year were women (Prentice et al., 1988: 46). In spite of (indeed, in large part because of) their small numbers, French women played a vital role in shaping the colony's spiritual and material beginnings. Among the first women to arrive were nuns, who established a network of missions, hospitals and schools essential to the fledgling colony's survival. Some, such as the Ursulines, expected to administer to the Amerindians, an expectation that was abandoned when homesick Native girls proved resistant to their 'civilizing' mission and fled back to their communities (ibid.: 38, 43).

A number of conditions – such as the overabundance of men and freedom from Old World constraints – coalesced to produce a high degree of independence among women in New France. The frequent absences of soldiers or traders compelled their wives to take complete charge of households, farms, military stores, trading operations, taverns and other businesses, and even to take up arms in skirmishes with the

Iroquois. French customary law, the concern of which was to ensure the rights of all members of the family, provided economic protection (if not gender equality) to wives and widows (Prentice et al., 1988: 51; Errington, 1993: 63).

From its beginnings, New France was a society divided by class and status distinctions (including hierarchies of military rank), which meant that relations among women were characterized by inequality as well as interdependence. The enslavement of both Amerindians and Blacks existed in New France as it did in the areas of present-day Ontario and the Maritimes, until it was abolished throughout the Empire by the British Parliament in 1833.

Over a period of 150 years, some 2,700 Amerindian and about 1,400 black slaves were recorded in Canada, most of whom were found in the Montréal region, with the remainder concentrated in Québec City and Trois Rivières (Knowles, 1992: 13). In contrast to the southern United States, however, Canada lacked the economic basis such as a (one-crop, gang-labour) plantation system to support slavery on a large scale. Slave labour was unprofitable for fishing and the fur trade, and for farming which in New France was organized in a quasi-feudal fashion where small farmers (*habitants*) worked for landowners (*seigneurs*). Most slaves worked as domestic servants for merchants, military officers and the religious community.

With the military defeat of the French Empire by the British in 1760, New France's ties with the mother country were severed, including those of migration. France perceived her overseas colony as a huge drain on her coffers, in which henceforth she had no interest. Most of the colony's leaders, merchants and their wives sailed back to France with the surviving French troops after the capitulation. Yet despite the exodus, by 1765 the French population of New France had climbed to nearly 70,000, largely through natural increase. For the next two centuries, the survival of Canada's francophone population was to depend heavily upon the 'revenge of the cradle', which hinged on Québec women having the highest rate of fertility in any western society (Maroney, 1992: 9). It was also made possible by a special constitutional accommodation which protected 'the collective, religious/educational and language rights of the two "charter groups" . . . even outside their respective territorial jurisdictions, in localities where their members constituted *numerical* minorities' (Kallen, 1990: 85, original emphasis).

British Settler Colonization

Aboriginal people are regularly obliged to point out that it was not the First Nations who were militarily conquered by the British in 1760 or at any other time (Dickason, 1992: 181; Mercredi and Turpel, 1993: 61). Rather, legal imperialism characterized the British Empire's strategy of expansion through cession of traditional territories, beginning with the Royal Proclamation of 1763. The Proclamation defined the contradictory nature of the Imperial government's, and later Canada's, relationship with indigenous peoples – a dual policy of 'recognition and assimilation' (Cassidy and Bish, 1989: 4).

Under the Royal Proclamation, King George III declared that 'the several Nations of Tribes of Indians with whom We are connected' were under the 'protection' of the Crown. Such protection was warranted by the political necessity of keeping the peace under settler colonialism, where settlement had resulted in 'Great Frauds and Abuses [having] been committed in purchasing Lands of the Indians, . . . to the Great Dissatisfaction of the said Indians' (quoted in Elliott, 1985: 53). The Proclamation strictly forbade the grant of settlement of new lands except as provided by treaty and with the express assent of the Crown. Lands 'not having been ceded to or purchased by Us' were to remain exclusively in the hands of Aboriginal owners to whom the Crown was extending its protection (Chartrand, 1992: 9).

Approximately one-half of Canada's lands came to be covered by treaties reached between First Nations and the British Imperial or Canadian governments. On the other hand, however, half of the Aboriginal peoples of Canada (primarily in British Columbia, Québec, the Maritimes and the Northwest Territories) have *not* signed treaties. Rather, their lands were simply expropriated by provincial governments, which offered in return reserve lands of varying, and usually low, quality and value. The illegal and unconstitutional seizure of Aboriginal lands has thus produced unresolved land and aboriginal rights claims, core features of contemporary Native politics.

Even before the extortion of Aboriginal lands was complete, however, British authorities were faced with land pressures from non-British immigrants. The period encompassing the fall of New France was a period of continuous political and military upheaval in Europe and North America that spawned a vast movement of peoples. Notable in this migration were the 40,000 to 50,000 United Empire Loyalists who travelled north to British North America as political refugees, fearing punishment for their support of the British during the American War of Independence. Interestingly, though primarily English-speaking and Protestant, the Loyalists were ethnically and racially heterogeneous (German, Highland Scottish, English, Abenaki and Six Nations Indians) and consisted of families headed by soldiers and frontier farmers (Knowles, 1992: 19–23).

Among the Loyalists were some 3,000 free blacks who had been emancipated by the British on condition that they served with the king's forces. These black migrants became the first large influx of freed and fugitive slaves to pre-abolition Nova Scotia, where they encountered what was to become a pervasive pattern of anti-black racism and segregation. However, in view of the relative unprofitability in Canada of slavery given the availability of alternative sources of cheap-wage labour, the former waned as an institution. Seeking the relative freedom of the Maritimes and Upper Canada, many American fugitive slaves made their way northward via the 'underground railroad', where they created communities (Krauter and Davis, 1978).

Given the American character of much of this early migration to British North America, explicit sponsored schemes were needed to promote settlement from the British Isles and to root British values into Canadian soil. Britain was quite willing to promote emigration to her self-governing colonies to relieve internal unemployment and social unrest, to reduce the number of persons of 'racially inferior' Irish stock who were flocking into British cities, and to provide a bulwark against absorption of the colony by the United States, a concern made acute by the War of 1812. The wheels of British migration and settlement in new parts of North America were greased by land companies and wealthy philanthropists.

Of particular concern to philanthropists were the growing numbers of single, impoverished women from the lower middle class. Family colonization schemes in the mid-eighteenth century thus came to be supplemented by plans to increase the population of the colonies with the emigration of single domestic servants. Such emigration schemes thus simultaneously 'solved' three problems for the imperial government and its colonies: alleviation of female poverty, the colonial need for domestic labour and the establishment of viable British overseas colonies (Roberts, 1979).

Although many of the British immigrants to upper and lower Canada and the Maritimes crossed into the United States, there is little doubt of the success of the British colonization efforts. By 1867, the year of Confederation, an estimated two-thirds of British North America's population was British in origin (Knowles, 1992: 30). Irish immigration between 1846 and 1854 alone, provoked by the horrific potato famine, brought approximately 400,000 persons to Upper Canada, tipping the population and political balance between the two Canadas. Poor Irish immigrants mostly found work in the lumbering, shipping and shipbuilding industries and in the construction of the massive Welland and St Lawrence canal systems, marking the beginnings of Canada's capitalist labour market (Pentland, 1981: 258).

As within the upper echelons of pre-Conquest society in New France, British women of means in the settler colony managed property, operated taverns and, if widowed, ran family businesses

(Errington, 1993: 65). However, part of the cultural baggage brought by British immigrants in the mid-nineteenth century were Victorian views regarding separate spheres for women and men suiting their respective 'natural' temperaments. This meant that women were increasingly excluded from the public sphere where the authorities – clergymen, magistrates, military and company officers – were all men. It also meant that while propertied, white men were increasingly active in politics, such as the elected assemblies established by British imperial authorities, all women were barred from participation in government.

The 'cult of true womanhood', which painted women as fragile, virtuous and subservient to menfolk and to domestic needs, reinforced the subordination of women under British common laws affecting sexuality, marriage and motherhood. As summed up by Prentice et al. (1988: 88), in British 'common law the husband and wife were considered one person and that person was the husband'. Between 1820 and 1860, as British North America developed economically and became socially more stratified, men's occupations were expanding in number, becoming more specialized and moving out of the household. In contrast, economic opportunities for women outside the home became increasingly constricted, unspecialized and poorly remunerated (Errington, 1993: 67).

The Protestant Victorian ideology of 'true womanhood' did not describe the harsh realities of the vast majority of women, who were required to perform hard labour – in their household or the household of others, the farm or family enterprise (ibid.: 84). In terms of paid employment, women could most easily get jobs as maids, cooks, laundresses and farm helps (ibid.: 66). Another avenue of employment for women was schoolteaching, initially in private homes (Prentice et al., 1988: 94). Finally, women's subsistence farm work, as well as production of goods for sale such as spun wool, woven goods and dairy products, also made possible the accumulation of capital in many farm families. Thus, women made vital contributions to the developing economy through their productive and reproductive labour, without which a capitalist labour market, industrialization or a healthy agricultural sector would not have been possible.

Race and Gender Policies in Nation-Building

In contrast to the revolutionary upheavals marking the birth of other independent nations, the dominion of Canada came into self-government by handshakes among businessmen-cum-elected members of the British-Canadian ruling class and a minority of the French elite in 1867. The spectacle of the conquered French enemies participating in the founding of the modern Canadian state is perhaps not so curious in a context wherein other threats to the survival and profitability of the British Empire (such as the possibility of an American invasion) necessitated alliance and accommodation with the surviving French in Québec. Indeed, although the aims of British policy at times vacillated between preserving and assimilating the French culture, the legal and institutional frameworks promoted formal respect for French cultural heritage. Both the 1774 Québec Act and the 1791 Constitutional Act accommodated the Québecois by respecting freedom of worship for Roman Catholics (who were chiefly of French descent), officially sanctioning the Catholic Church, retaining French civil law and the seigneurial landholding system, and granting the right of the (predominantly French) representative government to Lower Canada from 1791 to 1867.

In fact, the federal system created at Confederation and welcomed by Québec must be seen in part as an accommodation of 'the French fact', since the Anglo politicians of the time (especially Canada's first Prime Minister, Sir John A. Macdonald) would have preferred a unitary state for economic and security reasons. The understanding was that French elites and the Church would rule inside Québec, though this meant they would be rendered relatively powerless in the wider industrial capitalist project of Canada as a whole. Nevertheless, from that political compromise, the Québecois emerged with: a provincial state exercising jurisdiction over matters such as culture, language, education, immigration and civil law; the right to use French in the federal Parliament and courts; and what has turned out to be over-representation (relative to the proportion of the population) in the House of Commons, the Senate and Cabinets. These arrangements did not put the Québecois free and clear of the ultimate domination of the Anglo-Canadian state, as the institutions and constitution created were based on the British model and passed by her Parliament. It was around the time of Confederation, however, that the ideological construct of 'two founding races' or 'two founding nations' began to emerge. The concept would not only obliterate the history, role and claims of Aboriginal peoples, but also placate the Québecois and, for a time, forestall their own claims to national sovereignty.

The move to a more independent constitutional status of the nascent dominion did not in any way decrease the concern among the British-Canadian population, particularly its upper echelons, with the development of the British Empire and Canada's central place within it. Among the most urgent tasks facing the new Conservative government of Sir John A. Macdonald was the incorporation and settlement of British Columbia and the domains of the Hudson's Bay Company and the commercial linking together of what had heretofore been largely separate colonial regional economies and societies (Knowles, 1992: 45). Immigration policies and aggressive recruiting schemes of British women and children led by British-Canadian upper- and middle-class women were developed whose priority it would be to build a nation that was to be British in outlook and character (Roberts, 1979: 185–6). Fear of the physical deterioration of the 'Anglo-Saxon race', augmented by the rejection of recruits for the Boer War on the ground of physical incapacity, bred the belief among Britons and British-Canadians alike that 'Canada could become a regenerative force within the Empire, . . . "free from the blighting evils that afflict and torment older lands"' (Bacchi, 1983: 105).

The labour needs of an unprecedented wave of agricultural and industrial expansion, however, complicated the process of building a British settler colony in the new nation. The period from 1880 to 1920 saw the first recruitment of immigrants, who in varying degrees departed from the model of the ideal settler. Many of these newcomers had travelled from peasant villages in eastern, central and southern Europe, China, Japan and India. While immigration policy gave preference to farmers to develop the western wheat economy, many immigrants ended up working in mines, laying railway track or drifting into the urban working class.

Many migrants, like their predecessors a century earlier, saw themselves as sojourners earning money to improve the lives of their families back home. Among others, such as the Ukrainians, settlement during a key phase of Canadian nation-building generated a collective self-image as a 'founding people' that became an important aspect of ethnic consciousness (Swyripa, 1993: 5). Unfortunately, the Ukrainian peasant way of life was viewed by British-Canadians as rife with violence, pagan excess and idleness. The stereotypes of Ukrainian women as child brides, victims of male abuse, domestic drudges and beasts of burden were horrifying to middle-class, Anglo-Canadian women, who saw them as fundamentally destabilizing to Canadian society. While these distorted and incomplete images of Ukrainian women betrayed the class and ethnic biases of their creators, they, and similar negative stereotypes, became the basis for organized opposition to non-British immigration that quickly surfaced in the 1890s (ibid.: 34–5).

Although eastern and central European immigrants were treated with contempt and suspicion, deemed 'enemy aliens' during World War I, the most virulent and institutionalized forms of racism were reserved for non-white minorities and Natives. The consensus among British-Canadians, summed up by J.S. Woodsworth, a leading Methodist social reformer, was that Asians and blacks were 'essentially non-assimilable elements [that] are clearly detrimental to our highest national development, and hence should be vigorously excluded' (1909: 279). Systematically denied settler status and the rights of citizenship, the treatment of these groups fully expressed the Eurocentric contradictions of the British Empire's stance on race and rights. In the disposition of matters such as immigration and the franchise rights of Asians and blacks, the imperial philosophy of race-blind justice and equality before the law gave way to the sense of racial superiority of all things Anglo-Saxon.

Chinese migrants, who had first come to British Columbia in the late 1850s in response to the gold rush, were recruited in the 1880s to participate in the dangerous construction of the Canadian Pacific Railway. While some federal members of Parliament argued that as British subjects the Chinese ought to be shown 'fair play', the prevailing opinion among British-Canadians was typified by the sentiment of Prime Minister Macdonald uttered in 1885. He argued that 'we will have plenty of labor of our own kindred races, without introducing this element of a mongrel race to disturb the labor market, and certainly we ought not to allow them to share the Government of the country' (quoted in Stasiulis and Williams, 1992: 25). Racist fear of the 'yellow peril' pervaded all classes of the British population, but was most emphatically organized within the white, male working class, where cheap and coerced Asian labour provoked fear of undercutting and strike-breaking (Creese, 1988–89).

With a view to restricting entry and settlement of Chinese, progressively stiffer head taxes on the entry of Chinese were imposed, and from 1924 to 1947 there was an outright ban. This discriminatory immigration policy effectively kept the migration of Chinese women to a minimum and had a debilitating impact on the family lives of male migrants, who returned to China or settled in isolated enclaves in British Columbia and throughout the prairies. Only wives of Chinese clergymen and merchants were exempt from the tax. 'Slave girls', purchased from impoverished parents by Chinese businessmen, were also brought in to work as servants or prostitutes (Prentice et al., 1988: 115).

Later, other Asians who had settled in British Columbia were restricted from arriving in large numbers in ingenious ways. In 1907, Canada concluded a 'Gentleman's Agreement' with Japan to limit the emigration of Japanese to Canada to 400 a year. A year later, immigration from India was choked off by a 'continuous journey regulation', at a time when there was no direct steamship service from the Indian subcontinent to Canada (Knowles, 1992: 87–8).

Immigration of African Americans to western Canada was vigorously discouraged, through drafting in 1911 of 'the first racial exclusion ordinance in the Western Hemisphere' (ibid.: 86). This Order-in-Council, which was never implemented, was precipitated by the attempt of a group of black Oklahoma farmers to emigrate to Alberta in order to escape from Ku Klux Klan persecution in the United States. A 'sex-race panic', whereby white women homesteaders were viewed as endangered by the presence of black men, perniciously portrayed as 'over-sexed' and potential rapists, accounted for the vociferousness of the rejection in Alberta of even a small influx of Blacks (Valverde, 1991: 13). Henceforth, more informal exclusionary methods were utilized to exclude Black settlement until the 1960s, including resort to racist arguments concerning Black non-adaptability to the Canadian climate.

An active immigration promotional campaign by Clifford Sifton, the Laurier government's Minister of the Interior, brought unprecedented numbers of white American farmers and diverse Europeans (Ukrainians, Russian Doukhobors and Jews, Poles, Germans and Scandinavians) to push prairie wheat production to the top of the list of Canada's exports. Cultural stereotypes of white Americans as 'an intelligent progressive race' [*sic*] ensured them a warm welcome in the newly formed provinces of Alberta and Saskatchewan, where they would comprise the largest immigrant group (Knowles, 1992: 63).

A number of social reform movements – the social gospel, prohibition and women's rights – shared the view that the new immigrants posed a 'threat' to their common ideal of a homogeneous social order based on Protestantism and British 'democratic institutions' (Bacchi, 1983: 104–16; Palmer, 1982: 38). In western Canada, some suffrage organizations argued that British-Canadian women needed the vote to help offset the morally and socially detrimental effect of non-British immigrants on prairie society; in some instances, they even suggested that it was more important to restrict the franchise among immigrant men than provide the vote to white British-Canadian women (Palmer, 1982: 39). While such arguments did not secure the franchise for British-Canadian women, they did provide pressure on the state to enact a number of new coercive measures in immigration policy. These included the introduction of mandatory medical tests, new grounds for deportation and the greater policing of new arrivals, particularly unaccompanied women (McLaren, 1990: 46–67; Valverde, 1991: 104–28).

Opposition to the arrival of non-British immigrants was thus fuelled by an incendiary mix of race-sex fears, anti-Semitism, anti-radicalism, eugenics and 'nativism' (McLaren, 1990: 48). As described by Valverde, nativism which flourished in western Canada was a 'fantastical' term to invent a 'native' Anglo-Canadian people, and 'naturalize British ideas about law, the state and religion' (1991: 107–8). The most obvious effect was to erase the Métis and Native people who occupied western Canada.

The effort to obliterate Aboriginal and mixed-race communities in order to open the prairies to white settlement, however, required more coercive measures. In 1870 Prime Minister Macdonald declared that the Métis, 'these impulsive half breeds . . . must be kept down by a strong hand until they are swamped by the influx of settlers' (quoted in Bakan, 1991: 7) Repeatedly, in 1870 and 1885, federal forces were used ruthlessly to suppress the Métis and Native armed rebellions against incorporation into federal state control, which culminated with the execution of its most prominent leader, Louis Riel. The federal government also failed to honour a continuity of land tenures and native self-government promised in the Manitoba Act which marked the new province's creation. Where Métis individuals received land allowances, these were usually granted in 'scrip' (transferable equivalents), which unscrupulous speculators often bought at a fraction of their stated worth (Brown, 1988: 143).

The framework for a coercive policy towards Aboriginal peoples to remove their potential for hindrance of white settlement was established in 1867 with the British North America Act, whose Section 91 (24) gave jurisdiction over 'Indians and lands reserved for the Indians' to the federal government. In 1876 the consolidation of all existing legislation concerning Native peoples in the Indian Act provided a totalitarian 'cradle-to-grave' set of rules, regulations and directives to manage Native lives. It also imposed discriminatory and arbitrary standards for definition of who was or was not a 'status Indian', the result of which has been divisive and undermining of First Nations identity (Mercredi and Turpel, 1993). While the Act provided 'Indians' with a special 'status', its eventual goal was the loss of Indian status through a process that ironically was called 'enfranchisement'. This meant that Indians had to relinquish their Indian status, claims to land, hunting and fishing rights, and the right to live in reserve communities.

The Indian Act also ensured a differential impact of policies of protection, civilization and assimilation on women and men. Disregarding matrilineal or bilateral rules of descent and inheritance prevailing among many First Nations, the Act adopted a Eurocentric patrilineal principle of descent: 'Legal status was now transmitted exclusively in the male line from one generation to the next' (Weaver, 1993: 95). Moreover, for men enfranchisement would come with education and 'civilization' and 'was made virtually synonymous with the acquisition of private property (in contrast with the mere occupancy of reserve property, the title to which is held by the Crown)' (Jamieson, 1986: 119). By contrast, women, who were assumed to have no independent legal status from husbands, required only marriage to a non-Indian (or non-status man) to become enfranchised. This compulsory policy whereby women married to non-status men, and their children, lost

Indian status remained in place until challenged by courageous Indian women and their organizations, and finally overturned in 1985.

Leaving nothing to chance, Canadian federal and provincial governments passed a wide range of laws with the express purpose of suppressing Aboriginal political and civil as well as land rights. For example, a British Columbian provision of 1870 allowed any male over 18 simply to occupy 320 acres of land, but specified that 'such right of pre-emption shall not be held to extend to any of the Aborigines of this continent'; the Indian Act from 1880 to 1951 outlawed participation in Potlatches and other Indian festivals (which were forums for the conduct of politics); a 1920 law allowed the federal government to order 'enfranchisement' of qualified (male) Indians, whether they consented or not; every municipal and provincial Elections Act up to 1949 and every federal act up to 1952 specifically excluded Indians from voting (although they did not exercise the federal vote until 1961); and a 1927 amendment to the Indian Act made it illegal for any person to receive money from any Indian for claims-related activities.

Key to the federal policies of Indian protection and assimilation was a pass law which forbade departure from official reserve lands without the permission of government-appointed Indian agents. In effect from 1885 to 1930, this system became the model for the infamous pass and homelands systems, central elements in racial apartheid in South Africa. Indian and female forms of government were undermined by the superimposition of a federal male-led band council system, which in any case had little power *vis-à-vis* the new federal bureaucracy of Indian Affairs run by non-Natives.

On prairie reserves, promising Native large-scale agricultural developments, which threatened the profits of white farmers, were deliberately sabotaged through the imposition of a system of 'peasant' or subsistence farming (Carter, 1991). Other cruel and forcible measures of assimilation included the removal of Indian children from reserves into white residential schools and white foster homes. The tragic outcome of such extreme measures included high rates of youth suicide, sexual and physical abuse, and loss of Indian identity. Non-Native wives of farm instructors and missionaries became 'civilizing agents', providing domestic training for Native women and girls in cleaning, food preparation, sewing, and dairy and poultry production (White, 1987). Dire on-reserve living conditions, and the high incidence of disease such as tuberculosis, were attributed to the women's lack of housekeeping abilities. This legitimized increased state intervention which further disempowered Indian women. Thus, taken together, these and other measures denied Aboriginal people access to legal or political forums, and betrayed a clear and plain intention to destroy their cultures and economies, and indigenous forms of female autonomy, as well as to abrogate their citizenship and democratic rights.

Finally, in the period from 1880 to 1920, in the non-Aboriginal economy, clerical work overtook domestic service as the most common ghetto for women's paid work. As Canadian-born women came to shun the isolating and menial conditions of domestic service, ever-greater efforts were made to recruit immigrant and Native women to meet the unabating demand. Finnish women actually preferred domestic service over work in factories for the relative autonomy it offered, an independent stance these immigrant women also demonstrated in their vital contributions to Canadian socialism (Lindstrom-Best, 1988).

Wages for women in all paid work were kept low and generally below subsistence rates by relegation of women to segmented, 'unskilled' work. This tendency was buttressed by ideologies justifying the 'cult of domesticity', the 'family (male) wage', and the exclusionary practices of male unions. Ethnic divisions among women afforded further flexibility in labour practices of capitalist employers and relegated non-English-speaking immigrant women to the worst manufacturing jobs.

Postwar Migration

The depression of the 1930s and World War II provoked some of the most hostile reactions among dominant ethnic elites and the general population toward immigrants and ethnic minorities. Anti-Semitism existed among small but noisy minorities throughout the country, most notably in Québec (led by Adrian Arcand). It also existed within the federal Cabinet and among senior immigration officials who responded to the Nazi holocaust of European Jews with a refugee policy that decreed 'none is too many' (Abella and Troper, 1982). The chief innovation in immigration policy during the 'dirty thirties' was the honing of the bureaucracy of deportation to rid Canada of immigrant Communists and other radicals, or those who were simply indigent and unemployed (Roberts, 1988).

The internment and dispossession of Canadian Japanese during World War II revealed how multi-layered and deeply rooted were the bases for racism against Asians. In the case of anti-Japanese-Canadian sentiment, these included class interests (for example, resentment of successful Japanese-Canadian fishers and berry farmers among white small business and labour), international and domestic policies (western fear of Japanese military aggression), and the ideology of separate and 'unassimilable' races, long nourished in Canada's immigration policy (Sunhara, 1981).

The immediate post-World War II immigration policy towards refugees admitted (or failed to screen out) Nazis, while rejecting leftists.

It continued to be driven by a paranoid, anti-Communist Cold War stance, betraying Canada's common foreign policy objectives with the United States (Whitaker, 1987). Acute labour shortages in mining, agricultural work, lumbering, railway maintenance, hospital work and domestic service provoked the state to bring in postwar refugees (Polish veterans, Lithuanian, Latvian and Estonian Displaced Persons) and 'bulk order' Italians as indentured labour (Satzewich, 1989; Iacovetta, 1992: 44–5).

Postwar economic prosperity, augmented labour demand and the international discrediting of the pseudo-science of eugenics undoubtedly diminished certain forms of overt racism and provided the most auspicious material conditions for the growing acceptance of pluralist ideologies. These conditions were not sufficient, however, to dismantle the racial/ethnic hierarchy in the minds of Canadian elites and in immigration policy. In 1947 Prime Minister Mackenzie King, explicitly disavowing the notion of 'large-scale immigration from the Orient', stated his opinion that 'the people of Canada do not wish, as a result of mass immigration to make a fundamental alteration in the character of our population' (quoted in Ponting, 1994: 93). Continuity in racial/ethnic preferences meant that between 1940 and 1950 Canada continued to invest more effort in recruiting immigrants from the United Kingdom than any other country (Knowles, 1992: 135).

Remaining within a framework of European immigration, officials in Ottawa also made a sharp distinction between the 'culturally superior', 'Germanic' northern Italians and the 'inferior' southern Italians, viewed as better suited to hot climates and authoritarian regimes. These state preferences notwithstanding, southern Italian migration to Canada came to constitute the largest group of sponsored immigrants in Canadian postwar history, illustrating how immigrant networks utilizing enhanced sponsorship schemes defeated the intentions of officialdom (Iacovetta, 1992: 48).

Acute labour shortages in the professional and skilled categories provoked further liberalization in Canadian immigration policy in 1962 and 1967, removing the last vestiges of explicit racial and ethnic discrimination (but see Satzewich, 1991: 134–5). A points system of selection was introduced which tied selection criteria (occupational demand, educational levels and so on) more closely to the labour needs of Canadian employers. Administration of the policy, however, including location of Canadian immigration offices, continued to favour the 'traditional' source countries over 'non-traditional' third world ones. Nevertheless, the 'new era' of openness in immigration led to dramatic changes in the racial and ethnic character of the newcomers.

In the 1970s, the United Kingdom and the United States continued to top the list of source countries; however, by then leading source countries of immigration included India, Portugal, the Philippines, Jamaica, Vietnam, Hong Kong, Italy and Guyana (Knowles, 1992: 193). While European-born immigrants represented 90 per cent of those who arrived before 1961, they accounted for only 25 per cent of those arriving between 1981 and 1991 (Badets, 1994: 29). It is significant that of those 1.24 million immigrants who came to Canada between 1981 and 1991, 6 of the 10 top source countries were Asian, with Hong Kong and China in the top 3 reported countries of birth (ibid.). These trends, which bolstered the population that was ethnically neither of the two (British or French) settler groups, and particularly the historically feared and despised Asians, contravened the intent of a century and a half of immigration policy-making.

Unlike in the past, when immigration officials saw cheap and expendable labour as the only rationale for Asian entry into Canada, the nature and entry status of contemporary Asian migration to Canada have become extremely diverse. Thus, extremely wealthy Chinese immigrants from Hong Kong top the list of sources for the 'investor immigrants' (virtually an immigration policy for capital), as well as constituting the top source country for immigration overall. The major reason for the heightened interest in attracting Hong Kong business immigrants was the huge capital inflow into Canada, and particularly the west-coast city of Vancouver, they represented. One major Canadian bank estimates that the capital transfers into the country of Hong Kong immigrants totalled $6.3 billion (Canadian dollars) in 1989, or 4.1 per cent of all current account receipts (Cardoso, 1994: 48; see also Li, 1993). This novel Asian migration since the 1980s reflects emergent trends in the globalization and regional integration of the Canadian economy – in Vancouver's case, its growth fuelled by trade with the Pacific Rim, necessary for its establishment under the North American Free Trade Agreement (NAFTA) as the primary commodity gateway for the US market (Mitchell, 1993: 266).

In sharp contrast to Hong Kong Chinese business immigration was the roughly 77,000 Indo-Chinese refugees entering Canada between 1975 and 1981. While Canada accepted these refugees in order to honour international (United Nations) obligations and humanitarian objectives, the fate of the majority of these refugees does not reflect humanitarian aims. Instead, they have joined the ranks of the reserve army of labour, and have become among the most exploited sections of the working class. Thus, while only 7 per cent of all employed Canadian women in 1986 worked in product fabricating or processing/machining occupations, as many as 41 per cent of Indo-Chinese women were found in these jobs (White, 1994: 4).

This class-variegated character of current Asian migration illustrates how complicated articulations of race/ethnicity with class and gender have become in the contemporary Canadian political economy. These Chinese business immigrants have been the targets of hostility from white Canadians. Public and media perceptions have tended, according to Li, to view the new immigrants and their demand for opulent houses at the root of a 'housing crisis in Vancouver . . . characterized by high real estate prices, overbuilt neighbourhoods and rapid urbanization that destroyed traditional residential communities and the [white, British] heritage they represented' (1994: 20). Notwithstanding this novel form of scapegoating Chinese immigrants, the class position of these business migrants has mostly shielded them from the extensive and institutionalized racism experienced by Black, South and East Asian populations from less privileged backgrounds in major Canadian cities (Stasiulis, 1988).

Contemporary global migration trends and Canadian immigration policies bring to Canada's shores large numbers of third world migrants who are funnelled into the most precarious and low-wage jobs – as foreign domestic workers, labourers, janitors, garment industry homeworkers and agricultural seasonal workers. The immigration policy continues to reproduce these class disadvantages among (temporary) migrants and immigrants by denying them the political and social status of free-wage labour, and guarding access to citizenship.

This process is also profoundly gendered and continues to reveal an antiquated, British settler colony notion of separate male and female spheres. Women are more likely than men to be processed as 'family class', 'dependant' entrants. As such, they are restricted from full access to official language and skills training through the legal fiction that 'dependant immigrants' rely on male breadwinners and are not destined for the labour market (Boyd, 1986; Estable, 1986). Systemic racism has forced many non-English-speaking and non-white women into declining industries such as the garment trades and hospital sectors, where employment is threatened by NAFTA. Female, mostly third world domestic workers brought in on a two-year indenture programme are arguably the most exploited and disenfranchised of Canadian workers (Bakan and Stasiulis, 1994, 1995). Globalization of the Canadian economy and migration have thus not undermined the importance of race/ethnicity and gender for shaping the social structure. They have simply meant that the threads of the social order of the settler colony have been pulled apart and rewoven in new and more complicated patterns.

Contemporary Politics: Symbolic Re-ordering of Ethnic and National Identities

The current politics surrounding racial and ethnic diversity in contemporary Canada is a lesson in how settler societies and the legitimacy of assumed racial/ethnic hierarchies eventually come undone. The struggles of First Nations, Québec sovereignists, racial/ethnic minorities and women for symbolic recognition and claims on state resources (or in some cases, separate states) have severely undermined the assumptions about race and gender of the British white settler colonization model. Aboriginal, Québec and ethnic/racial minority politics also illustrate the practical impossibility of integrating divergent ethnocultural identity claims within the same political, territorial, administrative and institutional framework (Salée, 1994a).

Irreconcilable ethnocultural claims are perhaps posed most acutely by the confrontation in claims of francophone Québeckers and First Nations people within the province of Québec. The development of Québec nationalism is complex and has been tied to many divergent projects of social reform ranging across the political spectrum. Prior to the 1960s, Québec represented a primarily agrarian society, dominated by Roman Catholic clergy and controlled by a Montréal-based English elite. The past 35 years, beginning with the so-called Quiet Revolution of the 1960s, have seen the modernization of the Québec state and economy. Francophone Québeckers, in the flush of newly awakened nationalism, sought to overturn the fact that in a province where 80 per cent of the population was francophone, the language of higher education, management, finance, business and labour relations was English. They therefore set about building a virtual state within the Canadian state through the considerable powers permitted to provincial governments under federalism.

Provincial autonomy and linguistic distinctiveness have provided francophone Québeckers with the political apparatus, state intellectuals and resources to assert their ethnocultural distinctiveness, build a Québec bourgeoisie and lay their claims to political sovereignty. The territorial focus of Québecois nationalism on Québec and its state also stemmed from the fact that the population of French descent is becoming a receding minority in Canada as a whole (23 per cent in 1991). To ensure the survival of language, the core strategy of Québec nationalists has been to make Québec a unilingual society. To this end, francophone Québeckers have sought controls on immigration policy to maximize the number of French-speaking immigrants, and have passed laws that restrict the rights of children to English-language education, legislate the language of work and erase all public manifestations of English or languages other than French in commercial signage.

The memory of 'the Conquest', printed on every Québec licence plate ('*Je me souviens*', or 'I remember'), continues to mythologize the defeat of the Québec nation at a time when francophones are economically and politically an empowered majority in that province.

Currently, an economistic nationalism dominates the public agenda of Québec which articulates the desire of the francophone Québec business elite to better position itself first in the North American and then in the global market (Salée, 1994b). Powerful Québec capitalists have 'come to look on the Canadian market, and their cultural and political links with the English Canadian business class, as a historical left-over, a relic of a time when they, as Québecois, were the hewers of wood and drawers of water' (Ignatieff, 1993: 114). Similarly, Québec mass media, educational institutions and popular culture refer to Québec exclusively when referring to society in general: 'Books have been published on "Québec mushrooms" or "Québec small game", as if there were frontiers for morels and rabbits!' (Gagnon, 1994: 3).

Contemporary francophone Québec identity that draws selectively on traditional imagery of a rural and colonized past, yet exudes the confidence of Québec's captains of industry, is not coterminous with all those who occupy Québec. As Salée (1994b: 15) has observed, this imagined community of a 'founding nation' excludes those identities that are frequently discounted (immigrants), silenced (First Nations; those at the economic margins such as the poor, youth and many women), or oppositional (the Anglo Québec 'conquerers'). However, it is Aboriginal political claims that pose the major threat to francophone Québec's claims for special recognition.

Several issues have brought Québec nationalism into conflict with the nationalism of particular First Nations – hydroelectric development, the role of the Québec police in the armed confrontation with Mohawk warriors at Kanesatake and Kahnawake (or Oka) in the summer of 1990 (York and Pindera, 1991), and constitutional negotiations (Jhappan, 1993). For the Québec government, the James Bay hydroelectric project is a central symbol of Québec's modernization and represents the core of its competitive advantage in the North American economy; for the Cree, it is an invasion in their homeland (Ignatieff, 1993: 124–5).

The claims of First Nations in Québec (and Canada as a whole) to self-determination and self-government, an adequate territorial base and control over resources rest on inherent rights 'since time immemorial'. If recognized by the Canadian government, such claims made by representatives of Aboriginal peoples across the country would mean a fundamental restructuring of the Canadian federation to accommodate entirely new governments and sovereign territories. In Québec, First Nations' aspirations 'delegitimize the very foundations upon which Québec has built its claims for special status within the Canadian federation' (Salée, 1994a: 4). In fact, bitter animosity was activated between Aboriginal leaders and Québec politicians during the constitutional reform process of 1991–2, when the former finally succeeded in displacing the 'two founding nations' mythology with a new construct, 'three founding nations' (Jhappan, 1993: 238–42).

Of course, Québec has not been the only province to deny Aboriginal territorial and political claims; all of the provinces have abrogated aboriginal rights with the result that there are outstanding claims all over the country. Indeed, in some ways, up to the 1990s, Québec's legislative Native policy, especially under Parti Québecois (sovereignist) governments in the 1970s and 1980s, has been more progressive than that of most other provinces (Gourdeau, 1993). Since 1983, Québec governments have at least formally operated on the basis of 15 principles which essentially recognize that the Aboriginal peoples of Québec are distinct nations which have a right to their cultures, languages, customs and traditions, as well as the right to benefit from and govern the lands 'ascribed' to them (Salée, 1994a: 39–40). In practice, however, Québec nationalists and Aboriginal peoples are each making claims to forms of sovereignty over substantially the same territory, and this has produced 'a highly conflictual dynamic which considerably strains any hope of social and cultural coexistence' (ibid.: 4).

Whereas the Québecois see themselves as oppressed *vis-à-vis* is 'English Canada', Aboriginal peoples have been oppressed by both. Unlike francophone Québeckers, who have at their disposal a provincial state which provides substantial legislative and institutional autonomy, as well as significant economic power, Aboriginal peoples do not have the bargaining power to force concessions from *either* the provincial *or* the federal states. Moreover, the particular history of marginalization of Aboriginal peoples, the institutionalized and societal racism levelled at them for several hundred years, their geographic dispersion and, crucially, the fact that they, unlike Québec, are claiming ownership of lands all over the country are factors which put them in a vastly inferior bargaining position *vis-à-vis* both Québec and the rest of Canada.

Despite such an overwhelming imbalance of power, Aboriginal peoples in Canada have employed a range of strategies in pursuit of their claims, some of which have brought important victories. A series of legal challenges in the 1980s and 1990s, for example, have won declarations from the highest courts that Aboriginal and treaty rights are pre-existing legal rights which must be honoured or disposed of with the consent of the First Nations concerned (Jhappan, 1991). Such legal advances have been complemented by several historic political innovations, most notably the creation of Nunavut, a settlement of an Inuit land claim which will give the Inuit self-government over one-fifth of Canada's land mass in the eastern Arctic by 1999. It must be noted, however, that these victories are largely localized to specific tribal groups. While others may be empowered by them, in general Aboriginal peoples still suffer from ingrained discriminatory practices, and find themselves at the top of virtually every index of socio-economic distress.

The racial and ethnic heterogeneity of the settler population and the continued importance of immigration in Canada have led to a dramatic reshaping of the racial and ethnic composition of the population. In the 1991 census, of a population of 27 million, the proportion of Canadians of (single) 'other' origins was 31 per cent, higher than the proportions of British (21 per cent), French (23 per cent), Aboriginal (1.7 per cent) or combined origins (rounded percentages, 1991 Canadian Census). Notwithstanding their relative numbers, however, the politics of the 'others' – non-British, non-French and non-Aboriginal groups – are far less destabilizing insofar as they do not take the form of demands for self-determination, autonomous political or administrative institutions, or separate territory and control of resources (Salée, 1994a: 2). The struggles of racial, ethnocultural and immigrant minorities in Canada have encompassed a broad range of issues speaking to the aspirations of these minorities for equity, protection from discrimination and symbolic recognition of the reality of ethnic and racial pluralism. These include anti-racist, affirmative action and fair immigration and refugee campaigns, and efforts to bring racial and ethnic democracy within the institutions of the public service, law enforcement, education, representative political institutions, trade unions and women's movements.

The geographical dispersion and heterogeneity of minority groups makes them far less cohesive in their demands upon the state, and hence easier to ignore. The symbolic recognition of these groups' presence in Canada has chiefly taken the form of multiculturalism policies and agencies developed at the level of the national and most provincial states. Multiculturalism policy (as distinguished from the socio-demographic reality of ethnic diversity) arose as a result of protests by ethnic minorities over the settler society construct of a 'bilingual and bicultural' Canada, reflected in cultural and official language state policies. Since its establishment as official federal government policy in 1971, the central tenet of multiculturalism has been the promotion of racial/ethnic harmony and equality through respecting individuals' cultural differences.

Since the mid-1980s, popular and elite opinion on multiculturalism has become increasingly negative and developed into a virtual assault on the existence of the policy and its assumptions (Abu-Laban and Stasiulis, 1992). After a brief period whereby the administrative and legislative status of the policy had been elevated, the federal government in 1993 abruptly submerged the federal multiculturalism bureaucracy into an amorphous new department called Heritage Canada (Tepper, 1994: 103).

Although the arguments for rejecting multiculturalism are themselves diverse, there is little question that increasing numbers of
Canadians are willing to discard government policies that promote a
'cultural mosaic'. The policy has long attracted vocal opposition from
Québec, where francophone Québeckers have claimed that multiculturalism denies the cultural integrity of Québec society, and by
relativizing culture, masks the 'national question' that has otherwise
dominated federal politics (Rocher, 1973; Labelle, 1991). Members of
ethnic and racial minorities have faulted the policy for its failure to
alleviate racism or discrimination, for ghettoizing ethnocultural
communities' justice and equity concerns, and for handicapping the
movement of 'ethnics' into the mainstream (Abu-Laban and Stasiulis,
1992: 376–8).

The inextricable link of multiculturalism to immigration (the source
for diversity) also means that the growing hostility to multiculturalism
since the mid-1980s expresses the abhorrence of many white Canadians
to the predominantly third world origins of most immigrant newcomers. The broad wave of deindustrialization that has gutted Canada's
(Ontario–Québec) industrial heartland since the early 1980s, financial
deregulation, the accompanying corrosion of the welfare state, and the
further decline in Canadian living standards associated with NAFTA
are trends which have heightened the anxiety of many groups. The
result has been a backlash against so-called 'minorities' by those whose
majority or dominant status is perceived as under economic or cultural
threat, and whose politics draw on a refurbished arsenal of images and
metaphors associated with the racial/gender/class order of the white
settler colony.

Women's Politics

The national/ethnic/racial concerns as they articulate with gender and
class inequities evinced in the movements discussed above have
informed women's politics in novel and complex ways. Aboriginal
women have consistently tied their politics to the survival and empowerment of their communities. In the 1970s and 1980s, the struggle of
First Nations women to rid the Indian Act of Section 12 (1) (b), the
clause containing its discriminatory definition of Indian status,
involved many separate court cases, and coordinated protests of women
such as the Maliseet women from the Tobique Reserve in New
Brunswick (Silman, 1987). Bill C-31, An Act to Amend the Indian
Act, was perceived to be a victory for the many women who had invol-
untarily been stripped of their Indian status. The fact that it revised
rather than abolished the totalitarian, divide-and-rule Indian policy,
and left some forms of discrimination intact while creating new ones,

has meant that Bill C-31 has not won universal support among all First Nations' political organizations and women (Mercredi and Turpel, 1993: 83, 88; Weaver, 1993: 97–105).

Recently, some First Nations' struggles, where women have played a central role, have achieved national and even international attention. These have included the resistance and leadership of Kanienkehaka women in the face of police and military occupation during the Oka crisis of 1990 (Goodleaf, 1993), and battles to reach a fragile balance of collective aboriginal rights and individual rights for First Nations women in the constitutional forum. The politics associated with the Charlottetown Constitutional Accord revealed the divergent positions taken by Inuit women leaders (whose influence was reflected in their presence at the First Ministers' bargaining table) and by women involved in organizations representing non-status women, Métis, non-status and status Indians. Other types of Native women's activism have been relatively less visible, such as healing movements working from within communities to deal with the problems of social deterioration and violence that have been the fruit of decades of colonization and marginalization (Kaye, 1990; Pierre-Aggamaway, 1983).

The gulf between Québec and the 'rest of Canada' in women's politics is represented in the organizational split between two feminist umbrella bodies – the Fédération des femmes du Québec (FFQ) and the National Action Committee on the Status of Women (NAC). Feminism in Québec, which draws from a long tradition of French-Canadian women's autonomy and involvement in public affairs in Québec's history, was 'stimulated and nurtured' by the nationalism of the 1960s to the present (Dumont, 1992: 89; Dumont et al., 1987). Québec feminists, emboldened by Québec's relatively progressive legislation concerning women's rights and their profound mistrust of the federal government, have tied their feminist project to the Québec state, whose jurisdiction and power they have sought to expand (Vickers, 1993: 267). This has brought the FFQ to loggerheads with NAC over the latter's 'No' position on the referendum to decide the fate of the Charlottetown Accord. NAC's position had, in turn, largely been motivated by its concern over the Accord's weak protection of Aboriginal women's rights.

The most public, organized and 'legitimate' face of feminism in Québec represents (white) francophone feminists. The concerns and identities of First Nations women, immigrant and racial minority (francophone, anglophone and 'allophone'), and Anglo-Canadian women in Québec are relatively marginalized at this level of women's politics. Their marginalization reflects the difficulty among (francophone, Québec) women, who structure their politics around a combined sense of their own gender and national/linguistic oppression in the context of

Canada (de Seve, 1992), to come to terms with the racial/ethnic exclusions flowing from their involvement as the mothers and shapers of a subordinated white settler society.

For their part, women of colour and immigrant women have been organizing, sometimes through their ethnocultural networks, and sometimes in broader alliance with other women, to redress the conditions of their oppression and the racism faced by their communities. For instance, third world women homeworkers in the garment trades and live-in foreign domestic workers are two groups that have been developing creative new models of organizing that reflect their unique and isolated circumstances (Bakan and Stasiulis, 1994, 1995; Dagg, 1992). Grass-roots pressure by women of colour workers has forced trade unions to take up campaigns that simultaneously address racism and sexism in hospitals and other sectors where racial minority women are concentrated (Leah, 1989). The recognition that global restructuring and continental economic integration through NAFTA have produced shared interests and the need to develop common strategies among vulnerable Canadian, Mexican and US women in common sectors has also fostered international solidarity and coalitions (for example, Mujer à Mujer (Nadeau, 1992).

The question of diversity and racial/ethnic hierarchies, while barely visible until the 1980s, has since rocked women's movements in many parts of Canada outside of Québec. The efforts of organizations dominated by white, Anglo-Canadian women to become more inclusive of the concerns of racial and ethnic minority and immigrant women have led to divisive, highly emotive battles. Dealing with issues of racism has made it incumbent upon white women individually and collectively to come to terms with the history of white, Anglo-Celtic women's organizations. As this chapter has shown, in critical formative stages (for example, 1890s to 1930s), that history was xenophobic and motivated in part by the perceived need of white women to stem Anglo-Saxon 'race suicide'.

The at least partially successful efforts to incorporate an anti-racist sensibility within 'mainstream' feminist organizations are increasingly apparent, however. They have reshaped abortion rights campaigns to take up analyses of the broader racist/sexist set of mechanisms (involuntary sterilization, Depo-provera, sex-selection technology, female genital mutilation) which have restricted the reproductive rights of women of colour and third world women (Egan and Gardner, 1994; Thobani, 1992: 19–22). In publishing, much greater room has been made for the voices of women of colour by the previously white-dominated Women's Press, following a period of explosive race politics (Stasiulis, 1993).

This trend towards anti-racist pluralism is best seen in NAC, the largest umbrella feminist organization, where women representing minority and other marginalized identities 'now constitute almost half of the executive and hold several major leadership positions' (Vickers, 1993: 269). The result has been that NAC's policies are increasingly being shaped to reflect the anti-racist feminist analyses, issues, positions and strategies advanced by previously unrepresented minority and First Nations women. A major challenge in the women's movement remains to define a specifically *Canadian* women's politics of diversity, which reflects complex and changing racial/ethnic hierarchies and contending forms of nationalism, and rejects imported (US black/white) dualisms and new forms of racial/gender essentialism.

Conclusion

Canada's failure to confront the profoundly colonialist, racist and sexist white settler ideologies which have driven its history has ensured an enduring legacy of deeply rooted conflicts. While political elites have acknowledged and attempted to accommodate the competing claims of French Canadians in the form of the 'two founding nations' construct, this mythology has served to exclude other identities and trivialize their contributions to the development of the country. Moreover, the overwhelmingly masculinist cast of the white settler and later nationalist ideologies has negated the varied and essential contributions of women, wilfully ignoring their status as one of the 'two founding genders'. In such a context, attempts to foster a sense of national unity are bound to be frustrated, and Canada's political culture can be expected to become increasingly fragmented.

References

Abele, Frances and Stasiulis, Daiva (1988) 'Canada as a "white settler colony": what about natives and immigrants?', in W. Clement and G. Williams (eds), *The New Canadian Political Economy*. Montréal: McGill Queen's University Press.

Abella, Irving and Troper, Harold (1982) *None Is Too Many: Canada and the Jews of Europe, 1933–1948*. Toronto: Lester & Orpen Dennys.

Abu-Laban, Yasmeen and Stasiulis, Daiva (1992) 'Ethnic pluralism under siege: popular and partisan opposition to multiculturalism', *Canadian Public Policy*, 18 (4): 365–86.

Anderson, Karen (1991) *Chain Her by One Foot: the Subjugation of Native Women in Seventeenth-Century New France*. New York: Routledge.

Bacchi, Carol Lee (1983) *Liberation Deferred? The Ideas of the English-Canadian Suffragists, 1977–1918*. Toronto: University of Toronto Press.

Badets, Jane (1994) 'Canada's immigrants: recent trends', *Canadian Social Trends, vol. 2*. Toronto: Thompson Educational Publishing.

Bakan, A. (1991) *Québec: From Conquest to Constitution. A Socialist Analysis*. Toronto: International Socialists.

Bakan, Abigail B. and Stasiulis, Daiva (1994) 'Foreign domestic worker policy in Canada and the social boundaries of citizenship', *Science and Society*, 58 (1); 7–33.

Bakan, Abigail and Stasiulis, Daiva (1995) 'Making the match: domestic placement agencies and the racialization of women's household work', *Signs*, 20 (2): 1–33.

Boyd, Monica (1986) 'Immigrant women in Canada', in R.J. Simon and C. Bretell (eds), *International Migration*. Towota: Rowman & Allenheld.

Brant Castellano, Mary (1989) 'Women in Huron and Ojibwa societies', *Canadian Woman Studies*, 10 (2–3): 45–8.

Brodribb, Somer (1984) 'The traditional roles of native women in Canada and the impact of colonization', *Canadian Journal of Native Studies*, 4 (1): 85–103.

Brown, Jennifer S.H. (1988) 'The Métis: genesis and rebirth', in B.A. Cox (ed.), *Native People, Native Lands: Canadian Indians, Inuit and Métis*. Ottawa: Carleton University Press.

Brown, Judith K. (1975) 'Iroquois women: an ethnohistoric note', in R. Reiter (ed.), *Toward an Anthropology of Women*. London: Monthly Review Press.

Cardoso, Andrew (1994) 'Index on multiculturalism', *Canadian Forum*, 71 (828): 48.

Carter, Sarah (1991) 'Two acres and a cow: "peasant" farming for the Indians in the northwest, 1889–1897', in J.R. Miller (ed.), *Sweet Promises: a Reader on Indian–White Relations in Canada*. Toronto: University of Toronto Press.

Cassidy, Frank and Bish, Robert L. (1989) *Indian Government: Its Meaning in Practice*. Victoria: Institute for Research on Public Policy and Oolichan Books.

Chartrand, Paul L.A.H. (1992) 'The claims of the aboriginal peoples in Canada: a challenge to the idea of two founding nations', paper, Federalism and the Nation State Conference, Centre for International Studies, University of Toronto, June.

Coates, Ken S. (1993) *Best Left as Indians: Native–White Relations in the Yukon Territory, 1840–1973*. Montréal: McGill-Queen's University Press.

Creese, Gillian (1988–89) 'Exclusion or Solidarity? Vancouver Workers Confront the "Oriental Problem"', *BC Studies*, 80: 24–51.

Dagg, Alex (1992) 'Organizing homeworkers into unions: the ILGWU Toronto experience', in *From the Double Day to the Endless Day*, Proceedings of a Conference on Homeworking. Ottawa: Canadian Centre for Policy Alternatives.

De Seve, Micheline (1992) 'Women, political action and identity', in C. Leys and M. Mendell (eds), *Culture and Social Change: Social Movements in Québec and Ontario*. Montréal: Black Rose Books.

Dickason, Olive P. (1992) *Canada's First Nations: a History of Founding Peoples from Earliest Times*. Toronto: McClelland & Stewart.

Dumont, Micheline (1992) 'The Women's Movement in Québec', in C. Backhouse and D.H. Flaherty (eds), *Challenging Times: the Women's Movement in Canada and the United States*. Montréal: McGill-Queen's University Press.

Dumont, Micheline, Jean, Michele, Lavigne, Marie and Stoddart, Jennifer [The Clio Collective] (1987) *Québec Women: a History*. Toronto: Women's Press.

Egan, Carolyn and Gardner, Linda (1994) 'Race, class and reproductive freedom: women must have real choices!', *Canadian Woman Studies*, 14 (2): 95–9.

Ehrensaft, Philip and Armstrong, Warwick (1981) 'The formation of dominion capitalism: economic truncation and class structure', in A. Moscovitch and G. Drover (eds), *Inequality: Essays on the Political Economy of Social Welfare*. Toronto: University of Toronto Press.

Elliott, David W. (1985) 'Aboriginal title', in B.W. Morse (ed.), *Aboriginal Peoples and the Law: Indian, Métis and Inuit Rights in Canada*. Ottawa: Carleton University Press.

Errington, Jane (1993) 'Pioneers and Suffragists', in S. Burt, L. Code and L. Dorney (eds), *Changing Patterns: Women in Canada*. Toronto: McClelland Stewart.

Estable, Alma (1986) 'Immigrant women in Canada: current issues', background paper for the Canadian Advisory Council on the Status of Women, Ottawa.

Gagnon, Lysiane (1994) 'How the word "nationalist" changed its meaning in the Québec lexicon', *The Globe and Mail*, Toronto, April 23: D3.

Goodleaf, Donna Kahenrakwas (1993) '"Under military occupation": indigenous women, state violence and community resistance', in L. Carty (ed.), *And Still We Rise: Feminist Political Mobilizing in Contemporary Canada*. Toronto: Women's Press.

Gourdeau, Eric (1993) 'Québec and the aboriginal question', in A.G. Gagnon (ed.) *Québec: State and Society*. Toronto: Nelson.

Iacovetta, Franca (1992) *Such Hardworking People: Italian Immigrants in Postwar Toronto*. Montreal: McGill-Queen's University Press.

Ignatieff, Michael (1993) *Blood and Belonging: Journeys into the New Nationalism*. Toronto: Viking.

Jamieson, Kathleen (1986) 'Sex discrimination and the Indian Act', in J.R. Ponting (ed.), *Arduous Journey: Canadian Indians and Decolonization*. Toronto: McClelland & Stewart.

Jhappan, Radha (1991) 'Natural rights vs. legal positivism: Indians, the courts, and the new discourse of aboriginal rights in Canada', *British Journal of Canadian Studies*, 6 (1): 60–100.

Jhappan, Radha (1993) 'Inherency, "three nations" and collective rights: the evolution of aboriginal constitutional discourse from 1982 to the Charlottetown Accord', *International Journal of Canadian Studies*, 7–8: 225–59.

Kallen, Evelyn (1990) 'Ethnicity and human rights in Canada: constitutionalizing a hierarchy of minority rights', in P.S. Li (ed.), *Race and Ethnic Relations in Canada*. Toronto: Oxford University Press.

Kaye, Marcia (1990) 'In the spirit of the family', *Canadian Living*, October: 131–8.

Knowles, Valerie (1992) *Strangers at Our Gates: Canadian Immigration and Immigration Policy, 1540–1990*. Toronto: Dundurn Press.

Krauter, Joseph F. and Davis, Morris (1978) *Minority Canadians: Ethnic Groups*. Toronto: Methuen.

Labelle, Micheline (1991) 'Le débat sur la culture ethnique, la culture nationale et la culture civile: réflexions sur les enjeux de l'intégration des minorités au Québec', communication, Colloque sur 'Culture Ethnique, Culture Civile et Culture National', Congrès de l'ACFAS, Université de Sherbrooke, May.

Leah, Ronnie (1989) 'Linking the struggles: racism, feminism and the union movement', in J. Vorst (ed.), *Race, Class, Gender: Bonds and Barriers*. Toronto: Between the Lines.

Li, Peter S. (1993) 'Chinese investment and business in Canada: ethnic entrepreneurship reconsidered', *Pacific Affairs*, 66 (2): 219–43.

Li, Peter S. (1994) 'Unneighbourly houses or unwelcome Chinese: the social construction of race in the battle over "Monster Homes" in Vancouver, Canada', *International Journal of Comparative Race & Ethnic Studies*, 1 (1): 14–33.

Lindstrom-Best, Varpu (1988) *Defiant Sisters: a Social History of Finnish Immigrant Women in Canada*. Toronto: Multicultural History Society of Ontario.

Littlefield, Loraine (1988) 'Women traders in the maritime fur trade', in B.A. Cox (ed.) *Native People, Native Lands*. Ottawa: Carleton University Press.

Maroney, Heather Jon (1992) '"Who has the baby?" Nationalism, pronatalism and the construction of a "demographic crisis" in Québec, 1960–1988', *Studies in Political Economy*, 39: 7–36.

McLaren, Angus (1990) *Our Own Master Race: Eugenics in Canada, 1885–1945*. Toronto McClelland & Stewart.

Mercredi, Ovide and Turpel, Mary Ellen (1993) *In the Rapids: Navigating the Future of First Nations*. Toronto: Viking.

Mitchell, Katharyne (1993) 'Multiculturalism, or the united colors of capitalism', *Antipode*, 25 (4): 263–94.

Mitchell, Nancy Marybelle (1992) 'From talking chiefs to a native corporate elite: the birth of class and nationalism among Canadian Inuit'. PhD dissertation, Department of Sociology and Anthropology. Carleton University.

Nadeau, Denise (1992) 'Women fight back', in J. Sinclair (ed.), *Crossing the Line: Canada and Free Trade with Mexico*. Vancouver: New Star.

Palmer, Howard (1982) *Patterns of Prejudice: a History of Nativism in Alberta*. Toronto: McClelland & Stewart.

Panitch, Leo (1981) 'Dependency and class in Canadian political economy', *Studies in Political Economy*, 6: 7–34.

Pentland, Clare (1981) *Labour and Capital in Canada. 1650–1860*. Toronto: James Lorimer.

Pierre-Aggamaway, Marlene (1983) 'Native Women and the State', in J. Turner and L. Emery (eds), *Perspectives on Women in the 1980s*. Winnipeg: University of Manitoba Press.

Ponting, Rick (1994) 'Racial conflict: turning the heat up', in D. Glenday and A. Duffy (eds), *Canadian Society: Understanding and Surviving in the 1990s*. Toronto: McClelland & Stewart.

Prentice, Alison, Bourne, Paula, Brandt, Gail Cuthbert, Light, Beth, Mitchinson, Wendy and Black, Naomi (1988) *Canadian Women: a History*. Toronto: Harcourt Brace Jovanovich.

Redbird, Duke (1980) *We are Métis: a Métis View of the Development of a Native-Canadian People*. Willowdale: Ontario Métis and Non-Status Indian Association.

Richardson, Boyce (1993) *People of Terra Nullius: Betrayal and Rebirth in Aboriginal Canada*. Vancouver: Douglas & McIntyre.

Roberts, Barbara (1979) '"A work of empire": Canadian reformers and British female immigration', in L. Kealey (ed.) *A Not Unreasonable Claim*. Toronto: Women's Press.

Roberts, Barbara (1988) *Whence They Came: Deportation from Canada, 1900–1935*. Ottawa: University of Ottawa Press.

Rocher, G. (1973) 'Les ambiguïtés d'un Canada bilingue et biculturel', in *Le Québec en mutation*. Montréal: Hurtubise HMH.

Salée, Daniel (1994a) 'Identities in conflict: the aboriginal question and the politics of recognition in Québec', unpublished manuscript, School of Community and Public Affairs, Concordia University.

Salée, Daniel (1994b) 'Le mondialisation et la construction de l'identité au Québec', unpublished manuscript, School of Community and Public Affairs, Concordia University.

Satzewich, Vic (1989) 'Unfree labour and Canadian capitalism: the incorporation of Polish war veterans', *Studies in Political Economy*, 28: 89–110.

Satzewich, Vic (1991) *Racism and the Incorporation of Foreign Labour. Farm Labour Migration to Canada since 1945*. London and New York: Routledge.

Silman, Janet (1987) *Enough is Enough: Aboriginal Women Speak Out*. Toronto: Women's Press.

Stasiulis, Daiva (1988) 'Minority resistance in the local state: Toronto in the 1970s and 1980s', *Ethnic and Racial Studies*, 12 (1): 63–83.

Stasiulis, Daiva (1993) '"Authentic voice": anti-racist politics in Canadian feminist publishing and literary production', in S. Gunew and A. Yeatman (eds), *Feminism and the*

Politics of Difference. St Leonards, New South Wales: Allen & Unwin.

Stasiulis, Daiva and Williams, Glen (1992) 'Mapping racial/ethnic hierarchy in the Canadian social formation, 1860–1914: an examination of selected federal policy debates', paper, Annual Meetings of the Canadian Political Science Association, Charlottetown, Prince Edward Island, June.

Sunahara, Ann (1981) *The Politics of Racism: the Uprooting of Japanese Canadians during the Second World War*. Toronto: James Lorimer.

Swyripa, Frances (1993) *Wedded to the Cause: Ukrainian-Canadian Women and Ethnic Identity, 1891–1991*. Toronto: University of Toronto Press.

Tennant, Paul (1990) *Aboriginal Peoples and Politics: the Indian Land Question in British Columbia, 1849–1989*. Vancouver: University of British Columbia Press.

Tepper, Elliot L. (1994) 'Immigration Policy and Multiculturalism', in J.W. Berry and J.A. Laponce (eds), *Ethnicity and Culture in Canada: the Research Landscape*. Toronto: University of Toronto Press.

Thobani, Sunera (1992) 'Making the links: South Asian women and the struggle for reproductive rights', *Resources for Feminist Research*, 13 (1): 19–22.

Trigger, Bruce (1985) *Natives and Newcomers*. Montréal: McGill-Queen's University Press.

Valentine, Victor F. (1980) 'Native peoples and Canadian society: a profile of issues and trends', in R. Breton, J.G. Reitz and V.F. Valentine (eds), *Cultural Boundaries and the Cohesion of Canada*. Montréal: Institute for Research on Public Policy.

Valverde, Mariana (1991) *The Age of Light, Soap, and Water: Moral Reform in English Canada, 1885–1925*. Toronto: McClelland & Stewart.

Van Kirk, Sylvia (1980) *'Many Tender Ties': Women in Fur-Trade Society, 1670–1870*. Winnipeg: Watson & Dwyer.

Vickers, Jill (1993) 'The Canadian women's movement and a changing constitutional order', *International Journal of Canadian Studies*, 7–8: 261–84.

Weaver, Sally (1993) 'First Nations women and government policy, 1970–92: discrimination and conflict', in S. Burt, L. Code and L. Dorney (eds), *Changing Patterns: Women in Canada*. Toronto: McClelland & Stewart.

Whitaker, Reg (1987) *Double Standard: the Secret History of Canadian Immigration*. Toronto: Lester & Orpen Dennys.

White, Pamela (1987) 'Restructuring the domestic sphere – Prairie Indian women on reserves: image, ideology and state policy, 1880–1930, PhD dissertation, Department of Geography, McGill University.

White, Pamela (1994) 'The Indo-Chinese in Canada' in *Canadian Social Trends: A Canadian Studies Reader. Vol. 2*. Toronto: Thompson Educational Publishing.

Williams, Glen (1976) 'Canada: the case of the wealthiest colony', *This Magazine*, 10 (1).

Woodsworth, J.S. (1909) *Strangers within Our Gates or Coming Canadians*. Reprinted Toronto: University of Toronto Press, 1972.

Wright, Ronald (1992) *Stolen Continents: the 'New World' through Indian Eyes since 1492*. Toronto: Viking.

York, Geoffrey and Pindera, Loreen (1991) *Peoples of the Pine: the Warriors and the Legacy of Oka*. Boston: Little, Brown.

5

Gendering, Racializing and Classifying: Settler Colonization in the United States, 1590–1990

Dolores Janiewski

The arrival of the first Euro-American settlers in the late sixteenth century marked the beginnings of a process of settler colonization on the North American continent north of present-day Mexico. This chapter focuses on the interactions between four major racialized cultures over the course of the four centuries since the inception of settler society in the geographical area that is now the United States: Native American, Mexican American, African American and Euro-American. Other significant racialized cultures exist in the United States, including African Americans of Caribbean origin, Chinese, Japanese, Filipinos and Polynesians. For reasons of space, however, these other racialized cultures will not be discussed. The following analysis pays special attention to the gender divisions and relations that exist within and between each of the four racialized cultures specified while exploring the interconnections between gender, race, ethnicity and class for the peoples who have coexisted on the North American continent for the last four centuries.

Although an emphasis upon 'American exceptionalism' has led many American scholars to avoid consideration of the United States as a 'settler society', it can, nonetheless, be usefully compared to other examples of settler colonialism (Limerick, 1987). Contained within its historical evolution are the three kinds of settler colonies identified by scholars: mixed settlement, plantation and pure settlement. From the onset of colonization, the colonial settlements shifted from mixed settlement, a colonial structure including European settlers and a relatively large indigenous population, towards a plantation system based upon coerced, imported labour and a pure settlement colony as the indigenous peoples were dispossessed. Like other settler colonies, the United States and its ancestral colonies developed forms of racial domination and distinct racialized communities through the interaction of its settlers with indigenous peoples and imported slaves. As expressed by Benjamin Ringer, a 'colonist society [which had imposed] a network of coercive legal, political, and economic constraints and a harness of racial subordination and segmentation on nonwhite minorities' was transformed into 'a nation-state rooted in the rights and sovereignty of the people' (1983: 16). Its founders simultaneously 'legitimated and perpetuated . . . the plural society of a racially bifurcated colonist America regulated by the normative code of a racial creed' (Ringer, 1983: 8). The Euro-American settlers reserved full citizenship to themselves within the new nation, but denied the members of the racialized cultures full citizenship. White or European, as defined in the first federal naturalization statute in the 1790s, corresponded to citizen; non-whites or non-Europeans could not aspire to equal citizenship until racially based definitions of citizenship began to erode over the last century.

The chapter will trace the development of Euro-American domination over the other cultures during three periods of the history of the United States: its colonial origins, its expansionist republican phase and its contemporary existence as an industrial nation. Rooted in different class, gender and racial configurations lay the diverse but interconnected political and sexual economies which developed within colonial America. Gender relations varied according to the racial and class arrangements of the particular region. The two frontiers, the Spanish frontier moving northward from Mexico and the Anglo frontier moving westward from the eastern coast, resembled the mixed settlement colonial pattern. Where the indigenous peoples were displaced as in California, the plantation settlement pattern established itself as a hacienda or cattle ranch. Once the indigenous inhabitants had been defeated and dispossessed, the Anglo frontier gave way to the pure settlement pattern in the northern colonies while the plantation replaced it in the southern colonies where racially based slavery was essential to the organization of the economy and the social order. In the northern colonies, family, indentured, slave and wage labour coexisted in a complicated interaction that formed its more elaborate class and racial hierarchy and economic dynamic. Power and resources moved from female and indigenous control to Euro-American patriarchal households while the racialized groups were subordinated to the economic and political power of Euro-Americans as the United States emerged from its colonial antecedents.

Built upon colonial foundations, the expanding republic primarily benefited the Euro-American men who formed and led it. Despite the emancipation of African Americans after the Civil War, the initial extension of full citizenship to male African Americans was later withdrawn. Native Americans and Mexican Americans lost control over land to the United States who seized their territory by war and legal manipulations. The very effort to isolate and segregate the subordinated racialized cultures from the dominant Euro-American nation ironically aided in the survival of those cultures. Native Americans, Mexican Americans and African Americans persisted as unassimilable cultures inside the dominant culture that could neither eliminate nor expel them despite the efforts of the settlers, the government and the military. The emergence of a woman's movement and a labour movement challenged gender and class domination but only within the Euro-American community.

When Euro-American elites recognized the closing of the 'frontier' in the 1890s, they sought ways to continue their expansionist endeavours. Engaging in extra-continental colonialism, they extended their economic power outside the North American continent into the Pacific and the Caribbean (Kolko, 1984). Applying exclusionary and racial ideology to the inhabitants of the newly colonized regions, they decided against full political incorporation of the Philippines and Puerto Rico, and considerably delayed it in the case of New Mexico and Hawaii (Williams, 1980; Ringer, 1983; Limerick, 1987; White, 1991). Racial enclaves persisted as reservations and villages in rural areas but also took urban shape as ghettos and barrios. When wars made replacements for white male labour essential, Mexican Americans, Native Americans, African Americans and Euro-American women found unaccustomed demand for their labour. Wartime gains, however, were usually eroded during peacetime and periods of economic downturn. In addition, the members of racialized groups bore disproportionately the effects of mechanization and the expansion of US industry overseas, which limited the demand for labour in American industry. Poverty and membership in a subordinated racial group remained closely associated together while gender subordination constrained the economic position of women.

By the mid-twentieth century, the position of the United States at the core of the international economy influenced its internal patterns of gender, race and class relationships even as these provided models for its interaction with other colonized peoples (Williams, 1980). Competition with the Soviet Union for the allegiance in Asia, Latin America and Africa turned domestic race relations into foreign policy issues in a post-colonial world. Citizenship and civil rights for those racialized groups previously allocated 'second-class' citizenship became international as well as paramount domestic concerns in the post-World War II era. Gender equality became a political issue as the victory for women's suffrage changed into a struggle for equal rights and the politicization of personal life (Evans, 1989). The emergence of new forms of mobilization enabled each group to advance its interests. Radical resurgence and racial repression developed together as the dominant Euro-American group confronted the 'others' which it had sought to subordinate economically, legally, socially and politically since its colonial formation (DeLeon, 1988; White, 1991).

Colonial America

The Native-American Experience
Before the arrival of European settlers, the more than three hundred Native-American societies displayed a varied range of gender relationships. Given the small-scale, communal organization of most societies, there was relatively little class differentiation, although the enslavement of war captives provides a group that sometimes existed outside the kinship system (Perdue, 1979). While men usually constituted the warrior group, and women were less likely to engage in combat, female warriors did participate in wars, particularly once the arrival of the settlers caused warfare to escalate. Women often shared decision-making power with men, including the assumption of the role of leader among some groups. While patrilineal and patrilocal cultures did exist, many cultures operated matrilineally and matrilocally. Women's power relative to men was enhanced by the usual practice of maintaining a close connection between labour and resources. Women, as the chief agriculturalists, controlled and distributed the crops they produced. Women also shared positions of spiritual power with men, including a common presence as the creator in the cosmologies of many indigenous religions (Albers and Medicine, 1983; Amott and Matthaei, 1991; Jaimes, 1992). Contrary to the European notion of the 'squaw drudge', indigenous women operated within a context that tended to privilege their economic, sexual and political autonomy in comparison to Euro-American patriarchal practices (Smits, 1982).

By the late 1500s, settlers moving north from central Mexico began the creation of the first colonies of settlement. In the area that would become the south-western United States, the oldest continuous cultures in northern North America became the first to encounter Euro-American settlers. The relative scarcity, however, of the Spanish settlers willing to travel north protected these indigenous peoples from full-scale incorporation within a settler society, as did the area's isolation. Cultural and military resistance, such as Pope's War from 1680 to 1693 and continual raids by the Apaches and Comanches, preserved much of the indigenous culture in the area that became the colonies of New Mexico and Texas. But, in California, the interaction between the original inhabitants and the settlers largely destroyed the more fragile societies that existed prior to the Spanish arrival.

As the Anglo frontier moved westward, similar developments transpired. Within the first hundred years of contact, nearly 90 per cent of the indigenous peoples living along the Atlantic coast had disappeared. Wars such as the Pequot War in 1637, Bacon's Rebellion in 1676 which originated in settler conflict with the Susquehannahs, Doegs and Piscattaways and Metacom's War in 1675–76 'demonstrated that some of the coastal tribes were prepared to risk extinction rather than become a colonized and culturally imperialized people' as well as that they 'were doomed whether they chose war or peace' (Nash, 1974: 127, 135; Morgan, 1975: 250–1). By the 1680s in the older colonies and by the 1720s in the newer ones, the coastal groups had lost population, land resources, political autonomy and economic independence. Some Native Americans were enslaved and entered the plantation and household economies of the settlers or as tenant farmers, day labourers and domestic servants. More fortunately placed, the Cherokees, Creeks and Iroquois maintained control over interior areas of North America by playing off one European group against another for 150 years after initial contact until the establishment of the United States reduced their ability to manoeuvre (Nash, 1974).

After an initial period of mutual exchange and dependency in the fur, horse and hide trade in which Native-American women played an active role, the indigenous cultures began to lose their economic, cultural and political autonomy through military conflict, the impact of disease and the destruction of resources upon which their societies depended (Klein, 1983; White, 1983). Carolyn Merchant (1989) discussed 'the colonial ecological revolution' which involved an agricultural shift from female horticulture to patriarchal, male-dominated family farms in the New England colonies. Quaker missionaries sought to lead the Iroquois from 'barbarism' to 'civilization' through the conversion of men into farmers and women into housewives (Rothenberg, 1980; Jensen, 1977). Government agents, missionaries and an acculturated elite, many of whom were the children of white traders, began a process of domestication among the Cherokee. Modelling itself on the US republic, the Cherokee legislature undermined matrilineal kinship and excluded women from the political process (Perdue, 1985). The arrival of European settlers completed the process by shifting power and ownership from the original inhabitants to the settlers and the governments they established. As elsewhere, gendered colonialism operated to remove resources and power from women to men, whose authority was apparently enhanced, but whose power was largely illusionary because control actually resided with white settlers, the military, economic interests and government authorities (Albers, 1983; Etienne and Leacock, 1980; Klein, 1983; Ortiz, 1982).

The Mexican-American Experience

In seeking to expand the empire northward from central Mexico, the Spanish colonial government, operating within a feudal or patrimonial political economy, transported settlers to the colonies located in what would become New Mexico, California, and Texas. The late 1500s witnessed a colonizing effort that would continue for two centuries. Settlers who were descended from marriages or liaisons between Spanish men and Native-American women occupied the middle of a racial and class hierarchy stretching from the Spanish at the top to enslaved Africans and Native Americans at the bottom. The Catholic Church, the military and Spanish settlers divided the land to establish haciendas, using forced indigenous labour. Migrants of mixed racial ancestry received smaller plots of land or worked as peons on the haciendas for the better endowed settlers (Mirande and Enriquez, 1979; Amott and Matthaei, 1991). The Spanish colonizers thus established the first racially and class-stratified societies within the boundaries of what would become the United States.

Gender interacted with racial and class relationships to create different patterns within each class and racial stratum. Among the wealthy, men oversaw the running of the haciendas and directed the labour of peons while women supervised domestic servants and tended to the domestic and spiritual needs of the hacienda labour force. Intermarriage between the Pueblos and the settlers provided a basis for cultural exchange, shaping gender relationships in a more egalitarian direction. Among the peons, males performed the heavy labour while women often worked beside their husbands or served as a domestic labour force, whether paid or unpaid. Legally, husband and wife shared rights in property acquired during the marriages; moreover, daughters inherited equally with sons in contrast to the Anglo legal system. Husbands were also more likely than Anglo-Americans to bequeath the bulk of their property to their wives (Deutsch, 1987). Rooted in the conception of marriage as the combining of two families rather than the establishment of a single patriarchal household, women exercised greater control of family resources than they did in the English colonies.

The African-American Experience

Brought to North America as an enslaved labour force, Africans initially experienced conditions somewhat analogous to those existing for indentured servants of predominantly British origin in the English colonies. Slavery was not always for life, nor was it always passed on to descendants. But groups of recently emancipated servants, impoverished and unable to secure land, became a source of class conflict in colonies such as Virginia where they participated in Bacon's Rebellion.

When British dominance in the slave trade increased the available supply of Africans in the late 1600s, the southern plantation colonies turned to the enslavement of Africans as the dominant form of labour control in place of the more troublesome and short-term reliance upon indentured European labour (Morgan, 1975). In the northern colonies, slaves retained the right to own property, bequeath and inherit legacies, and work for their own benefit during their free time (Nash, 1974). In the plantation colonies, laws gave almost absolute power to the masters, including the right to buy or sell slaves, to execute them if they disobeyed, and to extract deference from slaves. Slaves lacked the right to move without permission, to bear arms or to enjoy the legal protections of a free citizen. Whether north or south, slavery was now a permanent condition which would be inherited by the children born to slave women (Morgan, 1975).

As slavery became the dominant labour system in the southern colonies, a racial system based upon the regulation of sexual relations was also established. Sexual relations between African-American men and Euro-American women were outlawed, although liaisons between Euro-American men and African-American women received tacit toleration from the Euro-American men who framed the laws (Fredrickson, 1981, 1988; Kulikoff, 1986; Amott and Matthaei, 1991). By 1691 the first statute banned marriage between a European and 'a negro, mulatto, or Indian . . . bond or free' with the stated purpose of preventing that 'abominable mixture and spurious issue . . . by negroes, mulattoes, and Indians intermarrying with English or other white women'. Accompanying slavery as a labour system was the construction of a 'two-category system of race relations' which drew a clear line between Europeans and 'those with any known or visible African ancestry' (Fredrickson, 1981: 105). Slavery thus created a racial, class and gender system in colonial America that subordinated the slaves to their masters economically, sexually and legally.

Slave resistance was most often manifested by the creation of a distinctive African-American culture through religion, music, family life and their own beliefs and values (Nash, 1974). Some slaves chose more active forms of resistance such as escaping from their masters and malingering to reduce the burdens of labour (Mullin, 1972). Other forms of resistance included theft, active sabotage and arson. In addition, slave women contributed significantly to the slave resistance through domestic labour that could not be claimed directly by the master. Skilled, artisanal slaves used the skills and privileges associated with their status to subvert the system by passing as free blacks or by escaping. Rarely did slaves openly rebel but uprisings did occur – as in South Carolina in 1739 when a hundred slaves attempted to flee towards the Florida frontier. In the northern colonies such incidents also occurred and led to occasional panics by masters and to severe retribution (Nash, 1974). The interaction between the domination imposed by the master and the forms of resistance and response developed by slave women created more sexually egalitarian, but fragile, relationships between men and women who were not bound together economically or legally (Bush, 1990; Jones, 1985; Mullings, 1986). Under such conditions gender relations among the enslaved were determined in large part by the demands of the masters rather than by the custom or choice of African Americans.

The Euro-American Experience
The gentry or rising middle class of English society were key to the creation of colonies of settlement in North America such as Massachusetts Bay and Virginia. As the demand for tobacco grew, land-owning settlers turned to England for a supply of indentured servants to expand tobacco production. In turn, the money crop required expansion into the territory of the indigenous peoples. War, conflict and eventual dispossession of the original inhabitants followed. A shift from indentured servants to slaves completed the establishment of a plantation settlement system. In the decades between 1680 and 1750, slavery provided the basis for the rise of a gentry composed primarily of planters and a few merchants. Patriarchal families gradually replaced more sexually egalitarian families among this class. Another major class developed among the English settlers: yeoman farmers. These included indentured servants, who had lived through their indenture, and new arrivals. Men managed the plantation and usually worked the land while women took responsibility for domestic labour. In such households it was assumed that 'wives owed their husbands obedience and smooth operation of the household in return for the financial support needed to purchase the necessities of life' (Kulikoff, 1986: 183). If a wife violated these rules, chastisement was acceptable as a means for the husband to assert his authority but she was granted 'some protection by law, custom, and theology' against brutality (Mullings, 1986: 43). Thus, the private patriarchy was subjected to constraints and regulations by a public patriarchy that was created as the colonies matured.

In the middle and northern colonies, merchant elites, prospering in the trade of the late 1600s 'including the slave trade', became the economic centre of coastal cities. Greater social differentiation accompanied the accumulation of wealth. There emerged a class of the labouring poor who became increasingly subject to the rise and fall of the urban economy. Single women and widows could easily become members of this class should they become dependent on their own earnings. Shopkeepers and craftsmen would sometimes slip into this class during the periods of depression that began to recur as the urban economies became more tightly integrated into the world economy. Economic insecurity worsened as masters shifted from long-term arti-sanal contracts to wage labour. 'Social structure and social attitudes' moved 'along divergent paths with the rise of egalitarian sentiment, concentrated in the labouring classes, accompanying the restructuring of urban society along more rigid class lines' (Nash, 1979: 262). Out of this explosive mixture would come support for a break with Britain as well as internal challenges to gender, class and racial domination.

Gender patterns differed among the classes. While their husbands became more absorbed in the complex tasks of managing international trade, the wives of wealthy merchants withdrew from active involve-ment in their husbands' affairs to concern themselves with the oversight of servants, often single women of the lower classes. Artisans and masters, however, often included their wives in the operation of the family business which would allow their widows to continue the trade after their husbands' death (Mullings, 1986; Evans, 1989). In rural areas the sexual division of labour assigned to men the work of agri-culture and the control of the family's economic resources while women concentrated on the domestic realm. Closer to cities, however, women might engage in cash-earning enterprises. Generally, economic power remained firmly in male control as did political power while women increasingly became defined as the emotional and religious centres of the household as well as unpaid domestic workers (Evans, 1989).

The American Revolution resulted in the formation of a politically independent ruling class composed primarily of planters and mer-chants, who could utilize their political power against the other classes, including slaves and wage labourers. That victory simultaneously removed the restraining hand of Britain that had sought to slow the westward movement of settlers across the Appalachians and, hence, resulted in greater coercion directed against Native Americans who occupied the territory into which the settlers began to pour. The 'class' of yeomen farmers and planters thus benefited at the expense of the communal occupiers of the land they seized. At the same time shifts from artisanal to wage labour represented declining opportunities for the economic independence to be obtained by the eventual rise of jour-neymen to master artisans. This left the hope of westward mobility to become one of the major escapes from an increasingly class-stratified urban economy.

Not all Euro-Americans shared equally in the rewards of Euro-American dominance, although each enjoyed a privileged position *vis-à-vis* the members of the other racial communities. A 'slaveholding mentality' became 'the wellspring of white supremacist thought and action', giving all whites a stake in racial domination which persisted even after revolutionary ideals gave impetus to the end of slavery in the northern states (Fredrickson, 1981: 93). Gender, of course, also marked a form of 'difference' and 'inequality' within Euro-American society. Women did not receive equal citizenship or economic opportunities within colonial or revolutionary America. Yet the contradiction between claims of equality and the reality of women's lives even among the elite did stimulate the development of an 'ideology of citizenship that merged the domestic domain of the preindustrial woman with the new public ideology of individual responsibility and civic virtue' (Kerber, 1986: 269). Likewise, racial domination coexisted uneasily with revolutionary pretensions to equality and liberty. Newly empowered national elites began to build a nation out of a racially and gender-stratified population by restricting full citizenship to white, property-owning men.

The Expansionist Republic

The Native-American Experience
From the time of the American Revolution to the end of the 'Indian wars' in the 1880s, one Native-American nation after another found its territory invaded by the expansionist republic that had established its independence in a treaty that ignored the claims of the indigenous inhabitants (Horsman, 1981; Ortiz, 1982). Forced to cede territory by treaty, Native Americans became subject to the efforts of missionaries and governmental agents to transform their economic, political and sexual relationships (Rothenberg, 1980; Perdue, 1985). Tecumseh, a Shawnee leader, sought to organize a confederacy to stem the settler invasion. Turning to the British for support, the alliance lost to American forces at the Battle of Tippecanoe in 1811. The survivors, like other Native-American groups, moved westward to keep ahead of the settlers or, in the case of the Creek, Cherokee, Choctow, Seminole and Chickasaw, were forcibly removed under the auspices of the 1830 Indian Removal Act.

The presidents, courts and secretaries of war continued the same policies aimed at expelling Native Americans from the United States. In 1856 the Attorney-General ruled that 'Indians are domestic subjects of this Government' rather than independent 'nations' or 'citizens' (Williams, 1980: 812). Finally, in 1871, Congress declared that Native Americans no longer constituted independent nations with whom the United States would have to negotiate, nor would it honour formerly negotiated treaties. According to such rulings, the indigenous people had become wards under the 'paramount authority of Congress which could alter or abolish tribal governments without regard to treaty promises' (Williams, 1980: 813). As the United States extended direct control over western areas, federal agents, military officers, railroad and mining interests, and settlers sought to confine the original inhabitants to smaller and smaller territories while the rest would be 'opened' to white settlement and exploitation. Under the so-called 'peace' policy of the late 1860s and 1870s, the government assigned reservations to different missionary groups, expecting them to keep up the pressure for assimilation. Like other colonizing societies, the expansionist republic promoted gender transformation to create possessive, patriarchal households in which self-sufficient Christian farmers would live in nuclear family households while women, excluded from treaty negotiations and leadership positions, would occupy themselves with domestic duties.

A group of eastern reformers, including missionaries, government officials and educators, secured the passage of the 1887 Indian Allotment Act to divide all Native-American land into small individual plots while opening the remaining land to sale and settlement. The 'Indian' was to disappear into the white citizenry (Carlson, 1981; Hoxie, 1984; White, 1991). But the reformers' advocacy of the doctrine of assimilation or cultural annihilation met determined resistance. Unable to maintain economic or political autonomy, Native Americans found that survival lay in maintaining cultural practices, values and identity. Gender patterns, however circumscribed by governmental and missionary activities, provided a core around which a distinctive culture could survive (Jensen, 1977; Albers and Medicine, 1983; Janiewski, 1992; Jaimes, 1992). Such resistance was aided by the reluctance of Euro-American settlements or states to incorporate Native Americans as full and equal citizens. Neither the 'Indian' nor the reservation vanished, despite the hopes of the reformers or the hostility of the settlers.

The Mexican-American Experience
Four decades after the United States established its independence from Britain, Mexico became independent of Spain. The proximity of its northern borders to the expansionist republic spreading across North America made it a target for conquest. Mexican officials tried to regulate the flow of Anglo-Americans into Texas, New Mexico and California, but the attractions of trade for the local inhabitants stimulated the flow of traders. Settlers soon followed. Forming their own Anglo enclaves in Texas, the new settlers organized a revolt in the mid-1830s 'around the issue of local self-government, accelerated by racial, religious, and language conflicts' (Limerick, 1987: 230). After the establishment of the Texas republic, hostilities continued as Anglo-American settlers poured into Texas. A 'caste system' developed that placed Mexicans at the bottom, just above African-American slaves.

The constitution reinforced social subordination by denying citizenship or ownership of property to those who had opposed the revolt against Mexico. By the 1840s conflict began between Texas and the Mexican state of New Mexico. Soon this conflict enlarged into full-scale warfare between the United States and Mexico, which would lead, in 1848, to the loss of more than half of Mexican territory to the United States (Limerick, 1987; Barrera, 1979; Acuna, 1981). What had been northern Mexico became the south-western United States and the states of Texas, California, New Mexico and Arizona.

Ostensibly, the Treaty of Guadalupe Hidalgo guaranteed the rights of the 100,000 former citizens of Mexico to citizenship, language and land, but the guarantees proved inadequate protection against the desires of Anglo settlers and the legal interpretations of Anglo courts. Forming an alliance with the ricos, the wealthy elite, the Anglo settlers assumed control of the territorial and state governments and influenced policy in Washington. Soon, many Mexican Americans had lost their land and found themselves a labouring class. As expressed by Rodolfo Acuna, 'a conqueror–conquered relationship existed and, by the 1850s, even the elite publicly recognized their subjugated status and economic demise' (1981:105; see also Barrera, 1979). Like the indigenous Americans, the Mexican Americans had become a colonized enclave surrounded by the expanding colonizing power.

In villages, cities, fields and mining camps, Mexican-American 'expansion and initiative' continued as the expanding Anglo frontier brought new opportunities and constraints. Mexican Americans created 'a regional community bound by ties of kinship as well as economy . . . and a multitude of cultural frontiers' (Deutsch, 1987: 9, 10). Women's involvement in religion and in building networks of neighbours and kin acted as 'an integrating force for the community' while their 'productive work' provided them both an 'autonomous base' and 'integration into the community' (Deutsch, 1987: 51). Accustomed to a flexible sexual division of labour, men and women adapted to migration. Whether the women remained behind in the village or joined the men on their travels, they retained 'a mutuality of production without either sex's activities becoming more critical than the other to the survival of the family and community' (Deutsch, 1987: 56). But women, forced to live outside the 'sexual structure of family labour', found it more difficult to survive because gender inequality made it harder to live on female earnings (Deutsch, 1987: 57).

Despite evidence of cultural resilience, the incorporation of Mexican Americans into the expanding Euro-American nation can usefully be discussed as the formation of an internal colony in its economic and political aspects. As their control over land was eroded, Mexican Americans lost the space necessary to self-determination. As landless, and often stateless, subjects of the dominant nation-state, Mexican Americans entered the American economy at the bottom. By the 1880s Mexican-American women, as well as men, were being incorporated into the agricultural labour force 'as entire families entered the pattern of seasonal and migratory field work' (Barrera, 1979: 53). Responding to such pressures, some members of the Hispanic upper classes 'would collaborate in the interests of property and social order, even at the expense of their lower-class countrymen', which sometimes included attempts to 'Europeanize or "whiten" themselves [by] accenting a Spanish line of descent to distinguish themselves from mestizos' (Limerick, 1987: 239–40). The Mexican-American enclave was thus internally divided along class and 'racial' lines even as it was being drawn into the Anglo-dominated political economy on terms that favoured the interests of Euro-Americans.

The African-American Experience
Republican values began to erode the ideological support for slavery in some regions of the United States, but support for racial domination increased. By the 1830s states began to pass disenfranchising statutes while free blacks were systematically excluded from economic opportunities. Segregation of public facilities was also common. Indeed, according to Edgard McManus, 'emancipation in some ways strengthened the tyranny of race by imposing on blacks new forms of subordination that better served the economic interests of whites' (1973: 197). In the South, slavery took on a new vigour as cotton growing provided impetus for US expansion from the removal of the major Native-American groups to the annexation of Texas and the Mexican–American War. Aiding the westward movement was the domestic slave trade which made possible the opening of new lands to the plantation system as well as giving slaveowners in the less thriving eastern states a new economic stake in the slavery. The wealth that flowed from slavery led to the passage of new and more stringent laws depriving slaves of civil rights, self-defence, education or the right to gather together without white supervision (Franklin, 1980). Although such laws were not always enforced, their existence pointed to the intention of their framers to deprive slaves of economic, social or cultural autonomy. Separation between the races was enforced to prevent mutually supportive or egalitarian relationships such as marriage while pro-slavery ideologues defined African Americans as 'naturally' adapted to enslavement.

Beyond the law itself, the system required brutality in the form of corporal punishment to enforce discipline upon the enslaved. The forced sale and separation of family and friends were other inescapable consequences of a system based upon obtaining economic profit from slavery and the concomitant slave trade. Physical constraints cohered with ideological pressures such as a pro-slavery interpretation of Christianity to induce the slaves to respect and honour the will of their masters. The masters also reformed some of the harsher aspects of slavery as a way to counter abolitionist pressures and to resolve the demands of a system that organized a labour system in the form of slavery. In order to establish a stable system of labour relations, the masters had not only to coerce but also to conciliate their slaves (Genovese, 1976).

Although slavery and racial domination did not exclude entirely the emergence of classes among African Americans, it clearly limited the possibility for the vast majority of entering any other economic situation than that of an enslaved labourer who worked primarily in agricultural or domestic labour. About 5,000 blacks worked as industrial slaves in southern factories and others worked at various crafts and trades, but most slaves lived on plantations and farms. Among free blacks, legal and economic restrictions kept most working at the bottom of the working class engaged in heavy labour or domestic service. Some, however, did become skilled craftsmen; others, shopkeepers, ministers and merchants. In the South a few even became prominent slaveowners, although most black slaveowners actually owned family members. Generally, however, class and race overlapped among African Americans to create a mutually interacting identity: to be African American was also to be a labourer, either free or enslaved.

Racial segregation provided an external force that helped to create an African-American community. North of slavery, African Americans were developing a political movement that incorporated escaped slaves into the anti-slavery cause. The greater access to resources in the North enabled free blacks to organize independent black churches as one of the first expressions of the creation of a black community in the face of a hostile or indifferent Anglo-American majority. The greater rights they possessed also allowed them to organize and fight against their oppression, including the formation of anti-slavery societies in the 1820s which converted some whites to supporting abolition (Franklin, 1980). Spokespersons created an African-American analysis of slavery and racism. Martin Delaney, for example, writing in 1852, linked the African-American cause to 'our similarly oppressed brother, the Indian'. Delaney situated the African-American struggle within an international context: 'The white races are but one-third of the population of the globe – or one of them to two of us – and it cannot much longer continue that two-thirds will passively submit to the universal domination of this one-third' (Harding, 1983: 175, 187). Finally, one group of the internally colonized were beginning to connect their situation to other colonized groups.

As they had in colonial times, southern slaves found various ways to resist slavery. The abolition of slavery in the North made escape a more available method, especially to slaves in the Upper South and to those who lived in the port cities. Slave revolts and attempted revolts, such as the Denmark Vesey affair in 1823, the Nat Turner rebellion in 1831, and John Brown's aborted rebellion of 1859, represented the most violent forms of resistance. However, given the relative numbers of Anglo-Americans and African Americans, such events were less frequent in the nineteenth-century United States than they had been in the colonial era (Genovese, 1979). Sabotage, theft and various forms of reducing the amount of labour provided to the masters represented more common ways that slaves defied their masters' interests. Music, folk tales and humour offered still other effective means of criticizing their masters, affirming their own claims to freedom, and describing methods of resistance such as escape (Harding, 1983). Within the slave community, slave preachers operated as the creators of a belief system that 'fired' slaves with 'a sense of their own worth' by providing the 'spiritual emancipation' that was 'the necessary foundation for black collectivity' (Genovese, 1976: 283).

Gender relations among African Americans developed within the context of slavery and the partial emancipation that left them in a dependent economic position. Enslavement 'stripped men of all the normal attributes of male power: legal and social fatherhood, the control of property' and 'the ability to dominate households' (Fox-Genovese, 1988: 49). Living within a 'dual caste system based on race and sex' in which 'racial and patriarchal ideologies' were 'wedded to the pursuit of profit', slave women, like slave men, were exploited for their labour while slave women were also seen as essential to reproducing the supply of slaves. The slave adherence to a sexual division of labour which would assign women primarily domestic duties was 'a political act of protest' rather than merely an acceptance of female 'domestication' (Jones, 1985: 11, 12). More likely to be able to be hired out, males might also contribute to the household through the additional resources (Blassingame, 1972). Their greater mobility also enabled male slaves to be more likely to escape, especially as young, unattached men, and to foment open acts of rebellion. As preachers and as rebels, males helped to define an African-American culture in opposition to the one imposed by their masters while women socialized and nurtured the young into that culture.

The Civil War gave new scope to African-American resistance. The Emancipation Proclamation gave official sanction to the desire to escape slavery by making abolition a part of the Union's war aims. Nearly 200,000 African Americans, ex-slaves and free, served in the Union army. In that context, Frederick Douglass declared that the

African Americans were fighting for a 'solidarity of the nation, making every slave free, and every free man a voter' (Harding, 1983: 243). Such goals led to the formation of the National Equal Rights League, which pressed for the 'recognition of the rights of the colored people of the nation as American citizens' (Harding, 1983: 247). After considerable political pressure, the League persuaded Abraham Lincoln and his administration to put abolition into the war aims. Then it lobbied for full citizenship. From such pressures came the 13th, 14th and 15th amendments to the Constitution that ended slavery and supposedly extended full citizenship to African-American men.

After emancipation, African Americans sought to define freedom by changing the situation they had experienced under slavery. Whether by voting, organizing Union Leagues, withdrawing the labour of women and children from agriculture, or leaving the lands of their former masters, they expressed a sense of their own autonomy. Above all, they sought access to land, education, citizenship and mobility (Harding, 1983). The organization of independent black churches began the construction of African-American institutions such as schools and self-help societies. Yet white racism undercut their efforts to achieve economic self-sufficiency and full citizenship. They endured the 'white terror' in which the paramilitary forces of groups like the Ku Klux Klan destroyed the hopes of an African-American and Anglo-American lower-class coalition. The return of conservative Democrats to power in the southern states brought a 'progressive narrowing of blacks' political and social options . . . New laws . . . redefined in the interest of the planter the terms of credit and the right to property' (Foner, 1988: 592, 594). From that time to the end of the nineteenth century, black men remained politically active until another wave of violent disfranchisement in the 1890s and 1900s produced the so-called 'Solid South' in which few blacks could vote. Some black women joined the campaign for women's suffrage or battled against racial violence such as lynching. But, despite their efforts, under the auspices of the conservative, white political elite the 'South emerged as a peculiar hybrid – an impoverished colonial economy integrated into the national capitalist marketplace yet with its own distinctive system of repressive labour relations' (Foner, 1988: 596). Although slavery did not return, tenancy and sharecropping locked African Americans into a system that allowed them few opportunities for escape.

The Euro-American Experience
Having successfully established their own nation-state and united it by a contradictory commitment to racial domination and political equality, Euro-Americans had vastly increased their ability to encroach upon the territory of the indigenous inhabitants of the continent they

laid claim to under the slogan of 'manifest destiny' (Horsman, 1981; Fredrickson, 1981). The common Euro-American commitment to expansion, however, resulted in conflict: economic, ideological and military. Divided by class and region, an adherence to white supremacy could not prevent rivalries and eventually civil war from tearing the new republic apart. After the Civil War, a more unified nation-state provided the political and economic framework in which full-scale industrialization could take place. A brief period of movement towards racial equality for African Americans quickly yielded to a reconstructed pattern of racial domination that left Mexican Americans, Native Americans and African Americans as subjects, not citizens, in the nation that was on its way to becoming the centre of the world economy (Greenberg, 1980; Acuna, 1981; Barrera, 1979; Fredrickson, 1988; White, 1991; Jaimes, 1992).

Expanding economically and territorially, the Euro-American-dominated political economy was transformed from a predominantly agrarian base organized around family labour and plantation slavery to an industrial capitalist economy organized around wage labour between the 1780s and the 1880s with its dominant metropolitan centre located in the urban north-east and mid-west (Levine et al., 1989). Subordinated to the industrializing centre were the agrarian and extractive regional economies of the South and West, which were linked by an expanding network of roads, canals and, finally, railroads that allowed a national market to encompass the continent. The expanding cotton economy of the southern states sold its product to the textile industries of Britain and those developing in the north-eastern states. The arrival of transportation enabled western settlements to replicate the patterns of development further east. Plantations in the south-west and family farms in the mid-west became commercial enterprises employing slave labour in the southern case and family labour and agricultural machinery in the northern case. The need for credit tied both types of farm economies to the financial system centred in the north-east. New European ethnic groups arrived: Irish and Germans in the early to mid-nineteenth century, southern and eastern Europeans in the 1880s, and Asian immigrants in the West in the 1850s and 1860s. The subordinated racial-ethnic labour of African Americans, Mexican Americans and Asians facilitated the rise of Euro-Americans to dominant economic positions, although the working classes also incorporated large numbers of Euro-Americans. The Euro-Americans thus occupied a more diverse set of class and gender relationships than did the members of the subordinated racialized communities who were confined primarily to the low and unwaged sectors of the labour force.

Whatever the region, the pattern of development led to widening class, race and ethnic divisions and growing social tensions. Rising levels of urban violence, crime and alcoholism, together with the poverty, led to various attempts at reform and repression. Schools, workhouses, prisons and police forces developed in order to deal with some of the problems associated with an industrializing and urbanizing society periodically afflicted by depressions, business failures and unemployment. Labour organizations also emerged to campaign for public schools, land reform and the 10-hour day, and to organize strikes against recalcitrant employers. Such tensions were partially absorbed into the conflict over African-American slavery that wove together 'race, religion, family, property, political and legal philosophy, and partisanship' with conflict over 'the proper status and rights of labor' (Levine et al., 1989: 365). In the post-Civil War world, class divisions emerged still more strongly in the first nationwide strikes against the railroads in 1877 and in the rivalry of the Knights of Labor and the American Federation of Labor for the leadership of the newly formed industrial labour force (Freeman et al., 1992).

In urban and small-town America a middle class took shape. The men in such households conducted their business in offices, shops and factories separate from their homes. New patterns of gender relations developed in which women were assigned moral, religious, childrearing and domestic responsibilities while men took on the responsibility of earning the family income and supporting children through a lengthening period of education. Whenever possible, such families tried to keep the married woman from engaging in wage labour so that she might devote herself to domestic duties. The poorer members of the class merged into the ranks of the working class. Daughters, as well as sons, might be sent to work to provide necessary income. Among the Irish, domestic service became the chief occupation for many women. Taking in boarders was another means by which poorer families attempted to supplement the earnings of other members. Thus gender relations differed depending upon the class, marital status and ethnicity of white Americans in an urbanizing, industrializing society (Levine et al., 1989; Amott and Matthaei, 1991).

In the rural South and West, patterns of gender relations were organized around patriarchal households. As analysed by Elizabeth Fox-Genovese, 'the persistence in the South of the household as the dominant unit of production and reproduction guaranteed the power of men in society' (1988: 42). The women in the planter class exerted power over slaves, but also experienced greater subordination than did upper-class women in the North where the household had been defined as female space. In the West, particularly on the frontier, the sexual division of labour and space contributed to the making of 'separate worlds' for men and women. Domesticity for women was a part of the cultural ideal as was their nearly total exclusion from public life.

Gender united men who 'chose male representatives to make policy for, to administer, and to sanction the social and economic order of the midwestern patriarchy' which organized the state and the civil economy (Faragher, 1979: 118).

The major challenges to gender, class and racial domination developed in the north-east. Feminizing education and religion in the North, middle-class women also became activists in the campaigns for temperance, abolition and, still more rarely, women's rights. The first women's rights convention at Seneca Falls in 1848 led to other meetings that concerned themselves initially with property rights for women. After the Civil War, the extension of suffrage to African-American men inspired the creation of a movement for women's suffrage by women's rights advocates disgruntled by the use of the term 'male' to describe a citizen in the Fourteenth Amendment to the Constitution. By 1869 two suffrage associations existed: one opposed to the Fifteenth Amendment that granted suffrage exclusively to African-American men, and the other willing to concede enfranchisement to recently emancipated males but pressing for women's future inclusion. Working-class women joined labour organizations despite the fewer opportunities they had for time away from work or domestic duties. But where 'racial oppression and gender intersected' such movements failed to develop. The 'association between abolitionism and women's rights' particularly horrified southern ideologues who made sure that the South would not nourish either challenge to their system (Evans, 1989: 108). The expansion of the Women's Christian Temperance Union in the 1880s and the National American Woman Suffrage Association in the 1890s gradually unified Euro-American women's organizations, North and South, in common support for suffrage, and in opposition to the 'lower classes, to immigrants, and to blacks' (Evans 1989: 129).

Modern America

The Native-American Experience
The 'closing of the frontier' coincided with the last of the 'Indian' wars (Robbins, 1992). The period from 1890s to the 1930s witnessed the use of the Indian Allotment Act to dispossess Native Americans of much of their remaining land (Carlson, 1981; Hoxie, 1984; White, 1991). The granting of citizenship to Native Americans in 1924 represented only another of the mechanisms by which 'to extend absolute U.S. control over jurisdiction, land tenure, national allegiance, and governance over even the residues of indigenous territoriality'. The 1934 Indian Reorganization Act created 'tribal regimes, ostensibly operated by indigenous peoples' but ultimately influenced by non-indigenous

decisionmakers', thus concealing the reality of colonial self-administration' under the 'appearance of self-determination' (Morris, 1992: 69). However, Native Americans, like other colonized and racialized peoples, began to change the politics of racial domination into the politics of racial identity (White, 1991; DeLeon, 1988; Cornell, 1988; Jaimes, 1992). As migration increased to urban areas in the post-World War II era, 'urban supratribalism' emerged. Constructing an 'Indian' identity through such organizations as the National Congress of American Indians, Native Americans enlarged their own 'political capacities' (Cornell, 1988:146). Connecting their own situation to other colonized peoples, Native Americans formulated demands for self-determination in opposition to 'domination by a colonial or settler state' (Jaimes, 1992: 79). Native-American women shared in the formation of the politics of racial identity. Their experience as colonized peoples made them sceptical of the appeals advanced by Anglo-American feminists. As expressed by Pam Colorado, 'the feminist agenda is basically one of rearranging social relations within the society which is occupying our land and utilizing our resources to its own benefit' (Jaimes, 1992: 332). In the 1970s the American Indian Movement attracted men and women into its ranks as did the series of legal struggles that sought to reclaim the resources which had been taken from the original inhabitants.

The Mexican-American Experience

Having forcibly incorporated half of Mexico within its national boundaries, Anglo-Americans continued their efforts from the 1880s to the 1940s 'to perfect the incomplete conquest' in the face of 'continually evolving Hispanic strategies to prevent it' (Deutsch, 1987: 200). Seasonal migration became one response which would rely on women to sustain village life. Once they permanently severed their village ties, Mexican Americans faced the problems imposed by discriminatory employment and real estate practices. Women were especially victimized by their unequal earning power within the white-dominated economy. Gradually, political and economic forces transformed 'the culturally autonomous Hispanic homeland' into 'an increasingly besieged enclave, an internal colony' in the 1930s (Deutsch, 1987: 201, 208). Yet the same decade witnessed the resurgence of class-based activism among Mexican-Americans workers, including women as well as men (Ruiz, 1987, 1990; Barrera, 1979; Acuna, 1981). Such struggles continued into the contemporary era as barrios provided the basis for political power for urbanized Chicanos. Reclaiming the designation 'Chicano' as a term of pride and self-definition, a movement addressing social justice, equality, educational reforms, and political and economic self-determination' emerged in the 1960s and 1970s, inspired, in part, by the African-American movement for civil rights (Garcia, 1990: 418; see also DeLeon, 1988; White, 1991).

Chicana feminism developed out of an awareness of membership in a 'colonized group' which rendered their analysis different from the feminism espoused by Euro-American feminists. Rooted in their experience in the Chicano movement, women began 'to question their traditional female roles . . . Chicana feminists struggled to gain equal status in the male-dominated nationalist movements and also in American society' (Garcia, 1990: 419). They sought to challenge the patriarchal ideology of machismo from within the Mexican-American community and to redefine women as capable of 'equally active resistance to colonization' (Mirande and Enriquez, 1979: 242; see also Baca Zinn, 1975, 1989). By the 1980s Chicana feminism was seeking to develop 'an analysis that stressed the interrelationship of race, class, and gender' in explaining the experiences of Chicanas in American society (Garcia, 1990: 427–8). Once again a feminism that analysed the needs of women in a colonized community was taking shape.

The African-American Experience

African Americans experienced intense racial violence in the period from the 1890s to the 1920s. The gains made immediately after the Civil War were taken from them through a concerted white supremacy campaign (Franklin, 1980). The northern Euro-American elites had moved closer to 'the settler or white southern' perspective on racial matters by the 1890s (Fredrickson, 1981: 188). Class consciousness contributed to this development as the 'emerging labor movement and the prospect of class conflict . . . brought out the ideological limitations of their egalitarianism' (Fredrickson, 1981: 189). This combined with the extension of imperialist ideologies justifying the 'forced incorporation of nonwhites into a new American empire' to erode commitment to equality (Fredrickson, 1981: 190). The Supreme Court completed the ideological shift away from racial equality by endorsing segregation in its 1896 decision, Plessy vs. Ferguson. Disfranchisement in the 1890s and 1900s excluded African Americans from the political process (Franklin, 1980). Although African Americans led by spokesmen like W.E.B. DuBois formed advocacy groups like the National Association for the Advancement of Colored People (NAACP), they could achieve few results in the hostile environment of the early twentieth century (Broderick, 1971; White, 1985; Meier and Bracey, 1993). Accompanying the loss of citizenship was an 'elaboration of racial disabilities and a growth of the state racial apparatus' which reinforced the economic exploitation for African Americans in the 'southern states where most continued to live (Greenberg, 1980: 26).

Commercial farmers, businessmen and trade unionists cooperated with politicians in lending 'legitimacy to the racial order and racial domination' (Greenberg, 1980: 111; see also Janiewski, 1985; Fredrickson, 1981). The few African Americans able to secure jobs outside agriculture found themselves placed at the bottom of the labour force in jobs that required heavy labour or placed them in domestic service. Even when blacks migrated northwards as World War I produced a demand for their labour, the patterns of labour market segmentation continued to entrap them while white workers mobilized against them. Only the New Deal's shift towards greater protection and recognition of unions and the growth of industrial unionism in the 1930s allowed the creation of a racially integrated labour movement under the auspices of the Congress of Industrial Organizations, although most African-American workers remained outside the protection of the organized labour force (Fredrickson, 1981). At the same time New Deal agricultural programmes funded the displacement of black tenant farm labour by giving large landowners the necessary capital to purchase machines such as cotton-pickers. Tenants, now jobless and landless, poured into cities in search of non-existent employment. While offering blacks membership in a new political coalition and giving black leaders an informal position in the 'black kitchen cabinet', the Roosevelt administration did little to benefit directly the economic situation of most black Americans (Bernstein, 1972).

During wartime and defence-generated prosperity, the most fortunate African Americans found better-paying positions in factories, the federal clerical ranks or the military. Gaining political and economic power during the expanding economy fueled by World War II, African Americans found themselves better able to advance their claims for citizenship in the postwar world. A small, black middle class began to expand and became the institutional and financial support of the civil rights movement as it gained momentum in the 1950s and 1960s. The NAACP secured legal victories after fifty years of efforts to secure constitutional recognition of African-American rights to citizenship (Franklin, 1980). Within the context of the Cold War, which placed race relations in the United States in an international spotlight, President Truman responded by desegregating the armed forces. The war and the accompanying revelations of the virulence of racism began to alter Euro-American attitudes towards racial minorities within the United States. The Supreme Court decision in Brown vs. the Board of Education of Topeka declared segregation to be unconstitutional as a more progressive 'Warren Court' began to pursue a social agenda. Such victories inspired the formation of a civil rights movement which reached its high point in 1964 and 1965 with the passage of the Civil Rights Act outlawing economic discrimination and the Voting Rights Act which restored the franchise to many African Americans (DeLeon, 1988).

Successful in achieving legal equality, the civil rights movement failed to make a successful transformation into a 'poor people's movement' to achieve economic equality for subordinated groups (DeLeon, 1988). Growing frustration with a white-dominated political, economic and legal system fostered ghetto revolts and the growth of 'black nationalism' as a separatist ideology, but did not force Euro-Americans to concede a share of economic power to African Americans (Broderick, 1971). Two unequal societies developed within African-American society as a result of the extension of civil rights. A middle class escaped from urban ghettos, abandoning a black underclass to its fate of apparently hopeless poverty, unemployment and violence. Political mobilization 'along racial lines' had resulted in the enactment of reforms 'which dramatically restructured the racial order, reorganized state institutions, and initiated whole new realms of state activity', but eliminated neither racial nor economic domination which still imprisoned a majority of African Americans within the internal colonies called the ghettos and impoverished rural communities within the southern states (Omi and Winant, 1986: 138)

African-American gender relations reflected the economic deprivation that limited their ability to purchase and to provide for their own needs. 'Despite efforts to maintain a sexual division of labour, the lack of male privilege in a white-dominated society' meant African-American men and women were not separated by 'extremes of economic power or political rights' (Jones, 1985: 80, 95). Confined, for the most part, to the labouring and service occupations, African-American men and women found themselves excluded from higher prestige employment except in segregated institutions such as schools, churches and businesses serving the African-American community. African-American women, like African-American men, 'fashioned race into a cultural identity that defined and connected them as a people, even as a nation', but some discovered that the politics of racial identity failed to recognize the differences between them that gender, class and sexual orientation created (Higginbotham, 1992: 260). Out of such circumstances emerged a black feminism which understood that 'gender itself was both constructed and fragmented by race . . . in very different, indeed antagonistic, racialized contexts' (Higginbotham, 1992: 267). Attempting to construct a feminism that was grounded in the black female experience, African-American feminists encountered the difficulties of analysing the complex interactions of gender, race and class.

The Euro-American Experience
The twentieth century represented the triumphal rise of the Euro-American nation-state to the core of the world economy in a structural relationship with third world nations that replicated its own internal

organization (Kolko, 1984). Its presence at the centre of the world ideological, economic and political system brought challenges to its 'domestic' and 'international' interaction with colonized peoples. More than mere coincidence produced simultaneous conflicts in Vietnam and in urban ghettos and rural enclaves. Although the Euro-Arnerican-dominated state was able to mobilize its considerable repressive and hegemonic forces to suppress the challenge, the continued existence of these racialized communities threatens the unity of the nation. Successive conflicts with other colonized groups, despite the US 'victory' in the Cold War, keep the same issues alive internationally. True to its origins as the creation of settler colonialism, the United States continues to rely upon racial domination as one of its structural supports but cannot avoid the unpleasant consequences in internal and external conflict. The police at home and the armed forces internationally remain essential to the maintenance of US control over its internal and external colonies.

The same decades that produced attacks from without and within upon Euro-American dominance encompassed diverse and wide-ranging conflicts over class. Occasionally, in the 1890s, 1910s, 1930s and 1960s, the working classes were able to develop a political and economic power base in association with a left-leaning political party and intelligentsia. Generally, a period of reaction followed, often fueled by war-induced nationalism, that eroded the gains that had been achieved. Over the last two decades 'political stalemate and economic stagnation' have placed 'popular social movements . . . on the defensive', but the forces leading to the concentration of wealth cannot continue without threatening the social, economic and political arrangements of the nation (Freeman et al., 1992: 671; see also Davis, 1986; Dawley, 1989).

Two waves of feminist insurgency also marked the rise of the United States to global power. The first brought women closer to equal citizenship with the attainment of suffrage in 1920; the second began to raise more fundamental questions about the organization of personal and public life (Evans, 1989). Partly in response to the emergence of feminism among African Americans, Mexican Americans and Native Americans, the second wave of feminism began to explore the 'differences' that undermined female solidarity, whether based upon race, class or sexual orientation. It began to extend its analysis beyond the boundaries of the United States to explore 'gendered colonialism' as a process which tied the experiences of African-American, Mexican-American, Native-American and Anglo-American women to those of women of many other nations. These feminists contributed to the development of a feminism that would be able to recognize 'difference' as arising from the different locations of diverse groups of women

(Hewitt, 1990; Janiewski, 1985; Anthias and Yuval-Davis, 1983; Higginbotham, 1992; Joseph and Lewis, 1981; Palmer, 1983).

The power vested centuries ago in an overlapping structure of gender, racial and class domination remained sufficiently intact to support a counter-offensive against insurgencies by the subordinated groups. The New Right upsurge of the 1970s and 1980s represented a modern variation on the previous mobilizations by conservative forces to retard advances made by racialized communities, lower classes or feminists. Appeals to white racial solidarity remained particularly potent given the clarity of the boundaries that defined groups into racial categories and communities. Appeals to patriarchal ideology could be deployed against the feminist challenge (Gordon and Hunter, 1977–78; De Hart-Mathews and Mathews, 1986; Evans, 1989). Unions lost battle after battle as the New Right domination of the political agenda eroded their power and the protections inherited from the New Deal. Divided against themselves, the colonized groups found it more difficult to discover and defend their common interests against the Anglo-American economic elites which controlled the American political economy.

Conclusion

Parallel histories have led to similar, albeit separate, destinations. Each of the colonized groups moved towards a revived 'politics of identity' as a part of their challenge to their racially defined subordination. At the same time 'integration', offered only to the economically successful and culturally assimilated among their members, fragmented their unity. Initially, and so long as they maintained territorial control, successive groups of Native Americans resisted militarily. Eventually forced upon reservations, their relatively small numbers denied them the same political and legal weapons available to more numerous or concentrated racialized groups. Ten million self-identified 'Native Americans', scattered through the dominant population, are unable to attain the political power that their numbers might entitle them to exercise. Instead, cultural revival became their basic mode of resistance. Concentrated in certain states, Mexican Americans have attained some political power, but still experience attacks on their language, the denial of their rights to free movement across the borders that divide them by national origin, and economic restrictions that place them among the lowest-paid workers. African Americans, the group most fully incorporated within the political and sexual economies of the United States, can be described as the most subordinated racialized community. Yet their very subjection by law gave their advocates a judicial and constitutional framework within which to challenge their subordination. Despite divisions by class and location, they have gained the greatest share of political power among the racialized groups. Women in each group sought to develop a racially and class-inflected feminism that could offer them the essential understanding of their situation. The political, economic and ideological formation of the United States reveals interlinked connections between race, gender and class relations that date their origins to a colonizing process that began more than four hundred years ago.

References

Acuna, Rodolf (1981) *Occupied America: History of Chicanos*. New York: Harper & Row.

Albers, Patricia C. (1983) 'Sioux women in transition: a study of their changing status in domestic and capitalist sectors of production', in Patricia Albers and Beatrice Medicine (eds), *The Hidden Half: Studies of Plains Indian Women*. Washington: University Press of America.

Albers, Patricia and Medicine, Beatrice (eds) (1983) *The Hidden Half: Studies of Plains Indian Women*. Washington: University Press of America.

Amott, Tersa L. and Matthaei, Julie (1991) *Race, Gender and Work: a Multicultural Economic History of Women in the United States*. Boston: South End Press.

Anthias, Floya and Yuval-Davis, Nira (1983) 'Contextualizing feminism: gender, ethnic and class divisions', *Feminist Review*, 15: 62–75.

Baca Zinn, Maxine (1975) 'Political familialism: toward sex role equality in Chicago families', *International Journal of Chicago Studies Research*, 6: 13–26.

Baca Zinn, Maxine (1989) 'Chicago men and masculinity', in M.S. Kimmel and M.A. Messner (eds), *Men's Lives*. New York: Macmillan. pp. 87–97.

Barrera, Mario (1979) *Race and Class in the Southwest: a Theory of Racial Inequality*. Notre Dame: University of Notre Dame Press.

Bernstein, Barton J. (1972) 'The New Deal: the conservative achievements of liberal reform', in Barton J. Bernstein and Allen J. Matusow (eds), *Twentieth Century America: Recent Interpretations*. New York: Harcourt Brace Jovanovich.

Blassingame, John W. (1972) *The Slave Community: Plantation Life in the Antebellum South*. New York: Oxford University Press.

Broderick, Francis L. (1971) 'The gnawing dilemma: separatism and integration, 1865–1925', in Nathan Huggins, I. Huggins, Martin Kilson and Daniel M. Fox (eds), *Key Issues in the Afro-American Experience*, Vol. 2, *Since 1865*. New York: Harcourt Brace Jovanovich.

Bush, Barbara (1990) *Slave Women in Caribbean Society, 1650–1838*. Kingston: Heinemann.

Carlson, Leonard (1981) *Indians, Bureaucrats and Land: The Dawes Act and the Decline in Indian Farming*. Westport: Greenwood.

Cornell, Stephen (1988) *The Return of the Native: American Indian Political Resurgence*. New York: Oxford University Press.

Davis, Mike (1986) *Prisoners of the American Dream: Politics and Economics in the History of the US Working Class*. London: Verso.

Dawley, Alan (1989) 'Workers, capital and the state in the twentieth century', in J. Carroll Moody and Alice Kessler-Harris (eds) *Perspectives on American Labor History: the Problem of Synthesis*. Dekalb: Northern Illinois University Press.

De Hart-Mathews, Jane and Mathews, Donald (1986) 'The cultural politics of the ERA's defeat', in Joan Huff-Wilson (ed.), *Rights of Passage: the Past and Future of the ERA*. Bloomington: Indiana University Press. pp. 144–53.

DeLeon, David (1988) *Everything is Changing: Contemporary US Movements in Historical Perspective*. New York: Praeger.

Deutsch, Sarah (1987) *No Separate Refuge: Culture, Class and Gender on an Anglo-Hispanic Frontier in the American Southwest, 1880–1940*. New York: Oxford University Press.

Etienne, Mona and Leacock, Eleanor (eds) (1980) *Women and Colonization*. South Hadley: Bergin & Garvey.

Evans, Sara M. (1989) *Born for Liberty: a History of Women in America*. New York: Free Press.

Faragher, John Mack (1979) *Women and Men on the Overland Trail*. New Haven: Yale University Press.

Foner, Eric (1988) *Reconstruction: America's Unfinished Revolution, 1863–1877*. New York: Harper & Row.

Fox-Genovese, Elizabeth (1988) *Within the Plantation Household: Black and White Women of the Old South*. Chapel Hill: University of North Carolina.

Franklin, John Hope (1980) *From Slavery to Freedom: a History of Negro Americans*. New York: Knopf.

Fredrickson, George M. (1981) *White Supremacy: Comparative Study in American and South African History*. New York: Oxford University Press.

Fredrickson, George M. (1988) *The Arrogance of Race: Historical Perspectives on Slavery, Racism and Social Inequality*. Middletown: Wesleyan University Press.

Freeman, Joshua, Lichtenstein, Nelson, Brier, Stephen, Bensman, David, Benson, Susan Porter, Brundage, David, Eynon, Bret, Levine, Bruce and Palmer, Bryan (1992) *Who Built America? Working People and the Nation's Economy, Politics, Culture and Society*, vol. 2. New York: Pantheon.

Garcia, Alma M. (1990) 'The development of Chicana feminist discourse, 1970–1980', in Ellen Carol DuBois and Vicki L. Ruiz (eds), *Unequal Sisters: a Multicultural Reader in US Women's History*. New York: Routledge. pp. 418–31.

Genovese, Eugene (1976) *Roll, Jordan, Roll: the World the Slaves Made*. New York: Vintage.

Genovese, Eugene (1979) *From Rebellion to Revolution: Afro-American Slave Revolts in the Making of the Modern World*. Baton Rouge: Lousiana State University Press.

Gordon, Linda and Hunter, Allen (1977–78) 'Sex, Family and the New Right: anti-feminism as a political force', *Radical America*, 11–12: 9–25.

Greenberg, Stanley B. (1980) *Race and State in Capitalist Development: Comparative Perspectives*. New Haven: Yale University Press.

Harding, Vincent (1983) *There is a River: the Black Struggle for Freedom in America*. New York: Vintage.

Hewitt, Nancy A. (1990) 'Beyond the search for sisterhood: American women's history in the 1980s', in Ellen Carol DuBois and Vicki L. Ruiz (eds) *Unequal Sisters: a Multicultural Reader in US Women's History*. New York: Routledge.

Higginbotham, Evelyn Brooks (1992) 'African-American women's history and the meta-language of race', *Signs*, 17 (2): 252–74.

Horsman, Reginald (1981) *Race and Manifest Destiny: the Origins of Racial Anglo-Saxonism*. Cambridge, MA: Harvard University Press.

Hoxie, Frederick (1984) *A Final Promise: the Campaign to Assimilate the Indians, 1880–1920*. Lincoln: University of Nebraska Press.

Jaimes, M. Annette (ed.) (1992) *The State of Native America: Genocide, Colonization and Resistance*. Boston: South End Press.

Janiewski, Dolores (1985) *Sisterhood Denied: Race, Gender and Class in a New South Community*. Philadelphia: Temple University Press.

Janiewski, Dolores (1992) 'Learning to live "just like white folks": gender, ethnicity and the state in the inland northwest', in Dorothy O. Helly and Susan M. Reverby (eds), *Gendered Domains: Rethinking Public and Private in Women's History*. Ithaca: Cornell University Press.

Jensen, Joan (1977) 'Native American women and agriculture: a Seneca case study', *Sex Roles*, 3 (5): 423–41.

Jones, Jacqueline (1985) *Labor of Love, Labor of Sorrow: Black Women, Work and the Family from Slavery to the Present*. New York: Basic Books.

Joseph, Gloria I. and Lewis, Jill (1981) *Common Differences: Conflicts in Black and White Feminist Perspectives*. New York: Anchor Press.

Kerber, Linda (1986) *Women of the Republic: Intellect and Ideology in Revolutionary America*. New York: Norton.

Klein, Alan (1983) 'The political-economy of gender: a nineteenth-century Plains Indian case study', in Patricia Albers and Beatrice Medicine (eds), *The Hidden Half: Studies of Plains Indian Women*. Washington: University Press of America.

Kolko, Gabriel (1984) *Main Currents in Modern American History*. New York: Pantheon.

Kulikoff, Allan (1986) *Tobacco and Slaves: the Development of Southern Cultures in the Chesapeake, 1680–1800*. Chapel Hill: University of North Carolina Press.

Leacock, Eleanor (1980) 'Montangais women and the Jesuit program for colonization', in Mona Etienne and Eleanor Leacock (eds), *Women and Colonization*. South Hadley: Bergin & Garvey. pp. 25–41.

Levine, Bruce, Brier, Stephen, Brundage, David, Countryman, Edward, Fennell, Dorothy and Rediker, Marcus (1989) *Who Built America? Working People and the Nation's Economy, Politics, Culture and Society*, vol. 1. New York: Pantheon.

Limerick, Patricia Nelson (1987) *The Legacy of Conquest: the Unbroken Past of the American West*. New York: Norton.

McManus, Edgard J. (1973) *Black Bondage in the North*. Syracuse: Syracuse University Press.

Meier, August and Bracey Jr, John H. (1993) 'The NAACP as a reform movement, 1909–1965: "To reach the conscience of America"', *Journal of Southern History*, 59 (1): 3–30.

Merchant, Carolyn (1989) *Ecological Revolutions: Nature, Gender and Science in New England*. Chapel Hill: University of North Carolina Press.

Mirande, Alfredo and Enriquez, Evangelina (1979) *La Chicana: the Mexican-American Woman*. Chicago: University of Chicago Press.

Morgan, Edmund S. (1975) *American Slavery, American Freedom: the Ordeal of Colonial Virginia*. New York: Norton.

Morris, Glenn T. (1992) 'International law and politics: toward a right to self-determination for indigenous peoples', in M. Annette Jaimes (ed.), *The State of Native America: Genocide, Colonization and Resistance*. Boston: South End Press.

Mullin, Gerald W. (1972) *Flight and Rebellion: Slave Resistance in Eighteenth-Century Virginia*. New York: Oxford University Press.

Mullings, Leah (1986) 'Uneven development: class, race and gender in the United States before 1900', in E. Leacock and H. Safa (eds), *Women's Work: Development and the Division of Labor by Gender*. South Hadley: Bergin & Garvey.

Nash, Gary (1974) *Red, White and Black: the Peoples of Early America*. Englewood Cliffs: Prentice-Hall.

Nash, Gary (1979) *The Urban Crucible: Social Change, Political Consciousness and the*

Origins of the American Revolution. Cambridge, MA: Harvard University Press.

Omi, Michael and Winant, Howard (1986) *Racial Formation in the United States: From the 1960s to the 1980s*. New York: Routledge.

Ortiz, Roxanne Dunbar (1982) 'Land and nationhood: the American Indian struggle for self-determination and survival', *Socialist Review*, 63–4.

Palmer, Phylis Marynick (1983) 'White women/black women: the dualism of female identity and experience in the United States,' *Feminist Studies*, 9: 151–70.

Perdue, Theda (1979) *Slavery and the Evolution of Cherokee Society, 1540–1866*. Knoxville: University of Tennessee Press.

Perdue, Theda (1985) 'Southern Indians and the cult of true womanhood', in Walter J. Fraser Jr, R. Frank Saunders Jr. and Jon L. Wakelyn (eds), *The Web of Southern Social Relations: Women, Family and Education*. Athens: University of Georgia Press. pp. 35–51.

Ringer, Benjamin B. (1983) *We the People and Others: Duality and America's Treatment of Its Racial Minorities*. New York: Tavistock.

Robbins, Rebecca L. (1992) 'Self-determination and subordination: the past, present and future of American Indian governance', in M. Annette Jaimes (ed.), *The State of Native America: Genocide, Colonization and Resistance*. Boston: South End Press.

Rothenberg, Diane (1980) 'The mothers of the nation: Seneca resistance to Quaker intervention', in Mona Etienne and Eleanor Leacock (eds), *Women and Colonization*. South Hadley: Bergin & Garvey.

Ruiz, Vicki L. (1987) *Cannery Women, Cannery Lives: Mexican Women, Unionization and the California Food Processing Industry, 1930–1950*. Albuquerque: University of New Mexico Press.

Ruiz, Vicki L. (1990) 'A promise fulfilled: Mexican cannery workers in southern California', in Ellen Carol DuBois and Vicki L. Ruiz (eds), *Unequal Sisters: a Multicultural Reader in US Women's History*. New York: Routledge. pp. 264–74.

Smits, David B. (1982) 'The "Squaw Drudge": an index of savagism', *Ethnohistory*, 9 (4): 281–306.

White, John (1985) *Black Leadership in America, 1895–1968*. London: Longman.

White, Richard (1983) *Roots of Dependency: Subsistence, Environment and Social Change among the Choctaws, Pawnees and Navajos*. Lincoln: University of Nebraska Press.

White, Richard (1991) *It's Your Misfortune and None of My Own: a History of the American West*. Norman: University of Oklahoma Press.

Williams, Walter L. (1980) 'United States Indian policy and the debate over Philippine annexation: implications for the origins of American imperialism', *Journal of American History*, 66 (4): 810–31.

6

Miscegenation as Nation-Building: Indian and Immigrant Women in Mexico

Natividad Gutiérrez

Mexican nationalism has placed great emphasis upon *mestizaje*, the process of racial and cultural miscegenation which began during the Spanish conquest. Both ideologically and empirically, *mestizaje* has permeated Mexican society to the extent that 90 per cent of the country's population is now considered *mestizo*. Extensive literature exists on the opinions and viewpoints of Mexico's most prominent nationalists (for example, J. Sierra (1848–1912), A. Molina Enríquez (1868–1940), M. Gamio (1883–1960) and J. Vasconcelos (1881–1959)), to exalt the ideology of mestizoism (Basave Benítez, 1992). However, little academic attention has been given to unravelling the complex interplay of race, gender, ethnicity and class which reverberate behind the facade of the ideologized fusion of two cultural traditions, the Spanish and the native, officially imposed on the heterogenous Mexican community. The development of an introspective nationalism based on assimilation towards *mestizo* patterns has systematically excluded provisions favouring the cultural development or survival of minorities – whether indigenous or immigrant. Nevertheless, the 'cult' of *mestizaje* and its exclusive policies have not served to completely extinguish cultural or ethnic identities, or the discrimination deriving from these parameters.

In recent decades, indigenous peoples have been engaged in campaigns and organizations for the rejuvenation of their cultures, as well as the respect of and rights to their lands. A recent example of this was the armed uprising of peasants and Indians of Chiapas (January 1, 1994) with demands for social justice, democracy and an end to corruption in government. This conflict has shaken the entire Mexican society and caused concern among the international community, to such an extent that the only viable solution to the conflict would seem to be the redefinition of the traditional relationships between the state and the indigenous peoples, a relationship based on the practice of discrimination and the state's neglect of development. Yet not all Mexican immigrants have had to relinquish their ethnic or religious identities; for example, the Jewish community have continued to practise and transmit their ethnic and religious identity based on the identification with the concept, the people and the state of Israel, while coexisting with the dominant – *mestizo* – majority (personal communication: Ana Margolis, September 1, 1993).

This chapter explores the historical points of contact and the relationships between indigenous and immigrant women in Mexico. Five centuries of racial and cultural intercourse have created a complex pattern of social and cultural relationships between women of differing backgrounds. Over the centuries, Mexico experienced a prolonged period of colonization (1521–1810), and a nation-building process which can be divided into two stages: the first revolves around Mexico's political independence in 1821; the second, a period of national reconstruction, which began in the 1920s with an end to the violent revolution of 1910 and continues to the present day.

Following a brief overview of the development of Mexico's ethnic mix, the chapter is divided into three parts: the first analyses the patterns of migration associated with the formation of colonial society; the second examines the structural incorporation of female migrants and indigenous peoples within the framework of state policies of nation-building from 1945; and the third discusses the current politics of Mexican women from diverse racial and cultural backgrounds.

The Ethnic Mix

Mexico's population is formed by the descendants of a variety of indigenous cultural groups and 'nations' whose origins and cultures flourished long before the arrival of the Europeans, by several groups of immigrants and by the dominant *mestizo* majority. The economic potentialities of the most prosperous Spanish colony in the Americas, New Spain (Mexico), proved attractive to Europeans. The early years of colonialism, from 1521 onwards, witnessed a migratory movement by single Spanish men as well as an enslaved black labour force from Africa. It is now commonly acknowledged that the destruction, transformation and adaptation of Mexico's original indigenous societies were produced in tandem with varying levels of immigration, beginning with the arrival of the Spaniards in the early sixteenth century. One of the consequences of the colonial occupation was the eradication of complex religious systems through the imposition of European values and mores, and an exogamous legal-juridical system. The enforced introduction of new patterns of social organization radically transformed indigenous economic structures. A dramatic erosion of traditional indigenous society emerged from physical and cultural contacts between immigrant males and indigenous women. Indeed, a

salient feature of Spanish colonialism was the creation of a heterogenous *mestizo* race who now form the bulk of Mexico's present-day
population.

From the end of the sixteenth to the eighteenth centuries, Mexico's
colonization process was enhanced by the arrival of an increasing number of European women. These women, the relatives of early settlers,
expanded the Hispanic concept of the monogamous family. One's place
of birth served to differentiate the European population into '*creoles*' –
Spanish Americans – and '*peninsulares*' – Spaniards born in Europe.
This culturally based division of Europeans who shared a race, a language and a religion would eventually lead to calls for Mexican
sovereignty.

Following Mexico's political independence in 1821, European immigration decreased. Over the next two centuries, other American
countries, such as Canada, the United States, Brazil and Argentina,
attracted large numbers of immigrants who settled in those places by
reason of their economic prosperity. Mexico since independence, however, has not been characterized by an overwhelming influx of settlers.
The country's surplus of Indian labour and an absence of so-called
'empty' lands for colonization militated against such a scenario.

With the arrival of exiles from the Spanish Civil War and political
refugees during World War II, a second wave of immigration began;
and during the past two decades, other groups of political refugees
have found asylum in Mexico: indigenous people from Guatemala and
El Salvador have also entered Mexico in order to flee the violence,
hunger and human rights violations in their own countries. According
to the Mexican Commission for Assistance to Refugees, Mexico now
shelters some 46,000 Mayan refugees in 89 refugee camps and up to
one million illegal migrants from across Central America (Bonilla,
1993: 8).

By 1992, 87 million people inhabited the 'territorial' nation-state of
Mexico – the term is used to emphasize the lack of cultural unity between
its diverse indigenous and exogamous elements (Smith, 1986: 122) In
cultural terms, the majority (90 per cent) is *mestizo*, while the indigenous
peoples comprise 9.8 per cent of the total population; the remainder of
the population including 'whites,' Asians or blacks is unclear given that
the census does not include criteria such as 'race' or 'ethnic origin', but
linguistic criteria have been widely used to classify ethnic Indian groups.
Today 56 native ethnic groups, with an estimated population of about 8.5
million, are scattered across Mexico. But unlike in the colonial period, the
white population is now treated as if it were of European descent, regardless of birthplace or ethnic origins. The Asian population is primarily
formed by communities of Chinese and Japanese, who have settled in the
northern and southern regions of Mexico.

In 1882 US immigration law prohibited the entry of Chinese labourers once the construction of the railways was completed. In spite of this restriction and the anti-Chinese campaigns of 1899 and 1911 in northern Mexico (Knight, 1990: 96), Chinese people continued to enter America, and once they were disqualified by the US authorities they attempted to settle in Mexico. Japanese communities have a more recent history of settlement, and the reasons are largely economic due to the growing investment of Japanese firms in the Mexican economy, such as the car industry, oil exports and the establishment of '*maquiladoras*', manufacturing enterprises on the US–Mexican border (Rubio, 1992: 93). Chinese immigration has been predominantly male and they have largely intermarried with *mestiza* women; and the descendants of these mixed marriages have become fully assimilated into *mestizo* culture.

A more complex situation applies to surviving black groups due to their specific lack of recognition in the census. After the transportation of black slaves was terminated in the late seventeenth century, blacks gradually intermarried with indigenous groups; as a result, the remaining blacks preserve only some of their original ethnic and racial characteristics. One small group of Caribbean blacks has been recently recognized – but, again, by linguistic (they are speakers of the Garífono language) rather than racial criteria.

The following sections describe in greater detail the contribution of women to this ethnic mix and to Mexico's nation-building process.

The Formation of Colonial Society, 1521–1810

In the so-called 'discovery' of the New World, Spain did not find an uninhabited continent. The following comment from the first recorded western view of Mexico serves to illustrate, from the perspective of our time, the highly developed urbanization of a complex and self-contained society: 'With such wonderful sights to gaze on we did not know what to say, if this was real that we saw before our eyes. On the land-side there were great cities, and on the lake many more' (Díaz del Castillo, 1963: 216).

By the time of the European arrival, Mexico was inhabited by an estimated 20 million people divided into ethnic and/or political organizations (Borah and Cook, 1963: 46); they spoke a variety of languages, and each group had its own form of government. In addition to the well-known Aztecs in the central region of Mexico and the Maya on the Yucatán peninsula, there were also numerous smaller ethnic nations scattered across the present territory of Mexico.

The diversity of these indigenous societies makes it impossible to define one singular pattern of social and economic organization; the latter depended largely upon the availability of natural resources: for example, the Raramuri – Tarahúmara – led a nomadic life in the desert of the northern plateau, while the Mixteco, Zapoteco, Maya and Aztec economies were diversified through intensive agriculture, tribute from incorporated groups, and internal trade. Indigenous social structures were characterized by varying degrees of stratification, but a basic distinction prevailed between an aristocracy or nobility and the mass of the people. Such a structure of social differentiation can be seen in the most researched pre-Columbian social organization, that of the Aztecs.

The governance of the Aztecs' large territory depended on an authoritarian bureaucracy which was militaristic and adept in revenue assessment and collection (Gibson, 1960: 169). This elite, including also aristocracy and priests, could own land and demand services, labour and tribute from one or more communities. Conversely, the *macehual* or common people were forced to pay taxes, perform military and labour services, and cultivate through usufruct rights or on communal lands (Gibson, 1960: 169, 172).

From 1521 Spanish colonizers began dismantling centralized Indian authority, as well as abolishing military ranks and the native priesthood; some offices were eliminated or came under the control of the Spanish administration. In the provincial centres, the Indian nobility managed to adjust to colonial life and maintained honorary titles and privileges. Their noble rank was recognized by the Spaniards who needed their collaboration in order to both consolidate the political conquest and undertake their evangelizing mission. The nobility were thus strategically coerced and their lands were forfeited to the *conquistadores*; however, they survived by continuing to marry within their own ranks. Aristocratic women also intermarried with Spaniards. The vestiges of the Indian nobility finally disappeared with the advent of Mexican political independence, the spread of liberal ideologies and economic change.

The introduction of a European system of agriculture during the colonial period radically transformed the structure of Indian societies. The conquerors and colonists, who now owned and occupied the land, coerced and organized Indian labour into producing European foodstuffs. Towards the middle of the seventeenth century the shortage of land available to the Indians became acute, as the Indian population recovered from the devastating epidemics which had decimated the indigenous peoples during the sixteenth century. The diversification of agricultural production was organized to satisfy the domestic market. Economic expansion during the sixteenth and seventeenth centuries was largely financed by silver mining which became the colony's second most important economic activity after agriculture.

Despite the introduction of new economic activities such as mining and manufacturing, as well as the expansion of an internal market, New Spain did not adopt advanced forms of commercial organizations. Business ventures were *ad hoc* arrangements which were established for a finite period and were dependent on family enterprises. Specifically, the colony's economy reflected the dynamics of an internal market geared to satisfying the agricultural demands of the colonists. With the exception of silver mining, the economy reflected the Crown's lack of interest in expanding trade, and the commercial retardation fostered by colonial rule hindered the long-term development of independent capital accumulation in Mexico (Maclachlan and Rodríguez, 1983: 148).

Miscegenation is the key to understanding Mexico's pattern of colonization from the conquest of 1521. As Robert Padden (1976: 220) has argued: 'The primary conquest of Mexico was really more biological than military . . . although it cannot be proved or disproved, I would guess that the Spaniards commonly left more pregnancies in their camps than they did casualties on the field of battle'.

The large number of unions between Indian women and European or African men produced a *mestizo* or mixed race population, which was already a significant demographic feature of the country by the seventeenth century. Some *mestizos* were born from a few privileged marriages, but the majority were the result of the widespread rape and coercion of indigenous women (Morner, 1967: 36). All Indian women were subject to male domination, but one select group evolved with economic privileges and social status and, for their children, legitimacy. This designated group of *mestizo* women – descendants of *conquistadores* and aristocratic Indian women – were easily assimilated by the colonizers, were kept in seclusion and did not marry outside the elite. The experience of these women contrasts sharply with those of *macehual*, the general mass of women; the latter would also be exposed to another important racial contact with Africans, predominantly male, slaves who were introduced during the conquest, pacification and settlement of Mexico (140,000 in total from 1521 to the end of the seventeenth century) (Palmer 1976: 39).

Three factors accelerated miscegenation: (1) the early arrival of the African population; (2) the high ratio of black men to black women; and (3) the sharp decrease in the male Indian population due to both the spread of western diseases and forced labour. The miscegenation process which initially occurred between Spanish males and Indian females was continued by black males. The growth of the mixed population rendered the transportation of African slaves unnecessary by the final years of the seventeenth century.

The colonial experience of black females is another matter. As in the case of Indian women, there is no historical record with respect to their degree of economic integration; but one does find mention of their experiences in other settings such as those referring to bizarre cases of cruelty, and they were also depicted as practitioners of magic and sorcery (Palmer, 1976: 161; Frucht, 1971: 89). Some references concern African women in the context of long working hours, excessive physical work and physical abuse; they also suggest that black women were primarily placed in the household, workshops and convents (Pescatello, 1976: 223). The available information paints a stereotypical picture of black women as mistresses and providers of sexual services. By contrast, Indian women were viewed less negatively, and they were seen as a means by which blacks could overcome their low status and become part of the Indian communities.

While the burden of hard work and frequent physical abuse appears to have fallen upon women of African descent, a vision of sexual desirability is suggested by the references to *mulatto* women, who were the daughters of Spanish fathers and black mothers. An observation by the Dominican friar Thomas Gage who visited Mexico in 1625 provides an example: 'Many Spaniards of the better sort . . . disdain their wives for them' (Israel, 1975: 69). Distinctions in socio-economic status extended even to women's clothes, which served as precise indicators of status among the various racial groups. For example, a 1571 ordinance prohibited black women from wearing gold, pearls and silk – these were for the exclusive use of Spanish women, aimed at symbolizing their superior status (Castelló Yturbide, 1990: 75).

The migration of Spanish women was encouraged by the Crown once the territory was largely pacified. However, severe restrictions were imposed on the settlement of Jews and non-Christians in the New World; this was due to the importance Spanish ideology placed on preserving the 'purity of Christian blood'. Contact and coexistence with non-Christians was to be eschewed.

The settlement of the Spanish female population in the New World had two consequences: first, the practice of Spanish males marrying aristocratic Indian women educated as 'Spanish girls' declined, although unions between Indian women and Spaniards or Africans continued (Marshall, 1963: 168); secondly, Spanish women proved to be very efficient agents in the introduction of certain fundamental institutions into colonial society and in transmitting Christian values. These were largely based on the European model of the patriarchal family, an institution which received total support and encouragement from the Catholic Church.

White, usually Spanish, women were largely confined to the household or nunneries. The pattern of female behaviour was that of organizing the household and ensuring the monogamous integrity of the family amidst an ocean of miscegenation (Seed, 1988). The number of marriages among the white community and the growing *mestizo* population demanded a domestic work-force which was supplied by Indian and black women, but the Indian servant who became synonymous with the image of the Spanish home lived as a subordinate and was usually treated with patronizing disdain. However, domestic service did serve as a link between Spaniards and indigenous women and through it Indian women learned Spanish and became familiar with Hispanic customs, habits and lifestyles (Cuevas, 1928: 186). As a result, the 'new Spanish home', ruled by recently settled Spanish women became a recognizable 'centre of acculturation' for women of other races.

Participation in ecclesiastical life was conditioned by racial descent, economic position and social status. These factors also determined the quality of indoctrination and religious instruction received by women of differing races and castes; for example, 'purity of the blood' was a prerequisite for entering monastic life, such that only white women could take religious vows. The daughters and relatives of the Spanish and the *creoles* had exclusive access to the religious institutions which proliferated across New Spain (Lavrín, 1976: 39; Muriel, 1963: 46). Acculturated daughters of the Indian nobility, who had been raised in 'good Christian homes', could also aspire to a religious life, but only in institutions specially designated for them (Gallagher, 1976: 152; Muriel, 1963: 47). The majority of non-aristocratic Indian, black and poor *mestiza* women received only minimal religious instruction – a simple catechism, for example – through the evangelism of the Catholic Church. Hence, they had greater access to the Christian religion through their role as domestic servants and slaves in convents and nunneries for Hispanic women. This pattern of religious segregation in a milieu dominated by Catholic ideology illustrates the role of religious instruction in defining social status.

The vital role of white women in maintaining and reproducing core Spanish values, such as sexual honour and 'purity of the blood', helps to explain the origins of the deep rivalry between the Spanish *peninsulares* and the *creoles*. This antagonism was a prime mover behind the struggle for Mexican political sovereignty in the first decade of the nineteenth century.

Differentiation between these groups, based on place of birth, was not readily apparent; after all, both shared a similar ethnic background, spoke the same language and were products of the same cultural tradition overseen by Catholic ideology. Yet the distinction was revealed in social life: while some *creoles* were affluent, had access to an ecclesiastical education, and filled the intermediate and lower levels of the bureaucracy, they did not occupy key political and administrative posts. Instead, all the important positions in the executive and the church were reserved for *peninsulares* who were appointed from Madrid.

Spanish women who were born in Europe became synonymous with high social status, and thus aided the process of differentiation between the two groups. The notion of 'prejudice by birth', introduced prior to Mexican independence, precedes both the upsurge in political nationalism and the ideological project of cultural and racial unity. And support for this prejudice came from two eighteenth-century French 'naturalists', G.L. Leclerc and C. de Pauw, as a form of environmental determinism which derogated the so-called underdeveloped geography and unhealthy climate of the New World (Gerbi, 1946: 393; Gutiérrez, 1990: 106).

This line of argument was used to discredit *creole* attempts at dissolving a segregationist imperial policy of maintaining two 'republics', the Spanish and the Indian, and dismantling the indigenous hierarchy in order to secure native labour for *creole* economic needs. The circumstances surrounding one's birthplace and *creole* cultural links with the indigenous world formed the basis of European disdain for the New World and all its inhabitants. Such a sentiment was apparent from the remarks of Don Juan de Mañozca, a seventeenth-century Archbishop of Mexico: '. . . although the *creoles* do not have Indian blood in them, they have been weaned on the milk of Indian women, and are therefore, like the Indians, children of fear' (Israel, 1975: 116).

Mexican Women and the Nation-Building Project

Soon after Mexico gained political independence in 1821, both legal measures and the European ideology of liberalism were introduced to promote the development of a more egalitarian and united society to replace the racially based colonial system of stratification. Consequently, castes, slavery and privileges for the Indian nobility were excluded from the institutional organization of the newly created state. Mexico's first century as an independent entity was problematic: the new state underwent over forty changes of government between 1821 and 1876, faced two foreign invasions, Texas's secession and lost a considerable portion of its northern territory to the United States (1846–48).

The extent of the struggle to build the new independent republic was reflected in the limited number of foreign immigrants, with the exception of the arrival of some 10,000 Chinese towards the end of the nineteenth century (Monteon González and Trueba Lara, 1988: 22). Both political and economic factors discouraged European settlement. These factors included political instability; the Liberals' fierce defence of Mexican sovereignty against the French-inspired imposition of a Hapsburg emperor, Maximilian; a growing internal debt and lack of investment; a surplus of indigenous labour; and demographic pressures on land.

While 36 million European migrants were settling in the United States and Canada, and 8 million in Argentina and Brazil, only 8,000 to 10,000 Europeans migrated to Mexico and Central America between 1902 and 1914; although immigration was officially encouraged, the state of Mexico's economy continued to discourage European settlers (Torres, 1983: 35).

At the turn of the twentieth century, Mexico's was an export-led economy based on minerals, livestock and cashcrop production (Reynolds, 1970: 92). Foreign investment, mainly from Britain and the United States, did increase between 1877 and 1910; this helped to mobilize the indigenous labour force for railway construction and the exploitation of natural resources. With respect to the latter, mineral and oil exports thrived in the first four decades of the twentieth century to meet the demands of the industries established during World War I. This led to considerable industrial expansion, but given the sexual division of labour it was only of significance for the employment of Mexican males; women's social position continued to depend largely upon their cultural and racial origins. Education and skills were more evident among urban middle-class women who gradually entered the labour market as teachers, nurses and office workers. The majority of women, who had no access to education, had few such possibilities; they faced appalling conditions in low-paid jobs, prostitution and domestic service, and were largely dependent on male breadwinners (Soto, 1979: 5). The skills and trades of peasant and working-class women, normally from *mestizo* or indigenous backgrounds, remained largely unrecognized and unremunerated during this industrializing period. For example, women's salaries in the growing textile industry were one-quarter of those paid to men by oil companies.

The dictatorship of Porfirio Díaz (1876–1911) was overthrown by the Mexican Revolution which started in 1910. The revolution and its ideology were largely directed towards introducing constitutional amendments for presidential elections as well as wide-ranging land reforms and other social and civic guarantees. Due to the widespread chaos of the revolution, women experienced another violent period of rape, pillage and disruption to family life. As a result, women began to organize and defend their interests and those of the country in novel ways. In a united stand against the Díaz dictatorship, women of all classes and cultural backgrounds took up arms, formed resistance groups and fought side by side with men. For the first time, women also founded anti-establishment newspapers and journals in order to make a political contribution to rebuilding the nation. They also contributed to the debate concerning the protection and defence of the country against the foreign economic encroachments favoured by the Díaz administration (Soto, 1979: 130; Franco, 1989: 105).

But even after the violent turmoil of the revolution in the 1920s, political instability continued as did a number of regional uprisings. Moreover, Church and state were engaged in a bitter struggle through the latter's attempts to secularize important areas of national life which were traditionally under the Church's control, notably education. After a period of Catholic resistance and rebellion, especially in central and western parts of the country, a bilateral agreement was reached in 1929 and 1935 (Meyer, 1976: 385).

The so-called post-revolutionary governments engaged in formulating and implementing nation-building policies; these were based on considerably improving and extending mass communications, health, conscription and education, and on the legalization of all political parties. Government policies and new administrative institutions favoured economic recovery and sustained growth. By the 1930s some structural reforms were implemented; these centred on the nationalization of the railways and the oil industry as well as accelerating the progress of land reform.

The moral reconstruction of the country was encouraged through the formulation and spread of official Mexican nationalism. This twentieth-century ideology reconstituted the cult of the *mestizo*, the fusion of Spanish and Indian cultures, established as a cultural and ethnic yardstick which would act as a source of popular identification *vis-à-vis* a singular 'ethnic' nation. The ideology was thus directed at neutralizing pejorative views of the *mestizos* and their origins which had persisted since colonial times despite the increase in the *mestizo* population.

The nationalist ideology also had 'indigenist' overtones. This suggests the valorization and conservation of indigenous cultures, provided that indigenous peoples were prepared to assimilate themselves into national life in terms of *mestizo* dominance. Another expression of the nationalist programme was through the state's education policies: during the first two decades of the twentieth century, national reconstruction was to be facilitated through a policy of expanding education and literacy; primary school teachers – mostly female – were mobilized to teach the mass of the people (Blanco, 1977: 47).

Both ideology and policies were conceived as strategies for integrating indigenous ethnic groups through assimilation and inculcating the mores and values of *mestizo* culture. These included use of the Spanish language, adopting an urbanized way of life, identification with and veneration of national heroes, loyalty to state institutions and national symbols, defending the national sovereignty and pride in Mexico's achievements. Within this nationalist schema, there were no special provisions for the development or enhancement of other cultures, either Indian or migrant. This was understandable in the sense that foreign immigration, as has been noted, remained limited and official concerns rested with national reconstruction. New settlers were expected to tailor their traditions to Mexican nationalism which involved recognition of the Spanish language and heritage, and the 'glorification' of the indigenous mythological past.

With the outbreak of World War II, Mexico experienced a politically motivated migration from Europe comprising primarily Spaniards and Jews. In the case of the former, a significant number of intellectuals and well-educated professionals escaped to Mexico in 1939, following the end of the Spanish Civil War (Fagen, 1973: 7). These professionals were to play a significant role in reorganizing and enhancing Mexican academic and intellectual life, while revitalizing the Hispanic heritage of Mexican culture. The Jews were divided into three major communities: the Azhkenazi formed by Jews escaping Nazi aggression in Poland, Russia, Hungary, Lithuania and central Europe; the Sephardic community, including Jews from Greece, Turkey and the Balkans; and a community of Jews from Syria.

The Spanish exiles were on familiar ground in Mexico since they shared not only a common language with the majority of Mexicans but also their Hispanic traditions. Some rediscovered family businesses which had originated in the colony; they also held republican ideals and were sympathetic towards the Mexican Revolution of 1910. The degree of cultural incorporation of the exiles is evident from the fact that they neither favoured the indigenism of Mexican nationalism nor promoted Hispanic chauvinism which they considered to be reactionary (Fagen, 1973: 146).

Unlike the Spanish exiles, Jewish refugees found themselves a minority in a milieu imbued with Catholic values and mores, and the dominant trends of Mexican nationalism created a dilemma in the cultural integration of these settlers. The general pattern of Jewish integration was through their business expertise, but with the entry of future generations into the professions and important positions within those professions, the situation of the Jews as a cultural minority improved, and they have not abandoned their specific ethnic and religious identities (Herman, 1984: 16).

The integration of exiled Spaniards and Jews was generally successful with both groups attaining positions of high social status. This success was attributable to their shared situation as political exiles, family ties in the case of the Spanish refugees, as well as their business activities and entry into high-status professions. It is difficult to estimate the number and specific positions of Spanish and Jewish women migrants, but most likely they migrated as wives or relatives of male refugees, and their socio-economic status remained unchallenged or even improved with time.

The Economy, Migration and the Role of Women since World War II

From 1946 the government pursued a policy of import substitution industrialization. This development policy, which promoted large-scale urban industry and infrastructural expansion for the domestic market, was largely dependent on Mexico's abundant indigenous labour force. Consequently, manufacturing became the country's most important and fastest growing sector with the later addition of tourism. During the same period, population growth accelerated, and by the 1960s one-half of the population lived in urban centres. In the process, Mexico moved away from being mainly an exporter of raw materials and primary products to being a provider of manufactured goods and services such as tourism (King, 1970: 41).

The 'lost decade of the 1980s' was initiated, as the financial world faced a major crisis, when Mexico – the second largest debtor in Latin America after Brazil – defaulted on its debt repayments. A 'structural adjustment' programme was imposed on Mexico and the rest of the region by the International Monetary Fund. The so-called 'lost decade' had a dramatic effect on local incomes and material standards of living declined. At the beginning of the crisis, unemployment in Mexico doubled in the modern sector of the economy. Consequently, later employment was generated in low-productivity sectors and these were the only dynamic sectors capable of absorbing female labour. This meant increasing unemployment for women in the urban and modern sectors, and a serious erosion of the middle classes' welfare provisions.

Official policies encouraging economic self-sufficiency have increased Mexico's commercial ties with North American markets. The North American Free Trade Agreement (NAFTA), an ambitious 'common market' involving Canada, the United States and Mexico, came into force in 1994. This commercial project, conceived and dominated by transnational capital, has been subject to political pressures and censure in all three countries, while an a *priori* assessment of its functioning in terms of investment, labour and markets is difficult to gauge; once NAFTA is fully operational its impact should be felt in the industrial sectors of all the participating countries. The proposal in itself serves as a reflection of modern and recent links between transnational corporations, the transnational capitalist class and the transnational cultural ideology of consumerism (Sklair, 1993: 243).

NAFTA also marks a further episode in the often complex history of the United States's economic and political relationships with Mexico. This intricate history of suspicion and mutual hostility has involved territorial disputes, the violation of Mexican sovereignty, primarily in cases concerning drug smugglers and environmental problems, as well as emigration across the US border. One of the most heated disputes between the United States and Mexico involves the issue of legal and illegal migration; precedent-setting treaties between the two countries on this issue go back to 1945. In 1965, Mexico's 'Border Industrialization Programme' was created as a means to secure employment for Mexican citizens along the US border and to contribute to the recovery of the Mexican economy. At that time, Mexico's inflation rate was 50 per cent, debt servicing exceeded total foreign exchange earnings, unemployment was high and income distribution uneven (Seligson and Williams, 1981: 2–3). The programme provided an opportunity to attract foreign invest-ment and technology as well as to create large-scale employment opportunities. Joint US–Mexican programmes have relied heavily on the constraints of the Mexican economy and its incapacity to provide pro-ductive employment; they have thus depended on capitalizing on a reservoir of cheap Mexican labour.

A case in point involves the development in 1970 of the *maquiladora* industry – 'in-bond services', the second most important source of for-eign exchange after oil revenues. Originating in the Mexican border towns, the industry has now spread to non-border locations; by 1989 some 1,500 *maquilas* were dealing with electronics and the manufacture and assembly of equipment and products (Khosrow, 1990: 4). The socio-economic impact of *maquiladoras* has produced a large literature which reflects the complexity of the Mexican–US labour exchange processes. Debate has focused on the hiring of cheap female labour, whether women displace male workers and, if this is the case, why it has occurred – that is, what are the characteristics that transnational cor-porations expect from an 'ideal worker'? (Sklair, 1993: 172).

Within the *maquiladora* industry, rates of female employment have fluctuated due to the varying introduction of technology which usually favours the hiring of male workers. In 1970, 90 per cent of workers were women, by 1988 this had dropped to 51.6 per cent (Chrispin, 1990: 74). Industrialists and policy-makers, supporters of the view that the *maquiladora* industry provides an alternative means of integrating women into the formal Mexican economy, neglect to note the discrim-inatory practices involved in the hiring of low-income *mestiza* women and often single women with dependants. Since their emergence, border industries have undergone a process of technological expansion and diversification which has increased demands for skilled technicians and operators, and these opportunities have tended to benefit men at the expense of women (Sklair, 1993: 172). Moreover, while men are employed in better paid jobs in the motor industry, women have been relegated to performing more 'feminine' and more poorly remuner-ated tasks in the textile industry and routine assembly lines. Among the 'feminine' attributes which, it is argued, make women particularly suited to these tasks are: docility, dexterity, patience with routine, and a lack of interest in workers' rights. By and large, *maquiladoras* are not favouring 'feminine' attributes, rather they exploit the fact of a vulnerable pool of cheap unskilled labour, the most vulnerable of which are often poor women and youths; many have dependants and must be prepared to take any job which provides an income, no matter how low (Tiano, 1987: 35).

The *maquiladora* industry provides a graphic example of how the internationalization of capital is affecting the Mexican female labour market, as well as the role of North American investment strategies in the Mexican economy. Yet *maquiladoras* are but one example of the myriad relationships, exchanges and conflicts which have characterized the interlinked histories of Mexico and the United States. This history has been dramatically played out along 3,000 kilometres of shared border, one side of which is populated by a large, vulnerable and unstable labour force.

The large-scale industrialization of the 1940s initiated a massive expansion of the labour force; for example, 5.8 million people entered the labour market in 1940, 8.2 million in 1950, 11.3 in 1960, 12 in 1970 and 22 in 1980 (Esquivel Hernández, 1989: 93). Whereas in 1940 women represented only 2.2 per cent of the economically active population (EAP), by 1980 they represented 27.8 per cent. Despite the significant incorporation of females into the EAP over four decades, sustained industrialization did not alter the types of economic activities women were engaged in (Chant, 1991: 44). In 1980, 12 women in every 100 of the EAP were in the primary sector, 33 in the secondary and 37 in non-specified activities (Esquivel Hernández, 1989: 95). Noticeably, the major proportion of the female EAP continues to be absorbed by the tertiary sector, in non-specified activities like domestic labour, street vending and prostitution. Moreover, the employment of women in highly paid jobs decreased from 13 per cent in 1960 to 1.29 per cent in 1980 (Esquivel Hernández, 1989: 97). In the 1980s unemployment of female workers was growing in the public sector as a result of an increase in competition between men and women and a decline in the urban labour market.

The incorporation of women into varying productive sectors depends to a certain extent on their degree of acculturation and access to education. The ideology of nation-building implied that the use of ethnicity as a differentiating criterion would completely disappear from national discourse, policies, the media and school textbooks. Nonetheless, the daily experiences of working ethnic women reflects the importance still assigned to race by Mexican society. In general, poor indigenous females migrating from rural to urban areas, who are unskilled and barely literate, find work as domestic servants or street vendors of produce with low profit margins such as fruit and sweets, while single young Indian women or acculturated but poor *mestizo* women are employed in households. Domestic service is a stereotypical reminder of the socio-cultural inferiority fostered during the colonial period. As a result, only unskilled illiterate and, in many cases, mono-lingual and politically unrepresented women are engaged in these activities.

Migratory patterns normally involve indigenous women in search of an income, and they are often engaged in the tertiary and informal sectors as street vendors and domestic workers. There are three identifiable patterns of migration: (1) a small group of young men and women who migrate in the hope of upward social mobility; (2) young men who for varying reasons are unemployable in the primary sector; and (3) a large group of men and women in search of an income or other means of subsistence simply as a means of survival for their families. Indigenous women usually subscribe to this last pattern often in the form of seasonal and temporary migration (Arizpe, 1987: 228). As urban living conditions increasingly deteriorate, the provision of homes and services falls ever further behind demand while the population and land prices continue to rise (Ward, 1990: 173). Furthermore, wide-spread pollution and the increasing length of journeys to work reflect an attenuated urban situation incapable of satisfying the basic needs of rural migrants.

The situation is no better in rural areas: Indian and peasant *mestizo* women, who bear the burden of domestic work, are increasingly join-ing the masses of day-labourers due to a crisis in agriculture during the 1970s. The crisis was through the prioritizing of economic develop-ment at the expense of alleviating low wages and growing unemployment among the rural population. In 1980, one-third of the 4.5 million agricultural labourers were women (Leahy, 1986: 85); the domestic work of rural women consists not only of housework, but also unpaid agricultural labour on the family plot and employment as casual day-labourers. The lack of services and infrastructure in many rural areas means that Indian women also have to collect fuel and water for household consumption (personal communication: Roselia Jiménez Pérez, November 12, 1992).

The majority of the secretaries, teachers, administrative staff and nurses working in the modern urban sectors are likely to be descen-dants of *mestizo* people, to the extent that their degree of acculturation conforms to a 'national standard'; that is, they are Spanish speakers, identify themselves with Hispanic values and traditions, and are Christian. This large group of women have received some formal train-ing that at least provides them with the opportunity of qualifying for a minimal salary. In Mexico City, primary teachers are predominantly female (74.1 per cent); in rural areas, where teaching denotes social mobility and status, women are obliged to compete with men and thus their representation is lower (57 per cent) (Vega Valdés, 1989: 587).

In sharp contrast to the huge mass of anonymous women, there is a select group of elite, educated women of European heritage – or at least without any evident vestige of indigenous culture or language. These women, who occupy high government posts or are academics, artists and writers, at least have a voice of their own. While they do not suffer from racial discrimination, they are in the position of a minority within academia. Their major problem revolves around their subordinate position *vis-à-vis* men; four women out of every 10 applicants are employed as academics in higher education (Censo del Personal Académico, 1983), and the highest concentration of female academics is at Mexico's premier university – the National University of Mexico. But while women are over-represented in nursing (70.6 per cent), they are poorly represented in the so-called male disciplines; for example, only 5.6 per cent of engineers are women (Carreras, 1989: 614). The minority position of women prevents them from negotiating for better conditions; it is also reflected in the failure of the male world to recognize the body of knowledge produced by women.

A comprehensive ethnographic study of a wealthy industrialist family over five generations, the Gómez family, highlights the profile of upper-class women in contemporary Mexico. The family identify themselves with Catholic ideology, trace their cultural heritage and ancestry to Spain, and 'equate white skin colour with high social status' (Lomnitz Adler and Pérez Lizaur, 1987: 195). Women from this socioeconomic stratum are wives and mothers and do not engage in independent economic activity. Men and women who marry into the family are expected to be affluent and, obviously, race is a determining factor in these alliances.

The conditions of this small upper-class segment of white women contrasts radically with those of the majority of indigenous women. The dark appearance of the latter, their lack of education and their loyalty to non-European traditions and languages assign them a highly marginalized position in Mexican society. In the more flexible middle strata, a wide range of so-called *mestizos*, both male and female, can be found spread across a wide spectrum of economic activities; and they hold varying levels of education, training and specialization, as well as political representation.

The socio-cultural position of the *mestizos* is based on an important matrix: Spanish as the natal language or at least fluency in Spanish, formal education and an identification with particular cultural and ideological elements provided via the standardized school system. Strict classification on the basis of race is problematic, since most

mestiza women have 'dark' skin colour. Thus, the ambiguous and misleading criterion of 'good presentation' is required as prerequisite for
any employment other than that of domestic work. Such criteria as
physical appearance, dress code and linguistic facility are all explicitly
utilized in determining an applicant suitability for employment.

Political Protest and the Response of Women

The Mexican political system has enjoyed relative political stability
since the foundation of the governing Revolutionary Institutional Party
(PRI) in 1929. This party has ruled and dominated political life at the
expense of the development of alternative democratic structures.
Electoral campaigns are tightly controlled by the ruling party, as was
clearly shown during the 1988 and 1994 presidential elections when
computer-based fraud and media manipulation (exploiting the climate
of violence produced by the southern uprising of 1994 and the recent
assassination of official party leaders) ensured a PRI victory. The organization of the PRI is characterized by corporatism and
authoritarianism; for instance, the PRI maintains or establishes clien-
telist links encompassing the nation's three most important electorates:
workers, peasants and a loosely defined 'popular' sector. The PRI is
thus able to manipulate the unions, agrarian organizations and some
popular movements and associations.

The corporatist urban, rural and popular structures of the PRI are
always in a position to commandeer, coerce and capitalize on campaigns and demands emerging from the grass roots of society. In 1979,
when Mexican women began to articulate their political views and
demands for rights as part of a feminist agenda, through the organization of independent groups and associations, the PRI also decided
there was a 'need to increase women's participation in public life'
(Poniatowska, 1988: 11).

Although the PRI has a 'feminist section' and more women are
employed in important public sector positions, some women's organizations and campaigns have successfully initiated strategies to
circumvent the PRI's stranglehold; they have also remained independent of other political parties when their rights or demands have been
threatened. Several opposition parties, mainly the right-wing National
Action Party and the left-wing-orientated Party of the Democratic
Revolution, have ceased being mere pressure groups and, with the election of opposition governors and senators in 1988 and 1990, these
parties have become real political alternatives. Moreover, some
women's groups have succeeded in having their claims incorporated
into the policies of opposition parties.

One way of comprehending the role of Mexican women in the

existing political structure is to examine the negative stereotypes with respect to any form of female political opinion. A common belief prevails that women rarely participate in politics; for example, a 1952 survey carried out in Mexico City found that only 25 per cent of the women interviewed 'used to talk of politics at least occasionally', compared with 55 per cent of men, while only 8 per cent of women, compared with 23 per cent of men, had sought to influence legislation (Jaquette, 1975: 201). Yet in 1958, when Mexican women voted for the first time in presidential elections, the percentage of the total population who voted rose to 23.14 per cent from 13.38 per cent in the previous election (González Casanova, 1976: 289). This increment made clear women's potential as voters, a fact that was made visible by the female vote's monopolization of the official networks of clientelism and patronage. In fact, women's suffrage had been delayed in light of their alleged links with the Catholic Church during the implementation of the state's secular nation-building policies. This was a deliberate attempt to counteract the Church's dominance in the colonial period, and women and Catholicism were seen as allied against a male-dominated state. One consequence of this 'conspiracy' was the fabrication of a stereotype suggesting that women were more interested in family matters than the discussion or the exercise of politics. The latter, in fact, was seen as an exclusively male concern.

Women have challenged their traditional family role by involving themselves in campaigns, strikes and assemblies, and they have also created their own organizations which publicize themselves in print, fora, petitions and other forms of persuasion. Mexican women's styles of political action can be observed at two levels: the theoretical and critical feminism of middle-class women, and the substantial mobilizations of working-class and indigenous women, and the latter have not necessarily emerged as an adjunct to an earlier theoretical feminism. Largely due to the variety of campaigns and interests arising from their varying socio-cultural and class positions, realization of the demands of women's organizations has been extremely uneven. Nevertheless, middle-class feminist groups have supported popular movements, such as the demands of women living in squalid urban conditions, and working women who have struggled to form trades unions (Lamas, 1986: 337; Enloe, 1989: 171).

Mexican feminist discourse is now recognized, and is characterized as a 'movement of opinion of educated middle-class women' (Acosta, 1981: 234). Today there are about a dozen feminist groups in Mexico which encompass a variety of feminist perspectives, and feminist sections can also be found in trade unions and political parties. Respect for feminist discourse has been achieved through the support and assistance of educated women. Fora have been held, consciousness has been raised, public participation has grown and feminist journals are being published; the result is that the mass media can no longer ignore or neglect women's views. Most serious publications have sections or special supplements addressing a wide range of socio-economic issues which directly affect women's lives; for example, Mexico City's most influential newspaper, *La Jornada*, carries a feminist section, the 'Doble Jornada'. The opinion-forming role and the coverage of these publications has helped to instil a sense of confidence in non-educated women far beyond the confines of their nominal readership. Working-class women are now demanding their rights and attempting to stem the violence and sexual harassment which they undergo in both their public and private lives. The feminist journal *Fem*, founded in 1976, has played a prominent role with respect to documenting women's campaigns and organizations.

But feminism, as it is articulated and operationalized, is nevertheless linked somewhat ambiguously with the objectives and demands of working-class women. Briefly, much of the content of feminist discourse is concerned with the wholesale exploitation of women. It is 'not contentious nor individualistic and it is not against men' (Sefchovich, 1980: 104). The appalling living conditions of the majority of Mexican women as well as the lack of employment protection determine that feminist strategies have collectivist goals. Strategies thus involve demands to end poverty and increase basic services such as adequate housing and public services. This discourse, which seeks to protect women against all forms of sexism and oppression that presently characterize women's lives, is linked to the left wing or to the liberal platform of the official party, the PRI.

A somewhat different agenda has been presented by the campaigns launched by urban working-class women. These actions, which have been supported and articulated by feminist middle-class women and feminist journals, include demands for union recognition and employment protection; solidarity with male colleagues engaged in labour conflicts; public demonstrations against human rights violations and the persecution of opposition militants: information on dissidents who are '*desaparecidos*', the disappeared, and the release of political prisoners (Acevedo et al., 1980: 112). These largely urban expressions of dissent emerged in the 1970s and intensified during the 1980s as a result of the economic crisis, the external debt and the unilateral implementation of development policies insisted upon by the international financial institutions (Contardo et al., 1990: 242).

A significant case with respect to union and labour demands concerns the actions of female ticket sellers in the metropolitan underground of Mexico City who demanded union rights and the same benefits as men. In 1976, 60 per cent of Mexico's female telephone operators went on strike for improved working conditions, union rights and respect of formal contractual agreements; they also demanded female representation and voting rights in elections to the union's executive committees. Examples of women's solidarity with men were occasioned by labour disputes during the construction of major infra-structural projects. These large projects have forced large numbers of men to live and work in intolerable conditions, and women have orga-nized public demonstrations demanding the introduction of better working conditions for their husbands and relatives. Feminist demands for work-place rights have also included the sporadic organization of prostitutes demanding improved medical facilities. Lastly, women have led campaigns to stop the government's human rights violations and to call for the release of 'disappeared' militants.

Rural movements are also being initiated or supported by women, but feminist support has been less forthcoming where the agenda has not exclusively involved female issues. Moreover, the campaigns involv-ing indigenous women have emerged without any prior feminist input, such as the movements addressing the defence of collective ethnic and territorial rights.

Some Indian women have resented the interference of middle-class feminism *vis-à-vis* indigenous politics, and this has led to misunder-standings between indigenous women and urban feminists. To simplify, indigenous women have other political priorities from those of the middle-class feminists, such as land rights and the defence of their cul-tures. Other issues, such as the burden of patriarchy, indigenous sexism, rights over the body, and domestic violence, might be discussed by indigenous women, but they do not constitute a salient demand or a movement as they do for urban feminists. Most probably, indigenous women could incorporate the issues that concern urban feminism, once they have realized both recognition and respect of their basic needs for cultural survival.

Over the past decade, and in response to the celebrations to mark the five hundredth anniversary of the 'discovery of America', there has been an upsurge in the number of indigenous organizations, campaigns and demonstrations. These autonomous initiatives, framed within the parameters of indigenous thinking, make it possible to identify a revival of indigenous values and ideas which have long been dormant or repressed. They are, in fact, initiating a new political mobilization of indigenous opinion which is by degrees rejecting the state's paternalism and integrationist policies.

The participation of Indian women in this indigenous revival is par-ticularly striking; given that indigenous opinion is still mainly ignored by the larger society, Indian women have even more limited means at their disposal to articulate their views and interests than do their male colleagues. Some organizations as well as national and continental fora have now been established entirely by Indian women, such as the First National Congress of Indigenous Women, and the First Meeting of Indigenous Women of South and Central America in 1992. They are occasions for discussing and exchanging opinions and strategies that can be tailored to the specific cultural identities of indigenous women *vis-à-vis* the larger indigenous world and the rest of society (*Boletín SAAIC*, 1992 (1–2)).

The founding of independent publishing outlets for indigenous peoples, such as *Revista Etnias* in 1987 and *Nuestra sabiduría* 1991, has facilitated the presentation of a diverse range of indigenous women's perspectives. These include testimonies and articles written by women who for the first time are establishing reputations through the written word. New Mayan women writers are gaining recognition in the literary world due to their vigour and creativity which is aimed at the collective recovery of their ancestral cultures and traditions (Gutiérrez, 1993 : 15).

In general, Indian women are participating in the collective defence of their natural resources, culture, and human and ethnic rights. These have recently been advanced by the example of the 1993 Nobel Peace Prize winner Rigoberta Menchú Tum, a Mayan-Quiché refugee from Guatemala now living in Mexico. Feminist groups of educated women have supported and honoured her achievements in a number of fora and publications which have debated the role of indigenous women in the struggle for human rights, such as the Week for the Dignity and Rights of the Indian Peoples, Mexico City, March 29 to April 2, 1993.

Through these discussions, held within the framework of the United Nations 1993 International Year of Indigenous Peoples, feminist opinion and critiques of male violence, patriarchy, racial discrimination and sexual harassment were aired. The strength of this feminist critique was that it addressed the double subordination of Indian women in both indigenous and non-indigenous societies. While indigenous women may articulate these issues, their political priorities – they argue – rest on their need to reinforce the cultural constituencies which they represent.

In order to adequately measure the significance of the Indian women's struggle, one must consider the role assigned to the family in the durability of Indian cultures (Arizpe, 1978). The Indian peoples of Mexico are particularly disadvantaged in all areas of national life in comparison with the dominant majority. Political non-representation, economic exploitation, socio-cultural subordination and racial discrimination help to explain the decision by Indian women to set their political participation within an ethnic agenda. Given the extent of the discrimination against all indigenous groups, Indian women feel that to organize individually or to formulate a position irrespective of their menfolk would be politically divisive. Hence, it is not uncommon to find indigenous women advancing statements in their struggle for political emancipation which avoid the politics of gender: 'We have only one way, a common destiny and the same struggle to carry out' (Pérez Jiménez, 1987: 15). A similar view arose from the pronouncements of various groups of Indian women at the First Meeting of Indigenous Women of South and Central America in 1992: 'We indigenous women are advancing along with indigenous men in our struggle for the right to our territories and the control of natural resources, for the respect of our traditional laws. autonomy and self-government' (*Boletín SAAIC*, 1992 (1–2): 30).

It is well known that across all cultures, women are the key to the socialization and continuation of values, traditions, languages and customs which initially derive from the family. In the case of subordinated cultures, this role is even more pronounced in that it guarantees the survival and reproduction of the group in a constantly hostile and discriminatory environment. Indigenous women understand that they possess a certain cultural authority within the family; for them to undermine this position through the adoption of an alien ideology would be counterproductive, and such a move would lead to a loss of influence and respect among their families and communities. The following claim reflects the view of those indigenous women who have experienced political awareness and organizations: 'We do not allow non-indigenous women of bourgeois mentality to make decisions for us or become spokeswomen of our thinking – between them and ourselves there are great inequalities' (Pérez Jiménez, 1987: 16).

Conclusion

The modern Mexican nation traces its ethnic and cultural roots to both the pre-Hispanic and colonial periods. These cultural epochs gave rise to complex patterns of ethnic and racial diversity which still influence Mexico's present socio-economic structure. The cultural complexity of the modern Mexican nation stresses the survival of indigenous ethnic culture, albeit much diminished, fragmented and assimilated by both colonial and post-Independence nation-building policies. Government policies seeking to achieve economic development and modernization have focused on the ideal of creating a culturally unified nation. This long-term project has not produced the homogenization and integration of Mexico's diverse female population. On the contrary, there are at least three identifiable strata of women who can be distinguished in terms of race, ethnic origin and cultural assimilation; these characteristics determine their degree of education and training as well as their class position. Feminism as an ideology articulated by educated groups of middle-class women has helped to support the campaigns and demands of working-class women and, to a lesser extent, indigenous women.

In brief, *mestiza* women are engaged in all types of formal and informal economic activities; and their capacity to undertake these activities depends on their degree of acculturation as well as their levels of education. White or settler women with European ancestry who have links with business families or who are involved in academic activities or the public sector are more likely to occupy the few high-income jobs available to women. Finally, the vulnerable situation of Indian women demands that any analysis notes the proximity of these women to their communities. It is these links which ensure the survival of group identity and language. If loyalty to their traditions and cultures persist among Indian women, this is due to an awareness of their marginalization in a discriminatory environment, a scenario where the only work available is as domestic workers or urban street vendors and perhaps occasionally as workers in the *maquiladora* industry.

The correlation of both cultural origins and economic position in the situation of *mestiza*, white and indigenous women does not always provide an accurate indicator of political awareness. Short-term urban movements have developed the militancy of rural *mestiza* women, but Indian women are fighting for ethnic and territorial rights as the bases for the survival of their entire culture. In the case of indigenous politics, there is a radical tendency on the part of indigenous women to reject the so-called middle-class feminism advanced by educated and professional groups.

These ethnic and racial divisions among women do not invalidate the legitimacy and integrity of feminist discourse in helping to address the problems of male violence and patriarchy. Rather they reflect the fact that women may have differing priorities and interests when they become politically conscious and engaged in political activity.

With the obvious exception of the colonial period, immigration to Mexico has been limited. The strength of Mexican nationalism and its lack of constitutional guarantees for the development of separate immigrant cultures has determined the fact that minority settlers have been incorporated, if not assimilated, into Mexican society and culture. This situation demonstrates the official stress given to *mestizo* ideology as the framework for unifying the different ethnic groups into a modern nation-state.

Indigenous groups have managed to influence public opinion, especially academics and the highly educated. The results are as yet ambivalent, with the exception of the unprecedented change in 1993 to Article 4 of the Constitution which refers only to the fact of Indian people as forming part of the 'pluri-cultural composition of the Mexican nation'. Consequently, there exists a political willingness among the educated to encourage the development of ethnic diversity, both Indian and immigrant; if such a multicultural agenda were to be accepted nationwide, then the ideology of *mestizaje* would become a thing of the past.

References

Acevedo, Marta, Lamas, Marta, and Liguori, Ana Luisa (1980) 'Una bolsita de cal por las que van de arena', *Fem: 10 años de periodismo feminista*, 13 (April–May). México: Planeta. pp. 111–48.

Acosta, Mariclaire (1981) 'Perspectivas políticas del feminismo en América Latina', *Fem: 10 años de periodismo feminista*, 17 (February–March). México: Planeta. pp. 182–8.

Arizpe, Lourdes (1978) 'Familia, desarrollo y autoritarianismo', *Fem: 10 años de periodismo feminista*, 7 (April–June), México: Planeta. pp. 79–88.

Arizpe, Lourdes (1987) *Migracion, etnicismo y cambio económico*. México: El Colegio de México.

Arrom, Silvia M. (1985) *The Women of Mexico City 1790–1885*. Stanford: Stanford University Press.

Basave Benítez, Agustin (1992) *México Mestizo: análisis del nacionalismo mexicano en torno a la mestizofilia de Andrés Molina Enríquez*. México: Fondo de Cultura Económica.

Blanco, José Joaquin (1977) *Se llamaba Vasconcelos*. Mexico City: Fondo de Cultura Económica.

Boletín SAAIC (1992) (1–2). Berkeley, California.

Bonilla, Adela (1993) 'Free trade, unfree workers in Mexico', paper, Women, Development and Human Rights Conference, Madrid, February 26–7.

Borah, Woodrow and Cook, Sherbune (1963) *The Aboriginal Population of Central Mexico on the Eve of the Conquest*. Berkeley: University of California Press.

Carreras, Mercedes (1989) 'Pormenores del trabajo de las mujeres en la academia', in Jennifer Cooper (ed.), *Fuerza de trabajo femenina urbana en México: participación económica y política*. México: Universidad Nacional Autónoma de México y Porrúa.

Castelló Yturbide, Teresa (1990) 'La indumentaria en las castas del mestizaje', *Artes de México: la pintura de castas*, 8: 73–9.

Censo del Personal Académico (1983) Dirección General de Asuntos del Personal Académico. México: Universidad Nacional Autónoma de México.

Chant, Sylvia (1991) *Women and Survival in Mexican Cities: Perspectives on Gender, Labour, Markets and Low-Income Households*. Manchester: Manchester University Press.

Chrispin, Barbara R. (1990) 'Employment and manpower in the maquiladora industry: reaching maturity', in F. Khosrow (ed.), *The Maquiladora Industry: Economic Solution or Problem?* New York and London: Praeger. pp. 71–90.

Contardo, Eduardo, Benítez, Manuel and Cordova, Raúl (1990) 'Luchas y conflictos', in *América Latina hoy*. México: Universidad Nacional Autónoma de México y Siglo XXI. pp. 241–84.

Cuevas, Mariano (1928) *Historia de la iglesia en México*. El Paso: Editorial Revista Católica.

Díaz del Castillo, Bernal (1963) *The Conquest of New Spain*. Harmondsworth: Penguin.

Enloe, Cynthia (1989) *Bananas, Beaches and Bases: Making Feminist Sense of International Politics*. London: Pandora.

Esquivel Hernández, Maria Teresa (1989) 'Mujer y modernización: análisis estadístico', *Sociológica*, 10: 81–107.

Fagen, Patricia (1973) *Exiles and Citizens: Spanish Republicans in Mexico*. Austin: University of Texas Press.

Franco, Jean (1989) *Plotting Women: Gender and Representations in Mexico*. London: Verso.

Frucht, Richard (1971) *Black Society in the New World*. New York: Random House.

Gallagher, Miriam A. (1976) 'The Indian nuns of Mexico City's Monasterio of Corpus Christi 1724–1821', in A. Lavrín (ed.), *Latin American Women: Historical Perspectives*. Westport: Greenwood. pp. 150–73.

Gerbi, Antonello (1946) *Viejas polémicas sobre el nuevo mundo: en el umbral de una conciencia americana*. Lima: Banco de Crédito del Perú.

Gibson, Charles (1960) 'The Aztec aristocracy in Colonial Mexico', *Comparative Studies in Society and History*, 2 (January): 169–97.

González Casanova, Pablo (1976) *La democracia en México*, 8th edition. México: ERA.

Gutiérrez, Natividad (1990) 'Memoria indígena en el nacionalismo incipiente de México y Perú', *Estudios Interdisciplinarios de América Latina y el Caribe*, 2 (July–December): 99–113.

Gutiérrez, Natividad (1993) 'Escritoras mayas', *La Jornada Semanal*, February 14.

Herman, Donald L. (1984) *The Latin American Community of Israel*. London: Praeger.

Israel, J.I. (1975) *Race, Class and Politics in Colonial Mexico, 1610–1670*. Oxford: Oxford University Press.

Jaquette, Jane S. (1975) 'La mujer latinoamericana y la política: paradigmas feministas e investigaciones comparativas por cultura', in *La mujer en América Latina*. México: Sep Setentas.

Khosrow, Fatemi (ed.) (1990) *The Maquiladora Industry: Economic Solution or Problem?*, New York and London: Praeger.

King, Timothy (1970) *Mexico: Industrialization and Trade Policies since 1940*. Oxford: Oxford University Press.

Knight, Alan (1990) 'Racism, revolution and indigenismo', in R. Graham (ed.), *The Idea of Race in Latin America 1870–1940*. Austin: University of Texas Press. pp. 71–113.

Lamas, Marta (1986) 'El movimiento de las costureras', *Fem: 10 años de periodismo feminista en México*, 45 (April–May). México: Planeta. pp. 336–50.

Lavrín, Asunción (1978) 'Women in convents: their economic and social role in Colonial Mexico', in B.A. Carroll (ed.), *Liberating Women's History: Theoretical and Critical Essays*. Chicago: Chicago University Press.

Leahy, Margaret (1986) *Development Strategies and Status of Women: a Comparative Study of the US, Mexico, USSR and Cuba*. Boulder: Lynne Rienner.

Lomnitz Adler, Larissa and Pérez Lizaur, Marisol (1987) *A Mexican Elite Family, 1820–1980: Kinship, Class and Culture*. Princeton: Princeton University Press.

Maclachlan, C. and Rodríguez, J. (1983) *The Forging of the Cosmic Race: a Reinterpretation of Colonial Mexico*. Los Angeles: University of California Press.

Marshall, C.E. (1963) 'The birth of the *mestizo* in New Spain', in *Hispanic American Review*, 43: 161–84.

Meyer, Jean (1976) *La Cristiada*. tI. México: Siglo XXI.

Monteón González, H. and Trueba Lara, José Luis (1988) *Chinos y anti-chinos en México: documentos para su estudio*. Guadalajara: Unidad Editorial.

Mörner, Magnus (1967) *Race Mixture in the History of Latin America*. Boston: Little, Brown.

Muriel, Josefina (1963) *Las indias caciques de Corpus Christi*. México: Universidad Nacional Autónoma de México.

Padden, Robert C. (1976) *The Hummingbird and the Hawk; Conquest and Sovereignty in the Valley of Mexico*. New York: Harper & Row.

Palmer, Colin A. (1976) *Slaves of the White God: Blacks in Mexico*. Cambridge: Cambridge University Press.

Pérez Jiménez, Aurora (1987) 'La mujer en el contexto de la lucha indígena', in *Revista Etnias*, 1 (1): 15–17.

Pescatello. Ann (ed.) (1976) *The African in Latin America*. New York: Knopf.

Poniatowska, Elena (1988) 'Fem o el rostro desaparecido de Alaíde Foppa', *Fem: 10 años de periodismo feminista en México*, México: Planeta. pp. 7–21.

Reynolds, Clark W. (1970) *The Mexican Economy: Twentieth-Century Structure and Growth*. New Haven: Yale University Press.

Rubio, Luid (1992) 'Japan in Mexico: a changing pattern', in Kantam, Purcell S. and Immerman M. Robert (eds), *Japan and Latin America in the New Global Order*. London: Lynne Rienner Publishers. pp. 69–100.

Seed, Patricia (1988) *To Love, Honor and Obey in Colonial Mexico: Conflicts over Marriage Choice 1574–1821*. Stanford: Stanford University Press.

Seligson, Mitchell A. and Williams, Edward (eds) (1981) *Maquiladoras and Migration: Workers in the Mexico–United States Border Industrialization Program*. Austin: Mexico–United States Research Program – University of Texas.

Sefchovich, Sara (1980) 'América Latina: la mujer en lucha', *Fem: 10 años de periodismo feminista*, 12 (January–February). México: Planeta. pp. 102–4.

Sklair, Leslie (1993) *Assembling for Development: The Maquila Industry in Mexico and the United States*. Center for US-Mexican Studies: UCSD.

Smith, Anthony D. (1986) *The Ethnic Origins of Nations*. Oxford: Blackwell.

Soto, Shirlene Ann (1979) *The Mexican Woman: A Study of Her Participation in the Revolution, 1910–1940*. Palo Alto: Research Associates.

Tiano, Susan B. (1987) 'Women's work and unemployment in northern Mexico', in Vicki L. Ruiz and S.B. Tiano (eds), *Women on the US–Mexico Border*. Manchester, MA: Allen & Unwin.

Torres, Diana (1983) 'Migraciones internacionales entre paises de América Latina', in *Migraciones latinas y formación de la nación latinoamericana*, Caracas: Instituto de Alto Estudios de América Latina. pp. 469–479.

Vega Valdés, María Eugenia (1989) 'Las maestras de primaria del Distrito Federal: hacía un perfil sociológico', in *Fuerza de trabajo femenina urbana en México: participación económica y política*. México: Universidad Nacional Autónoma de México and Porrúa.

Ward, Peter (1990) *Mexico City: The Production and Reproduction of an Urban Environment*. London: Belhaven Press.

Warner, Judith Ann (1990) 'The sociological impact of maquiladoras', in F. Khosrow (ed.), *The Maquiladora Industry: Economic Solution or Problem?* New York and London: Praeger. pp. 183–99.

7

Five Centuries of Gendered Settler Society: Conquerors, Natives and Immigrants in Peru

Sarah A. Radcliffe

'Being sons of the conquerors of that empire [of Peru] and with native mothers . . . yet neither through the merits of their fathers nor by the nature and inheritance of their mothers and grandfathers, did they obtain anything.

(Inca Garcilaso de la Vega (seventeenth century) quoted in Brading, *The First American*, p. 268)

Fundamental to a settler society dynamic are the ways in which women and men articulate class and ethnic distinctions, and how in turn they are placed in national society. This chapter examines the ways in which gender, ethnicity and class constitute Peruvian citizens with distinct relationships with labour markets, laws and culture. The gendering of ethnic and class relations in Peruvian society reveals the inadequacy of dichotomous categories for the analysis of Peruvian society, as miscegenation, regional differences and various ethnic groups contributed to a complex situation. Debates around being 'Peruvian' have focused on the role of female natives and later black female slaves.

Peru's society throughout its modern history has been sharply divided along lines of race, ethnicity and class. Labour market participation, authority and status depend on complex race/ethnic/class hierarchies, interrelated in practice and images. Many of these hierarchies originated with the foundation of the Spanish colonial empire in the Americas after 1492. As the centre for the Spanish colonial empire for some 250 years, Peru was at the forefront of colonial labour arrangements, importing racialized labour and elaborating colonial discourses around race, gender and class. As elsewhere in the Americas, Peru was densely populated with indigenous groups which, despite suffering dramatic demographic collapse after conquest, remained a significant pool of exploitable labour. As in other Latin American countries, the development of sugar and cotton plantations on the coast depended on black slaves and then Asian labourers.

Despite these features of Peruvian colonial society, the term 'settler society' has not been widely utilized. By contrast, the sustained unequal relationship between a colonizing group and subordinate populations is discussed in terms of internal colonialism. Developed largely by Mexican sociologists and political scientists in the 1960s, internal colonialism argued that colonialism in culturally and racially heterogeneous situations created 'societies within societies', where a dominant ethnic group administered economic domination over spatially separated ethnic groups providing commodities and cheap labour (Kay, 1989). Internal colonialism usefully points to the organization of groups across space, along lines of race/ethnicity and class, yet it does not tend to consider the very varied positions of non-conquering immigrants, such as black slaves, Asian workers and other Europeans. Given its relatively early independence, the question arises whether Peru can be characterized as a settler society. The continuation of a society politically and socially 'fractured' (Weitzer, 1990: xi) along ethnic lines suggests a settler society remained in place after independence from Spain in 1821, although it can be usefully considered both as a case of internal colonialism and as a settler society. The settler society status of Peru is thus not simply a phenomenon of the last 100 years, but rather the result of a continuous process of migration and settlement.

Fundamental to the gendering of different racial and ethnic groups was a notion of the spatial distribution of various demographic groups over the territory of Peru. In other words, between 1532 and the 1990s strong images and discourses existed regarding geographical locations of different population groups. Although in many cases these 'mental maps' were regional, distinguishing white/*mestizo*/black coastal regions from *mestizo*/'Indian' highlands, and native Amazonia, they also occurred on a smaller scale. For example, urban areas were often divided along racial or ethnic lines, with different neighbourhoods and streets being associated with specific groups. Such geographical separations were not directly inscribed into colonial and republican government legislation (with minor exceptions). However, throughout Peru's history, the indirect effects of social, political and legal structures has been to associate particular groups with specific areas. In this sense it was not an enforced separation of groups, but a complex discourse about the appropriateness of certain geographical environments for 'their' populations.

The formation of racial/ethnic distributions owes much to the utilization of different groups' labour for distinct purposes in the colonial period and to a lesser extent in the republican era. For this reason, the organization of territory in Peru has been a continuous process of shaping power relations by various means: territory and power have been intimately connected through the spatial arrangements of constituent populations. Powerful groups gained central locations, close to political and administrative structures, while less powerful groups were allocated to areas which did not threaten elites, or were separated into smaller groups and located in marginal areas. Where close proximity has been permitted, it has involved close supervision and control over subordinate populations, such as in plantations under slavery or in the domestic sphere with servants. As discussed below, this association of certain groups with power and place was gendered.

Pre-Columbian Peru: Diversity and Conquest

The Inca empire, itself an amalgam of diverse ethnic groups, was a complex, hierarchical and highly differentiated society. When the Spanish arrived in the Americas, the Inca state encompassed 14 million people, making it the largest empire in the continent. The empire had grown through conquest and trade, incorporating groups into its state religion. In the course of growth, the Inca state articulated notions of power and authority in terms of gender and ethnicity. As Irene Silverblatt argues, the Inca state perceived itself as a masculine conqueror from 'outside', overthrowing local 'femininized' societies, which were thereby made subordinate (Silverblatt, 1987). The warrior state organized the efficient collection of tribute in labour and goods from agricultural and herding communities up to 1,000 miles away, goods which underpinned further conquest and consumption by an elite. In turn, territorial control was exerted through the forced movement of different ethnic groups, as 'colonizers' were sent into new areas for trade and agriculture, initiating a relation between ethnicity, power and place which has continued through Peruvian history.

Spanish Colonial Peru, 1532–1821

Through its discourse of conquest and submission, the Inca empire expressed power in terms of gender, class and ethnic hierarchies in a way recognizable to medieval Spaniards. Themselves recently 'victorious' over Moorish and Jewish populations in the Iberian peninsula, Spaniards instituted a colonial settler state. Within this state, *limpieza de sangre* (purity of blood, codified into law in the mid-sixteenth century) and white European origin became the markers of status, and the means for access to the central sources of power and prestige, namely Indian labour, land and Catholic legitimacy. Pizarro's conquest of Peru was carried out by a small band of 180 Spaniards and Indian soldiers brought from Honduras and Nicaragua (Newson, 1992). Moreover, the gender ratio was skewed such that Spanish men outnumbered Spanish women until the early seventeenth century. By 1614 there were still 120 white men per 100 white women, while in Lima in 1555 there were between 7,000 and 8,000 men and only 1,000 women (van Deusen, 1987: 9).

The pinnacle of colonial society resided in Lima, and recreated a hierarchy of race, ethnicity and class as the basis of rule. Until the eighteenth century, some 300 families are said to have run Lima, ranking first the *conquistadores* and their descendants, secondly the *peninsulares* (the peninsular Spanish, born in the Old World), and thirdly the merchants (Balmori, 1984) over black and Indian populations. The aristocracy laid claim to a privileged, white and Catholic link with Spanish history. In this context, merchant South American and European immigrants were allowed into the elite group through the accumulation of wealth and intermarriage with existing notable families.

Peru received some 50,000 European immigrants during the 1800s. These included Spaniards, the largest group; Italians who contributed about 26,500 immigrants; French who came to represent a tenth of Lima's population; around 2,700 Germans; and smaller numbers of English and Irish (Vazquez, 1970). By 1876, since some 85 per cent of foreign residents were male and wars had decimated the numbers of men, a high degree of intermarriage between new and older settler groups occurred (Vazquez, 1970: 85). However, the tracing of family origins back to the conquerors gained in importance, to demonstrate purity of blood and to claim antecedence over new arrivals and the increasingly large group of *criollos*. *Criollos*, or creoles, were of European descent born in the Americas, where they occupied the lower ranks of colonial administration. Forbidden to hold important administrative posts, they resented their minor status and led the wars of Independence.

In common with many European societies, the ritual tracing of origins took place through the male line: Spanish conquerors brought with them a patrilineal and strongly Mediterranean family system, favouring male control over female family members. Women's roles within the creole group were related to the tasks of maintenance of family honour, and forging links through marriage. Ties of marriage and blood formed a nuclear family-based defence of privilege and wealth, which not only unified Spanish American society, but also tied it to the *madre patria* (motherland) of Spain. For example, in the late sixteenth century the de Escobar sisters in Lima provided a linchpin uniting the commercial business of one brother in Seville and another in Chile (Balmori, 1984: 88).

It is probably as the wives and mothers of Spanish colonial authorities and nobility that white European women most shaped settler society in Peru. As women were the repositories of family honour, their virginity and fertility were closely supervised and carefully passed from father and brothers to husbands. The codification of concern for *limpieza de sangre* formalized a general regulation of white women in the New World. Creole sexual liaisons with Indians or blacks were governed by gendered and racialized double standards: while it was acceptable, even expected, of Spanish men to have Indian women as sexual partners, the notion of Spanish women choosing to have sexual relations with men of other races was unthinkable. In the early colonial period, conquerors married noble Indian women, providing them with some measure of wealth and status. In contrast, the majority of peasant women's liaisons were socially unrecognized and insecure (Silverblatt, 1987). Creole wives were placed in an invidious position in this gendering of settler social relations: often aware of their husband's parallel relations, they could only take out their frustration and anger on the servants (Francke, 1990: 96). In a few cases, creole women had relations with black men, although it was often assumed that rape initiated these exchanges, resulting in severe punishment for the slave (Hunefeldt, 1988). Women discovered to be complicit in these relations were often separated from their children and placed in a convent for life, or rapidly married to a socially mobile immigrant (Francke, 1990: 93). For those unwilling to enter into marriage (either with men or God), women of all racial and ethnic groups were encouraged by kin and social custom to place themselves in *casas de recogimiento* (refuge houses) run by Catholic orders (van Deusen, 1987). These houses distinguished between women entering as workers (indigenous, blacks) and whites and *mestizas* entering as 'conceptuals', or potential nuns.

Lima society was not exclusively European. An area known as the Cercado de Lima was designated exclusively for Indians (most dedicated to domestic service [Pérez Cantó, 1985]), and contained black slaves as well as the few remaining Inca nobility (Morner, 1967). One major group introduced to the Americas by Spanish settlers were blacks, first brought over in 1502. Most blacks lived as servants or artisans close to *criollo* areas. Between 1764 and 1876 sex balances in free and slave black were relatively equal (Hunefeldt, 1988: 6), unlike on the plantations where men outnumbered women. With a higher social status than legal position, black women attempted to negotiate freedom (if slaves), or greater economic security (if free), by entering liaisons with wealthy creole masters. Although the law did not allow men to free black mistresses, in practice women gained clothes, food and sometimes liberty. In effect by 1818 in Lima, black women made up 64.6 per cent of 'free castes' (caste, *casta*, refers to mixed blood populations), and only 7 per cent of slaves (Hunefeldt, 1988: 7). Moreover, as black slaves could earn money through wage work, they often represented an attractive alternative to a white wife whose role in her husband's eyes was to spend money. Children of black–white unions, although perceived by Catholic doctrine to be largely the fruit of the woman's womb (and hence slaves in some cases), were legally and effectively left to the father's whim, who decided whether to recognize children or to sell them. Offspring, regardless of skin colour, could be declared 'Spanish', although their mother might remain a slave. Owners could not prevent slave marriage, despite Church encouragement. However, illegitimacy among slave populations fluctuated between 35 and 48 per cent of births (Hunefeldt, 1988: 7).

In rural hinterlands and provincial towns, the development of the settler society followed a distinct trajectory, due to particular Spanish economic and political aims. As reward for conquest, soldiers were awarded access to Indian labour, slowly replaced with forced labour and cash tributes. Spaniards and their descendants accumulated large landholdings, haciendas, to demonstrate high settler status as much as for agriculture. In the early colony, white conquerors expressed fear about their small and vulnerable cities surrounded by indigenous rural hinterlands (Francke, 1990: 82). In this context, settlers used violence against native populations to reduce threats. They also relied upon indigenous labour to maintain living standards and class status; and as female labour was deemed to be more controllable, native women were preferred as domestic servants. By contrast, Indian men were restricted in their entry to *conquistadores*' towns, due to fears of public revolt. Although detailed data are not available, it is argued that 'at least as many women as men, if not more, entered the urban Hispanic world' (Burkett, 1978: 109).

The provincial imbalance of sexes among the Spanish, of whom only about 10 per cent were women, led to an immediate process of intermixing of populations. The violence of conquest involved indigenous women as spoils of war, as well as rape and the taking of indigenous women as gifts from native lords. The latter *caciques* attempted to ally themselves as brothers-in-law with Spaniards (Morner, 1967: 21). The Spanish imagery about Indian women was elaborate, with early chronicles recording how native women were expressing love for conquerors, causing jealousy among local men. As for indigenous women themselves, there is no direct record of their views of the new lords. Yet soon concubinage was numerically the most significant form of interaction between conquerors and native women, as rural estate-owners and provincial officials recruited women for domestic work. As labourers, women had few choices. From the start, domestic service was predominantly a female and indigenous/poor *mestiza* occupation. In 1684 women made up three-quarters of domestic servants in La Paz (Glave, 1987: 42).

Uneasy about cross-race sexual relations, the Catholic Church attempted to regulate the situation over which, however, it exercised little control. In the end, it appeared more acceptable and feasible to the Church to gain *mestizo* Catholics, than to baptize indigenous women before they became concubines (Morner, 1967: 21). As one Spaniard argued, 'the service rendered to God in producing *mestizos* is greater than the sin committed by the same act' (quoted in Morner, 1967). The Church encouraged marriage between landowners and *caciques'* daughters, a move explicitly permitted by the King in 1501, 'so that the Indians become men and women of reason' (quoted in Morner, 1967). Marriage was to be voluntary on both sides, to avoid coercing Indians into handing over property. Offspring of these unions, whether formalized or not, were recognized as legitimate, accepted as Spanish and permitted to inherit land.

However, by the eighteenth century, *mestizos* became closely associated with illegitimacy. The doctrine of racial 'purity' grew in significance as Peru's central position in the colonies disappeared, the number of white women increased, and competition for high status occupations rose (Pérez Cantó, 1985). *Mestizos* were viewed with contempt by peninsulars who attempted to protect socio-economic privilege and status through emphasizing blood ties with Spain. Only marriages with neighbouring racial/ethnic groups were encouraged by creole elites. The degree of 'proximity' between racial groups was carefully calculated with the assistance of tables, giving the appropriate ethnic label to the offspring of different unions: for example, 'español [Spanish] male mates with an Indian woman and produces a *mestizo*' (cited in Olien, 1973: 94). By calculating the outcome of 17 different unions, the *casta* system placed each individual within the social stratification system based on occupation, skin colour and a legal framework (Morner, 1967: 53–90). Interestingly too, sex as well as race was crucial in determining a child's status: it was assumed that men partnered women of a lower (or equal) race and class status to themselves, while women were not seen as active sexual agents. Moreover, offspring gained a social status intermediary to their parents': miscegenation produced a lower status than the father's, but higher than the mother's. Women as mothers remained at the lowest rank in race and social terms relative to partners and children, whether they were black, indigenous or *gente blanca* ('white people'). Under this system, race status was almost gender status in which contrasts between white/indigenous/black and male/female were played out in endless permutations.

Notions of 'legitimate' settlers and Catholic purity continued to resonate and shape discourses around origin, history and rights. Fundamental to this was the Catholic Church that framed debates around female morals and appropriate behaviour. The spread and uptake of Catholic faith was a central tenet of Spanish conquest in the Americas, and Jews and New Christians (converts from Islam or Judaism) were forbidden to settle (Laiken, 1992: 4–5). Encounters with indigenous groups triggered immediate efforts to indoctrinate the natives in the Catholic faith. In the Peruvian Andes, priests were sent to convert and baptize Indians, as well as destroy indigenous sacred sites.

The Catholic Inquisition was founded in Lima (and Mexico) in 1569 to hear cases against idolatries and 'dangerous thoughts' (Keen and Wasserman, 1988). The violence unleashed by the Inquisition was felt by both Indian and Jewish groups. For example, in 1639 several Jews in Lima were arrested, interrogated and burnt after confiscation of property (Laiken, 1992: 5). The 'extirpation of idolatries' was often highly gendered due to the opposition between male Catholic clergy and native female religious authorities. Among indigenous populations, women played a significant role in ritual but were accused of witchcraft by Spaniards (Silverblatt, 1987). Often forced into hiding in the remote Sierra, native women practised a new syncretic religion. Arrested for witchcraft, Andean women used their trials to resist Hispanic dichotomies of good and bad, Catholic and pagan, by identifying the 'Devil' of their religion as a wealthy and well-dressed Spaniard.

Black men outnumbered black women by some three to one, a factor which led to immediate intermixing of Indian women with black immigrants. Remaining under 5 per cent of Peru's total population until 1826, black slaves were concentrated largely on coastal plantation zones which became 'Afro-America' in a racial and cultural sense. For economic and cultural reasons, rates of manumission of slaves were higher in Spanish America than in North America, resulting in a situation whereby freed blacks and *mulattos* outnumbered slaves by the late eighteenth century (Keen and Wasserman, 1988; Morner, 1967). From the earliest colonial period too, black slaves escaped into the peripheries of the country away from plantation and commercial agriculture (Whitten and Torres, 1992: 17). Such *cimarrones* (maroons) formed settlements with indigenous and *mestizo* groups, prompting further racial mixture outside Spanish control. Due to severe gender imbalance in slavery, escaped male slaves often partnered Indian women.

As miscegenation continued, the administrative divide between 'Spaniards' and 'Indians' broke down. Although a division into a Republic of Spaniards and a Republic of Indians (*república de españoles*, *república de indios*) had aimed to protect Indians, miscegenation blurred the sharp social and spatial boundaries once laid between the two groups. Each group was legislated as separate, in response to theological debates (from the start of colonization in the Americas) about the desirability of keeping Indians away from corrupting influences (Morner, 1967: 47). Originally, Indians were resident in villages or specific urban districts, and European ownership of Indian lands forbidden. However, *mestizos* and creoles accumulated land through real and fictive (god-parenthood) kin ties during the colonial period. Moreover, Indians were highly mobile, moving to escape labour and tribute obligations, although the majority remained culturally separate from urban, Catholic and Europe-oriented society. While elite women in Lima bought the latest fashions from Paris (Tristan, 1986), Andean village women wove traditional cloth and elaborated a new culture. Provincial Indian and poor *mestiza* women continued, if only to a limited extent, to work in the market: women owned and managed popular corn-beer houses, and produced bread and cloth (Glave, 1987: 46). After the forced economic interchange of the colony, the nineteenth century saw increasing isolation of indigenous groups and downward social mobility among rural *mestizo* groups, who were listed as Indians for census and administrative purposes (Kubler, 1952).

Over approximately three centuries, Spanish colonial rule *engendered* a hierarchical society, largely constructed in terms recognizable to settler societies around the world (Denoon, 1983; Weitzer, 1990; Lodge, 1986). As in other Latin American countries with large indigenous populations, racial/ethnic intermixing was incomplete and riven with fear, mistrust and frequently violence (Weitzer, 1990: 25).

The Early Republican Period, 1824-1900

Peruvian independence initiated a debate around the issues of national identity, based on the interactions between gender, race/ethnicity and class hierarchies. Although many laws changed, the everyday structures of settler society bequeathed by the Spanish largely remained: the imagined geographies (Said, 1978) of territory and power of the colonial period were slow to change, while gender divisions of labour and authority maintained disparities in opportunity and income.

During the nineteenth century, a complex system of hierarchy based on class and racial lines distinguished high-status creoles from other population groups. Racial ideologies of social Darwinism became increasingly influential in Peru, as elites interlocked increasingly with European powers through dependent capitalism and intellectual currents in Britain and France (Graham, 1990). Policies of social engineering stressed the importance of European racial inputs, and presidents such as Ramón Castilla in mid-century encouraged German settlers to colonize Amazonia, a process which displaced pre-existing Amuesha groups. Ironically however, the importance of 'race' declined in Andean areas, as intermixing of populations and increasing poverty gave rise to social distinctions based on income and culture, rather than race. For this reason, the terms 'Indian' and '*mestizo*' referred, as they still do today, more to class and *ethnic* status than race difference. (Currently, *mestizo/a* refers in provincial small towns and hamlets to those with some urban consumer goods, and political leverage through sponsorship of rituals and urban resources.) From 1791 to 1876, the proportion of Indians increased while *mestizos* declined from 26.6 to 24.8 per cent of Peru's total population (Kubler, 1952).

The wars of Independence brought renewed attention to the question of racial difference in Peruvian nationhood. Both national 'liberators', Generals San Martín and Bolívar, declared that the entire population was 'Peruvian', and for a short period imports of slaves were abolished. However, these early hopes for equal citizenship were soon undermined by a tribute system, known as the *castas*' contribution, which divided the population into non-paying creoles and tribute-paying *castas* (blacks, *mestizos*, indigenous).

By 1893 Peru was officially a country of 'free immigration', only allowing entry to free migrants. When slaves were freed in 1854, the need for alternative sources of labour encouraged Peruvian landowners and plantation companies to look to the other side of the Pacific, where large populations were beginning to migrate internationally. Japanese migration to Latin America began in Peru, followed closely by Brazil where large numbers eventually settled. In the early 1890s, a group of 790 Japanese were contracted to work on coastal plantations, in the first recorded case of Japanese settlement in Peru. The Japanese contractor specified workers were to be 25 to 40 years old and of 'good moral character', which attracted a largely male group of poor farmers and labourers (Irie, 1951). Initially, Japanese workers were contracted by large sugar plantations owned by Peruvians, although later groups moved into independent farming and waged work in Amazonia and Bolivia. Japanese migration continued throughout the early twentieth century, and by 1991 there were some 76,000 Japanese in the country. Located largely in urban areas, Japanese immigrants worked in retail, small crafts and services such as barber shops. Nevertheless, the link with agriculture continued, as Japanese migrants settled in the coastal cotton valleys. Knowledge of agriculture and commerce permitted Japanese to climb socially, encouraging adoption of Catholicism and Spanish names (Olien, 1973). President Alberto Fujimori (elected 1990) was exemplary of such a history: his parents arrived from Japan in 1934, and he was Rector of the Agricultural University before his election.

Contract workers were also brought from China. Between 1849 and the late 1860s, some 80,000 Chinese were contracted to work alongside Japanese in sugar plantations, in guano fields and as servants (Morner, 1967: 131; Olien, 1973: 134). Chinese immigration was exclusively male, resulting in rapid intermarriage with all local populations, including in some cases with creole elites, and in the adoption of Catholicism (Olien, 1973: 135–6). Over time, Chinese descendants settled throughout Peru, concentrating in the Colonia China in Lima, working in small retail, cooking and restaurant trades. In the provinces, their assimilation into local society was widespread as their mothers were local *mestizas*, and their intermediary role between coast and peasantries provided an economic niche (Vazquez, 1970).

As a consequence of demographic and economic changes, women of different social strata experienced widely differing work and status positions. Elite women, located largely in the towns, saw increasing restriction in their movements and were expected to conform to a domestic wifely figure (Keen and Wasserman, 1988). Employing servants to carry out heavy work, wealthy creole women became administrators of domestic and family economies, overseeing the organization of child care, cooking and consumption. By such gender and ethnic divisions of labour, elite women freed themselves for developing social networks which underpinned elite class status. Indian, black and poor *mestiza* women made up the bulk of the domestic service class: by 1894 servants, two-thirds of them women, made up 30 per cent of Lima's population (Vazquez, 1970: 86). Elite women remained pawns in games of alliance and resource accumulation between wealthy families. However, with increasing European immigration and industrialization, the variety of marriage strategies pursued by wealthy elites grew (Balmori, 1984: 225).

In the highland areas, provincial women saw different dynamics of settler society because of distinct economic and marriage relations and demographic ratios. In the province of Tarma, elite European women married local Peruvian soldiers (defending the area against Amazon tribes) and European immigrants (Wilson, 1984). With much emphasis placed on large families, women were pawns in a reproductive strategy among elites to build networks for trade and commercial agriculture by intermarrying with Italian, German and Argentine male entrepreneurs. While families stressed the desirability of foreign marriage partners, they relied upon Amazon and Chinese slave labour, and indentured Indian and *mestizo* traders for operationalizing elite lifestyles and fortunes (Wilson, 1984).

Violence by provincial elites and state authorities towards local populations was increasingly criticized by intellectuals. In Peru's *indigenista* literature, attacks were made on clergy, wealthy landowners and rural strongmen who between them exploited Indian female labour at home and Indian male labour in the fields. Among pro-indigenous writers, Clorinda Matto de Turner (1854–1909) used her novels and newspaper editing to make strong attacks on unequal racial, ethnic and class relations.

On the eve of the twentieth century, the political instability which had characterized early independence Peru was over. Population mobility, largely in the form of permanent moves, had increased cohabitation among different population groups, especially on the coast, but many areas of Amazonia and the southern highlands remained remote and relatively self-contained. Peru's settler society remained in place, despite dramatic demographic, economic and political changes.

Peru in the Late Twentieth Century

Due to its uneven state presence and relatively poor communications (Slater, 1989), Peru by the early 1990s comprised a set of regional cultures, each with its associated class, ethnic and racial composition shaped by the process of *mestizaje*. Ideologically in this regional patchwork, the coast was seen as a creole area, wealthy and culturally more 'western'; the Andean zone was perceived as an area of culturally 'backward' Quechua or Aymara Amerindian peasants; and Amazonia was seen as the region outside Hispanic urban norms and inhabited by tribal groups such as Campa, Aguaruna, Shipibo and Piro.

In demographic terms, the largest group were the *criollos* who, whether of Spanish, *mestizo*, Chinese or black descent, were culturally fully 'Peruvian'. *Criollo* as an adjective was used to qualify those 'typical' aspects of Peruvian culture such as music, food and attitude taken as the epitome of national identity. The other major group were the *andinos*, Andeans, whose resistance and ambivalence to creole culture generated alternative discourses around nationalism (Flores Galindo, 1987) and popular cultures (Rowe and Schelling, 1991; Degregori and Francke, 1990).

At one remove from this interacting pair of *criollo–andino* lay Amazon *nativos* widely perceived by themselves and others to live at a remove from 'Peruvianness'. In terms of social organization, religious beliefs, economic activities and semi-nomadic existence they placed themselves beyond the norms of 'civilian society' and thus outside the 'nation' (Shoemaker, 1981). Rejecting Hispanic, western notions of literacy, social mobility and class awareness, many *nativos* resisted colonization and cultural hegemony. Although originally forced into labour camps by settlers in Amazonia, Indian groups in the 1980s organized for their rights through such groups as the Campa Congress, the Amuesha Congress, the Aguaruna–Huambiza Federation and the Shipibo Federation (Varese, 1988). Amazonian women were active in this political process, taking part in local organizations, and creating links with indigenous highland women through the CCP (Confederación Campesina del Perú) national peasant confederation (interview with author, 1988; SAIIC, 1991). For example, a 1988 meeting held in Maynas attracted 150 women, many bringing children by boat on three-day journeys to voice concerns over high food prices, malnutrition, poor health and education services, and absence of effective government.

Nevertheless in the 1990s, Peruvian society remained riven by racisms (Manrique, 1991), further exacerbated by segregated labour markets. While sharing experiences of racism, Indian and black women and men were differentially placed in labour markets, and in politico-social structures. The franchise excluded illiterates until 1980, disproportionately marginalizing poor *criolla* and *andina* women. Moreover, the Peruvian labour market was highly gender segregated: the 1981 census figures indicated one of the lowest female labour force participation rates in Latin America. However, this masked high female participation in informal sector work (domestic service, street selling, preparation of food) and in agriculture, especially in Andean small-holdings. While not so well documented, the division of labour by ethnicity and race was also notable, with whites/*mestizos* occupying professional and managerial positions, while Indian and black groups worked in manual occupations.

The consequences of Peruvian settler society remained visible. Increasingly recognized was the legacy of Spanish domination and its racial–gender–class hierarchies; Carlos Degregori notes the 'abysmal mutual misunderstandings between *andinos* and *criollos*, the violence, the racism and the authoritarianism' (Degregori and Francke, 1990: 187). As noted previously, this mutual misrecognition was gendered, as women and men were positioned differently according to their class and race.

Contemporary Gender, Violence and Politics

The construct of 'Peruvian society' around dominant notions of gender, race, ethnicity, class and geographical location generated its opposite, articulated by the radical Maoist terrorists of Shining Path. In its violent and intolerant actions, this movement held up a mirror to previous relations between Hispanic settlers and native populations. Shining Path, or *Partido Comunista del Perú Sendero Luminoso*, developed in the divisive politics of the mid-1970s in the central Sierra (Poole and Rénique, 1991). Drawing its rural focus from Mao, Sendero aimed to end Peru's 'semi-feudal, semi-colonial society': its ideology was Maoist, with no ethnic or racial connotations. However, unlike most parties, Sendero made consistent efforts to raise the issue of women's rights. By 1968 the party had organized a Women's Front in its stronghold (Kirk, 1990). Female leaders wrote on 'Mariátegui's Marxism and the Women's Movement', organized women in mining villages and translated Alexandra Kollontai's 'Love in a Communist society (Andreas, 1990–91: 22). By publishing pamphlets and holding meetings in Spanish and Quechua, Sendero's message was carried to *andina* women who previously had been excluded from national debates conducted in Spanish, and from village decision-making (compare Bourque and Warren, 1981). Market women in the Sierra also initially supported Sendero, for the party's policy on the subsistence economy (Isbell, 1986).

In 1980 Sendero declared war against the government and boycotted the general election, the first after 12 years of military rule. Although little is known about Sendero's membership, it has been argued that it recruited from among young, poor *mestizo* or peasant provincial groups, while leaders were mostly provincial intellectuals. It was these groups that stood most to gain from increased education provision in the 1970s, yet whose hopes were blocked by post-1975 economic collapse and urban racisms. Among provincial migrants to highland cities and the coast, resentment at the wealth and status of Lima, the marginalization of central and southern provinces, and hierarchies of ethnic difference gave rise to a call for change, expressed through armed insurrection. Over the years since Sendero's appearance, some 25,000 people have been killed, over 1,000 have disappeared and around two-thirds of the national territory has been under military control.

In the military–terrorist conflict, poor peasant and *mestiza* women played a crucial role, challenging Catholic and Hispanic notions of feminine behaviour. The emergence of a female Sendero cadre, estimated at 40 per cent of the total, also alienated urban feminist groups only beginning to address issues of racism and class inequalities between women (Vargas, 1991). Whether or not Sendero attracted more female than male followers is speculative (Andreas, 1990–91), yet around one-third of those held in prison on terrorism charges associated with Shining Path are women and the party claims that one-half of its cadre are women, as it expressly aims to recruit them (Kirk, 1990; Castillo, 1991). Among those recruited were housewives, peasants, students, market vendors, domestic servants – young, largely impoverished women responsible for families and kin, yet faced with rising prices and discrimination. One female Senderista argued that women were particularly hit by economic decline: 'Who is it who suffers most from this country's crisis? It is the woman, who has to leave her house to work, to fight to bring bread home to her children' (quoted in Kirk, 1990).

However, Sendero also carried out actions which had gender-specific connotations. In 'popular' courts set up by Sendero, punishment was meted out to rapists and landowners who abused female domestic workers, while philandering and absent husbands were warned about their behaviour (Andreas, 1990–91: 27). Moreover, armed actions were led by female leaders, who often initiated the shooting and killing. Within Sendero structures, women were expected to maintain high moral standards, partnering fellow Senderistas, renouncing motherhood and treating the leader, Abimael Guzman, as father-chief (Vega-Centeno, 1992).

Shining Path's development prompted a profound shift in the inter-class relations bound up in ethnic difference in Peru, especially in domestic service, where *andina* and black women were historically permitted into the daily lives of the elite and middle class. Due to the historical trajectory of rural–urban, white–indigenous interaction, domestic service in Peru historically comprised a relation in which metaphors of parent/child, national/non-national expressed relations of control (Radcliffe, 1990). In other words, the least powerful groups of contemporary Peruvian society, young poor *andina–mestiza* women, were allowed into the private spheres of the wealthiest, most powerful groups.

With the rise of Sendero Luminoso, these relations of power, place, gender and ethnicity were rearticulated. With a notable recruitment of *andina* women into its ranks, Shining Path changed the parameters of power around ethnicity and gender. Whereas previously *andina* women were powerless in practice and in ideologies, they were then perceived as potentially subversive, as Sierra groups were viewed as likely Sendero members by coastal *criollos*. The domestic service relation, given its basis in subordinating female *andina* labour, was greatly transformed. As the national press sensationalized Sendero's female recruits, so elite households became reluctant to take on women who were not known and 'trustworthy' (that is, subordinate).

However, although Sendero drew support from marginalized women, many in the same situation rejected that movement's ideological narrowness. Other very varied, forms of rural poor *mestiza*/indigenous women's organizations were not engaged in violent expressions of alternative 'nations'. Rather they were involved in grass-roots, open movements with close links to democratically elected leaders and, in some cases, to feminist organizations such as the Flora Tristan and Manuela Ramos groups. In low-income areas throughout the country, women attempted to provide themselves and their families with cash, services and political leverage through numerous neighbourhood committees and women's clubs. Through alliances across race, ethnic and class lines, women's movements struggled continuously against the violence promoted by Sendero, as in the demonstration by 22,000 women in September 1991 against the assassination of Juana Lopez, a popular *mestiza* leader. In certain cases, these organizations explicitly addressed the questions of interacting gender, ethnic and class relations. For instance, the first South and Central American Indian women's gathering in March 1991 drew Peruvian participants from the Amazonian Shipibo and Aguaruna, highland Quechua and Aymara, as well as indigenous women from around the continent. Calling for 'traditional forms of law, autonomy and self-government' for themselves and kin, the women criticized racist policies of forced sterilization of indigenous groups (SAIIC, 1991). Another organization was the self-declared Indian women's organization, the Micaela Bastídas Female Community, founded in 1976. Promoting a pro-communal indigenous society in which women played an equal role to men, the Bastídas community drew its membership from *andina* women brought to Lima as domestics at a young age, and attempted to change servants' work and education. Challenging creole notions of culture, they argued for 'autochthonous culture and languages' and tried to persuade young women to remain in the Andes and not migrate (interview with author, 1988). Similarly, the Domestic Servants Union's activities challenged racism and stereotypes about *andina* society which underlay domestic service employment (Radcliffe, 1990). Their version of 'Peruvianness' called for an acceptance of cultural and ethnic diversity, and women's rights to retain *andino* culture in the city.

Conclusion

Marfil Francke argues that gender subordination, ethnic stratification and class structure form a triple spiral of domination in Peru, underlying institutional forms, relations of reproduction and production, and daily life (Francke, 1990: 85). Clearly, the triple spiral had its origin in settler society, where relations of subordination and domination were expressed through the overlap of social and spatial difference. Relations between groups were not haphazard, as they referred back to one specific discourse around class, gender, ethnic and race relations. At a symbolic level, this discourse engaged with the meanings around female/male, insider/outsider, local/foreign and, with the blurring of these dichotomies by miscegenation, rural–urban migration, cultural syncretism, regional interactions and settler institutions. Moreover, these relations were articulated through the association of certain groups with particular spaces.

However, what has emerged in Peru in the early 1990s is a situation in which various political groups attempt to articulate an alternative discourse of national development and identity in which a gendered encounter between cultures is transformed. As in the historic nationalism of creole masculinity dominating native femininity, the dimensions of these newly emerging (and as yet fragile) identities are voiced in terms of gender, ethnicity and place. Yet the recent gendered-ethnic nationalisms represent a symbolic reversal of official nationalism as they foreground femininity (albeit of a militaristic, intolerant and aggressive kind in Sendero's case) and *andina–mestiza* ethnic groups. In Sendero, rearticulation of Peruvian gendered nationalism is expressed in a violent, intolerant movement rejecting all that Peruvian history made of the country and projecting onto the future a utopian 'new democracy' for the populations and areas disempowered by settler society. By contrast, grass-roots *andina* women's organizations express a non-racist, collaborative ideal in which women are active, equal and articulate actors constructing a popular culture from a valued indigenous and slave past, human rights discourse, and demands for equal labour market conditions.

While the impact of these developments remains uncertain, it appears that class–ethnic relations between women, and between women and men, remain unresolved. Nearly 500 years after the foundation of settler society in Peru, the consequences of hierarchically structured relations between insiders, outsiders and the children of native mothers are being played out on an ever-violent stage. Given the long-term dynamic of settler society in Peru, while it is difficult to identify one particular collectivity which has emerged directly from the settlers, certain assumptions and discourses about gender, racial and ethnic difference and class persist.

Acknowledgements

Many thanks to Gina Vargas, Nira Yuval-Davis, Daiva Stasiulis and members of the Centre for Developing Areas Research (Royal Holloway, University of London), who took time to read and comment on earlier drafts of this chapter.

References

Andreas, C. (1990–91) 'Women at war', *NACLA Report on the Americas*, 24 (4): 20–7.
Balmori, D. (1984) *Notable Family Networks in Latin America*. Chicago: Chicago University Press.
Bourque, S. and Warren, K. (1981) *Women of the Andes*. Ann Arbor: University of Michigan Press.
Brading, D. (1991) *The First American*. Cambridge: Cambridge University Press.
Burkett, F. (1978) 'Indian women and white society: the case of sixteenth-century Peru', in A. Lavrín (ed.), *Latin American Women: Historical Perspectives*. Westport: Greenwood.
Castillo, R. (1991) 'La mujer terrorista', *Mujer/Fempress*, 118: 17.
Degregori, C.I. and Francke, M. (1990) *Tiempos de ira y amor*. Lima: DESCO.
Denoon, D. (1983) *Settler Capitalism: the Dynamic of Dependent Development*. Oxford: Clarendon Press.
Flores Galindo, A. (1987) *Buscando un inca: identidad y utopía en los Andes*. Lima: IAA.
Francke, M. (1990) 'Género, clase y etnía: la trenza de la dominación', in C.I. Degregori and M. Francke (eds), *Tiempos de ira y amor*. Lima: DESCO. pp. 79–106.
Glave, L.M. (1987) 'Mujer indígena, trabajo doméstico y cambio en el virreinato peruano, siglo XVII', *Bulletin de l'Institut Français d'Etudes Andines*, 16 (3–4): 39–69.
Graham, R. (ed.) (1990) *The Idea of Race in Latin America, 1870–1940*. Austin: University of Texas Press.
Hunefeldt, C. (1988) *Mujeres: esclavitud, emociones y libertad. Lima, 1800–1854*. Lima: IEP.

Irie, T. (1951) 'History of Japanese migration to Peru', *Hispanic American Historical Review*, 31: 437–52.

Isbell, B.-J. (1986) 'Sendero Luminoso', Institute of Latin American Studies Seminar, London.

Kay, C. (1989) *Latin American Theories of Development and Underdevelopment*. London: Routledge.

Keen, B. and Wasserman, M. (1988) *A History of Latin America*, 3rd edition. Boston: Houghton Mifflin.

Kirk, R. (1990) 'Women warriors at core of Peruvian rebellion', *San Francisco Chronicle*, November 11, 1990.

Kubler, G. (1952) *The Indian caste of Peru, 1795–1940*. Westport: Greenwood Press.

Laiken, J. (1992) 'Colonial legacy of anti-Semitism', *NACLA Report on the Americas*, 25 (4): 4–7.

Lodge, T. (ed.) (1986) *Resistance and Ideology in Settler Societies*. Johannesburg: Ravan Press.

Manrique, N. (1991) 'Sendero Luminoso: la violencia y el imaginario social en el Perú', Institute of Latin American Studies Seminar, London.

Morner, M. (1967) *Race Mixture in the History of Latin America*. Boston: Little, Brown.

Newson, L. (1992) 'Indigenous populations under colonial rule: Honduras and Nicaragua', paper, Society of Latin American Studies Conference, Southampton.

Olien, M. (1973) *Latin Americans*. New York: Holt, Rinehart & Winston.

Pérez Cantó, M.P. (1985) *Lima en el siglo XVIII: estudio socioeconómico*. Madrid: Universidad Autónoma de Madrid.

Poole, D. and Rénique, G. (1991) 'The new chroniclers of Peru', *Bulletin of Latin American Research*, 10 (2): 133–91.

Radcliffe, S. (1990) 'Ethnicity, patriarchy, incorporation into the nation: female migrants as domestic servants in Peru', *Society and Space*, 8: 379–93.

Rowe, W. and Schelling, V. (1991) *Memory and Modernity: Popular Culture in Latin America*. London: Verso.

Said, E. (1978) *Orientalism*. Harmondsworth: Penguin.

SAIIC (1991) 'First South and Central American Indian Women's Gathering', *Newsletter*, 6 (1–2).

Shoemaker, R. (1981) *The Peasants of El Dorado: Conflict and Contradiction in a Peruvian Frontier Settlement*. Cornell: Cornell University Press.

Silverblatt, I. (1987) *Moon, Sun and Witches: Gender Ideologies and Class in Inca and Colonial Peru*. Princeton: Princeton University Press.

Slater, D. (1989) *Territory and State Power in Latin America: the Peruvian Case*. London: Macmillan.

Tristan, F. (1986) *Peregrinations of a Pariah*. London: Virago. (1st edition, 1835.)

Van Deusen, N. (1987) *Dentro del cerco de los muros: el recogimiento en la época colonial*. Lima: CENDOCC-Mujer.

Varese, S. (1988) 'Multiethnicity and hegemonic construction: Indian plans and the future', in R. Guidieri (ed.), *Ethnicities and nations*. Austin: University of Texas Press. pp. 57–77.

Vargas, V. (1991) 'The women's movement in Peru: streams, spaces and knots', *European Review of Latin American and Caribbean Studies*, 50: 7–50.

Vazquez, M.C. (1970) 'Immigration and *mestizaje* in nineteenth-century Peru', in M. Morner (ed.), *Race and class in Latin America*. New York: Columbia University Press. pp. 73–95.

Vega-Centeno, I. (1992) 'Género y política: a propósito de la mujer en Sendero Luminoso', *Socialismo y participación*, 60: 1–6.

Weitzer, R. (1990) *Transforming Settler States*. Berkeley: University of California Press.

Whitten, N. and Torres, A. (1992) 'Blackness in the Americas', *NACLA Report on the Americas*, 25 (4): 16–22.

Wilson, F. (1984) 'Marriage, property and the position of women in the Peruvian central Andes', in R.T. Smith (ed.), *Kinship, ideology and practice in Latin America*. London: University of North Carolina Press. pp. 297–325.

8

Constructing Race, Class, Gender and Ethnicity: State and Opposition Strategies in South Africa

Elaine Unterhalter

Elements of the apartheid state in South Africa came to an end in May 1994, with the inauguration of the first parliament chosen in a non-racial democratic election. The old state had been constructed by people who claimed descent from European settlers, and had used these claims over four centuries as one component of their political and economic domination over the indigenous peoples of South Africa and other racialized immigrant minorities. More than a decade of internal resistance, international isolation and economic collapse are frequently cited as the reasons for dominant social forces in South Africa seeking to negotiate with opposition movements (Bazzili, 1991; Friedman, 1993). However, in addition to noting these material conditions, it is evident from the very process of negotiation in the early 1990s that the identities of indigenous peoples, 'settlers', and other immigrants who were not perceived as settlers, have been through a process of reformulation. One intention of this chapter is to illustrate that this process was not unique to the end of the century, but has long been an aspect of South African society.

The notions of race, class, ethnicity and gender that are woven through South African history are neither standardized nor homogenous. In fact they have been highly mutable, shifting dramatically in different periods. Even in the heyday of apartheid (*c.* 1960–90) when the entire population was classified according to race on supposedly biological grounds, every year the *Government Gazette* published lists of people who had been reclassified from one race to another. Martin West tabulates for 1986 the 1,624 applications for reclassification according to 25 different permutations of racial classification (West, 1988: 104).

Studies of the state in South Africa have tended to look at relationships based on race, on class and, to a much more limited extent, on gender and have not, on the whole, been concerned with the ways in which shifts in the definition of these relationships have occurred (Magubane, 1979; Wolpe, 1988). These analyses have tended to focus on homogenizing relationships and generalizing their effect on the state. Similarly, some of the major debates in South African political economy – for example, the debate between liberals and Marxists on the rationality or irrationality of race in relation to the development of South African capitalism – tend to take notions of race, class and gender as unproblematic and unchanging givens (Lipton, 1986; Greenberg, 1980).

Nonetheless, the process through which these relationships have been constructed has begun to be documented (Goldin, 1987; Marks and Trapido, 1987; Walker, 1990a). These studies explicitly question the simple analytical category of race, and begin to problematize notions of ethnicity and historicize the form of gender relations. This chapter is premised on a similar range of questions. One intention is to highlight the different ways in which race, gender and ethnicity have been defined in the course of South African history. A second intention is to examine how, in different periods, competing definitions have held sway. A third intention is to look at the way in which constructions of race, ethnicity and gender were shaped by, and in turn shaped, state institutions.

Broadly four phases in the construction of gender, race and ethnicity can be delineated:

1 a prenational phase (from the period of earliest settlement to *c.* 1750)
2 a phase of African kingdoms establishing national projects (*c.* 1750–1898)
3 a phase of colonial rule (1652–1910)
4 a phase of settler rulers establishing a national project through the structures of the state of the Union of South Africa (1910–60) and the Republic of South Africa (1960 to April 1994)

Although these phases are set out here sequentially for ease of explication, it is important to stress that they do not denote a chronology of events, but a series of processes. For example, the pre-national phase does not finish at the end of the eighteenth century, when societies evincing these characteristics become less dominant; it continues, for some of these societies, to the present. Similarly, although national projects associated with African kingdoms are reasonably well documented from the end of the eighteenth century, there is evidence from archaeology and linguistics to indicate they probably existed much earlier. Furthermore, the national projects of African kingdoms continued after their subjugation by colonial or settler forces, but in different form.

The Pre-National Phase

The earliest societies in South Africa are described as pre-national because of their lack of ideologies and politico-economic structures that delineate their interests as superior to that of other societies. While there may have been keen notions of difference between societies and strong competing claims to territory, these were not informed with notions of the supremacy of one society with regard to another. In these societies the forms of social organization ranged from small-scale groups of gatherer-hunters or herders to large-scale settlements with mixed economies based on agriculture, animal husbandry, metal working and other crafts. All were probably characterized by a sexual division of labour and a differential access to the means of production, but probably differed in the degree of rigidity of these divisions and the extent of reciprocity across gender and class lines.

According to Jeff Guy, all the societies of southern Africa, at the time of the first written records and probably before, were based on the appropriation of women's labour by men (Guy, 1990: 33). Production was organized in homesteads headed by a man. Wealth was accumulated in cattle, which were not owned by women. A man exchanged cattle for a woman through a payment of *lobola* or *bohali* (brideprice) to another homestead head. Women's productive and reproductive power were essential to social reproduction. but were closely controlled by men. The *lobola* exchange, however, was not a simple payment. It signified a relationship between homesteads that would last for a generation or more (Guy, 1982). There were distinctions between women in terms of age and the status accorded their marriage. A homestead head could designate one of his wives as the woman whose sons would inherit the homestead and its lands.

It appears that these pre-national societies were relatively tolerant of what were later to be construed as racial and ethnic difference (Mostert, 1992: 115). While the Khoi at the Cape were critical of the first Dutch settlers and viewed them pityingly as slaves, the Europeans perceived the Khoi with unpitying derision as semi-animals (Mostert, 1992: 107–8).

In pre-national societies it seems that differences of language, custom and appearance were no barrier to newcomers being accepted as members of a homestead, although they may well have been incorporated in subordinate roles. Noel Mostert comments on the hospitality shown by the Xhosa of the eastern Cape to Europeans shipwrecked along the eastern coasts. Many of these became members of local homesteads and refused to leave when rescue missions arrived (Mostert, 1992: 196–7).

However, relations between gatherer-hunter San and mixed farmers indicate strong notions of difference and dominance. In some areas there was a symbiotic tolerance between the two economies. In others, San hunters were forced to recognize the dominance of mixed farmers who demanded tribute either in kind or in service in return for allowing the San access to hunting grounds. In the area of the Sotho peoples, San women were married by homestead heads in order that a homestead might gain access to what was viewed as San land (Thomson, 1990: 28–9).

In this pre-national phase, while gender relations and the control of women's productive and reproductive powers were central to the political economy, notions of race and ethnicity appear not to have impinged greatly on the form of the polity or its institutions. It appears that there were no barriers to granting land to men of what were later to be construed as different racial and ethnic groups. Women who were physically or linguistically different were incorporated into homesteads. While they had lower status than other women, all women were subject to male control of their productive and reproductive potential.

The Establishment of National Projects in African Kingdoms

Possibly from the tenth century in certain regions, and in a sustained development from the mid-eighteenth century in some areas of South Africa, kingdoms developed with a ruling clan assuming a much more vigorous dominance over homesteads, compared to earlier eras. The emergence of these kingdoms was associated with the assertion by dominant groups of a national identity, a common founding father, a common language, new religious rites and new forms of social organization. A national identity, containing within it notions of superiority to neighbours, was advanced by the dominant clan to legitimate seizure of land from neighbours and demands for labour from subjects.

The process of forging kingdoms and national identities entailed the formation and reformation of the polities of the region. It also coincided, often violently, with the expansion of European settlement. The national projects of these African rulers shaped the nature of colonial rule in South Africa but equally they were shaped by colonialism and conquest. Particularly in the second half of the nineteenth century, the balance of forces turned against the African kingdoms. The kingdom of the Venda, the last independent African kingdom in South Africa, was conquered by settlers in 1898.

Gender relations in the African kingdoms of the nineteenth century continued to be primarily informed by the appropriation of women's productive and reproductive powers by male homestead heads. However, their rights to the labour power of women were often superseded or mediated by the rights of chiefs or kings to demand women to work on their land and to sanction women's marriages. This tendency was most marked in the Zulu kingdom, but elements of it have been noted among the Basotho and the Swazi (Unterhalter, 1981; Bonner, 1983; Kimble, 1983).

The formation of hierarchically organized kingdoms with a national focus and special political, economic and religious functions vested in a monarchy entailed a process of what came to be viewed as ethnic differentiation between the different African kingdoms. In the areas of what are today Kwazulu and Natal, in imposing the hegemony of the Zulu clan Shaka and his heirs obliterated the use of the different Nguni dialects. All speakers of these languages were to come to identify themselves as Zulu. Similar trends can be noted all over the region.

Another ideological element in the process of ethnic differentiation was the construction of a common ancestry for all the members of the kingdom. In this process the mythical ancestor of the dominant clan, or a symbolic beast associated with this group, came to be seen as the symbol of the polity for all its members whether they shared a common history with the dominant clan or not (Thomson, 1990: 25).

While the process of ethnic differentiation can be noted from the time of the development of African kingdoms, it is important to stress that this trend was not uniform throughout the country, as not all indigenous peoples were subjects of the kingdoms of the region. Moreover, this process was to be made considerably more complex by the imposition of colonial notions of ethnic identity on the indigenous population.

An important component of the national projects of African kingdoms were the wars fought with antagonists in other clans or kingdoms. However, this process went side by side with the openness to incorporating new ideas brought by Europeans who were missionaries, traders and hunters. Land was granted to people who were religiously, linguistically and culturally different to the subjects of the king, providing they were prepared to recognize the king's authority. In this manner a number of European traders became subjects of African kings and missionaries were able to establish stations. In addition refugees from wars between polities or from the system of slavery at the Cape might find themselves incorporated into an African kingdom. Thus the process of ethnic differentiation still proceeded side-by-side with an openness to people from other ethnic backgrounds.

In this interchange there were no notions of race. However the incursion of settler and colonial forces against the African kingdoms forced them to formulate a racially inscribed notion of their attackers as 'the European' (see, for example, Webb and Wright, 1976: 96–8).

The state structures of the African kingdoms were shaped by their assertion of ethnic difference. But the state remained relatively weak as the political economy of the homestead survived and was able to accommodate to the demands of the king. While homesteads came to acknowledge an ideology informed by notions of ethnic unity, their gendered structure remained permeable to the incorporation of people of different racial and ethnic origins. This placed limits on the power of the monarchy to assert too vigorous an ethnic hegemony. However, in the subsequent period, when African kingdoms were subjected to colonial conquest, in the face of military attack, royal lineages were, much more successful at asserting, a national identity and ethnic difference.

Colonial and Settler Projects: Race, Gender and Ethnicity, 1652–1910

The period of colonial and settler rule by the Dutch and British in South Africa extended from 1652 to 1910 entailing a range of differing and overlapping colonial and settler projects. Examples included the settlements fostered by the Dutch East India Company during the period the Cape was under its suzerainty (1652–1795), and by the Afrikaner Trekkers who settled in the interior republics of the Transvaal and Orange Free State (1836–1902). In the Cape and Natal under British colonial rule (1815–1910) there were some congruences, but many gendered economic, political and ideological differences between the descendants of Dutch settlers, the newer British settlers and the administrators. The large numbers of European immigrants who came to work the mines in Kimberley from 1867 and the Witwatersrand from 1886 added a new range of settler perspectives.

The Development of Mercantile Capitalism: Dutch Colonization, 1652–1795

The initial colonization of South Africa in the seventeenth century took place as part of the expansion of Dutch mercantile capitalism to the East Indies. In 1652 a small refreshment station was established at the Cape under the command of an official of the Dutch East India Company. By the end of the century a small settler population had established itself in Cape Town. This was composed of Dutch, French Huguenot and German settlers.

   The settlers' initial contacts with the indigenous people at the Cape – the Khoi and the San – had been limited to exchanges of livestock. But the settler extortions became heavy. Between 1662 and 1713, 14,363 cattle and 32,808 sheep passed from the Khoi settled around what is today Cape Town to the Dutch East India Company (Thomson, 1990: 38). A war of resistance by the Khoi in 1673 was suppressed.

White settlers established wheat and wine farms on land to which the indigenous people's title was not recognized. In early wars of conquest some Khoi and San people were captured and taken as slaves. Others were forced to sell their labour, as the settlers undermined their political economy. Many San and some Khoi moved away from the settler enclave into the eastern and northern Cape, and even further to the Drakensberg Mountains. Throughout the seventeenth and eighteenth centuries settlers increased the amount of land under their control. These migrant settlers, known as Trekboers (travelling farmers), for the most part practised a subsistence economy based on the herding of cattle and sheep. As they moved further from Cape Town, the political authority of the Dutch East India Company became more and more attenuated.

Labour for settler farms and the artisanal workshops that were established in Cape Town and the neighbouring small towns was extorted from slaves. These were bought both from Dutch and African slave traders working along the west and east coasts of Africa and from the Dutch authorities who sold as slaves the people they captured during the uprisings against their rule in Indonesia and other captives they took in Malaya, Sri Lanka, India and Madagascar. By the end of the eighteenth century there were rather more slaves than settlers at the Cape; in 1793 they numbered 14,744, compared to 13,830 settlers (Thomson, 1990: 36). Slaves were forbidden to marry and had no legal rights over their children.

In contrast with the settlers' views of the Khoi, travellers and traders who encountered the Xhosa further along the east coast described them in admiring terms, praising their strength, gentleness and complex social organization (Mostert, 1992: 189, 196, 271). In my view these different racial constructions of different groups of indigenous people turn on political and economic factors. The Khoi and the San at the Cape were obstacles to the Company establishing its base in the area. They refused to become Company servants, work the land for Company officials, and supply the Company with endless cheap stocks of cattle and game. The brutality meted out to them and to imported slaves who were denied rights to wages, accommodation and even their children, could only be 'justified' if they were considered inhuman (Mostert, 1992: 174).

On the other hand, in the seventeenth and early eighteenth centuries the very small number of European settlers was in no position militarily, politically or economically to make any claims on Xhosa society. The settlers were in fact dependent on the goodwill of Xhosa rulers. Under these conditions the Xhosa were described in glowing terms that emphasized their similarity to an idealized vision of rural Europeans.

The impact of these constructions of race on gender relations was twofold. First, the denial of human features to the Khoi and the slaves and their lack of economic and political rights meant that sexual harassment and abuse of these women went unchecked (Mostert, 1992: 113–14). Secondly, gender relations in settler households, which confined women's work to agriculture and the domestic sphere, were imposed on slaves. Slave women worked primarily in the homes of their owners or in the cultivation of their lands. They were not employed in herding, nor were they trained in artisanal crafts.

The nature of women's organization in this period remains under-researched. There appears to be a lack of women's organization outside the domestic sphere, but this may reflect the lack of investigation in this area. Within the domestic sphere in settler society there appears to have been cooperation between women defined by the same race and class, and a marked lack of perception of common gender among women perceived as belonging to different races and classes (Ginwala, 1989).

While notions of racial difference underscored gender relations between colonialists, settlers and indigenous peoples, ethnic differentiation does not appear to have been a feature of Cape society. The employees of the Dutch East India Company were drawn from all over Europe and no special privileges appear to have accrued to people of Dutch origin. To the indigenous population ethnic differences between the settlers were of no consequence, although by the end of the period it was clear to the Khoi and the Xhosa that there were different classes, political groupings and factions among the colonialists. One of the themes in the history of the subsequent period of British rule concerned attempts by indigenous people to manipulate these differences to secure their own futures.

The slave population was ethnically extremely diverse. But with the exception of the Muslim population, who preserved their sense of ethnic identity in their religion, other slaves forged bonds with each other, speaking common languages like Portuguese Creole and the patois that was to evolve into Afrikaans. Promises of manumission were often made conditional on conversion to Christianity. The development of this common religion further flattened ethnic distinctions.

Colonists and settlers in the period perceived the Khoi, the San, the Xhosa and their slaves very differently. In these differences, I believe, lie the origins of what was to be a persistent theme throughout the period of colonial and settler rule – that is, the tendency to exaggerate as 'ethnic' difference the social, political and linguistic diversity of the dominated population, while simultaneously officially downplaying similar diversities among the settler population.

British Colonial Rule: The Expansion of Mercantile Capitalism, the Growth of Finance Capitalism and the Conquest of African Polities, 1806–1910

During the course of the Napoleonic wars Britain seized the Cape from the Netherlands (in 1795 and again in 1806). As part of the Treaty of Vienna in 1815 the Dutch possessions at the Cape were ceded to Britain. Under the British, during the first half of the century increasing areas of the eastern and northern Cape were brought piecemeal under colonial rule.

In the 1830s, 6,000 settlers, predominantly, but not exclusively, the descendants of Dutch settlers, impatient with the Colonial Office's opposition to slavery at the Cape and what they perceived as its inability to protect them from attack by the Xhosa, moved into the interior of South Africa in an effort to establish an independent settler state. This move, known as the Great Trek, resulted in the establishment of Trekker republics independent of British rule in the interior and the British annexation of the coastal region of Natal. Settler states were established in the Transvaal and Orange Free State, which remained in varying degrees politically independent of the Colonial Office until the outbreak of the Anglo-Boer War in 1899.

Politically, the establishment of British colonial rule in the Cape and Natal signalled a departure from the institutions put in place by the Dutch East India Company. Although overall political and military policies for the country were formulated in London, the powers of the local high commissioner and his magistrates to make and maintain laws expanded markedly. These came to include 'Native Administration' – that is, the governance of all indigenous people who were brought under colonial rule through either conquest or migration.

In 1853 some legislative powers were devolved to male voters in the Cape. A property qualification was introduced, which had the effect of enfranchising the majority of settlers and some indigenous men and some descendants of immigrant slaves. All decisions of this parliament were subject to veto in London. A legislative body elected only by male settlers defined as white was established in 1856 in Natal.

Within the interior settler republics, more extensive rights of political participation were vested in men deemed white. Thus, the Orange Free State adopted a constitution in 1853 which enfranchised all white males who had been living in the territory for more than six months. The South African Republic (in the area of the Transvaal) adopted a similar constitution in 1860.

The economy of South Africa in the first half of the nineteenth century was primarily agricultural. The settlers claimed large tracts of the land brought under their political dominance. The indigenous population in these areas lost all title to lands acquired by settlers in this manner. However, the small numbers of settlers were usually not able to utilize all the land they claimed, and much of the indigenous population remained as the occupants of the land, paying rent either in kind or in labour for what had been their territory. Not all land was owned by settlers. In the British-ruled territories, reserves were established under the rule of appointed chiefs for indigenous people deemed Native. Some indigenous peoples and ex-slaves were also able to buy land. The owners of these freehold lands, sometimes termed 'emancipated natives', were not always subject to chiefly rule.

A very dramatic shift in the nature of the economy took place in the second half of the century. In 1867 diamond mining began in an area in the northern Cape around what is today Kimberley. It soon became evident that extensive diamond deposits were available. Thousands of prospectors from all over South Africa, Europe and America flocked to the diggings. Britain overruled the different claims of Trekkers and local chiefs to the area and annexed Kimberley as part of the Cape Colony in 1871.

Technical problems in extraction and the 'free' market in plots led to a concentration of ownership. By 1880 a monopoly, De Beers Consolidated Mines, with backing from the Rothschild banking interests in London, acquired control of all mines. The wealth accumulated by De Beers in Kimberley ensured it a pivotal role in South African history. Cecil Rhodes, who became the major shareholder in the company, became Prime Minister of the Cape. When rich seams of gold were found along the Witwatersrand in the South African Republic in 1886, De Beers became a major investor in the mines that were established. Finance capitalism became pivotal to this phase of history.

The successful development of a capitalist mining industry depended on enormous supplies of semi-skilled labour. To secure the conditions for extracting this labour from the indigenous population, the colonial government engaged in a series of wars to bring all the African kingdoms under its dominance. Once conquered, a system of taxation was put in place that forced homesteads to send young men to work in the mines, and on the railways and other infrastructural and service projects associated with the development of the mining industry.

Very bitter and bloody wars were fought. The British and the Boers were defeated in some battles, most notably by the Sotho at Thaba Bosiu in 1858, by the Venda in 1867 and by the Zulu at Isandlwana in 1879. But it was difficult for African kings to sustain victory beyond a single battle. They could not maintain troops in the field for long periods and did not command the field of diplomacy, as the British did. All African kingdoms, once conquered, were placed under the rule of chiefs, whose authority was subject to the sanction of the colonial authorities. Special legal institutions in the form of what was termed 'Native law' were devised to govern the subjects of African kings. The process through which old rulers were transformed into agents of colonial and settler domination was an uneven one (see, for example, Marks, 1970; Guy, 1979; Unterhalter, 1981; Beinart, 1982; Kimble, 1985; Delius, 1989; Burman, 1990). Generally, colonial economic authority was more easily established than political or ideological hegemony.

Changing political and economic relations in South Africa were accompanied by waves of immigration, each different in character. Commercial immigration schemes were used to secure settlers to populate advancing frontiers of colonial rule in the eastern Cape and Natal. Both these annexations of territory were accompanied by attempts to 'plant' settlers in the land recently brought under colonial control. However, relatively few settlers came to South Africa under these schemes compared with contemporaneous British immigration to Australia and North America.

Throughout South Africa, in the middle of the nineteenth century the settler presence was numerically small. There were 2,000 settlers in the Cape in 1707, and just before the British annexation they numbered 13,830 (Thomson, 1990: 47). In 1865, when the first census was taken at the Cape, the settler population was estimated at 180,000; if account is taken of the settlers then living outside the jurisdiction of the Cape authorities, the total settler population of South Africa could be estimated as 250,000. The 1865 Cape census estimated the indigenous population at 300,000. On the basis of this, and the figures contained in the first national census of 1911, one could suggest the total indigenous and non-settler population in the middle of the nineteenth century numbered 3 million (Thomson, 1990: 66, 243). Settlers thus made up approximately 8 per cent of the population of South Africa at mid-century.

The second wave of nineteenth-century immigration to South Africa was that of indentured workers brought to Natal from India to work on the settler-owned sugar plantations. The plantation owners had had little success in securing local labour, as relations of production in the homestead had not been significantly disrupted by British annexation. The terms of indenture forced the workers to work for five years for a single employer for very little remuneration; thereafter they could enter wage employment. Between 1860 and 1866, 6,000 workers from India came to South Africa. Virtually all elected to stay after the expiry of their indenture (Thomson, 1990: 99–100).

The third wave of immigration was associated with the development of the mining industry, first in Kimberley and then on the Witwatersrand. Very large numbers of immigrants came from Europe

and North America as prospectors, miners or workers in the large ser-
vice sector that grew up in association with the development of mining.
While much of this migration had an oscillating nature with many
prospectors and miners remaining only a few years at a stretch in South
Africa, a considerable proportion of immigrants settled permanently in
South Africa.

In order to take control of the Witwatersrand gold-fields, Britain
fought and won the Anglo-Boer War (1899–1902). The defeat of the
Boer generals meant that the Trekker republics were brought under
British rule. Lord Alfred Milner, British High Commissioner in South
Africa, intended to use the period of British rule in the former Boer
republics to introduce a sweeping policy of Anglicization, backed up by
widespread immigration from Britain. He hoped to grant self-government to the territories only when they had been anglicized. In the event
the large-scale British immigration failed to materialize. In 1907 a
Liberal government in Britain, wary of imperial expansion, acceded to
requests from settlers for self-government. This was achieved with the
establishment of the Union of South Africa in 1910.

In the period of British colonial rule, as the whole country came
under colonial and settler dominance, so notions of racial difference
and European superiority became hegemonic. Sometimes these notions
became inscribed in economic or political institutions; these institutions then formalized the equation of white race and power. For
example, 1872 saw the enactment of the Kimberley diamond diggings
prohibitions against diggers and traders who were construed as black.
Racially inscribed laws defining skill and governing employment in the
mines followed soon after and were later adopted on the
Witwatersrand.

The 1856 constitution of Natal vested the franchise in male settlers.
This numerically small group of men used the political power they
acquired to pass laws expressly forbidding anyone who was subject to
Native Law or under the political authority of a chief from voting for
the legislative assembly. Indigenous families who were viewed as emancipated from Native Law were placed under the authority of chiefs. The
constitution had required the Legislative Assembly to spend a minimum of £5,000 per year raised from revenue on education and
agricultural development for indigenous people. The Assembly consistently failed to spend this minimum amount, even though indigenous
peoples in Natal contributed more than £10,000 a year in taxes to the
colonial treasury (Thomson, 1990: 98–9). Thus, an equation developed
between what was defined as a white race, access to political power and
the privileges that power bought.

It is evident that the expansion of colonial rule and capitalist relations of production proceeded hand-in-hand with constructions of

notions of a white and a black race. These races, however, were internally divided by class, region, language, religion and political affiliation. Nonetheless, state institutions tended to assume a homogeneity among these races. This was accompanied by a process of what may be termed a forming of ethnic identification. This had become marked by the end of the period, but was complex and changing.

The attempt of successive colonial administrations to manipulate the politics of the South African Republic from 1877, and ultimately to go to war with the settler republics in 1899, resulted in the majority of settler inhabitants who worked on the land of these republics viewing themselves as Boers, whether or not they were of Dutch origin or members of the Dutch Reformed Churches. The British attack on the settler republics in 1899 also had the effect of making British subjects view themselves as Boers, particularly those in the Cape and Natal who spoke Dutch or Afrikaans and/or identified with the settler resistance to British annexation. Twelve thousand men from the Cape Colony joined the armies of the Boer generals.

On the Witwatersrand, however, the trend among skilled miners and many immigrants working in the service sector was towards support for the British. Many immigrants, despite their diverse European or American origins and their range of faiths from Judaism to Catholicism, viewed themselves as British and supported British imperial ambitions in the region.

While in this period two major ethnic identities became available to South African settlers, the conquest of African kingdoms and the imposition of chiefs and Native Law inflicted a multitude of ethnicities on indigenous peoples. These tended to be described by the colonial authorities in terms of language, and what was deemed the ethnic identity of a chief, although often with scant attention to local histories and the complexities of identity.

Ethnicities formed in the opposition to colonial conquest and fostered by the colonial rulers militated against the formation of a common African identity among indigenous peoples. This was partly because the need to defend their polities against colonial conquest had led to enhanced support for African kings from the homesteads under their suzerainty. This support remained, despite and possibly because of their defeat. However, no African kingdoms were able to unite together against colonial attack. The support base of the rulers who could put up any form of military resistance was local, based on regional political economies.

Attitudes to the ethnicities fostered by colonial rulers were complex. Many indigenous Christian converts, often descended from people who had been persecuted in the process of the formation of African kingdoms, found employment in the Colonial Civil Service. Despite their personal histories and the nature of their employment, they identified with the resistance led by the African kings. They claimed an ethnic identity that was melded in with their adherence to universalist notions of Christianity, African unity and what was believed to be the liberalism of the Empire. For example, the architects of the African National Congress (ANC), formed in 1912, sought to carry rulers of defeated kingdoms like the Zulu king Dinuzulu and Dalindyebo of the Pondo into an organization which looked forward to a different form of polity. They also simultaneously hoped for justice that they believed was inherent in the governance of the Empire and despaired at the treatment of African political aspirations (Meli, 1988: 36–46).

The constructions of race and ethnicity that developed in this period of colonial rule had profound implications for gender relations. Jacklyn Cock has shown how, on the eastern frontier, women who were subordinate workers in settler households were construed as racially inferior (Cock, 1990). Similar trends probably characterized attitudes to domestic workers in most settler households and militated against the development of any perception of a common sisterhood, even among women who spoke the same language or were members of the same church (Gaitskell, 1981; Gaitskell et al., 1980).

Notions of race informed gender relations with regard to political participation. The franchise was a preserve of male property-owners, predominantly those deemed white. No political power or authority was vested in settler women, mirroring their lack of access to economic and ideological authority.

As in the earlier phase of colonial rule, the nature and form of women's organization remain largely undocumented. However, there are some accounts of schools and church organizations run largely by women (Gaitskell, 1981). In these the strong influence of ideologies of 'improvement' for indigenous women aspiring to an ideal embodied by settler women, and for settler women aspiring to an ideal embodied by a woman living in metropolitan Europe, is evident. Gender ideologies were thus deeply inscribed with notions of race.

While the intention of these organizations of settler women was to bring indigenous women into the orbit of the Empire, albeit in a subordinate position, the intention of some organizations of indigenous women within the kingdoms that opposed settler and colonial conquest appears to have been to maintain the forms of homestead ritual that sanctified the king or the chief and provided him with labour and troops, thus assisting his opposition to conquest and cementing a form of ethnic identity. For example, the support of women subjects for the Zulu king Cetshwayo in his opposition to British conquest has been noted (Guy, 1979: 181).

The construction of the subjects of African polities as Natives ruled by chiefs, the extortions made on them for tax, and the subsequent development of migrant labour restructured gender relations in the homesteads. While the form of homestead production was maintained, increasingly as more and more young men were forced into labour migration, and heavier revenue demands were made on the homesteads, the sexual division of labour within the homestead shifted. Greater demands were made on women to labour in communal fields and women increasingly lost access to the product of their vegetable gardens. Legal stipulations on a high level of *lobola* sometimes led to homestead heads forcing women into marriage (Unterhalter, 1981).

The mobility and rights of residence outside the homestead of women deemed 'Native' were severely restricted under colonial law. A congruence of interest in controlling these women emerged between chiefs, homestead heads and colonial rulers. For the latter the political and economic objectives of this control were overlaid with notions concerning the need to protect women from what was deemed urban squalour and the licentiousness believed to ensue when women were outside the control of a male relative (Kimble, 1983).

The construction of ethnicity by colonial and indigenous rulers led to a further subordination of women in terms of what was termed traditional law. In first Natal and later Zululand, the Shepstone Code, which purported to be a codification of traditional, Zulu law, defined women who were not Christian and not married to private property-owners as perpetual minors, and prevented them from gaining access to or owning land or entering into any contract in their own right. In other ethnically defined chieftaincies, the somewhat more flexible negotiations concerning law and gender, which had been a feature of the previous period, transmuted into written documents, underwritten by the power of the colonial authorities. In these, women were formally barred from participating in councils, subject to the authority of their husbands with regard to ownership of property, and punishable by flogging for offences (Simons, 1968; Burman, 1990; Kimble, 1985).

As in earlier periods competing notions of race and ethnicity co-existed and impacted differentially on gender relations. These helped form the colonial and settler state and became enshrined in institutions, particularly those governing political participation, employment and land ownership. While ethnic differentiation evolved between settlers who viewed themselves as Boers or British, this division was given no institutional sanction in this period. By contrast, ethnicities ascribed to the former subjects of African rulers were central to the way in which they were ruled, and hence to their access to land and to the labour market. These ethnicities also came to structure gender relations, and women's organizations were marked by divisions of race and ethnicity.

The National Project of Settler Rulers: The Union of South Africa, 1910–1960

The legislation that established the Union of South Africa in 1910 sought to create a national sovereign state out of the colonial and settler-ruled regions of the previous era. The form of this new state preserved the racially inscribed and gender-biased franchise arrangements current in the four provinces of South Africa. In the Transvaal, Natal and the Orange Free State all men deemed white could vote, and all men deemed not white were excluded from the franchise, bar a handful; in the Cape a larger number of men considered black had franchise rights, but in 1908 85 per cent of registered voters were classified as white (Thomson, 1990: 150). Women considered white won franchise rights in 1936. From its inception the South African nation-state was largely the project of settler interests.

In this period South Africa constitutes a form of racialized democracy. That is, in the whites-only parliament the executive and judiciary were subordinated to the legislature; all political parties were legal (although the Communist Party was proscribed in 1950); there were rights of association, rights to demonstrate, a free press and an organized trade union movement. However, male workers who carried passes – that is, primarily those who were subject to Native Law – were prevented from joining registered trade unions and thus unable officially to engage in collective bargaining.

The National Party (NP) came to power in an election in 1948. During the 1950s the NP enacted many of the laws which came to be viewed as the pillars of apartheid – that is, laws enforcing racial classification, residential and educational segregation, strict controls on the movement of people classified as Africans and laws preventing marriage and sexual intercourse between those classified white and those classified non-white.

However, much of this legislation made *de jure* what already existed *de facto*. Institutions and associations that developed after 1910 entailed constructions of a unified white race, and what came to be construed as non-white races of Africans, Coloureds and Indians.

The economy of South Africa was based on the extraction of minerals and the export of agricultural produce. While the country was largely self-sufficient in food, it was heavily reliant on imports of capital and manufactured goods. However, during World War II there was an expansion in local industry, a trend which continued afterwards.

Mining, industry and the service sector were heavily reliant on migrant labourers who were paid low wages. These workers were largely denied access to training and hence viewed as unskilled. They were virtually all defined as Native (or African). However, not all unskilled or low-paid workers were deemed black. Throughout the 1920s and 1930s governments were concerned with the problem of what were described as poor whites. These were primarily impoverished rural families, descendants of settler farmers, who were forced to leave the land and migrate to the cities. Extensive social welfare and training projects were established to integrate them into the industrial economy.

This concern contrasts sharply with the way in which the state ignored the impact of migrant labour on the reserves and farms where people classified as African lived. The combination of labour migration and lack of land had begun to impact negatively on rural populations on farms and in the reserves. There was a steady growth in conditions of poverty and the number of people dependent on the wages of a migrant worker, which no longer supplemented, but became the main source of, income for a homestead (Bundy, 1977; Murray, 1981). Legislation assisted settler farmers to secure labour service from their tenants and to force down the wages of farm workers. All men classified Native were required to carry passes. Legislation was enacted that limited their rights to settle in urban areas. In the 1950s attempts were made to extend this legislation to women similarly racially classified, but intense opposition led by women's organizations made the laws unworkable until the next decade.

The Union of South Africa between 1910 and 1960 gave legislative form to the notion of a white race. It did this primarily by identifying not *who* was white, but what constraints limited all who were not. Thus, controls on the movement of labour were enforced for black workers, not white. (South Africa welcomed immigrants from Europe and America, and only began to impose quotas on immigration for Jews when considerable numbers started coming to the country in the mid-1930s.) There were stringent barriers to land ownership for anyone other than those deemed white in areas demarcated for whites. Much of the impetus for social welfare projects for poor whites after the depression stemmed from a concern that poverty would degrade them and make them equivalent to 'non-whites' (Christie and Gordon, 1992).

Divisions between the 'non-white races' were initially inscribed in legislation regarding ownership of land and mobilization of labour. From 1913 a range of legislation began to be introduced that limited where these 'non-whites' could own land. Much of this began to differentiate them as Asiatics, Natives and Coloureds.

The formal division of land ownership primarily on grounds of 'race' was effected in the 1913 Native Land Act. This prevented 'Natives' (that is, the subjects of chiefs and people administered through Native Law) owning or acquiring land outside scheduled areas (which comprised 14 per cent of the country). It also prohibited acquisition of land in these scheduled reserves or certain proclaimed urban areas by people deemed white, Coloured or Indian.

Labour legislation also carried with it ascriptions of racial identity. The pass laws which controlled access to the labour market and rigidly limited the mobility of labour were applied only to those subject to Native Law and under the authority of chiefs. The 1911 Native Labour Regulation Act made it a criminal offence for those defined as African (that is pass-bearing) farm and mine workers to leave their jobs without the permission of their employers. The 1924 Industrial Conciliation Act excluded 'pass bearers' from the definition of an employee. This prevented African men forming legally recognized trade unions.

The notion of a largely homogenous 'black race' implied in the South Africa Act was as much a fiction as was that of a 'white race'. Differences of class, gender, religion and political affiliation were marked. The utilization of structures of indirect rule in the conquered African kingdoms and chieftaincies and the system of migrant labour maintained and often reinforced regional and local identities (Bozzoli, 1991; Delius, 1989). While some subjects of these polities settled permanently in urban areas and maintained strong links with their rural origins, others, many of them women who had left to evade control by chiefs and homestead heads, forged new hybrid identities in a different context.

Throughout the period the racial category of Coloured was being defined. At the beginning of the twentieth century the term was used to denote all people not deemed white. Ian Goldin demonstrates how, by 1905, a stratum of wealthy educated people living in the western Cape, who did not perceive themselves as white, mobilized themselves ideologically and politically to forge an identity for a Coloured population, distinct from impoverished unskilled indigenous people, whom they perceived as Natives and later Africans (Goldin, 1987: 162–3). In the 1905 census, Coloureds are distinguished as a separate racial group. This census sought to delineate as Coloureds those descendants of ex-slaves brought to the Cape from the East Indies, many of whom were Muslim, certain descendants of the Khoi and San peoples, and some literate Christians and skilled artisans with a mixed racial and ethnic heritage (Goldin, 1987: 12–13). This new racial category was given institutional effect throughout the period as people deemed Coloured were exempt from carrying passes, from restrictions on urban residence, and from barriers that limited access to artisanal training. There was often a very thin line between people deemed Coloured and those deemed white, particularly if the latter were long-established in the country. They shared a common language in Afrikaans and often shared family relations. When the 1950 Population Registration Act of 1950 forced a firm legal boundary between *wit en bruin* (white and brown) Afrikaners, many personal tragedies ensued.

The constitutional legislation entailed a political concept of the descendants of Indian indentured labourers and other immigrants with affiliations with India as non-whites. From 1910 to 1947 the Union government was locked in bitter wrangling with representatives of this population and the Indian government over the legal status of people termed Asiatics and later Indians. This racial categorization represented a simplistic unity. These immigrants came from very different regions of India, and some had been settled in the Middle East or East Africa. They were divided by gender, class, political perceptions, religion, the length of time they had been in South Africa, and the region they lived in. Yet they were viewed as a homogenous and separate Indian 'race' by the state. Specific laws like the 1946 Asiatic Land Tenure Act regulated where they could own land, to whom they could sell their land, and where they could trade.

Thus far I have indicated how the constructions of racial difference among dominated people were formulated through laws emanating from the settler parliament. However, partly as a defence against this enforced subordination, the population classified as non-white mobilized politically and ideologically in organizations that simultaneously both opposed segregation under imposed racial categories and entrenched a racial identity. For example, the ANC, officially launched in 1912 under the leadership of a middle-class intelligentsia with the support of the heirs of former African kings, developed out of widespread opposition to the racial discrimination contained in the 1910 Constitution. It attempted to bring together all the subjects and former subjects of chiefs and kings to oppose the racially inscribed franchise laws. During the period of Union it opposed the discriminatory land and labour laws. In doing so it began to forge the notion of an African nation united in opposition to the attacks on indigenous rights enacted by the settler state. Further examples of this construction of racial difference are evident in the political organizations and trade unions which were developed to protect the interests of people who viewed themselves as Indians and Coloureds (Swan, 1987; Goldin, 1987).

There were some attempts at building alliances across 'racial' boundaries. In the 1920s a radical trade union leadership among those classified Coloured in the western Cape united with workers classified as African in the large nationally based Industrial and Commercial Workers Union (ICU). In the late 1940s Indian radicalism made common cause with the ANC. However, many of these initiatives were fragile.

From the late 1940s the ANC forged alliances with Indian Congresses, the Coloured People's Congress, the white Congress of Democrats and the non-racial South African Congress of Trade Unions (SACTU). The Congress Alliance mobilized a number of popular and extremely successful demonstrations throughout the 1950s in which Africans predominated, but people of other 'races' participated. However, the ANC leadership's support for non-racialism was not without its critics. In the late 1950s the organization split, and an Africanist movement, which rejected the participation of whites and Communists (sometimes seen as equivalent) in African opposition politics, emerged in the form of the Pan-African Congress (PAC).

The process of constructing race was intensely contradictory. On the one hand, South Africa portrayed itself as a nation-state made up of many racial groups. However, as the ANC pointed out in its submissions to the 1919 Versailles Conference, while black South Africans were considered part of the nation when there was a need for troops, they were not given this identity when it came to government (Meli, 1988: 54). There were similar contradictions in the labour movement, in which notions of socialism and universal brotherhood coexisted with strong mobilization to protect the privileged position of white workers and prevent black workers from gaining skills. This contradiction is encapsulated in the banners displayed during the General Strike of 1924, which read: 'Workers of the World unite for a white South Africa.'

The unity of the white 'race' constituted through the constitutional legislation of 1910 was fragile. This population was divided as much as the 'non-white' by class, gender, religion and region. In this phase an ethnic nationalist mobilization of Afrikaners gained ground. Some of the origins of this movement lay in the harsh treatment meted out by the British to the Boers during the Anglo-Boer War (1899–1902). This was compounded by Milner's zeal for Anglicization in the former Boer republics, which resulted in suppressing the use of Dutch and Afrikaans. The war had left many Boer farmers destitute and disillusioned with their leaders. Many lacked the skills to compete for work with British immigrants. A nationalist movement grew up among whites who viewed themselves as Afrikaners engaged in a struggle to defend and advance the use of Afrikaans and to build up Afrikaner-owned companies, Afrikaner trade unions and Afrikaner access to education. Afrikaner nationalism was antagonistic to what was seen as the moderate approach to segregation of the South African Party (SAP), which, it was felt, did not adequately protect white workers from black competition or secure to white farmers adequate supplies of labour (O'Meara, 1983). A view of racial difference was thus deeply embedded in the construction of Afrikaner identity in this period.

The development of ethnic identity in this period was not unique to the Afrikaners. The system of Native Administration continued to foster ethnic divisions among the African population. The system of migrant labour helped to maintain ethnic identities and regional affiliations, as workers were forced to return to their home districts every year. Many large employers, like the mines, maintained ethnically segregated hostels forcing workers to adopt an ethnic identity.

Ten main African languages were given standardized orthographies and grammars in this period, and the segregated education that existed for Africans perpetuated regional linguistic differences. These further contributed to ethnic perceptions.

The ANC, from its inception, had been aware of the need to unite disparate African ethnic groups. Its inaugural conference succeeded in bringing together delegates from all the different ethnically defined sectors of the African population. The upper house of the organization consisted of seven paramount chiefs, who were appointed honorary presidents in a move to gain support from those whose interest remained in continued ethnic division.

However, the ANC was not uniformly strong in all the regions of the country. In this period, with the majority of the population still rural, the effect of universalizing ideologies such as African nationalism, socialism and Christianity was strongly counterpointed by local affiliations which carried within them ascriptions of ethnic identity. Belinda Bozzoli's study based on the life histories of women migrant workers from the western Transvaal brings out this tension very clearly (Bozzoli, 1991).

Ethnicization proceeded in this period among people deemed white and among those deemed African, but in the numerically smaller 'races' of Coloureds and Indians, despite the diverse origins of the population and very different faiths, ethnic differences did not take a political form. It may be that the imposition of Coloured and Indian identities through state institutions and popular organizations militated against further division of these groups. There were few political and economic objectives to be gained by developing an ethnic identity and the state did not impose this.

The emergence of strong lines delimiting racial and ethnic difference impacted forcefully on gender relations. The impact of residential segregation and the emergence of ideologies of racial purity among whites, of Africanism and of Coloured and Indian identity all led to a tendency to control women's reproduction to ensure the maintenance of race identity. These informal family controls were given legislative force when the Immorality Act and the Prohibition of Mixed Marriages Act became law in 1950, forbidding sexual relations and marriages across what were viewed as racially defined boundaries.

However, the entry of many more women into wage employment in this period tended to weaken patriarchal controls over reproduction. Tensions between a woman's wish to marry or form a sexual relationship across ethnic or racially constructed boundaries and the pressures of a family forcing conformity have been noted in a number of auto-biographies and collections of life histories (Bozzoli, 1991; Kuzwayo, 1985: 124; Russell, 1990: 299).

The ascription of racial identity to African women superimposed a colonial version of 'traditional law' on the social structures of the homestead. The Union of South Africa meant that this law, termed 'customary law', was extended to all African women not deemed emancipated. This law entailed that all African women were perpetual minors subject to the authority of father or husband. They could not enter into contracts or own property in their own right (Simons, 1968: 122–38).

The creation of ethnicity impinged powerfully on the construction of gender for Afrikaner women. In the development of Afrikaner nationalism the icon of the *volksmoeder* evolved, levelling differences of class and region, and transmitting a powerful message regarding the importance of Afrikaner women's submission to their menfolk and loyalty to the Afrikaner *volk* (Brink, 1990). The promotion of Afrikaans was linked with the publication of magazines that celebrated special Afrikaner home values (Hofmeyr, 1987). Research still needs to be conducted on whether similar processes informed the construction of an ethnic identity for English-speaking South Africans, African subjects of ethnically distinct chieftaincies, and the ethnically or racially constructed minorities of Coloureds and Indians.

This period saw the emergence of women's organizations based outside the domestic and religious sphere. Women's trade unions, political movements, professional associations and social welfare groups all developed, many growing from local or regional to national structures (Walker, 1982, 1990b: Kuzwayo, 1985: 100–4; Berger, 1992; du Toit, 1978; Hooper, 1960; Ginwala, 1988; Wells, 1982; Spink, 1991; Joseph, 1986). Most of these organizations embodied a tension. They were divided between the dominant ideological construction of gender, where, as Cherryl Walker has pointed out, the concept of 'woman' was organized around domesticity, subordination to male authority, child-bearing and child care (Walker, 1990a: 25), and a new construction of gender inherent in the organizational work, where women worked to further the aims of their organizations, sometimes together, but often in direct conflict with, men of the same class and 'race'.

However, while organization outside the domestic sphere worked to redefine gender relations, the general tendency was for these organizations to comply with dominant formulations of 'race', and to a more limited extent with those of ethnicity. Thus, all the major women's organizations formed in this period worked within the boundaries of racial differentiation constructed by the state and the predominantly male opposition organizations. The most striking example of this is the suffrage movement, where white women strategically decided to focus their organization on demands for the vote for themselves, to the exclusion of other disenfranchised groups, that is men and women termed 'non-white' (Walker, 1990b).

The nation-state of South Africa was founded on a notion of unequal power and racial division. However, the notions of race and ethnicity propounded by the state and popular organizations were not uniformly accepted. Universalist notions about equality, citizenship and non-racism were expressed by a relatively small number of organizations, but by the late 1950s these notions appeared to be gaining mass support. In 1959–60 there was a countrywide series of strikes and demonstrations against the government on a range of issues, both local and national. A growing demand was for an end to apartheid with its implicit and explicit racism; this demand entailed the creation of a new state on the basis of universal franchise. These uprisings were suppressed by the imposition of a state of emergency, and the imprisonment of the leadership of most of the organizations. With its major opposition severely weakened, the ruling party moved to utilize the state apparatus to entrench the demands of Afrikaner nationalism and shape the state to fulfil the objectives first of Afrikaners and only secondly of all deemed white.

Fulfilling the Objectives of the Afrikaner Nation-State: Race, Ethnicity and Gender in the Republic of South Africa, 1960–1993

The 30 years of the repressive apartheid state (1960–90) began and ended with the imposition of states of emergency, mass detentions and widespread killings of demonstrators by police. This period saw a continuation of a racialized parliament, which was democratic only in form. Increasingly, the legislature and the judiciary were subordinated to the executive, and in the 1980s to the military. Political opposition parties demanding majority rule were outlawed after 1960; the press was subjected to rigid censorship; powerful instruments to support the ideology of white supremacy were put in place in the education system; rigid restrictions on rights of association and demonstration were enacted. From 1976 violent police and later military power were used to enforce these. Detention without trial, torture and assassination – that is, terror – were common instruments of state power.

The period was marked initially by a boom, with large-scale foreign investment and an expansion of production and employment. The economy went into recession in 1976, following the brutal suppression of the schoolchildren's uprising that began in Soweto. Thereafter, corporate capital undertook a restructuring, floating and finally abolishing the colour bar that had prevented the employment of black workers in skilled jobs. The work-force in mining and agriculture was reduced with large-scale investment in mechanization.

From 1960 industry began to expand dramatically both as an employer and as a contributor to GDP. While the number of locally owned corporations increased, the economy remained heavily dependent on importations of capital. From the mid-1980s a long period of recession began. In the late 1980s and early 1990s the country experienced negative growth and very high rates of unemployment.

The state and its legislative apparatus maintained the racial divisions constructed in a former era until 1990. The 1945 Native (Urban Areas) Act and the 1950 Group Areas Act were vigorously applied to enforce the residential segregation of the African, white, Coloured and Indian populations. Educational segregation carried with it sharp differentials in spending on the different racially defined population groups. While huge investments were made in white education, there was markedly less spending on Coloured and Indian education, with derisory amounts being invested in African education. Education was not compulsory for African children, and only became so for all Coloured and Indian children in 1979–80. English-language universities, which had admitted a small number of students classified not white, were forbidden to continue with open enrolments. New racially divided universities were established for Africans, Indians and Coloureds.

The pass laws were applied with great vigour to men and women in an attempt to maintain the African work-force as migrant and unskilled with minimal labour protection.

The trend that had begun in the earlier period for the reserves to become overcrowded and underdeveloped accelerated. Starved of resources, suffering a heavy increase in population because of the policy of forcibly removing workers from farms and from the urban areas – approximately 3 million people were removed between 1960 and 1985 – reserves became areas of horrific poverty (Platzky and Walker, 1985; Unterhalter, 1987). People living on them suffered excessively high rates of infant mortality, malnutrition and disease. Remittances from migrant labourers and scant welfare payments became the only source of support for homesteads.

These areas described as 'homelands' by the government and 'Bantustans' by the opposition became central to the strategy for political repression. Repressive administrations were put in place which were nominally self-governing. The Bantustan strategy was intended to establish South Africa as a country without African nationals. In the early 1980s four Bantustans had been granted what was termed independence. Their citizens (approximately 20 per cent of the population) became officially aliens in South Africa subject to severe restrictions on employment and accommodation.

This harsh institutionalization of racism had many contradictions, partly because of the realization by the government that it could not remain in power without the support of sections of the dominated races and without the leadership of corporate capital. Large corporations perceived the declining productivity of the economy to be the result of controls on the mobility of labour and the lack of skill among black workers. In an attempt to address these concerns, while simultaneously maintaining a commitment to black subordination, the government pursued contradictory policies. Thus, while racial division was being legally entrenched and advanced, officials turned a blind eye as employers disregarded legislation that imposed a colour bar and hence allowed black workers to carry out skilled work previously forbidden them. Although the African population was terrorized by officials enforcing the pass laws, employers were allowed to evade these regulations.

The African population, faced with starvation in the rural areas, defied the pass laws, and daily risked arrest and imprisonment in order to gain access to the wage economy in the urban areas. This mass defiance over decades made the pass law system unworkable. In addition, capital grew increasingly impatient with the pass laws, which artificially limited their access to skilled labour. In the mid-1980s the pass laws were abolished. However, this did not signal the end of migrant labour. The lack of housing in urban areas and the very poor conditions in which squatters were forced to live sometimes meant that wage earners were forced to remain as migrant workers.

The government found allies amongst some Bantustan leaders and Coloureds and Indians, who were prepared to give credence to a new constitutional dispensation. In 1983 the tricameral parliament was inaugurated. Coloureds and Indians were enfranchised and granted the right to elect representatives to two subordinate houses of parliament.

The establishment of the tricameral parliament and the enfranchisement of Coloureds and Indians, while Africans, the majority of the population, were denied this vote, unleashed the largest wave of opposition since 1959–60. The Indian and Coloured population were strongly divided on whether to participate in the tricameral parliament and support apartheid institutions or not. Those who rejected this joined the mushrooming anti-apartheid organizations.

Mass-based opposition had re-emerged in the early 1970s. It grew up first in black trade unions, which enlisted thousands of members. In the 1980s mass opposition to apartheid expanded into new spheres. A range of locally based housing and urban action organizations (civics), repression monitoring groups, religious groups, sports groups and women's groups openly defied the regime, opposing apartheid legislation in their areas. In some of these groups there was an attempt to organize across racially constructed boundaries. Two very large national non-racial bodies emerged in the United Democratic Front (UDF), which brought together a wide range of local and regional organizations, and the Congress of South African Trade Unions (COSATU).

Although some Coloureds and Indians did vote for representatives in the tricameral parliament, not all members of these racially constructed minorities opted to be identified with a white political project. Some Coloureds and Indians viewed participation in the tricameral parliament as a betrayal of Africans who had no vote. From 1983 to 1993 significant numbers of Indians and Coloureds identified themselves with the aspirations of Africans for majority rule, participating in the work of the UDF, COSATU and the ANC.

The forging of organizational links across racial barriers within the country echoed a trend that had been begun by the ANC, in exile and underground. At its conference in 1967 in Morogoro, the ANC opened the membership to all South Africans. An internal opposition group with an Africanist orientation, the Azanian Peoples Organization (AZAPO) had developed from the 1970s, uniting Africans, Coloureds and Indians together in an assertion of what was portrayed as black political unity. The notion of 'black' delineated a common experience of oppression and became widely used in a broad range of opposition movements. With this meaning it gained a particular ideological force for opposition organizations as the regime attempted to co-opt the term 'black' to describe the section of the indigenous population it had once disparagingly termed Native.

Despite the draconian measures of the state of emergency imposed in 1986, and in spite of attempts to divide the anti-apartheid opposition, the regime was unable to suppress what amounted to a national uprising. In 1990 it was forced officially to unban the ANC, the South African Communist Party (SACP), PAC and a number of other proscibed organizations, release large numbers of political prisoners, and allow home an exiled political leadership. This move signalled an awareness by the Afrikaner Nationalist leadership of the NP that it was impossible to ensure either economic or political survival in South Africa without some form of political accommodation with the majority of people who lived in the country. From 1990 to 1994 the ANC, the NP and a number of smaller parties engaged in complex, protracted negotiations on a future political and economic settlement for South Africa.

By the 1990s commitment to the institutional framework of racial division had waned in the dominant classes. The economic weakness, international isolation and political instability of the country were all seen to be consequences of apartheid. In an attempt to reverse all these negative tendencies, President de Klerk attempted to normalize political conditions, lift repressive legislation and abolish the so-called pillars of apartheid, the Population Registration Act, the Group Areas Act, the Separate Amenities Act and the Land Act. However, this legislation represented only the tip of the iceberg out of which racial differentiation and discrimination had been carved. Moreover, racism had penetrated economic and ideological relations which were not governed by law.

The contradictory construction of race in this period was paralleled by a similar contradictory construction of ethnicity. The forced removal of millions of Africans into the Bantustans was accompanied by a forced ascription of ethnic identity. The majority of people classified African had strong attachments to their language and history (partly as a result of imperial conquest). I would like to counterpose this informal assumption of ethnicity, which I believe is based on processes by which an individual constructs an identity, with the forced ascription of ethnicity imposed under apartheid legislation. This latter trend was different in degree from less coercive forms of ethnicization linked to rule by chiefs and Native Administration in the previous era.

In this period an arbitrary ethnicization of the African population was carried out, forcing people to be subjects of a particular Bantustan, whether they spoke the language of the rulers of that Bantustan or not. In most Bantustans there were people speaking a different language or with a somewhat different culture to that deemed dominant. In a number of Bantustans these minorities were sometimes terrorized and forced to flee, as was the case in Bophuthatswana in 1978.

The ascription of ethnic identity was not confined to the Bantustans. By the 1960s large numbers of Africans were living outside these areas and many had permanent rights of urban residence. Many families were not ethnically homogenous. A Xhosa-speaker might be married to a Zulu, a Sotho to a Tswana. The ethnicization of the previous periods had been intermeshed with other integrative forces of church, school or employment, facilitating marriages and associations across ethnic barriers. Nonetheless, housing and schooling were allocated on the basis of a perceived ethnicity. All Africans settled in urban townships were zoned into ethnic areas, and their children forced to attend the schools deemed appropriate for their ethnic group.

The strategy of ethnicization of the African population was based on a simple notion of divide and rule. It was pursued side by side with a range of policies which sought to overcome the ethnic divisions that had developed between whites in the previous period. This trend emerged in 1976. In the 1960s and early 1970s there had been a vigorous attempt to assert Afrikaner independence from the metropolitan centre, seen to be symbolized by the Commonwealth. This was accompanied by an Afrikaner wresting of control of political, economic and ideological institutions from English South Africans. However, from 1976 when crucial foreign investment was first withdrawn in response to the repression of the schoolchildren's uprising, it became clear to sections of the NP leadership that it would be impossible to achieve Afrikaner dominance without the support of corporate capital, still largely controlled by English-speaking South Africans. As the decade progressed, so the regime attempted to mobilize not only corporate capital, but also all whites, in what was termed a 'total strategy' to preserve minority rule against what were perceived as the threats of internal insurrection and international isolation (Moss, 1980; O'Meara, 1983). Thus, while Africans were being divided as the subjects of Bantustan governments, whites (both English and Afrikaans, women and men, of all religions) were being mobilized to support the apartheid project through a heady mixture of supposed threats to their property and stability posed by 'terrorists' and 'Communists', by conscription into the army and by isolation from the rest of the world.

The advancement of racial and ethnic divisions in this period became of great importance to the constitution of gender relations for a majority of the population. Two areas can be considered. First, all African women were forced to carry passes until their abolition in 1986. The pass laws meant these women were extremely vulnerable in relation to employment, accommodation and mobility. They were deemed the 'superfluous appendages' of male workers, and were viewed as the breeders of an unwanted African urban population (Simons, 1968: 282). As such, they were forced to remain in the Bantustans by a whole array of laws which subjected them to the authority of Bantu Affairs Administration Boards with extensive powers to control and enforce where women could live and work. As illegal workers in urban areas, women, often employed as domestic workers, were isolated and subject to enormous exploitation (Cock, 1989). As illegal urban residents, women were often forced into dependency on a male with access to accommodation. The abolition of the pass laws did not end the fragile position of a majority of African women with regard to employment or accommodation. Their impoverishment, partly the result of the breakdown of redistributive structures in the rural areas, and partly the result of the apartheid-imposed barriers to their employment, has ensured a continuation of the exploitation they suffered before 1986.

Secondly, the mobilization of whites around what was perceived as a threat to their survival and the organization of opposition forces around the cause of national liberation had strangely similar effects in terms of gender. Both led to a predominance of conservative views in relation to maintaining existing gender relations, particularly in the domestic sphere and within political organizations. To challenge these was viewed as a threat to the projects of building unity to which each was dedicated.

White women who joined the NP and served in the army were forced to accept subordinate roles and collude in ideological representations of themselves still restricted to the domestic sphere (Goodwin, 1984; Cock, 1992). Although the UDF, COSATU and the ANC made programmatic commitments to advancing and defending women's rights in the 1980s, their success in giving effect to this in their organizational practice was limited (Ginwala, 1987; Mtintso, 1992; Manzini, 1992). In all three organizations there was a tension about how women's demands should be advanced. The debate centred on whether there should be a two-stage approach to the gender question or, whether in demanding national liberation, women should also demand an end to their subordination.

By 1990, however, the view had become widespread within sections of the ANC and the NP that there could be no two-stage approach to women's emancipation. Women intervened in the discussions about constitutional change, demanding that gender be put on the agenda (Bazzili, 1991; Biehl, 1993). This consensus united women across political parties, but their success in achieving this was marred to some extent by party-political ties and differences on how to prioritize the range of issues under scrutiny (Biehl, 1993; Friedman, 1993).

In the process of shaping a new South Africa, the dominant conception of gender came under severe ideological pressure. To some extent this was the achievement of women's groupings within trade unions, political organizations and pressure groups; it was also the result of contact with international women's organizations (Unterhalter, 1988; Russell, 1990; Mabandla, 1991; Mtintso, 1992; Biehl, 1993). In the majority of these organizations there was a strong commitment to attempting to organize across the apartheid-created racial barriers. However, the difficulties of doing this were manifold, although rarely acknowledged in the literature.

In counterpoint to the national trend to try to overcome 'racial' divisions in women's organizations and attempt to construct new gender relations, a defence of the older construction of gender was mounted by a number of women's organizations which placed great emphasis on ethnicity. Thus, for example, the Inkatha Women's Brigade continued to extol the importance of women's role in the domestic sphere, which it characterized as part of Zulu identity.

Enormous contradictions also confronted the ANC in negotiating with traditional leaders over a new constitution. The concept of citizenship and equal rights for women contained in the draft bill of rights ran counter to the perceptions of this powerful grouping within the

ANC's constituency. Agreement that customary law should be subject to the equality clause of the bill of rights was only reached 24 hours before the establishment of the Transitional Executive Council (TEC) in November 1993. This represented a considerable victory for women's groups, particularly the National Women's Coalition which had campaigned on this issue.

The major contradiction of this period was that forced racial and ethnic delineation and intense repression of women spawned their opposites. Partly in reaction to repression and economic decline, a strong commitment to a deracialized form of the state emerged, not only among dominated classes where this was based on principle, but also within corporate executives and the leadership of the NP, where it was based on pragmatism. A significant achievement of women's organization was that the move to build a deracialized state was accompanied by a constitutional framework that sought to overcome gender inequalities.

Conclusion

This chapter has surveyed different phases in the construction of race, ethnicity and gender in South Africa. In each phase different elements have had greater influence than others. However, it is striking that the period of the most rigid state enforcement of racial and ethnic difference (1960–90) was also the period of gender relations marked by an increasing economic, political and ideological subordination of women.

The process of giving institutional effect to changing notions of gender, race and ethnicity has been highly contradictory. The intentions of dominant groups have not always been implemented, or, in the implementation, the opposite tendency to that intended has been nurtured. But old formulations of gender, race and ethnicity do not disappear in new conjunctures and supporters of an older order have vigorously contested new definitions in new conjunctures.

At the time of writing the new constitution for South Africa was under negotiation. The period of transition (1990–94) was marked by a very high level of violence. Two of the greatest threats to the success of negotiations were as follows. First, there was the determination of some white South Africans to retain their power through violent acts like the assassination of Chris Hani or through organizational intransigence in institutions like the army, the police force and sections of the bureaucracy. A second major threat was posed by volatile localized attacks in poor communities, which were frequently interpreted in ethnic terms. Nonetheless, neither succeeded in preventing the first democratic elections taking place in April 1994, and Nelson Mandela, the President of the ANC, being inaugurated as State President and head of a government of national unity the following month.

Constructions of race, class, ethnicity and gender were central to debates over establishing a deracialized constitution and bill of rights In the aftermath of the ratification of these documents and the formal establishment of a deracialized state in South Africa, there remains at issue how, given the bitter history of minority dominance on the grounds of categories of 'race', class, ethnicity and gender, a new state can be constructed which both takes account of this history, attempting some redress, and posits new relationships based on notions of citizenship, equity and equality. The Reconstruction and Development Programme, which forms the basis of ANC policy in the new era, is an attempt to undertake this task. Doubtless there will be intense struggles over its implementation because of the powerful legacy of some of the older identities discussed in this chapter.

References

Bazilli, Susan (1991) *Putting Women on the Agenda*. Johannesburg: Ravan Press.

Beinart, William (1982) *The Political Economy of Pondoland, 1860–1930*. Cambridge: Cambridge University Press.

Berger, Iris (1992) *Threads of Solidarity: Women in South African Industry, 1900–1980*. London: James Currey.

Biehl, Amy (1993) 'Dislodging the boulder: South African women and democratic transformation', unpublished paper, Community Law Centre, University of the Western Cape.

Bonner, Philip (1983) *Kings, Commoners and Concessionaires: the Evolution and Dissolution of the Nineteenth-Century Swazi State*. Cambridge: Cambridge University Press.

Bozzoli, Belinda (1991) *Women of Phokeng: Consciousness, Life Strategies and Migration in South Africa, 1900–1983*. Johannesburg: Ravan Press.

Brink, Elsabe (1990) 'Man-made women: gender, class and the ideology of the *volksmoeder*', in C. Walker (ed.), *Women and Gender in Southern Africa to 1945*. Cape Town: David Philip. pp. 273–92.

Bundy, Colin (1977) 'The Transkei peasantry, *c.* 1890–1914: "passing through a period of stress"', in R. Palmer and N. Parsons (eds), *The Roots of Rural Poverty in Central and Southern Africa*. London: Heineman. pp. 201–20.

Burman, Sandra (1990) 'Fighting a two-pronged attack: the changing legal status of women in Cape-ruled Basutoland, 1872–1884', in C. Walker (ed.), *Women and Gender in Southern Africa to 1945*. Cape Town: David Philip. pp. 48–75.

Christie, Pam and Gordon, Adele (1992) 'Poverty and education in rural South Africa', *British Journal of the Sociology of Education*, 13 (4).

Cock, Jacklyn (1989) *Maids and Madams*, 2nd edition. London: Women's Press. (1st edition, 1980.)

Cock, Jacklyn (1990) 'Domestic service and education for domesticity: the incorporation of Xhosa women in colonial society', in C. Walker (ed.), *Women and Gender in Southern Africa to 1945*. Cape Town: David Philip. pp. 76–96.

Cock, Jacklyn (1992) *Women and War in South Africa*. London: Open Letters.

Delius, Peter (1989) 'The Ndzundza Ndebele: indenture and the making of ethnic identity, 1883–1914', in P. Bonner et al. (eds) *Holding their Ground: Class, Locality and Culture in Nineteenth- and Twentieth-Century South Africa*. Johannesburg: Ravan Press. pp. 105–40.

Du Toit, Bettie (1978) *Ukubamba Amadolo: Workers' Struggles in the South African Textile Industry*. London: Onyx Press.

Friedman, Steven (ed.) (1993) *The Long Journey: South Africa's Quest for a Negotiated Settlement*. Johannesburg: Ravan Press.

Gaitskell, Deborah (1981) 'Female mission initiative: black and white women in three Witwatersrand churches, 1903–1939', PhD dissertation, School of Oriental and African Studies, University of London.

Gaitskell, Deborah, Kimble, Judy, Maconachie, Moira and Unterhalter, Elaine (1984) 'Class, race and gender: domestic workers in South Africa', *Review of African Political Economy*, 27–8.

Ginwala, Frene (1987) 'Aspects of women's resistance in South Africa', paper, Women, Colonialism and Commonwealth Seminar, Institute of Commonwealth Studies, London.

Ginwala, Frene (1988) 'Women and the ANC, 1912–1943', paper, Societies of Southern Africa Seminar, Institute of Commonwealth Studies, London.

Ginwala, Frene (1989) 'Women's responses to colonialism in the seventeenth and eighteenth century', paper, ANC Women's Section History Study Group, London.

Goldin, Ian (1987) *Making Race: the Politics and Economics of Coloured Identity in South Africa*. London: Longman.

Goodwin, June (1984) *Cry Amandla! South African Women and the Question of Power*. New York: Africana Publishing.

Greenberg, Stanley B. (1980) *Race and State in Capitalist Development: Comparative Perspectives*. New Haven: Yale University Press.

Guy, Jeff (1979) *The Destruction of the Zulu Kingdom*. London: Longman.

Guy, Jeff (1982) 'The destruction and reconstruction of Zulu society', in S. Marks and R. Rathbone (eds), *Industrialization and Social Change in South Africa: African Class Formation, Culture and Consciousness, 1870–1930*. London: Longman. pp. 167–94.

Guy, Jeff (1990) 'Gender oppression in southern Africa's precapitalist societies', in C. Walker (ed.), *Women and Gender in Southern Africa to 1945*. Cape Town: David Philip. pp. 33–47.

Hofmeyr, Isabel (1987) 'Building a nation from words: Afrikaans language, literature and ethnic identity, 1902–1924', in S. Marks and S. Trapido (eds), *The Politics of Race, Class and Nationalism in Twentieth-Century South Africa*. London: Longman. pp. 95–123.

Hooper, Charles (1960) *Brief Authority*. London: Collins.

Joseph, Helen (1986) *Side by Side*. London: Zed Press.

Kimble, Judy (1983) '"Runaway wives": Basotho women, chiefs and the colonial state, *c.* 1890–1920', *Women in South African History Bulletin*, no. 2.

Kimble, Judy (1985) 'Migrant labour and colonial rule in southern Africa: the case of colonial Basutoland, 1890–1930'. PhD dissertation, University of Essex.

Kuzwayo, Ellen (1985) *Call Me Woman*. London: Women's Press.

Lipton, Merle (1986) *Capitalism and Apartheid: South Africa, 1910–1986*, 2nd edition. Aldershot: Wildwood House. (1st edition, Gower, 1985.)

Mabandla, Brigitte (1991) 'Promoting gender equality in South Africa', in S. Bazzili (ed.), *Putting Women on the Agenda*. Johannesburg: Ravan Press. pp. 75–81.

Magubane, Bernard (1979) *The Political Economy of Race and Class in South Africa*. New York: Monthly Review Press.

Manzini, Mavivi (1992) 'Women and power: implications for development', in World University Service, *Women and Power: Implications for Development*. Cape Town: World University Service. pp. 3–11.

Marks, Shula (1970) *Reluctant Rebellion: the 1906–8 Disturbances in Natal*. Oxford: Oxford University Press.

Marks, Shula and Rathbone, Richard (eds) (1982) *Industrialization and Social Change in South Africa: African Class Formation, Culture and Consciousness, 1870–1930*. London: Longman.

Marks, Shula and Trapido, Stanley (eds) (1987) *The Politics of Race, Class and Nationalism in Twentieth-Century South Africa*. London: Longman.

Meli, Francis (1988) *South Africa Belongs to Us: a History of the ANC*. Harare: Zimbabwe Publishing House.

Moss, Glenn (1980) 'Total Strategy', *Work in Progress*, no. 11.

Mostert, Noel (1992) *Frontiers: the Epic of South Africa's Creation and the Tragedy of the Xhosa People*. London: Jonathan Cape.

Mtintso, Thenjiwe (1992) 'Race, class and gender', in World University Service, *Women and Power: Implications for Development*. Cape Town: World University Service. pp. 31–4.

Murray, Colin (1981) *Families Divided: the Impact of Migrant Labour in Lesotho*. Cambridge: Cambridge University Press.

O'Meara, Dan (1983) *Volkskapitalisme: Class, Capital and Ideology in the Development of Afrikaner Nationalism, 1934–1948*. Johannesburg: Ravan Press.

Platzky, Laurine and Walker, Cheryl (1985) *The Surplus People: Forced Removals in South Africa*. Johannesburg: Ravan Press.

Russell, Diana E.H. (1990) *Lives of Courage: Women for a New South Africa*. London: Virago.

Simons, H. Jack (1968) *African Women: Their Legal Status in South Africa*. London: C. Hurst.

Spink, Kathryn (1991) *Black Sash: The Beginning of a Bridge*. London: Methuen.

Swan, Maureen (1987) 'Ideology in organized Indian politics, 1891–1948', in S. Marks and S. Trapido (eds) *The Politics of Race, Class and Nationalism in Twentieth-Century South Africa*. London: Longman. pp. 182–208.

Thomson, Leonard (1990) *A History of South Africa*. New Haven: Yale University Press.

Unterhalter, Elaine (1981) 'Religion, ideology and social change in the Nquthu district of Zululand, 1879–1910'. PhD dissertation, School of Oriental and African Studies, University of London.

Unterhalter, Elaine (1987) *Forced Removal: the Division, Segregation and Control of the People of South Africa*. London: International Defence and Aid Fund for Southern Africa.

Unterhalter, Elaine (1988) 'Class, race and gender', in J. Lonsdale (ed.), *South Africa in Question*. London: James Currey. pp. 154–71.

Walker, Cherryl (1982) *Women and Resistance in South Africa*. London: Onyx Press.

Walker, Cherryl (ed.) (1990a) *Women and Gender in Southern Africa to 1945*. Cape Town: David Philip .

Walker, Cherryl (1990b) 'The women's suffrage movement: the politics of gender, race and class', in C. Walker, *Women and Gender in Southern Africa to 1945*. Cape Town: David Philip. pp. 313–45.

Webb, Colin and John Wright (eds) (1976) *The James Stuart Archive of Recorded Oral Evidence relating to the History of the Zulu and Neighbouring Peoples*. Pietermaritzburg: University of Natal Press.

Wells, Julia (1982) 'The history of black women's struggle against the pass laws in South Africa'. PhD dissertation, University of Columbia, New York.

West, Martin (1988) 'Confusing categories: population groups, national states and citizenship', in E. Boonzaier and J. Sharp (eds), *South African Keywords: the Uses and Abuses of Political Concepts*. Cape Town: David Philip. pp. 100–10.

Wolpe, Harold (1988) *Race, Class and the Apartheid State*. London: James Currey.

9

Gender Divisions and the Formation of Ethnicities in Zimbabwe

Susie Jacobs

Zimbabwe is a classic example of a settler society. From the 1890s, white – predominantly British – settlers colonized the area that was to bear the name Southern Rhodesia and then Rhodesia. Like other such settler minorities, 'Rhodesians' laid strong foundational claim to the state and to society, forcibly attempting to establish their hegemony over African peoples. Unlike many others, when the Rhodesian settler minority found itself under threat from the worldwide move towards national independence, it declared UDI (Unilateral Declaration of Independence) from Britain in 1965. This resulted in guerrilla war and in negotiated independence in 1980. This chapter seeks to analyse racial and gender divisions in Zimbabwe in a more complex manner than the simple, racialized categories 'black/white' or simple dichotomies between men and women can afford. This will be done, where sources permit, by paying attention to ethnic* as well as to class and racial divisions. Zimbabwe is a heavily male-dominated society for all 'races' and ethnic groupings. Along with other chapters in this volume, this one argues that racial and ethnic divisions do not have the same resonance for men and for women.

A note on sources and on the aims and limitations of this chapter is in order here. There is now a well-established literature documenting the strength of gender divisions in pre-colonial, colonial and independent Zimbabwe (see, for instance, Batezat et al., 1988; Cheater, 1981; Jacobs, 1989a; Jacobs and Howard, 1987; Muchena, 1979; Pankhurst, 1991; Pape, 1990; Schmidt, 1991, 1992; Weinrich, 1979, 1982). Other sources (for example Arrighi, 1973; Bush et al., 1986; Cousins et al., 1992; Mandaza, 1986; Phimister, 1988; Stoneman and Cliffe, 1989) document

---

* In Zimbabwe, the term 'tribal' rather than 'ethnic' is often used to signify political conflicts based on (presumed) pre-colonial units of organization. Here I do not continue this use because of the association of 'tribalism' with other pejorative terms such as 'primitive'; moreover, the term 'tribe' does not correspond to contemporary units of organization, and may be misleading when applied to pre-colonial organization, based upon lineage groups.

the growth of class divisions in Rhodesia and Zimbabwe. A small literature focuses more specifically on the intersection of class with gender
divisions in Zimbabwe (Adams, 1991; Jacobs, 1989b; Pankhurst, 1991;
Weinrich, 1979, 1982).

Much writing, of course, details the racial divisions which were bru-
tally imposed with colonialism. Several sources discuss the creation
and/or existence of ethnic identities and groupings (see Hodder-
Williams, 1974; Kennedy, 1987; Kosmin, 1980; Mandaza, 1979;
Murphree, 1988; Ranger, 1983, 1985b, 1990a, b) among both Africans
and Europeans. However, the literature on ethnicity either omits mention of women or mentions them only in passing. In this chapter I
address this gap, and discuss the relation between gender and ethnic
divisions; where possible, I include discussion of class divisions. The
discussion of ethnicity among non-African groups is disproportionate
to their numbers in the population. This is necessary for two reasons.
The first is simply the relative lack of sources dealing with ethnicity
among African peoples. The second is an explicit attempt to break
down dichotomous notions of 'race' and to indicate how processes of
construction of (gendered) ethnicities and of racist ideologies may
occur among all sectors of the population.

The chapter will also argue that, at present, there exists a disjuncture
between the economy of the country, still dominated by the settler
minority and by transnational corporations (despite the rapid growth
of a black bourgeoisie), and its political/ideological structures and
processes. The latter are controlled in the main by the Zimbabwe
African National Union, the party which forms the government and
which controls other institutions such as the military and the media.
Although the condition of the African masses is not dramatically
changed, to be 'black' now affords the possibility of political power and
of upward mobility for a few, as did being 'white' during the settler
regime. Independence has, to an extent, given new life to racialized
categories constructed during colonialism.

Pre-Colonial Societies

Three main African linguistic or ethnic groupings exist in present-day
Zimbabwe. The groups today called 'Shona' constitute about 75 per
cent of the population (Sylvester, 1991: 38). The Tonga, by far the
smallest grouping, constitute less than one per cent of the population
(Murphree, 1988: 125). Living in the north of the country, they were
originally one people with the Zambian Tonga and, like them, engaged
in wetland cultivation in a decentralized system. They were cut off
from Zambia, first by the creation of an international border and then
by the flooding of the Zambesi Valley in the mid-1950s. Historically,

they have been least assimilated into capitalist 'development'. Groups speaking SiNdebele constitute 19 per cent of the population (Sylvester, 1991: 138) and live mainly in the west and south of the country. The rest of the African population consists of migrant workers, refugees (from Mozambique) or fragments of other language groups such as the Shangaan in the south-east.

If these groups can today be considered as ethnic entities, the ethnicities at least of the Shona and Ndebele are of post-colonial origin. The term 'Shona' relates to peoples or groupings speaking a group of related dialects: in the nineteenth century there did exist a common language and political culture across a wide area – what is most of Zimbabwe today – but there was not a common 'Shona' ethnic identity. People were defined politically, as subjects of particular chiefs (Ranger, 1985b: 4; see also Beach, 1980). Previously, these peoples had lived in a centralized kingdom under 'divine' rulers; this system had disintegrated by the eighteenth century, but the mode of production based on lineages continued relatively undisturbed (Weinrich, 1979, 1982).

Likewise, Ndebele ethnicity had no pre-colonial currency. The Ndebele state originated from cattle-herding peoples who migrated north to evade more dominant peoples (later constructed as the 'Zulu'). It was created by the incorporation or the subordination of dozens of peoples who were *not* linguistically or culturally related. In the nineteenth century the Ndebele state was a polyethnic organism defined politically: to be Ndebele was to be a subject of Mzilikazi or Lobengula (Ranger, 1990a: 5–6). The economy was based mainly on cattle herding, with a highly centralized political system. Military youth were regularly deployed to raid the Shona and Tonga for cattle and grain. Ranger points out, however, that the 'Ndebele' were themselves raided for cattle by other groups. The widespread and often reported 'memory' of Ndebele raids upon the Shona is mainly a product of school history lessons (Ranger, 1985b: 4).

Before attempting to discuss the position of women in pre-colonial societies, it is well to note that the form that social relations took in precolonial societies is a matter of much debate in contemporary Zimbabwe. This controversy is due in part to the fact that interpretations of the past are relevant to current gender struggles. The evidence, however, which forms the basis of such discussions is exceedingly thin, being based upon (usually racist) accounts written by colonial administrators, missionaries and traders as well as on the few ethnographic accounts available.

From these accounts it seems that women's position varied between the three groupings. The Tonga are matrilineal, and women probably had somewhat more autonomy than in the other groups. For instance, they had rights to their own fields before the period of resettlement

(Colson, 1971). Strong gender divisions existed within pre-colonial Shona and Ndebele societies. Both were male-dominated; nevertheless, women had a limited range of rights and a degree of autonomy. Both societies were patrilineal, patrilocal and polygynous for those men who could accumulate the bride wealth. Men had authority over land use and could convert any surplus into livestock and eventually into more wives. Women could own cattle, but had no right to husbands' herds. Within the household, they had responsibility for meeting needs for food but men had the power to allocate resources. Women acquired status through bearing children, especially sons; a barren Shona wife could be divorced and would thereby lose access to the resources mentioned and would lose custody of children aged over seven.

Schmidt (1992: 42) notes that, although Shona women were subordinate to men, a female hierarchy existed: age, marital situation and socio-economic situation (as well as number of children) were important determinants of women's status. A small minority of women, generally older ones, achieved positions of authority as diviner/healers, midwives, spirit mediums and head-women. At the other extreme were women of low socio-economic position who were vulnerable to being taken hostage or to being used as pawns to pay debts. For the majority of women between these extremes, the main hope of higher status lay in their ability to manipulate kinship positions as mothers-in-law or grandmothers.

Weinrich (1982) argues that Ndebele society was even more highly male-dominated than that of the Shona, due to the relative lack of importance of women's labour in agriculture, their consequent dependence upon men and the militaristic nature of the society. Although the position of women did not differ markedly between the two societies, in at least a few respects Ndebele beliefs were less harsh for women. For instance, an Ndebele woman could not be divorced for infertility. And Ranger (1985b) quotes a disapproving Native Commissioner early this century who observed that an Ndebele girl could choose 'whom she likes, when she likes and as often as she likes'.

Settler Colonialism: Some Early Processes

Cecil Rhodes and the pioneer column of the British South Africa Company (BSAC) marched northward from South Africa and established the colony of Rhodesia in 1890. Hence began the long period sometimes known as the European Occupation. The white settlers' hopes of mineral wealth soon evaporated, so they turned to ranching (in the west and south) and to agriculture in more fertile regions.

With colonialism came the creation of new, unifying ethnicities for the Shona and Ndebele. The processes whereby peoples who identified politically came to hold ethnic identities involved many agents. These ethnicities, as Ranger has pointed out forcefully, were in the first instance inspired by Europeans. Colonial states and officials, backed by anthropological theories, recognized only hierarchically ordered, territorially linked and patriarchal 'tribes' with rulers, not loose confederations of lineages. Thus, the inventors of 'Ndebele' ethnicity were, in the first instance, colonial administrators from Natal who expected them to be like their image of the Zulu (Ranger, 1985b). Ndebele chiefs readily accepted this glamorous and authoritarian identity (Ranger, 1990a: 9). Part of the colonists' justification for the occupation of Zimbabwean territory was that the majority Mashona were being protected by the British from Ndebele raids. In line with this justification, the Ndebele were seen as brave, fierce warriors, while the Shona were viewed as passive, fearful and virtually devoid of their own social structure, if also more open to 'civilizing' influences. Ranger cites a diarist in 1886: 'No one likes the Mashonas, dirty, cowardly lot. Matabele bloodthirsty devils but a fine type' (Ranger, 1979: 3).

European employers also played an important part: Ndebele speakers were considered superior to Shona speakers and better suited to supervisory positions; hence, many workers were eager to claim Ndebele tribal identity. In later work, Ranger (1990a, b) emphasizes *African* agency in the construction or 'imagining' (Anderson, 1983) of ethnicity. African aristocrats and chiefs, mission-educated and other intellectuals, cultural nationalists and (later) those with an inclusive vision of democratic Ndebele society all played a role in the (still ongoing) construction of Ndebele identity.

The herding economy of the western 'Ndebele' peoples was undermined by the colonists' demands for cheap labour and by the imposition of forced labour (Weinrich, 1982). The result, in 1896, was the uprising or *chimurenga* which ended in defeat. The most fertile land was soon confiscated; many were forced to become wage labourers on ranches or mines. Thus, the political, military and economic fabric of Ndebele society largely disintegrated after 1896.

The initial contact of the Shona peoples was of a different order. More successful cultivators in more fertile regions were able to meet settlers' demands for food, and some Shona men turned to cash-cropping (Muchena, 1979: 4). The 'peasant option' (Ranger, 1985a) – itself based upon female labour – was the preferred one for Shona farmers, despite settler plans to create a proletariat through imposition of measures such as hut taxes. But confiscation of Africans' land escalated when it became apparent the settlers would not find gold and the Shona – to the whites' amazement – joined the Ndebele in the *chimurenga* war.

By 1902 three-quarters of African land had been expropriated (Arrighi, 1973: 195), although this proportion was later reduced somewhat. Various taxes – a poll tax, even a tax on dogs – were imposed to try to increase the number of people living in low-quality 'reserves' and to lessen African agricultural competition. African men in most areas were forced into wage employment in mines, agriculture and European households.

In 1923 Rhodesia became a self-governing colony. Economically, big capital remained dominant, particularly in mining, railways and citrus production (Phimister, 1983: 268). Politically, the white settlers dominated, and racial segregationism became even more marked. The 1930 Land Apportionment Act established exclusive European rights over half the total land. The Maize Control Act established legal discrimination against Africans who marketed crops. These laws became the cornerstone of white rule (Palmer, 1977).

African Women and Settler Colonialism

The majority of people left behind in reserves were women, children and elderly men. In many areas, women became the main farmers when large numbers of able-bodied men worked elsewhere, sending home remittances when they chose to. Early on, virtually the only wage labour opportunities for women were in prostitution, which was encouraged in areas such as mining compounds (van Onselen, 1980: 174–82).

African women's treatment under settler colonialism should not be seen purely as the result of policies imposed by the colonial state. As various authors have commented, this approach does not pay sufficient attention to internal social, particularly gender, conflicts (Bozzoli, 1983; Folbre, 1988; Schmidt, 1991). Instead, indigenous and European structures of male domination reinforced one another. Most colonial authorities saw African women in highly negative terms. Schmidt points out that colonial records are filled with adjectives describing African women as indolent, lazy, slothful, immoral, frivolous, savage, uncivilized and (in the words of one official) 'extraordinarily inferior to the men' (Schmidt, 1991: 735). Women's status was also undermined by the loss of religious, professional and political roles which were denigrated or else outlawed by the colonial system (Schmidt, 1992). This meant that status differences among women actually diminished through early colonialism, through a levelling-down process.

The state's motivation was also economic: it was seen as necessary to control female sexuality in order to ensure a male labour supply in times of shortage. For instance, laws such as the 1916 Natives Adultery Punishment Ordinance, which rendered adultery with a married African woman a criminal offence, sought to reassure men that their sexual interests would be protected in the reserves if they migrated to work outside the rural areas. Chiefs, headmen and older men welcomed attempts to restrict women to rural areas since women in urban areas were widely thought to be beyond male control (Folbre, 1988; Schmidt, 1991).

Younger men able to engage in wage labour and to earn cash to pay for their own bride-wealths were for the first time able to partially escape from constraints imposed by the community and by their lineage elders (Chigwedere, 1982). Relations between husbands and wives became more individualized (Gaidzanwa, 1992). In particular, this meant that it became much easier for men to divorce wives, and that women had little recourse to protection by the man's family (Pankhurst, 1991), and so male power and female dependence increased.

The codification of Customary Law was a major step in increasing women's subordination. However one views women's pre-colonial situation, this development certainly diminished women's customary rights (Snyder, 1982; May, 1983; Kazembe, 1986). Most African women were deemed unable to make contracts, to represent themselves in court, to marry without the consent of a male guardian, and to have custody of children because women were defined as legal 'minors'. This ignored the fact that, in pre-colonial society, all members of society except the elders were, in a sense, 'minors' (Milroy, 1983). Hence African women lost rights such as that to their *mavoko* property (literally in Shona, 'of her own hands'), including money from wages and from petty commodity production (Holleman, 1952). Customary Law was created by colonial officials, but with the active participation – indeed, the connivance (Snyder, 1982) – of Shona and Ndebele elders and chiefs. Settler colonialism had deprived African men of their political domination but tried to enhance male authority *within* households to avoid outright (male) rebellion.

However, some African women attempted to escape from the control of husbands and elders, mainly by moving to urban areas on a temporary or permanent basis. Women migrated in order to seek economic independence, to escape unsatisfactory or violent marriages, and – at times with the consent of their guardians (Barnes, 1992) – to earn cash in whatever ways were possible, including prostitution, so that they might send some back to dependent families. Although formally the state disapproved of female migration, it tacitly tolerated it because it was recognized that male migrant workers expected females to be available to service their domestic needs. Even in 1936 when legal measures were aimed at curtailing the presence of single women, these were largely ignored (Barnes, 1992). But numbers of African women were low: Barnes estimates that some 13 per cent of the Salisbury township population was female in 1938 (Barnes, 1992: 607). Her figures also indicate that in 1936 6 per cent of Salisbury African women were in formal waged employment. One of the reasons that this percentage was not higher was that in Zimbabwe the great majority of domestic workers, 86 per cent in 1948 (Pape, 1990), were male (see below).

The relative homogeneity of black women's class position began to differentiate from the late 1930s, along with the general growth of class divisions among Africans (Ranger, 1985a; Phimister, 1988; Schmidt, 1992). New petty bourgeois strata of 'progressive' farmers and mission-educated intellectuals began to emerge. Native Purchase Areas, where land could be bought freehold by Africans, were set up; however, less than 3 per cent of the population lived in such Areas. Some men succeeded in becoming wealthier peasants or even small capitalists, often through the strategy of marrying numerous wives and using them as 'cheap labour' (Weinrich, 1979; Cheater, 1981). In this instance, men's entry into the petty bourgeoisie obviously did (and does) not imply that their wives share the same class position.

In other cases, African women did better their class positions, mainly through marriage to Christian teachers, clerks, artisans and evangelists (Schmidt, 1992: 181), and a small number of women became nurses and teachers in their own right. The few female domestic workers were also usually privileged in relation to female peasants/housewives. At the other end of the class 'scale', women came to be employed on white commercial farms for exceedingly low wages and in exceedingly poor conditions (Clarke, 1977).

From the early 1950s, the situation changed somewhat for African women. Because of reformist attempts to establish a system of permanent black wage labour in towns, it was obvious that 'family settlement' of some black people in towns would have to be permitted, and so married women with permits were allowed to reside in urban areas. However, the position of most black women was unaffected by these developments.

White Women and Settler Colonialism

Female migration was necessary for white men to become settlers rather than simply colonists (Kirkwood, 1984: 143). At first, women were forbidden to trek with men, but in 1891 the ban was lifted and by 1911 the sex ratio was 100 males to 51 females; by 1941 this had decreased to 100 to 88 (Kirkwood, 1984: 146). Most early settlers were, of course, British, but a large minority of Afrikaners and small numbers of Germans, French and Portuguese also migrated, as well as a substantial minority of Jews. J. Lloyd's *Rhodesia's Pioneer Women, 1859–96* attempts to list all women migrants to Southern Rhodesia (Lloyd, 1974). Of approximately 1,020 names, 242 are Dutch, 10 German and 10 Jewish.

From the beginning, class and ethnic divisions among whites were important, as demonstrated in the field of immigration policy. Kennedy (1987) describes how the BSAC wished to recruit 'small' men with agricultural experience. However, the high capital requirements imposed by the state debarred the very class of farmer desired, for fear of being 'swamped' by poor Afrikaaners, to whom the British felt superior and whom they suspected of disloyalty. Nevertheless, large numbers of Afrikaaners, along with South African migrants of British origin, did enter the country with little capital. Hodder-Williams (1974) notes that, until the 1960s and UDI, the social lives of these Afrikaaner settlers were almost entirely segregated from the British.

Of necessity, immigration policy changed and subsidies were granted to unskilled and semi-skilled British workers to enable them to settle. Men of public school, professional and landed backgrounds also continued to enter, in smaller numbers, eventually coming to form the elite of settler society. Social interaction among (British-originated) whites occurred more readily and with less attention to status than within Britain, and this served to bolster a myth of 'classlessness' as well as solidarity against Africans. However (as in the United States), this myth, served to obscure marked class divisions, made even more oppressive by the small scale of white Rhodesian society (Kirkwood, 1984: 161): Europeans never constituted more than 5 per cent of the population.

Southern Rhodesian white society was highly gender as well as class and ethnically divided. This was a man's world, and the role of 'frontiers-man' able to wield power over all women and over black men was likely to have been a positive incentive to many white men (Phillips, 1992). White women were seen predominantly as wives whose destiny was to support men and as mothers whose duties were to increase the settler population and to raise young Rhodesians. Women had a particular role in maintaining what was termed racial 'prestige' with regard to Africans; they also played a significant role in the reproduction of class and status divisions on an everyday basis.

In early colonial times, Lloyd (1975) notes a high demand for the labour of single women. Women worked as barmaids, nurses, teachers and nannies – the last so that white children would not be under the tutelage of Africans. Of white married women, only 10 per cent worked by 1946 (Kirkwood, 1984: 158); these found it easy to obtain employment in the sex-segregated areas of education, medicine and office work (Kirkwood, 1984: 156).

For white housewives, the ability to lead lives that consisted mainly of managing households, gardening, morning tea parties and afternoon bridge depended upon the labour of African servants, who were mainly male. This feature of colonial society is curious since it meant (and means) that white women and black men were in nearly constant, close proximity. Although, as elsewhere, white men asserted their dominance through sexual access to black women (with or without their consent), the possibility of sexual relations between white women and black men was (again, as elsewhere) viewed with horror and termed the 'black peril'. Pape (1990) details how the 'black peril' was from early on detected on the slightest of evidence; fear of it reached hysterical proportions, with numerous miscarriages of justice, often leading to the gallows (Pape, 1990; Kennedy, 1987; Ranger, 1979).

The 'black peril' served to distract from the far more prevalent 'white' peril, or sexual relations between white men and black women. While the violence of white men was rarely mentioned in public, from 1912 it was considered a serious enough matter to receive official attention (Pape, 1990: 711). Although the welfare of black women was not considered of great importance, the ire of African fathers and the growing presence of a mixed-race population was: the latter was a particular threat in a society struggling to maintain racial boundaries. White women were not unaware of the activities of white men; however, in spite of what were seen as sexual, social and racial betrayals, they were constrained to appear to support 'their' men in the interests of white privilege. Nevertheless, in 1921 over half of the white female population signed a petition advocating that sexual relations between white men and black women be criminalized (Pape, 1990: 715). This never came to pass and no white was ever executed for a sexual crime against a black woman. Despite women's marked failure in this respect, it is likely that the continued presence of male domestics not only reflected settlers' true fears as to which 'peril' was greatest (Kennedy, 1987), but also represented a victory for white women in keeping the 'temptation' of black women away from – or at a greater distance from – husbands and other male relatives (Schmidt, 1992). The victory was both personal and political, in the sense of maintaining European women's prestige *vis-à-vis* Africans and their symbolic sexual position, crucial to settler society.

Did contact between white and African women in any way soften white domination? Evidence is slight and anecdotal. White farmers' wives were in an unusual position since farm workers usually lived in family units. Wives of farmers had to have some knowledge of the hybrid patois offensively known as 'kitchen kaffir', and had to develop some rapport with their staff in order not to lose servants (Kirkwood, 1984: 150–1). They often opened rudimentary primary schools. Most other white women, however, had virtually no contact with black women. Nevertheless, it could be said that the two groups were connected through racist sexual imagery, since colonial belief systems implicitly counterpoised the ideal of white womanhood to that of the degraded African woman.

Lastly, a women's homemaking movement began in the 1940s, led by middle-class whites. The movement was aimed at rural Africans, whom it sought to teach 'home economics'. It was led by the white Women's Institutes, but some middle-class black women (for example, wives of teachers) also participated. Black women usually viewed such activities as patronising. Weiss quotes a nurse, speaking of a white woman who assisted with disabled children in townships:

> She was a white woman like any other, friendly but detached, as though I wasn't there . . . To me, she always seemed a helpless sort of person . . . [These women] didn't even change their children's nappies, yet they would come to our women's clubs and teach us floral arrangements . . . They knew nothing about our problems. (Weiss, 1986: 61–2)

These organizations were nevertheless the forerunners of today's Women's Clubs. These are grass-roots African women's organizations which operate mainly in the rural areas, running on a fairly democratic basis, promoting income-generating activities and providing some opportunity for rural women to discuss problems without men present.

What of groups of minority white women? Such evidence as there is points to their identification with the dominant white culture. Kirkwood notes that after Southern Rhodesia became a self-governing colony, there was a growing sense of Rhodesian nationalism. After World War II the British government agreed to establish the Central African Federation (of the Rhodesias and Nyasaland) in order to increase settler influence in the region. Efforts were made to attract immigrants, and many came (see below) including Greeks and ex-Portuguese colonists. References to tensions between 'old' and 'new' immigrants are found in several places, and these intertwined with ethnic differences.

The Jewish 'Community'

I use the example of the Jewish minority in Southern Rhodesia to illustrate the complex intertwining of different forms of racism, nationalism and allegiance: anti-Semitism, anti-African racism, British imperial identity and Rhodesian patriotism. In contrast to other groups such as Greeks or Asians, a published history (Kosmin, 1980) exists for the Jewish community; unfortunately, this study ignores women.

A relatively large proportion of Jews took part in the early Occupation. This was in part because Rhodes favoured Jewish settlement, stereotyping Jews as 'constructive, far-seeing and persistent' so that in the early period little anti-Semitism existed. The overriding identification of all settlers was as 'white' and Jews identified with British imperialism (Kosmin, 1980: 21). In the early 1900s the composition of the Jewish population changed. The first settlers were largely

English and German; the second wave was Eastern European. The national difference of the new Jewish settlers, their poverty, the growing normalization of settler life, and general anti-alien feeling during World War I all contributed to a rise in anti-Jewish racism. Many Jewish men were forced back into their traditional economic niches in the service industries and small trade. In 1912, Jews owned over one-third of all retail outlets in the country (Kosmin, 1980: 41). Their role as middlemen invited (further) anti-Semitism from the British, who saw them along with Greeks as lowly and their sometimes informal contact with Africans as diminishing white prestige. Anti-Semitism came too from some Africans, to whom Jews were the most directly visible exploiters.

After European immigration was halted in 1914, the Jewish population stabilized at 4 per cent of Europeans, being the second largest white minority. Jews were by then mainly concentrated in larger cities. Many occupational avenues remained closed or restricted to them, but a few, mainly young people, were beginning to enter professions. The 'community' itself was divided between European (Ashkenazi) Jewry and oriental (Sephardic) Jews, mainly from Rhodes: the latter faced additional discrimination, and were sometimes known to Ashkenazim as 'black Jews'.

With the growth of fascism in Germany, the racially and ethnically exclusive basis of the Southern Rhodesian state provided fertile ground for growth of anti-Semitism and British xenophobia. The main focus was the debate on European immigration. Huggins's United Party (which won the 1939 general election), the populist white Labour Party and the few fascist candidates all campaigned against European immigration, especially from 'commercial races'. Relatively few refugees were allowed in before or during World War II. Anti-Semitism and xenophobia both survived the war intact and culminated in the 1946 Aliens Act, which established that British citizens were to make up 90 per cent of immigrants, with no other country providing more than *one per cent* of all entrants.

During the 1950s the position of Rhodesian Jews was to undergo a great change. With industrialization, many small Jewish traders were able to become manufacturers. In general, Jews moved into primary production, now including farming, ranching and mining, and the number of Jewish professionals grew rapidly. Jews lent disproportionate support to the United Party and to the Central African Federation from 1953 to 1963. The Federation represented to many a 'modern' state with laissez-faire economic policies, racist but nevertheless opposing explicit apartheid and with some socio-cultural autonomy promised to black and white ethnic groups.

The Federation failed due to African opposition and to the growing reaction of white settlers. Ian Smith of the Rhodesia Front (RF) –

itself heavily supported by Afrikaaner migrants – was elected in 1964 and UDI followed. With the increased racialization of society, anti-Semitism grew, but paradoxically the RF also courted Jews (apparently, particularly women) in the name of white unity. With the failure of the Federation, many Jews emigrated, so that the proportion of the white population dropped to 2 per cent after UDI (Kosmin, 1980: 132); those remaining largely accepted it.

Thus, despite the existence of racist attitudes and discrimination, the Jewish community gained from and supported the racial privilege available to all whites. Sometimes this took on tragic – nearly inexplicable – turns. In one case known to the author, one of the few survivors of Dachau, saved due to his work as a skilled watchmaker, migrated to Southern Rhodesia to join his family, only to become assimilated as a racist Rhodesian. While anti-Semitism, anti-Greek feeling and other forms of racism were important in determining the position of white ethnic minorities, the existence of ethnic divisions did not strongly affect white men's and women's identification with Rhodesia and with white nationalism. In general, despite deep gender, class and ethnic differences which threatened to separate them, whites united in order to defend their (precarious) domination over Africans.

Asians, Coloureds and Ambiguities

As in South Africa, rigid racial categorization operated so that people were grouped as 'European', 'African', 'Asian' or 'Coloured'. Pass laws, never as important as in South Africa, were abolished in the 1950s. Nevertheless, all groups lived in racially segregated areas and attended racially segregated schools. The Asian and Coloured communities were accorded a legal and social status between that of Africans and Europeans.

The Asian minority is small, half of one per cent of the population (Weinrich, 1982), and is mainly of Indian origin. These small numbers can be attributed to white fear of competition: early in the sixteenth century, the white population pressed for legislation to curtail Asian entry. The most militant racists took direct action, torching Asian shops in Umtali (now Mutare) (Kennedy, 1987: 51). As elsewhere, and like Greeks and Jews, Asian families were heavily concentrated in commerce, shopkeeping and middlemen activities. Frequent commercial contact existed among these groups; if this extended to social contact, it is likely that mainly men were involved.

Coloureds in Zimbabwe are a heterogeneous grouping, consisting of descendants of mixed-race people and of relationships between Africans and Europeans or Asians. Unlike in South Africa, the Coloured community is a small one, one-third of one per cent of the population (Brand, 1981: 37). However, it was granted social privileges denied to blacks, such as specially allocated schools and the right to settle in cities. It was advantageous, then, for mixed-race people to identify as Coloured rather than as African. People of 'Coloured' origin do not have a homogeneous 'ethnic/class' position, but many are engaged in a range of waged and 'informal' urban occupations.

Asian and Coloured people present – as do European ethnics to a lesser extent – particular definitional 'problems' due to their ambiguous racial status. This is perhaps particularly so for Coloureds, visibly the products of mixed unions in a society in which ethnic endogamy is the official norm. It can be hypothesized that it is this grouping which is most marginalized in a society in which legal and folk definitions of 'race' are crucial.

Ethnic Differences among African Women

While many aspects of life for African women under colonialism can be generalized, important ethnic differences did (and do) exist. Whatever the origins of Ndebele ethnic identity, Weinrich (1982) writes that as a minority they suffered most under colonialism. By 1948, for instance, 60 per cent of Ndebele men participated in wage labour, compared with about 40 per cent of Shona men (Weinrich, 1979: 16), because Ndebele land was less fertile and so few opportunities for cash-cropping existed. And whereas Shona men tended to work in urban centres, Ndebele men tended to work on ranches for lower pay. Weinrich's figures show for 1975 that while the average Shona household had Rhodesian $30 disposable income per month, Ndebele households on average disposed of $12 (Weinrich, 1979: 49). In Rhodesia, most black education was provided by Christian missionaries: unlike the highly Christianized Shona, most Ndebele showed little interest in conversion, and so missed out on the only education available. In the early 1980s, nearly all men with secondary or higher education in rural areas were Shona-speaking, even in the west of the country (Weinrich, 1982). In general, then, Ndebele people were more highly proletarianized and on worse terms, less educated, less Christianized and more poverty-stricken than the Shona.

Differences in educational attainment provide a good example of differences among ethnic groups which affect women. In the late 1970s one-quarter of Shona and 37 per cent of Ndebele women had *no* formal education, and *no* Ndebele women surveyed had over eight years of education (Weinrich, 1982: 42). Since only one Tonga person with a university degree was thought to live in the country in the mid-1980s (Murphree, 1988), it seems likely that very few Tonga women have any secondary education. If relatively few male professionals are Ndebele-speakers, the number of Ndebele female professionals can be expected to be far fewer.

In other respects which directly affect gender relations, institutions and practices differ between the ethnic groupings. I draw heavily upon Weinrich's work because her research provides the only source of comparison between women in different ethnic groups. Bride wealth payments are smaller among the Ndebele than among the Shona, among whom they have escalated, and while nearly all Shona pay bride-wealth nearly one-fifth of Ndebele pay none (Weinrich, 1982: 37). Polygyny rates differ significantly among the two groupings. Weinrich gives polygyny rates for the Shona as being 10 per cent and, for the Ndebele, less than 2 per cent (Weinrich, 1982: 141). Concerning family planning, Ndebele husbands held far less negative attitudes than did Shona husbands. Lastly, Weinrich's study found divorce rates to be highest among Ndebele peoples and least high among the Shona (Weinrich, 1982: 57). The picture given, then, is of an Ndebele society more individualized than that of the Shona and, by implication, less cohesive and more 'western'. However, and perhaps paradoxically, Weinrich also reported the existence of some distinctly 'unmodern' features. For instance, the 'modern' idea of companionship between spouses was less developed among the Ndebele, who, unlike the Shona, spent little leisure time together (Weinrich, 1982). She also reports that cases of extreme violence – which are common (Mabazeke, 1986) – were most numerous in impoverished rural Matabeleland districts.

Although Weinrich's work was carried out shortly before independence, it is likely that the type of ethnic differences described persist. Ethnicity is also likely to play a strong role in class formation. However, the extent to which nearly all African women are severely disadvantaged should be emphasized. This situation cuts across class divisions, since only a tiny minority of women are financially secure, let alone wealthy, in their own right. Women greatly fear male violence and, even more, divorce and desertion. Divorce, which is common, is likely to bring destitution and loss of custody of children. Such fears play a large part in determining women's lives (Mpofu, 1983; Pankhurst and Jacobs, 1988).

Women and the Independence Struggle

Following UDI in 1965, guerrilla war by African nationalists began from the late 1960s. The two main groups involved were the Zimbabwe African National Union (ZANU) under Chitepo (and later Mugabe) and the Zimbabwe African People's Union (ZAPU) under Nkomo. ZAPU support was mainly in Matabeleland while ZANU drew support from Shona-speaking areas. While the two forces' military operations were usually geographically separate, there were regions of overlap and clashes occurred not only between nationalists and Rhodesian forces but also between nationalists themselves. ZANU was returned to power in 1980 and has formed the government since independence (see below).

What of women's role in the struggle? The guerrilla war prompted whites to unite even more strongly. White Rhodesian women did not participate in formal military capacities but played a servicing role, for instance, fund-raising and running canteens for soldiers. Some African women, almost exclusively young ones, did participate as guerrillas and some achieved high military rank. More commonly, women participated in a servicing capacity, carrying food and water and hiding guerrillas in their homes. Young women (*chimwidos*) acted as messengers for the guerrillas, as did young boys (*mujibas*). However, *chimwidos* were expected to cook for the freedom fighters and also to service their sexual needs, often without choice.

The public lore regarding women in the war is that they participated willingly, and for many this was no doubt true. In Staunton's collection (1990) one woman commented, 'The lives of the comrades were in our hands.' Obviously, most were pleased and relieved at the victory of nationalist forces. The 30 accounts in Staunton reveal courage but also much ambivalence; many women (and men) were simply caught between two different forces and sometimes between all three. Whatever their political affiliations or lack thereof, the women interviewed focused overwhelmingly on the grief and pain they experienced over the death, torture, injury and rape of children and spouses.

Kriger's innovative analysis (1992) is also based upon oral testimony and is located in Mutoko, an area of ZANU support. She argues that peasants were, at best, reluctant supporters of the guerrillas, participating because of threatened or actual coercion. Her analysis, after Debray, is in terms of 'revolutions within the revolution'. Thus pre-existing structural conflicts within peasant communities became entangled with support for the guerrillas: different groups had their own motives and agendas in the struggle. She outlines four different types of conflict:

1   Between *youth* and *parents*: *youth* tried to overthrow rigid age-based hierarchies. Of the four, the support of *youth* for the war was most whole-hearted and important
2   Between people from *stranger* lineages and those from local 'royal' lineages
3   Between poorer and wealthier peasants and between all peasants and the rural black elite
4   Between married women and their husbands

I elaborate only upon the last type, as it is most relevant here. ZANU was wary of attacking African 'custom' and of thereby alienating male support. Thus, for instance, it never introduced family planning in its camps. However, married women were able to mobilize around one gender issue, in the sense of enlisting guerrilla support against wife-beating. Hence, for a time, guerrillas who found a woman being beaten by her husband would publicly beat the man in retaliation (Kriger, 1992: 195). Over time, however, men's appeals for control over their 'private' lives prevailed and gender issues were pushed to the back of the agenda.

These works indicate much ambiguity, both concerning women's responses to the war and concerning official responses to gender struggles. Nevertheless, gender as well as class, generational and other conflicts can help to motivate revolutionary participation.

Some Notes on Changes since Independence

The war led people – both men and women – to expect or at least to hope for better lives. For most Africans, such improvement was not couched in terms of abstract racial equality but in terms of issues perceived as more immediate, for example, land, jobs and schools. Both women and men hoped for improvements in living standards, but many women also hoped for improvements in their domestic situations, their legal status and their social entitlement *vis-à-vis* men, such as the right to hold land (Zimbabwe Women's Bureau, 1981) and legal equality in the spheres of marriage, divorce and child custody (Jacobs, 1989a). While the former demand has not been met, the government has moved to ameliorate women's legal position by a series of laws dealing with matters such as women's right to vote at the age of 18; (by implication) with the matter of legal minority; with the rights of children in matters of custody; with conditions for divorce and for maintenance; and with rights to inheritance of marital property. However, in practice such welcome reforms are likely to be taken up almost exclusively by urban middle-class women (Kazembe, 1986).

After independence, a Ministry of Community Development and Women's Affairs was set up. Its creation was seen as an important symbol; however, it was hindered by poor resourcing and by lack of prestige. Recently, the government placed the Ministry under the jurisdiction of the Senior Minister for Political Affairs, a move hardly calculated to strengthen pro-woman forces (Sylvester, 1991: 150). Another organization, ZANU Women's League, has always been seen as a support group for the ZANU (Patriotic Front) government and has little independent voice in policy-making. A small, multiracial women's organization with largely professional membership, the

Women's Action Group (WAG), was formed in 1983 after a government 'clean-up' (that is, systematic arrests and imprisonment) of women out on the streets and labelled 'prostitutes' (see Jacobs and Howard, 1987; Jacobs, 1989a). In 1984 WAG organized a large national conference which attempted to include women from all races, classes and ethnic groups and which provided a forum in which women could speak out on the issues of most concern to them. However, the gathering was met with vilification and did not receive official support (Batezat et al., 1988: 169). Indeed, there are allegations that the group has been under surveillance by the Central Intelligence Organization (CIO), the state intelligence agency. More recently, WAG has turned to researching and advocating issues concerning women's welfare and health: for instance, a Women's Health and Information Project was begun in 1989 (Women's Action Group, 1989). Another organization, Women in Law and Development in Africa, has also been active in campaigning in recent years.

The general erosion of civil liberties in recent years has made it more difficult for women, like other groups, to organize in any way the state perceives to be a threat. However, women's resistance and protests do continue. No doubt this resistance has contributed to the legal changes which have been enacted. And the struggles of the war years have left some legacy. To give two examples: violence against women is endemic and continues in private. However, during my own fieldwork in 1984, I found that women exhibited much anger about the matter, and that most men would not admit to approval of violence against women. On a wider scale, in November 1992, nationwide protests and activities occurred against a school headmaster who allegedly raped four girls (*Ms.*, 1993). Thus, although male violence is normal, it may no longer be the norm and is now a matter for public discussion.

Another shift in gender relations is a general opening up of white-collar work, because of 'Africanization' and partly as a result of the exodus of about half of the settler population (see below). There has been little change in the gender division of labour as such. The new opportunities for African women are mainly in the service and the retail sectors, and in some 'female' professions. Numbers of educated females are growing due to the emphasis on education by government and by popular feeling. Primary schooling is technically free in rural areas (fees have been imposed in urban areas since the adoption of the Economic Structural Adjustment Programme); university is state funded and new universities have been recently opened – one, in Bulawayo, in Matabeleland. The third and related change is the growth of a new African middle class: middle-class females are still a tiny proportion of the population although their existence is seen as a threat by many (Jacobs and Howard, 1987).

However, the situation of the majority has changed little since independence. Stringency imposed by the International Monetary Fund has meant high and growing unemployment and the erosion of many welfare measures enacted after independence; the latter is particularly detrimental for women. In times of drought and hunger such as have occurred recently, the impoverishment of the population and especially of women will be greatly exacerbated.

The growth of class divisions among Africans is perhaps the single most important development in independent Zimbabwe, but this is not without its ethnic dimension. ZANU dominates the government, even after 'Unity' with ZAPU. It is largely, although not exclusively, a party of Shona-speaking people. The guerrilla activity which occurred from 1982 to 1987 in the south-west of the country was associated in part with interparty (ZANU/ZAPU) conflicts and in part with ethnic conflicts. Hence many reports were heard of wholesale suppression of 'dissident' areas, where Ndebele people live. Boston (1992) cites the figure of 40,000 killed in Matabeleland during this period; more than the number of Africans who died in the independence struggle. It is also alleged that recent food shortages are more severe in the west not only because it is drier but also because of the state's failure to build dams there. It is often alleged that Ndebele-speakers face discrimination and find it difficult to obtain jobs. It is likely, then, that most of the growth of middle-class employment among women has been taken up by Shona-speakers.

Other shifts have occurred. The white population has declined to about 2 per cent of the whole (Stoneman and Cliffe, 1989) although those who remain are still highly privileged and continue to dominate the economy. However, the decline in their numbers means that whites have to an extent had to turn to intermediate groupings for social purposes: it is reportedly not uncommon now for whites, including white women, to invite Asians and occasionally Coloureds for tennis or to tea.

If 'whites' have become, ironically, not-quite-purely-white, then today 'black' peoples are not solely composed of Africans. An ideology of black unity exists, but this identity too is malleable, historically constituted. Many young Coloureds and Asians consider themselves black people: indeed, some mixed-race people do not acknowledge their ancestry. Interestingly, their identification appears to be contested by both 'sides' of the racial divide.

Matters of importance are not always discussed openly in any society. In Zimbabwe, gender issues are much debated and growing class divisions are acknowledged to some extent. However, it is not a society notable for free speech – witness the recent wholesale closure of the university in Harare – and ethnicity (as opposed to 'race') is rarely discussed. In fact ethnic as well as class divisions among black groups are likely to grow as – eventually – the white population declines in size and as the country becomes more Africanized. Admirable as is the ideal of unity, rhetoric of unity may serve to obscure division. Open acknowledgement of social divisions is a prerequisite for struggle against the inequalities they produce. Not only gender and class but also ethnic divisions were in part shaped by settler society, but they are also produced and reproduced in independent Zimbabwe.

References

Adams, J. (1991) 'Female wage labor in rural Zimbabwe', *World Development*, 19 (2–3): 163–77.

Anderson, B. (1983) *Imagined Communities*. London: Verso.

Arrighi, G. (1973) 'The Political Economy of Rhodesia', in G. Arrighi and J. Saul, *Essays on the Political Economy of Africa*. New York: Monthly Review Press.

Barnes, T. (1992) 'The fight for control of African women's mobility in Colonial Zimbabwe, 1900–39', *Signs*, 17 (3).

Batezat, E., Mwalo, M. and Truscott K. (1988) 'Women and independence: the heritage and the struggle', in C. Stoneman (ed.), *Zimbabwe's Prospects*. London: Macmillan.

Beach, D.N. (1980) *The Shona and Zimbabwe, 900–1850*. London: Heinemann.

Boston, R. (1992) 'A country dying of thirst', *The Guardian*, September 2.

Bozzoli, B. (1983) 'Marxism, feminism and South African studies', *Journal of Southern African Studies*, 9 (2).

Brand, C. (1981) 'The anatomy of an unequal society', in C. Stoneman (ed.), *Zimbabwe's Inheritance*. London: Macmillan.

Bush, R., Cliffe, L. and Jansen, V. (1986) 'The crisis in the reproduction of migrant labour in southern Africa', in P. Lawrence (ed.), *World Recession and the Food Crisis in Africa*. London: James Currey.

Cheater, A. (1981) 'Women and their participation in commercial agricultural production', *Development and Change*, 12 (July): 349–77.

Chigwedere, A. (1982) *Lobola*. Harare: Books for Africa.

Clarke, D. (1977) *Agricultural and Plantation Workers in Rhodesia*. Gweru: Mambo.

Colson, E. (1971) 'The impact of the colonial period on the definition of land rights', in V. Turner (ed.), *Colonialism in Africa*, vol. 3. Cambridge: Cambridge University Press.

Cousins, B., Weiner, D. and Amin, N (1992) 'Social differentiation in the communal lands of Zimbabwe', *Review of African Political Economy*, no. 53: 5–24.

Folbre, N. (1988) 'Patriarchal social formations in Zimbabwe', in S. Stichter and J. Parpart (eds), *Patriarchy and Class: African Women in the Home and the Workforce*. Boulder: Westview.

Gaidzanwa, R. (1992) 'The concepts of citizenship and nationality and their applicability to southern Africa', forthcoming in *Alternatives*.

Goldin, I. (1987) *Making Race: the Politics and Economics of Coloured Identity in South Africa*. Cape Town: Maskew Miller.

Hodder-Williams, R. (1974) 'Afrikaners in Rhodesia: a partial portrait', *African Social Research*, 18 (December).

Holleman, J. (1952) *Shona Customary Law*. Cape Town: Oxford University Press.

Hughes, A.J.B. and van Velsen, J. (1954) 'The Ndebele', in D. Forde (ed.), *Ethnographic Survey of Africa: Southern Africa*, Pt IV. London: International African Institute.

Jacobs, S. (1989a) 'Zimbabwe: class, state and gendered models of land resettlement', in

J. Parpart and K. Staudt (eds), *Women and the State in Africa*. Boulder: Lynne Rienner.

Jacobs, S. (1989b) 'Gender relations and land resettlement in Zimbabwe'. DPhil thesis, Institute of Development Studies, University of Sussex.

Jacobs, S. and Howard, T. (1987) 'Women in Zimbabwe: stated policy and state action', in H. Afshar (ed.), *Women, State and Ideology*. London: Macmillan.

Kazembe, J. (1986) 'The Woman Question', in I. Mandaza (ed.), *Zimbabwe: the Political Economy of Transition*. Dakar: Codeseria.

Kennedy, D. (1987) *Islands of White: Settler Society and Culture in Kenya and Southern Rhodesia, 1890–1939*. Durham: Duke University Press.

Kirkwood, D. (1984) 'Settler wives in Southern Rhodesia: a case study', in H. Callan and S. Ardener (eds), *The Incorporated Wife*. London: Croom Helm. pp. 143–64.

Kosmin, B.A. (1980) *MaJuta: a History of the Jewish Community in Zimbabwe*. Gwelo: Mambo.

Kriger, N. (1992) *Zimbabwe's Guerrilla War: Peasant Voices*. Cambridge: Cambridge University Press.

Lloyd, J. (1974) *Rhodesia's Pioneer Women, 1859–96*. Bulawayo: Rhodesia Pioneers and Early Settlers Society.

Lloyd, J. (1975) *Experiences of Rhodesia's Pioneer Women*. Bulawayo: Rhodesia Pioneers and Early Settlers Society.

Loney, M. (1975) *Rhodesia: White Racism and Imperial Response*. Harmondsworth: Penguin.

Mabazeke, M. (1986) 'Violence against wives: a crime *sui generis*', *Zimbabwe Law Review*, 4: 88–111.

Mandaza, I. (1979) 'White settler ideology, African nationalism and the "coloured" question in southern Africa, Southern Rhodesia/Zimbabwe and Nyasaland/Malawi, 1900–78'. DPhil thesis, York University. Cited in I. Goldin (1987) *Making Race: the Politics and Economics of Coloured Identity in South Africa*. Cape Town: Maskew Miller.

Mandaza, I. (ed.) (1986) *Zimbabwe: the Political Economy of Transition*. Dakar: Codeseria.

May, J. (1983) *Zimbabwean Women in Customary and Colonial Law*. Gweru: Mambo.

Milroy, R. (1983) 'Customary law and legal majority', *The Herald*, Harare, February 27.

Mombeshora, S. (1990) 'The salience of ethnicity in political development: the case of Zimbabwe', *International Sociology*, 5 (4): 427–44.

Mpofu, J. (1983) 'Some observable sources of women's subordination in Zimbabwe', Centre for Applied Social Studies, University of Zimbabwe.

Ms. (*International News*) (1993) 'Zimbabwe: mother/daughter/sister, 3 (5): 11.

Muchena, O. (1979) 'The changing position of African women in Zimbabwe', *Zimbabwe Journal of Economics*, 1 (2) (NS).

Murphree, M. (1988) 'The salience of ethnicity in African states: a Zimbabwean case study', *Ethnic and Racial Studies*, 11 (2).

National Federation of Business and Professional Women of Rhodesia (1976) *Profiles of Rhodesia's Women*. Salisbury: National Federation of Business Women.

Palmer, R.H. (1977) *Land and Racial Domination in Rhodesia*. London: Heinemann.

Pankhurst, D. (1991) 'Constraints and incentives in "successful" Zimbabwean peasant agriculture: the interaction between gender and class', *Journal of Southern African Studies*, 17 (4).

Pankhurst, D. and Jacobs, S. (1988) 'Land tenure, agricultural production and gender relations: the case of Zimbabwe's peasantry', in J. Davison (ed.), *Agriculture, Women and Land: the African Experience*. Boulder: Westview.

Pape, J. (1990) 'Black and white: the "perils of sex" in colonial Zimbabwe', *Journal of Southern African Studies*, 16 (4).

Phillips, P. (1992) Personal communication, Leeds, January 22.

Phimister, I. (1983) 'Zimbabwe: the path of capitalist development', in D. Birmingham and P. Martin (eds) *A History of Central Africa*, vol. II. Harlow: Longman.

Phimister. I. (1988) *A Social and Economic History of Zimbabwe, 1890–1948*. London, Longman.

Pitts, M. (1991) Personal communication, Stoke-on-Trent, November 25.

Ranger, T.O. (1979) *Revolt in Southern Rhodesia: 1896–7*. London: Heinemann.

Ranger, T.O. (1983) 'The invention of tradition in Colonial Africa', in E. Hobsbawm and T.O. Ranger, *The Invention of Tradition*. Cambridge: Cambridge University Press.

Ranger, T.O. (1985a) *Peasant Consciousness and Guerrilla War in Zimbabwe*. London: James Currey.

Ranger, T.O. (1985b) *The Invention of Tribalism in Zimbabwe*. Gweru: Mambo.

Ranger, T.O. (1990a) 'Ethnicity and nationality in southern Africa: Eastern European resonances', unpublished, St Antony's College, Oxford, June.

Ranger, T.O. (1990b) 'The origins of nationalism in rural Matabeleland: the case of Wenlock', unpublished, St Antony's College, Oxford, October.

Schmidt, E. (1991) 'Patriarchy, capitalism and the colonial state in Zimbabwe', *Signs*, 16 (4).

Schmidt, E. (1992) *Peasant, Traders and Wives*. London: Heinemann.

Snyder, F. (1982) 'Colonialism and legal form: the creation of "customary law" in Senegal', in C. Sumner (ed.), *Crime, Justice and Underdevelopment*. London: Heinemann.

Staunton, I. (1990) *Mothers of the Revolution*. London: James Currey.

Stoneman, C. and Cliffe, L. (1989) *Zimbabwe: Politics, Economics, Society*. London: Pinter.

Sylvester, C. (1991) *Zimbabwe: the Terrain of Contradictory Development*. Boulder: Westview.

Van Onselen, C. (1980) *Chibaro: Mine Labour in S. Rhodesia, 1900–1933*. London: Pluto.

Weinrich, A.K.H. (1977) *The Tonga People on the Southern Shore of Lake Kariba*. Gwelo: Mambo.

Weinrich, A.K.H. (1979) *Women and Racial Discrimination in Rhodesia*. Paris: UNESCO.

Weinrich, A.K.H. (1982) *African Marriage in Zimbabwe*. Gweru: Mambo.

Weiss, R. (1986) *The Women of Zimbabwe*. London: Kesho.

Women's Action Group [1989?] *Women's Health Information Project*. Harare: Women's Action Group.

Zimbabwe Women's Bureau (1981) *Black Women in Zimbabwe*. Salisbury: Zimbabwe Women's Bureau.

10

Between 'Becoming M'tourni'* and 'Going Native': Gender and Settler Society in Algeria

Anissa Hélie

Historical analysis of nineteenth-century western colonialism in Algeria invokes a simple dichotomy as a first point of departure: the colonizers versus the colonized. This dichotomy blurs other social relations which are significant, particularly with regard to women's politics in Algeria after independence. There are three compelling reasons for scholars of Algeria and other settler societies to reject a dichotomous framework.

First, this dichotomy implies that the history of the colonized started with the process of western colonization, thus obscuring and misrepresenting pre-colonial times as well as previous colonizations. In the Algerian case, this would mean ignoring the colonization by the Romans and Turks. Hence, pre-colonial, colonial and post-colonial periods become viewed as distinct and separate historical periods, ignoring the continuities and discontinuities between them. Secondly, the class, racial, ethnic, religious, gender and other schisms among the colonized as well as the colonizers are rendered far less salient, and their social and theoretical implications are ignored. These differences between and within colonizers and colonized are crucial for understanding the socio-historical processes of colonization and their implications.

Last but not least, different types of colonization created different bases for the development of the colonizer–colonized relationship. Attention should be paid to the impacts that both the concept and the reality of a settler society had on the construction of nationalist claims as well as on the post-independence problematic.

The objective of this chapter is to analyse the period of French settler colonization of Algeria (1830–1962) in order to establish the effects of the above considerations for the formation of Algerian national and gender identities. More specifically, this chapter will highlight the formation of gender identity in Algeria in the context of the formation of

*Literally means 'turned', in other words: renegade, turncoat.

a settler society and the elaboration of a nationalist discourse – both of which sought to obliterate gender differences. Understanding the challenges of the contemporary Algerian feminist movement, including the possibilities for strategic alliances with European women's movements, necessitates an analysis of the historical reality of the settler colony as well as of the limitations imposed by Algerian nationalism. Algerian feminists are compelled to analyse the various racial, ethnic, religious and class relations dominating different phases of Algeria's history as a colonized society in order to place in perspective their current orientations, strategies and challenges.

Specific points are important to bear in mind when investigating this particular settler experience. First, the presence of long-term settlers is as politically significant in Algeria as in the case of South Africa or Israel. The fundamental difference, however, lies in the fact that, with the emergence of an independent state, no European settlers remained there after 130 years of French occupation. The settler society dispersed almost completely with the breakdown of the colonial system in 1962.

Secondly, European colonizers confronted a specific mosaic of religious/ethnic/racial/class groups which had existed in Algeria prior to colonization. For the purpose of this chapter, however, the analysis will be limited to four major groups: European settlers, Jews, Arabs and Berbers. It will not include groups who have not settled permanently in Algeria, such as the nomadic Tuaregs in the Sahara or French civil servants residing temporarily in the country. Despite the complexity of the social structure, each group has defined itself in opposition to the others. In the colonial lexicon Algerians were usually labelled 'indigenous', 'Arabs' or 'Muslims', depending on whether the colonizers wanted to emphasize racial, ethnic or religious difference at a particular time and for a particular purpose. Similarly, the Algerian population referred to all Europeans as 'the French' – sometimes even 'France' – or as '*Roumi*' ('*Roumia*' for women, a term meaning 'foreigners' with the implicit connotation of 'non-Muslim'). Interestingly, to define themselves primarily as distinct from European rulers did not lead Algerians to ignore their own ethnic differences. Berbers, for example, revindicate a specific identity up to the present time.

Finally, the multi-ethnic character of the settlers also introduces nuances in the definition of 'Europeans' as a monolithic entity. Settlers by no means originated only from France. At the time of independence, only around half of the European population was composed of French citizens. Most of them had acquired citizenship only recently, compelled by the fact that in 1962 the French authorities denied assistance in repatriation to many Europeans, precisely on the grounds that they were not French citizens. The frequent reference (particularly in the settler literature at the end of the nineteenth century) to a 'European melting pot' should not obscure the divisions in economic and social status between French citizens and the Maltese, Spaniards or Italians.

Political orientation provided another source of division linked to the multi-ethnic composition of the European settler population. Between the mid-nineteenth and mid-twentieth centuries, Algeria provided shelter for Europeans fleeing undemocratic regimes; at the same time it was seen by the French metropolis as a site to dump undesirable activists. Both these forms of population transfer explain why Algeria has been labelled the 'red colony'. The leftist wave of French settlers was a minority component. According to Ageron (1992), the republicans deported by French authorities in 1852 numbered no more than 6,200. This was followed by the migration of the *Communards*, expelled from Paris in 1870. Other Europeans, such as the Spanish refugees who sought asylum after the fall of Madrid in 1936, joined the fray.

The leftist tendency of the colony is evidenced by the strong membership of European migrants in the Algerian Communist Party (PCA). It is significant, however, that this political identification has not prevented most settlers, French and 'foreigners' together, from adopting racist discourse and attitudes embodied in the colonial system. Furthermore, a colonialist lobby (particularly strong among the landed aristocracy) was opposed to all efforts at integration of the indigenous population within civil society. Only a few instances in the process of integration led to the adoption of a less restrictive status for Algerian subjects.

This complexity of interactions between the various actors, in everyday life as well as institutional political practice, led to the construction of several dichotomies in which one party was always inferior. The 'classical couples of the cultural–ethnic exclusion [were] defined as Muslims/Roumis, M'tournis/Muslims, Jews/Europeans, European Jews/Algerian Muslims' (GRENAMO, 1987: 12). Two crucial elements can be underlined here. The first is the system of (mutual) exclusion that successfully prevents the dominant hierarchy from being challenged. The second is the interdependence on which the whole settler society lies, with one category being systematically defined relative to another.

I will refer to the colonial categories of the 'Europeans' (French and other Mediterranean country citizens) and the 'indigenous'. In the colonial lexicon, the latter category was subsequently changed to refer to Jews, Berbers and Arabs. However, I will retain this term to refer to its literal definition, that is, the autochthonous population of a country. None of the available terminology – that is, Muslims, Arabs and Algerians – refers to the original population. Where appropriate, I will also distinguish among ethnic groups.

This chapter is divided into three sections. The first section gives an overview of the ethnic and class structure which existed in Algeria before and during colonization. It analyses ethnicity and class as interwoven and mutually reinforcing elements of divisions and alliances in the struggle for political and economic power.

The second examines the impact of racial and religious dichotomies on the construction of collective identities and different national projects in the colonial and post-colonial context. It focuses on the colonizers' definition of citizenship, as well as on the role of religion, ethnicity and gender relations in the struggle for independence.

The third section examines how women's subjectivity/agency led them to reproduce or resist what was expected of them in ethnic, religious, class and/or racial terms. Finally, the chapter concludes with an analysis of the consequences of Algerian pre-colonial, colonial and post-colonial diversities on the women's movement in Algeria.

The Algerian Settler Society: Social Structures

Algeria in Pre-Colonial Times: a Multicultural Society
In pre-historic times, the native population of Algeria comprised the ethnically homogeneous Berbers. The Berber territory stretched to the north-west quarter of the African continent. Their presence is first attested to in Egyptian written sources in 1227 BC, although contacts with ancient Egypt occurred even earlier. With the exception of the appearance of camel drivers during the fourth millennium, this proto-historic group did not experience any invasions after the eighth millennium.

As a result of its strategic location on the Mediterranean coast, Algeria was later the site of many waves of invasions: Greeks, Phoenicians, Romans, Arabs and Turks followed one another. Some of these early colonizers settled and mixed with the native Berber population. Given the relatively small numbers of these settlers, their presence failed to modify the ethnic unity of the Berber population. Berbers remain numerically predominant to the present day. However, the presence of Judaized and Islamicized, partly Arabic-speaking, communities is at the core of Algerian history.

There is evidence of Berber conversion to Judaism as early as the fifth century. It was the Arab wave of colonization, however, between the mid-sixth and the eleventh centuries which introduced changes on a larger scale. Arab conquerors were relatively few in number. The main wave of invasion, led by Hillalien tribes in the eleventh century, did not bring more than 60,000 people. Nonetheless, the introduction of Islam and the Arabic language had a major social and cultural impact. Jewish minorities were relegated to a subaltern status as they were non-Muslims, while most Berbers adopted an (adapted) Islamic faith. Islamization was globally achieved around the thirteenth century.

These social transformations demonstrate that the 'natives' became a heterogeneous entity in terms of culture, religion, social status and ethnicity. The mutual influence of various groups of early inhabitants occurred not only in sharing and interacting in the same public space, but also in terms of the transmission of culture. Some groups shared the Arabic language (spoken by those of Arab descent, Jews and a certain percentage of Berbers), while others shared the Islamic faith (observed by both Berbers and Arabs). At the same time, each community managed to preserve elements of its own cultural specificity. Up to the present day, Berbers have preserved their own language, script and social organization, such as the tribal structure. They have also retained traditions through rituals, lullabies, agrarian legends and a particular form of geometric art. Although subjected to restrictive legislation, the Jews have enjoyed the right to live according to their own religious and communal rules.

Cultural norms and religious traditions have had implications for the position of indigenous women. Jewish and Muslim women were especially expected to observe culturally specific gender guidelines. However, substantial ethnic and class variations exist among the Muslims. For example, although Muslims practised common traditions such as the dowry, there were also clear differences among the unveiled Kabyle farm-woman, the veiled urban woman, the secluded M'zabite and the nomadic Targuiya. These variations are attributable to differences in interpretation of Islamic precepts according to cultural values and economic realities. The strong influence of Berber *kanoun* (customary laws), for example, has sometimes interfered with the dominant *sharia* (Muslim religious laws).

These differences manifest themselves among women in practices pertaining to the veil. The definition of female roles and variations in donning of the veil were linked as much to the economic mode of production, urban/rural and class distinctions as to differences in ethnic background. The active involvement and unencumbered physical movement required of most rural women in agriculture facilitated the discarding of the veil. Female urban elites were expected to wear the veil much more than their urban working-class counterparts. There were, however, also regional differences between the thin, white, *haik* veil in Algiers and the heavy, black, woollen veil of Constantine, as well as between the various ways of wearing it (either concealing only the lower part of the face or the whole face with the exception of one eye). The same observation applies to the seclusion of many urban Muslim women. The economic prosperity of the family increased the likelihood of seclusion, but some women of the working classes were also secluded.

In pre-colonial Algerian society, geographical location and class were tightly connected with religious and/or ethnic membership. Most Berbers were tied to their village communities and were involved in agricultural work. In contrast, as a legacy of their role as intermediaries for the Turkish potentates, Arabs were concentrated in the urban centres of the northern part of the country. Jews were also more numerous in the cities, mainly in the western regions of the country. Apart from religious leaders and rabbis, the urban Jewish population was mostly involved in trade, handicrafts (textile and leather) and the medical professions, while their rural counterparts could be found travelling through the country as itinerant merchants.

Class differentiation existed not only in the secular world, but also in the dominant religious sphere. The *Ulemas* – the urban Muslim aristocracy in charge of interpreting and promoting Islamic texts – played an important role in the emergence of nationalist movements. Another level in the Muslim hierarchy consisted of the *Marabouts*, local saints integrated in small communities and venerated in the popular faith.

The juxtaposition of Jews, Arabs and Berbers, their geographical and cultural location, and their class and gender differences shaped the society invaded by the French colonizers in 1830.

Colonization: Overcoming Divisions within the European Community

The need to confront Turkish–Muslim power in Algiers, which threatened European trade on the Mediterranean Sea, was invoked by France as justification of the 'Algiers expedition' in 1830. In fact the conquest was more powerfully motivated by internal difficulties faced by the July Monarchy, which the French power hoped to divert attention from by a glorious territorial expansion.

Contrary to the original intentions of French political leaders, Algeria gradually became a colony of settlement. Once this informal process began, the French authorities claimed that their objective was to establish a 'Greater France' 'from Dunkerque to Tamanrasset' – from the northernmost French town to the southernmost Algerian one. Officially, Algeria was to become one of the French territorial circumscriptions, that is, not a colony but an integrated part of the French territory. The Mediterranean Sea was perceived merely as an internal lake to this Greater France. The geographical proximity of the 'African France' to mainland France was seen as an advantage in the settlement process.

Because of the strictly political and military motivations of the conquest, the colonizers did not design any global plans for Algeria's economic development. Historians are presently debating the economic profitability for France of its Algerian colony. According to Marseille (1984), French investments in Algeria, between 1830 and 1900 and from 1900 to 1962, exceeded the capital gained by the metropolis flowing from Algeria. Moreover, the local revenues were never sufficient to sustain the development of the colony. Marseille argues that, during the 130 years of French domination, only the decades spanning 1900–50 were prosperous ones. Even during those years, however, most sectors of the economy were subsidized by the metropolis. On the grounds that colonization is far from a philanthropic enterprise, other historians take a different position. They argue that French authorities would have given up Algeria if it was so evident that they could not materially benefit from it.

Appropriation of agricultural production was a constant trend in the colonization of Algeria, and agricultural products constituted the colony's major exports to France. The resulting commerce was clearly not to the advantage of the metropolitan market. Cereals, wool and, above all, wines and liquors were already produced in sufficient quantity in France. Moreover, Algeria did not constitute a particularly desirable market for French exports, apart from some textiles, clothing and mechanical industrial goods.

Nonetheless, capitalists from both sides of the Mediterranean were most able to profit from the colonial encounter. The cheap indigenous labour available was certainly profitable to the whole metropolitan economy. Immigration of Algerian workers increased after World War I and continues to be important to the present day. During both world wars, France also took advantage of the reserve army constituted by the indigenous population. Indeed, 25,000 indigenous persons died in the first conflict alone. The Algerian territory was also used as a safe strategic base for the Allied troops in 1945.

Such advantages to the colonizers became possible through the enforcement of French rule. However, early French settlement was made difficult by indigenous resistance. Even after the 1847 surrender of the coalition led by Abd El Kader, significant insurrections took place – in the Kabylie (1871), the Aurès (1879, 1916), and southern Algeria and Oranie (1881). The complete 'pacification' of the country, including the Sahara (whose conquest was to facilitate links with French possessions in Sudan), was not completed until the end of the nineteenth century. Because penetration by the French army in southern Algeria had been slowed down by such resistance, the northern regions constituted the core of the European presence.

The period spanning 1870–1900 was characterized by growing economic prosperity of the settler society. Algeria offered potential settlers the image of a promised land. By 1896 the number of Europeans born in Algeria exceeded the number of immigrants. In 1888 the protectorate of Tunisia assured a place for European settlers on the eastern frontier. In 1912 the French protectorate of Morocco established French military supremacy over the whole of North Africa. The effort to 'make Algeria French' (Prochaska, 1990) was key in attracting immigrants and modifying the average settler's profile.

From the 1830s to the 1840s, early French settlers came as individuals – a pattern which was to become characteristic of other European immigrants. Subsequently, 'official colonization', a more organized form of settlement, was put into operation by the French metropolis in order to ensure the establishment of its own citizens. This policy favoured French people willing to settle as farmers in Algeria. 'Colonial villages' were built, following the model of the 'colonial Panthéon' which included family-unit houses, church, town hall and school.

There is no historical evidence of restrictive legislation limiting female emigration. On the contrary, the European population was balanced in terms of sex ratio. By their mere presence at the beginning of the colonization process, married European women in Algeria 'confirmed the status of their husbands as settlers in a "new" country' (Kirkwood, 1984: 143).

The imperial power was interested in ensuring long-term settlement. Hence, there was the strategy of providing free plots of land. Although this failed to create an agricultural population (Ageron, 1992), it ultimately facilitated the immigration of families on the grounds that a single person was unable to perform the necessary reclamation work. Plots of land were specifically allocated to French citizens, but some Spaniards, Maltese and Italians (the 'foreigners') also benefited from this. Attracted by the seasonal work in agriculture, they settled and formed significant minorities. Next to the French, the Spanish constituted the largest European ethnic group. In 1848, out of the 115,000 Europeans, between a third and a half were of Spanish origin. The European population gradually increased but retained its multi-ethnic character.

Due to their geographical isolation from each other, these various European ethnic groups remained as separate communities. The Spaniards were concentrated in the west, while the Italians were more numerous in the east. French and Maltese were more evenly spread, with more of the latter residing in the coastal cities. In places where various European sub-groups were represented, they lived in distinct neighbourhoods. Notwithstanding intermarriage between Europeans of different origins at the very end of the nineteenth century (Ageron, 1992), this spatial distribution pattern remained during the whole settler period and was further reinforced by the emergent class divisions.

The pioneer wave of immigrants was characterized by the lack of training and qualifications, a fact which is not specific to the Algerian case (see Hammerton 1979: 53, for Australia and South Africa). Subsequently, the development of the settler society contributed to a modification of the average immigrant profile, from the 'male uneducated generalist (Kirkwood, 1984) to young professionals of both sexes. The expansion of urban centres, to accommodate the increase in business and service industries as well as professional occupations, helped create an urban middle class. Gender differentiation, enhanced by women's supposedly inherent civilizing mission, enlisted in the colonial project, led most middle-class women to concentrate upon 'feminine occupations' in education, in health care and as lower-level bureaucrats, such as post-office employees.

Although Algeria's economy was primarily reliant on the agricultural sector, the authorities in Paris failed to establish a stable, small-scale peasantry. Instead, they favoured the emergence of a landed aristocracy, a group that was to become quite vocal in political debates. Not surprisingly, most *grands propriétaires* (large landowners) were French, while the agricultural workers were mainly European 'foreigners'. They constituted a cheap labour force, not only in the agricultural and mining sectors but also in the urban areas as well. According to Ageron (1992), during the period 1870–1900, 260,000 foreigners, mainly Spaniards, settled in the cities to join the labour force for public works. Some immigrants, such as Maltese merchants or Italian fishermen, set up their own small businesses. The female working class played a significant role as factory workers. For instance, Spanish women worked in the tobacco industry in the Algiers and Oran regions. The other alternative was centred around home-based work (dressmaking, laundry and so on).

While the division of labour emphasized divisions among Europeans, the school system reinforced the notion of a collective identity. In 1881–82 legislation was introduced which emphasized the 'compulsory, free and secular' character of primary education. These educational reforms did not lead to the breakdown of the implicit hierarchy that regulated relations between those who were 'French by race' and 'foreigners' (and later on, Jews). But it did make possible alliances. 'The Algerian melting pot did not dissolve individual European ethnic differences, but instead created a heady new Mediterranean stew – what later came to be known as the Pied-Noir community' (Prochaska, 1990: 155). This community created its own specific dialect (the Pataouet) incorporating words and sentence structures borrowed from various Mediterranean idioms (Lanly, 1963).

The emergence of a common culture allowed the European community to dream of a future made up of a 'common destiny' – the myth of a common origin being out of reach. The settlers started to define their identity as specific:

> The work of French immigrants in Algeria is not restricted to its material results. The French race, implanted in Africa, has acquired special qualities of boldness and initiative. But it is also welcoming, attractive to others and rapidly assimilates the foreign population who lives amongst them. A new race is thus being formed, bearing both the stamp of the French imprint and the outlines of its destiny. (Bernard and Redon, 1923: 104)

The growing sense of national belonging that Europeans experienced led them to redefine their links with the mother country. In 1901 they acquired responsibilities in managing Algeria's budget. As a result of the colony's increasing autonomy, the European population of Algeria, and more specifically the landed aristocracy, even tried to secede in 1945 – following upon the successful attempt of the white South African community. However, the strong opposition in France, and the virtual lack of industry in Algeria, making the latter country vulnerable to an industrial embargo, led the French colonial microcosm to be obedient to the mother country. Settlers were clearly dependent on the imperial power, particularly on an economic level, with Algerian outlets relying heavily on the French market.

Colonization: Reinforcing Divisions Among the Indigenous
The intimate interdependence of the two communities – colonizers and colonized – was evident in many aspects of social and economic life. Settlers disrupted indigenous communities through French military actions, displacing village populations and implementing land policies. At the same time, the numerical superiority of the 'indigenous masses' led Europeans to concentrate in the northern and urban areas. In 1870, 60 per cent of Europeans lived in cities; in 1926, the figure was 71.6 per cent.

Economically, the colonial experience modified the relations of the indigenous community to the labour market. But it also affected the relations between the different ethnic and class groups within the indigenous population. The pauperization of people in the countryside started with the expropriation of indigenous land. Between a quarter and a third of the agricultural land was to be concentrated in French hands. These inequities were exacerbated by the exploitative character of the *grands domaines* (large agricultural estates). The impossibility of competing with the colonial, large-scale agricultural sector led many indigenous peasants to become day labourers or waged agricultural employees. Pressure on the land also forced people to migrate to the coastal cities or even to France. Urban centres provided work opportunities for what were seen as typically male activities. Thus the construction sector employed many Kabyles (Berbers from the north) in Algeria as well as in France.

If colonization modified the participation of indigenous women in the economic sphere, it did not reduce traditional female involvement in the agricultural sector. The main factor that induced changes in indigenous female employment was the colonial demand for domestic servants, concentrated in cities where there was European settlement.

These data should not, however, be allowed to blur the class relations within the indigenous population. An indigenous ruling class, land-lords and the educated elites were all established before colonization. The situation was partly modified by colonization, but male and female members of the wealthy as well as the *maraboutic* families generally did not work.

Class formations were interwoven with ethnic divisions. The development of the European settler society in Algeria led to the constitution of political and economic intermediate groups that served the colonial interests. The Jewish minority, which was granted French citizenship in 1870, had much easier access to education than any other indigenous group. It led many Jews to achieve a 'middleman' position that could only please the colonial power, as supported by this quotation from a 1923 primary school textbook: 'Today most of the Algerian Israelites dress, work and live according to European standards. No population has so quickly achieved, through contact with the French, such a beneficial evolution . . . Knowing perfectly the Arabic language and customs, they are the natural intermediaries between the Europeans and the indigenous' (Bernard and Redon, 1923: 158). This quotation also shows the wilful and strategic ambiguity among French authorities between the 'European' and 'French' categories.

The collusion of some indigenous leaders with the rulers also underlines the role that the Arab and Berber bourgeoisie tried to play. Their often explicit pro-colonialist and pro-assimilationist position caused them to be labelled 'M'tournis' (that is, those who have turned) by other indigenous people. Notwithstanding the heterogeneity experienced within both European and indigenous communities, the major gap between colonizers and colonized remained unchallenged. The processes which facilitated the schisms between these groups will now be examined.

Boundaries of Identity

Colonial times: 'L'Algérie, c'est la France'
('Algeria is France')
The colonial authorities tried to include European settlers in the nation-building process while excluding the indigenous population from it. The national project, as understood by the European

community, relied on the claim that Algeria 'has been made' by the joint efforts of the settlers. Consequently, the benefits of its development should be reserved for Europeans. Further stemming from this colonial logic was the assumption that only Europeans should have influence on Paris's direction of Algerian economic and political development. 'The Arabs' had no right to be heard.

In order to consolidate their supremacy on a long-term basis, the colonial rulers promoted policies of unification among various European ethnic groups; obversely, they emphasized the divisions among the indigenous people. This was articulated around the notion of citizenship which allowed a legal juxtaposition of French citizens and indigenous subjects. However, males of both categories were expected to undergo French military service. In this domain there was again racial segregation and inequities. While the length of service for French men was 18 months, it was two years for indigenous males.

The Europeans were subject to the French Civil Code, while in all matters concerning civil life (inheritance, marriage and so on) the indigenous were subject to a special Code de l'indigènat derived from Islamic laws. Until 1949 education was also racially segregated.

It was not only the indigenous who received the attention of French rulers in Algeria. The 'European melting pot' appeared to be problematic as well. Behind the hypocrisy of the dominant discourse promoting an ideal image of the unified European society, the facts were otherwise. In 1876 there were actually more other European 'foreigners' than French settlers in Algeria, an unbearable situation for the latter group. A remedy was provided on the centenary of the French Revolution. In 1889 an assimilationist law provided automatic French citizenship to all children born in Algeria from foreign (that is, non-French and European) parents, except for those who explicitly refused it. According to Ageron,

> This fundamental law, which would create around 190,000 French citizens in the twenty years to come, was considered at that time as the true birth certificate of the French people in Algeria. It allowed for an increase of the number of French and 'neo-French' in relation to 'the foreigners'. (1992: 73)

With this citizenship law, the dream of 'French Algeria' appeared more attainable. To ensure its realization, however, the French employed a divide-and-rule policy towards the indigenous population. They identified, among the indigenous, a group who would be easier to 'assimilate' because of their religion and ethnic background. In 1870 the Jews became French citizens under the Crémieux décret. Such legislation (which affected 37,000 Jews in 1870) strengthened the European community on a quantitative level. By the mid-twentieth century, Jews represented not less than 12.7 per cent of the European population.

Two types of policies further defined the relations of Europeans with Arabs and Berbers. Firstly, the French government developed in Algeria a strategy based on the 'assimilation theory'. The indigenous *Francisés* (Frenchified locals), who resembled the Europeans in their manners and lifestyle and who were willing to abandon their specific status (based on Islamic laws), could request French citizenship. In fact, the complexity of the process as well as the explicit requirement to abandon one's cultural identity meant that only an insignificant number of people were 'naturalized'.

When this assimilationist policy proved unworkable, the authorities relied on the 'theory of association', which assumed that the 'natural' inferiority of the indigenous would be reduced through contact with European civilization and French culture. Here, again, colonial discourse denied the indigenous a common identity, Berbers and Arabs being virtually constructed as each other's antagonist: 'The pure Berber provides a better output than the Arabized Berber who is himself superior to the pure Arab' (Guernier, 1950: 224, vol. 2).

But another, even greater division was to be established between Europeans and indigenous. In 1872 a young metropolitan woman was denied the right to marry Si Ahmed Tidjani, leader of the powerful Tidjanyat confederacy. The Governor General of Algeria officiating at that time refused to put aside the legislation forbidding inter-racial marriages, arguing that the *rapprochement des races* (bringing the races together) was not on the agenda (Hélie, 1990). This episode underscores the perceived need among the Europeans for European women to serve as reproducers of identity boundaries (Anthias and Yuval-Davis, 1987: 9). It also highlighted the fear related to the emergence of a *métis* (coloured) group. Such a mixed group threatened the clear distinction between European and indigenous. Policies which distinguished women from each group were therefore developed.

Colonial Times: Taking Advantage of Gender
Gender as well as race has influenced the process of nation-building. European women in Algeria were expected to perform a particular role as settlers and were held responsible for the physiological and cultural reproduction of the European microcosm. Because of their supposed 'civilizing attributes', they were seen as representatives of the 'progress' symbolized by the mother country. This implied specific gender guidelines for moral and sexual regulation.

The fear of 'going native' as well as the fear of sexual assaults by 'Arabs' – perceived as motivated by the mythical attraction of indigenous for 'white' women – reinforced the need for all European women to observe and inculcate 'proper' behaviour. But the impact of such an ideology was even stronger in the case of women employed by the state. Women teachers, for example, were encouraged to develop 'female qualities' in their students in order to 'educate' the mothers of their indigenous pupils into European notions of domesticity and femininity. Their ability to enter the private sphere more easily than their male counterparts gave them a specific role as active agents of colonization.

Colonial policies towards indigenous women were clearly based on the idea of penetrating a society through its women. Alloula (1981) acknowledges this colonial desire to 'unveil Algerian women' in his analysis of the 'exotic' postcards (fashionable under colonial rule) portraying indigenous women. Acculturation of Algerian women was the goal and the strategy of colonizers, as it was to become also for the later Muslim fundamentalists. This is particularly clear in regard to education: the approach towards the schooling of indigenous girls demonstrates the will of the colonizers to take advantage of ethnic/religious differences. The first targets were those ethnic groups assumed to be more readily assimilated to western culture. Thus, immediately following the conquest and the completion of 'pacification', primary schools were opened, for Jewish and Kabyle girls respectively.

Indigenous women were also used by the colonial army secessionists who led the coup against Paris in May 1958. A public unveiling of Algerian women took place in Algiers, consistent with the policy to promote 'fraternization' of the colonized and the colonizers against the metropolis. The public burning of veils instigated by French officers illustrates how the colonizers had positioned 'Algerian women as living symbols of both the colony's resistance *and* its vulnerability to penetration' (Woodhull, 1991: 119, original emphasis). Along the same lines, Algerian women's access to the vote in 1958 was, according to Woodhull, intended primarily as 'a divisive tactic to promote women's support for a French rather than an independent Algeria' (Woodhull, 1991: 119). But in 1958 the indigenous had their own project of resistance. Indeed, by 1954 the nine 'historical leaders' of the Algerian Revolution – all males – had initiated the armed struggle.

Algerian Nationalism: Before Independence
The Algerian national project was created around factors that were supposed to unite all Algerians. Among the most important of these, religion was defined as the pivot and framework of national identity. Women were generally perceived and represented as 'the preferential symbol' (Hélie-Lucas, 1993) of national and religious identity. The cohesive role of Islam, however, does not blur the fact that Algerian nationalism and its links with Arabization have been based on ethnic as well as gender exclusions. The identification of the independent socialist

state with the third world did not prevent the new rulers from constructing their own third world. In other words, decision-making processes came to exclude large segments of the Algerian population whose oppression was instrumental to the reinforcement of their power.

In the colonial context, where Algerians in general were deprived of basic rights, the issue of cultural identity was of primary importance for national survival. Hence, the manipulation/definition of 'cultural roots' during the liberation struggle was crucial in constructing a homogeneous community from disparate peoples. The fact that more secular political programmes (such as that of Ferraht Abbas) and forces did not ultimately gain as much support as those emphasizing Islam may be related to the need of those labelled 'Muslims' by the settlers, to affirm their separate identity.

The creation of the Association of Reformist Ulemas in 1931 reinforced the quest for a return to 'Islamic roots'. Its slogan expressed the spirit of Algerian nationalist struggle for decades. Its programme clearly melded national, cultural and religious identities: 'Islam is my religion, Arabic is my language, Algeria is my fatherland.' Such a formula, however, denies the multidimensional character of Algerian society. It obscures the presence of Berbers, whose mother tongue is not Arabic and whose tribal links extend beyond state boundaries. It also ignores Jews whose religion is not Islam. The reference to a supposedly homogeneous Islam obscures the fact that, in melding cultural traditions, Muslim religious guidelines shaped and were shaped by very diverse realities. The nationalist rallying cry, quoted above, was not yet linked to a later independence goal, but to the enhancement of an Algerian-ness rooted in Arabo-Muslim identity.

The massacre of Sétif, on May 8, 1945, was a turning point in raising national consciousness. An official ceremony was held to celebrate the Allies' victory over the Nazis. Aware of the important role they had played in fighting alongside French troops, numerous indigenous ex-servicemen demonstrated with Algerian flags, demanding better conditions and the recognition of their status. Although independence as such was not yet on their agenda, this demand was seen as a provocation by French colonial authorities who reacted violently, the outcome of which was that more than 40,000 were killed in and around only the city of Sétif. Consequently, political mobilization increased and nationalist movements formed to pursue the goal of independence. At the 1948 National Assembly elections, the Movement for the Triumph of Democratic Liberties (MTLD) was promising the 'departure of the French and the Spanish, an Arab government, Arab prefects and our flag'.

Women's roles, in the eyes of the male independentist leaders, were primarily oriented towards the defence of cultural values and the reproduction and education of the youth. The liberation war (1954–62) further reinforced the subordination of sexual identity to the national cause. 'Whether we want it or not, the Algerian woman would never evolve as long as Algeria is submitted to the French colonialist yoke,' claimed the MTLD in 1949 (Amrane, 1991: 32).

Molyneux (1985) turns the question of the relationship between gender and national struggles upside down: 'If women surrender their specific interests, in the universal struggle for a different society, to what are these interests rehabilitated, legitimated and responded to by the revolutionary forces or by the new socialist state?' (Molyneux, 1985: 229). Answering this question reveals that the exclusion of both women and so-called minority groups is embodied in the roots of Algerian nationalism. This becomes evident in the demise of the settler society whose racial divide had hidden other power relations.

Following upon the Soummam Congress in 1956, Jews were urged by the National Liberation Front (FLN) to join the struggle and denounce the divisive Crémieux décret by their active involvement. Some members of the Jewish community did join the underground forces and sent letters to the French government proclaiming their identity as Algerians. However, these were a minority: the pre-colonial and colonial history of Jews in Algeria was successful in enhancing divisions between indigenous Jews and Muslims.

On the Berber side, the participation was very strong: it was Berbers who initiated the armed struggle. The population was particularly active in the Kabylie and the Aurès. The mountainous character of these areas, their poverty and the very limited European settlement may explain why they were at the forefront of the underground actions. But the benefits gained by these groups on independence were minor in contrast to their involvement.

Algerian Nationalism: After 1962

Immediately following the proclamation of independence, there was a dramatic exit of almost the entire settler population. July 1962 took the form of a true mass exodus. Around one million Europeans fled Algeria within the space of a few weeks. Fights to obtain seats on any boat leaving the country were common. The desperation characteristic of these few weeks can be found in the Pied-Noir expression, 'We've left one hand in front, one hand behind' (that is, being left naked!). The refugee settlers, including the Jews, departed mostly for France, although more than one-third of them had never set foot in France before. The only group that was not able to leave as quickly as the Europeans were the *Harkis* – those indigenous who were forced to collaborate with the French army during the Algerian liberation struggle. Abandoned by their former allies, several thousands of them were executed by the Algerian national forces.

Algeria's 'specific socialism' (or 'Islamic socialism') reinforced the tensions between 'tradition' and 'modernity'. It attempted to reconcile the transformation of economic/political structures in line with the project of the new socialist state with traditional identity politics. As the 'guarantors of national identity [rather than simply] traditional values, . . . and the supreme threat to that identity, insofar as the endemic instability can be attributed to them, women were the first to be affected by these contradictions' (Woodhull, 1991: 114).

After their active involvement in the liberation struggle, women were sent back to their homes and domestic duties. The return to their role as housewives was denounced by Fadela M'rabet as early as 1965. M'rabet asked if 'socialist revolutionaries' should act this way, before drawing a comparison with the colonial experience:

> The matter is to enhance privileges: like the most miserable Pied-Noir during the colonial period, the poorest Algerian [man] has a tremendously superior position to the one of the Algerian woman . . . Here is the definition of racism and we know its function: perpetuate, while justifying it and making it acceptable, the exploitation of the other. This is what the colonialists did with the colonized, the merchants with the slaves, the bosses with the workers, the anti-Semites with the Jews – and the Algerians with women. (1965: 23)

Following independence, however, the ruling elites used references to the colonial experience, mainly to silence potential opposition. Being accused of having links with the Hizb Franca (literally, 'the party of France') meant being labelled as traitors to the nation. In fact, any of the French-speaking bourgeoisie or any person suspected to be in favour of a 'western modernist' project was viewed as traitorous. This kind of accusation goes beyond ideological disagreement, particularly in times of crisis. From April 1993 onwards, several cases of assassinations of intellectuals have occurred. In the midst of such a wave of terror, a comment made by Abdesslam, the chief of the government, has had far-reaching consequences. His denunciation of the '*laïco-assimilationnistes*' (secular assimilationists) suggests an endorsement of a policy aimed at liquidating all political alternatives other than fundamentalist or military. But Abdesslam's public stand goes further to sound an appeal to murder.

Such state 'diabolization' of critical political practice is by no means new. In 1981, upper middle-class women protested against the state's edict forbidding women to leave the national territory on their own, without a male chaperon. But the official interpretation of this reaction was that these were *Francisées* Algerian women trying to imitate the *Roumia*. The same strategy is repeated by the fundamentalists today. In December 1989, in Algiers, the Islamic Salvation Front (FIS) called for 'the abolition of the colonial laws that require, for administrative documents, identity pictures of women without the veil' (Bessis and Belhassen, 1992: 199).

The assumption of power by a local Algerian intelligentsia had far-reaching consequences not only for the position of women, but also for ethnic and class oppressions. The exclusion of Berbers from political life was quickly implemented. With the adoption of one-party rule in 1963, Berber opposition was silenced. The first constitution of the independent state defined Arabic as the only official language, denying recognition of Berber as an official language.

Far from suppressing the class structure, the policies of the new socialist government deepened economic inequalities. With the help of the one-party rule system, a national bourgeoisie arose and succeeded in maintaining the country under its control for 30 years, while the powers of the military rested on the legitimacy of the FLN. As stated by the historian Harbi, 'the other countries have an army, the Algerian army has a country.'

The actions of this powerful but corrupt elite have contributed to the deepening of the economic crisis. By 1992 unemployment had reached 25 per cent of the active population, while inflation was estimated at 35–40 per cent. External debt consumes, annually, around three-quarters of export receipts. This background of economic deterioration, allied with historical precedents such as the use of religion in the nationalist discourse, has fostered a climate supportive of the fundamentalists. In this context, women have again become the first target. As Woodhull remarks,

> If North African feminists are right to argue that the current political function of mysogynistic customs is to forge solidarity among men, who are otherwise deeply divided, while maintaining what is perceived as a crucial distinction between Muslim and Western society, then it is reasonable to say that the oppression of women has become *the* national necessity in Algeria. (1991: 115, original emphasis).

Women's responses, *vis-à-vis* such trends, have obviously been historically conditioned. The following discussion examines relationships between European and indigenous women during colonial times and during the liberation struggle. It then explores alliances Algerian feminists have tried to promote with external women's movements after 1962.

Women's Activities and Political Organizations

The Colonial Era

Under French colonialism, the population was clearly racially segregated. In 1948 there were no more than 0.9 per cent of the European settlers who lived in the *communes mixtes* ('mixed districts' – one of the three administrative divisions of the territory in which the European component was very marginal). Class divisions reinforced the racial divide. Lack of social interaction between colonizers and colonized was the rule. The combination of racial and sexual boundaries led most European women to experience even fewer contacts with indigenous than their male counterparts. There were, however, exceptions.

Chaudhuri and Strobel's book illuminates the contradictions that characterize the experiences of western women in the colonies, in 'exploring both their complicity with colonialism and their resistance to it' (Chaudhuri and Strobel, 1992: 5). I will refer here to two examples where Europeans came into contact with indigenous women: as employers of domestic servants and as school teachers.

As housewives and mothers, European women were in direct contact with the indigenous; the domestic realm provided them with one of the few spaces for inter-racial contacts. As members of the elite, taking advantage of an unending supply of cheap labour, most European women were employers of indigenous nannies or female house servants. The condescending attitudes often adopted towards domestic servants were an illuminating example of how European women's social life embodied the ruling ideology.

European women employers of domestic servants may be viewed as accomplices of the colonial domination by the very fact that they participated in the oppression and exploitation of women of other ethnic groups. However, my intention is not to refer to a stark portrayal – very likely to be false since individual women might embody different attitudes in varying combinations – but to point to the ambiguity of European women's position in Colonial Algeria. They appear as 'oppressed oppressors' – and if such an expression sounds problematic, it is because of the absence of a 'language that articulates what it means to be pained via gender even as you are privileged via race and class' (Childers and Hooks, 1990: 62).

The role performed by school teachers can be seen as more ambiguous. It should be noted that the impact of education on the indigenous was very marginal – and again gendered: 13 per cent of Algerian boys were literate in 1954, while only 4.5 per cent of girls knew how to read and write (Amrane, 1991: 27). However limited in scale their role was, European women as teachers were able to interact more often with the indigenous than the average female settler. The political implication of schooling in Algeria was strongly embodied in the system: race and sex stereotyping was prevalent in the value system as well as the curriculum material (Bernard and Redon, 1923). Although they did not necessarily disagree with this specific orientation, some European teachers explicitly encouraged Algerian girls to become autonomous women.

Here are the arguments given by some of my sources (Hélie, 1988) in favour of female education: 'They should be able to survive by themselves'; 'They should not depend solely on their husbands'; and 'They should be able to work and rely on themselves in case of unhappy marriages.' These teachers believed that to provide intellectual skills to their female pupils would arm them with a means to break with traditional patriarchal standards. European teachers were thus not mere reproducers of existing power relations. Although they operated within a system that attempted to produce and reinforce an *a priori* negative attitude towards 'Muslim culture', it provided a space for them to 'want to socialize immature daughters to their adult rights and responsibilities' (Ramusack, 1992: 120). Some European women teachers have introduced subversive elements in that process.

It is not surprising, therefore, that a significant number of those Algerian women who took part in the liberation struggle were former pupils of these European teachers. In both the Algerian nationalist and the French colonial histories, Zohra Drif, Hassiba Benbouali and Djamila Bouazza are renowned for their spectacular actions; all three were trained by European female teachers.

The above argument is in disagreement with Amrane's view according to which 'the old Mediterranean legacy and the Berber culture marked the Algerian society with an entrenched patriarchy which accords women a lower status. Far from modifying women's position, Islam – interpreted in the same way – supported masculine hegemony. The colonization affirmed this situation by forbidding any evolution' (Amrane, 1991: 17). The example of European women teachers, involved simultaneously in an emancipatory as well as oppressive process, suggests that some indigenous women may have enjoyed some advantages from the colonial encounter. The interest in being literate, even in a foreign tongue and with the risk of acculturation, cannot be dismissed in a country where no education was available to girls prior to colonization.

Legislation forbidding child marriage and regulating divorce, in opposition to repudiation (exclusive, unilateral divorce on the male initiative), may also have contributed to the indigenous women's struggles against these practices. Woodhull, for instance, subscribes to a similar view, although she mainly refers to middle-class women. She points to the 'Algerian women's successful manipulations of the ambiguities within both the Muslim and the French legal codes, and their productive exploitation of conflicts and gaps between those codes, to improve their economic and social conditions' (Woodhull, 1991: 120). We should not, however, simplify the short- and long-term consequences of colonization on the indigenous women's position nor should we deny the indigenous women's capacity to resist both settler authorities and indigenous cultural practices. Nevertheless, the dichotomized social structure in which European and indigenous women lived is largely responsible for their general lack of alliances.

The images European and indigenous women held of each other influenced their inter-racial relations. Clancy-Smith explains how

> in Algeria white women defined social distance from, and political control over, the Muslims. Islam was intrinsically inferior to Western civilization precisely because of female status in the Other holy-land and culture. The women were the measure of all things, particularly in the last decade of the [nineteenth] century when a new socio-cultural synthesis finally emerged, that of the Pied-Noir community. (1992: 69)

Colonization was in part justified by the French civilizing mission towards indigenous women who were systematically portrayed as victims. It is this notion of the indigenous woman as powerless, and the colonial focus on her subordinated position (through emphasis on practices such as the veil, seclusion or forced marriages), that limited collective strategies.

In her study of colonial wives in Uganda, Gartrell indicates that 'the forms of oppression of women were so specific to each stratum that attempts, by women, to reach across the social barriers between colonizers and colonized inevitably had a degree of artificiality' (Gartrell, 1984: 183). Hatem, however, has another approach based on her Egyptian case study. She points to the factors that overshadowed commonalities between indigenous and European women but does not deny that these commonalities exist. 'The danger that cultural nationalism posed for women is that it prevented them from developing an appreciation for the varied mechanisms of control developed by different patriarchal systems' (Hatem, 1992: 55). Such a hypothesis highlights the fact that by picturing themselves as much more liberated than the indigenous women, European women in Algeria avoided analysing the limitations that their own society imposed on their lives – in the family, in their access to the labour market or by denying them the possibility of marrying if they undertook 'male' occupations.

These ideological traps explain the difficulties indigenous and European women had in relating to each other's experiences and in identifying common issues. Examples from the period of liberation struggle demonstrate the impact of these positions. Amrane shows that in the 1950s opposition parties such as the PCA did not succeed in bringing in women of various origins because of 'European-based recruitment criteria' (Amrane, 1991: 39). As a result, European Communist women joined mixed cells in which Europeans of both sexes and Algerian men worked together, while the few Algerian women involved met in all-female cells. Another example is the method used for the dissemination of party guidelines. Women activists who were sent to meet potential female recruits were mostly European, did not speak Arabic and were hence accompanied by an indigenous translator. The persuasive character of the dominant/subordinate power structure thus remained untouched.

Furthermore, very few European women supported the Algerian women's demand for the right to vote. In 1947 the Communist-linked Algerian Women's Union (UFA) led a protest. According to a participant, a march organized in Bel Abbes attracted more than a thousand women. At most, fifty were European women (Amrane, 1991: 42). It should be remembered that French women had only been granted political rights two years before, in 1945.

On the Road towards Partnership?
History, nevertheless, provides some examples of women reaching across cultural barriers. The interest of European women in indigenous women often took the form of ethnological studies. Although often distorted by colonial stereotypes, these writings sometimes offered valuable insights. For example, in 1900 Hubertine Auclert, a female French writer and traveller, deplored the fact that in Algeria 'only a very small elite minority of Frenchmen would place the Arab race in the category of humanity'.

Racial segregation was mainly reinforced during the liberation period (1954–62). But in a minority of cases, attempts by European women to express support for the Algerian Revolution were developed on a more equal basis. Such women shared with Algerians a common denunciation of imperialism and its militarist methods. The social construction of the 'Muslim terrorist' and the violence against the European population in Algeria made alliances difficult. Nonetheless, there were individual cases of European women – from France rather than the settler community – involved in the struggle.

The relationships experienced in jail by women prisoners of various origins (French metropolitans, settlers of various European nationalities and indigenous) demonstrated the strength of their solidarity. Despite the jail and the administration's divide-and-rule strategy, women prisoners succeeded in maintaining a common front. In El Harrach jail, for example, European women were expected to sew while Algerian women were expected to weave baskets. This unequal ethno-cultural distribution of tasks showed, however, that the prison authorities recognized their commonality as women. Neither indigenous nor European women were given 'hard labour', that is, male tasks. The women organized their own lives in jail. Those who were literate gave lessons to their comrades. Both Arabic and French were part of the curriculum. In one jail the daily newspaper-reading sessions entailed one woman reading in French, a second translating it into

Arabic, and a third into Kabyle. In some places, women organized social activities which included dance and singing lessons. 'In the song notebook of Fatima B., an Algerian intellectual activist of the Algerian People Party (PPA), one can find the same songs as in the notebook of Rose, an Algerian Communist activist of Spanish origin. The Algerian patriotic songs fused with "Carmela", the Spanish republican song, and "Les partisans", the French song from the Resistance against the Nazis' (Amrane, 1991: 193).

Some initiatives were designed to alert public opinion in France about the repression in Algeria. In 1961 the well-known French feminists, Simone de Beauvoir and Gisèle Halimi, published a book denouncing the use of torture by the French army, 'Djamila Boupacha: the story of the torture of a young Algerian girl which shocked Liberal French opinion'. Their appeal on behalf of this heroic figure is, however, the only example of cross-cultural solidarity that received nationwide attention.

After independence, however, mobilization inside Algeria as well as links with women's movements outside the country became more difficult to implement. Until 1989 the one-party system did not allow room for any opposition. The so-called 'women's organizations', such as the National Union of Algerian Women (UNFA) and the Association of Former Moudjahidates (female freedom fighters) were, if not directly colluding with the dominant power, at least effectively silenced by the FLN. Lacking any formal structure, women attempted to organize collectively to address issues of common concern. The struggle against the legalization of the Family Code was their main battle for 20 years. In June 1984 the Family Code was adopted, defining women as legal minors. This makes it the most restrictive code in all of North Africa.

The identification of the Algerian nation with the third world also led Algerian women to concern themselves with struggles abroad, such as that centred in Vietnam. More recently, the struggle of the Palestinians, characterized by anti-imperialist and pro-Arab official political discourse, has attracted Algerian women's support. But it was not until July 1989, when political pluralism emerged and independent associations were legalized, that more effective alliances were made possible.

July 1989 brought a tremendous mobilization of civil society. Various political parties, such as the Socialist Forces Federation (FFS, led by Ait Ahmed and representing Berber political demands) and the Islamic Salvation Front (FIS), as well as numerous associations have emerged. Women's consciousness has also dramatically been raised. At least 20 women's organizations were established between 1989 and 1991, although only one was independent of the political parties. When, in January 1992, fundamentalist leaders condemned western feminism and accused Algerian women of 'blind imitation', women succeeded in organizing a demonstration in Algiers that brought hundreds of women together. Such a level of participation was a tremendous success by Algerian standards, for there was no tradition of mass mobilization in the decades after independence. Also, both the low level of female employment and the high rate of illiteracy (according to 1990 data, 56.66 per cent of women could not read and write and only 365,000 were in paid work) are not factors that facilitate organizing. Despite this, women's associations have undertaken numerous actions in recent years to denounce the wall of silence built around aggression against women. One prominent leader of the FIS, Abassi Madani, highlights the fundamentalist response to their activism. In an interview with the Agence France Presse in December 1989, he stated that the 'recent demonstrations of women against violence and intolerance are one of the greatest dangers threatening the destiny of Algeria [for they are] defying the conscience of the people and repudiating national values. These women are the spies of neo-colonialism and the fireguard of cultural aggression.'

These new organizational networks have also facilitated the development of links with the outside world. The forms of these links, however, also illuminate the government's emphasis on 'our common Arab roots'. The relations established with the 'Arab sisters' demonstrated more global feminist concerns. In March 1990 Algerian women participated in the coordination of the North African women's movement, held in Tunis, that protested against the legal murder of women suspected of adultery in Baghdad. During the Gulf conflict in 1991, the 'Arab women's boat for peace' – an attempt to set up an international anti-war force – was welcomed in Algiers by a large female group and an Algerian delegation took part in this action. In July 1992 the banning of the Arab Women Solidarity Association (AWSA) by the Egyptian authorities led Algerian feminists to invite the organization to hold its third international conference in Algiers. Unfortunately, recent political developments have not allowed this invitation to be realized. For several years Algerian women have been living in a terror-ridden atmosphere and witnessing an increasing number of attacks on female students in university dormitories, widows and divorced women. Blind terrorism now targets unveiled women and teenagers in the streets. In January 1992 several women's groups expressed their concern in launching an appeal for 'the defence of women's rights and democracy'. At the time, they sought solidarity from individual women in North Africa (including Egypt), Palestine, Turkey, Syria and Lebanon.

The 130 years of the French presence in Algeria has also influenced women's recent strategies to forge alliances with French feminists as well as Algerian immigrants living in France. The issue of 'mixed' marriages has opened a whole range of common preoccupations for women of both countries, such as custody of children. In Algeria the *sharia* systematically gives custody rights to the father, while in France women are usually awarded custody of their children. In cases of divorce or separation, children of some French mothers and Algerian fathers have been abducted by the men. It has taken more than 10 years of unceasing legal struggles for the 'Mothers of Algiers' to obtain, if not the custody, at least the right to visit their children detained in Algeria. French women are being subjected, through their children, to the same Islamic law that limits Algerian women's rights on the other side of the Mediterranean. The identification of a common oppression has been acknowledged on both sides. A delegation of Algerian women welcomed the 'Mothers of Algiers' during the summer of 1989. This action indicated a growing awareness among Algerian feminists of what they can gain by supporting other women's struggles and transcending the nationalist discourse. The courage of these Algerian women – required to support their bothersome, controversial European guests – must also be understood in the context of the violent racist discourse against Europeans, which is particularly virulent against the French. For their part, the strategies of the European mothers have been careful to avoid any racist attacks against 'the Arabs'. International networks, such as the Women Living Under Muslim Laws, insist precisely on the need for this two-way solidarity.

Several cases of abduction of young migrant women, for the purpose of forced marriages in Algeria, have also been recently resolved by joint efforts. With the help of women's groups based in Algeria, campaigns concerning abduction cases have received effective support from feminist circles in France. Two French-based organizations, the Support Association to Women Victims of Forced Marriages and the Enfants d'ici et d'ailleurs association (concerned with abduction of children) have helped to strengthen these links. More recently, Algerian women's groups concerned with avoiding the drift towards totalitarianism, from which women would be the first to suffer, have started seeking support from European feminist and human rights organizations. Not surprisingly, it is mainly women's groups in France that initiated, in coordination with Algerian democratic women, solidarity campaigns and networks.

Conclusion

The settler experience which marked the country for 130 years modified the internal dynamic of the pre-colonial society. Furthermore, its impact on both France and Algeria did not disappear with independence of the colony in 1962. Privileged political and economic relations exist between the two states and a number of cultural links are the legacy of French colonialism in Algeria. Some of the long-term consequences of the colonial encounter include the immigration phenomenon. More than one million Algerians settled in France. Also notable is the influence of the French media in Algeria. Algerians have access to French television and other media (two major daily newspapers are published in French). An unfortunate legacy of colonialism is the increasing reference to the Algerian youth as 'bilingual illiterates', that is, people who are not able to speak either Arabic or French correctly.

However visible the contemporary repercussions of historical factors, the (often bitter) fruits of the colonization period have not yet been fully absorbed by either Algerians or French. There is a parallel here between the settlers' attempts to deny the Algerians any role in the colonial picture and the modern Algerian state's desire to ignore the impact of both the French and the Jewish communities. Hence, Algerian identity is constructed in opposition to the Other, the denigrated European, the *Roumi*. The instrumental role played by religious specificity in the rise of nationalist claims has structured the post-independence period. Algerian women, for example, have been forbidden to marry non-Muslims since 1967.

Algeria's inability to deal with its settler past finds echoes in France's inability to come to term with its Algerian past. The recent public debate on citizenship in France demonstrates the persuasive difficulty of including 'the Arabs' (born in France in this case) in a notion of citizenship – a fact underlined by the problematic integration of the 'second generation' of immigrants in France. Furthermore, Pied-Noirs as well as *Harkis* refugees were resented as aliens when they reached France in 1962. Some 30 years later, they are still not fully integrated into the French nation. Most Pied-Noirs retain their collective identity, constructed as separate from the 'French from France'. Large annual events, numerous local associations and publications as well as political lobbying bring them together. The position of those *Harkis* who managed to escape from Algeria to France is also significant. Despite obtaining French citizenship, their descendants are still stigmatized, as evidenced in the riots led by second-generation *Harkis* in 1990. Interestingly, the Pied-Noir lobby has been able to make alliances with the first-generation *Harkis* and support the demands of those who, as they see it, remained 'loyal' to France.

As exemplified in this case, the question of definition of identity can either limit or enhance the ability to identify issues of common concern. Algerian and French feminists must not close their eyes to those developments, for these are part of their past, present and future struggles. The latest dramatic political events make compulsory the need to re-examine the past. The present emphasis on the fundamentalist dimension cannot hide the fact that the chaos Algeria is facing today has roots in the rejection of a common history. It seems the current crisis acts as a catalyst and brings back old dichotomies that were not dealt with. Significant examples can be found within the Algerian society itself as well as in the ways some of its components now relate to the outside world. Problematic enough was the fact no room was ever given to the Jewish community as part of national history. But now the public stand taken by some political leaders shows that anti-Semitism is openly on the rise. Similarly, the ethnic dichotomy between Algerians of Arab and Berber descent is increasingly shaping the political agenda. The unique Berber chair, part of the Tizi-Ouzou University, was stopped as early as 1964 (to deny further the liveliness of this culture, the professor in charge was transferred to Algiers and relegated to the ethnological museum!). But the Berbers' reaction cannot be as effectively silenced any longer. The FFS, the party that brings together most of the Berber opposition, organized 'democrats' rallies' or an 'autonomous democratic forum' back in 1990. Finally the recent abductions and murders of foreigners performed by fundamentalist armed groups show the successful attempt made to define all individual Others as potential threats to the whole of Islam. It is not surprising then that French interests and citizens have particularly been a target for such terrorist acts. Furthermore, the numerous Algerian women and men whose assassinations were revindicated by fundamentalist groups were precisely those who did not fit into the narrow fundamentalist definition of what Algerianity should be.

In this context, democrat women try to bring together what is left of civil society. The demonstration called for on March 22, 1994 by several women's organizations aimed at denouncing both the state-sponsored violence and the violence performed by fundamentalist armed groups. While political parties are more and more caught up in contradictory strategies, Algerian women are still showing their ability to go beyond dichotomies.

References

Ageron, Charles-R. (1979) *Histoire de l'Algérie contemporaine*, Vol. 2. Paris: PUF.

Ageron, Charles-R. (1992) 'De quoi était fait le peuplement français d'Algérie?', in *L'Evènement du Jeudi*, 383, 5–11 March: 72–4.

Alloula, Malek (1981) *Le harem colonial*. Genève and Paris: Spatkine.

Amrane, Djamila (1991) *Les femmes algériennes dans la guerre*. Paris: Plon.

Anthias, Floya and Yuval-Davis, Nira (1987) *Women–Nation–State*. Basingstoke: Macmillan.

Bernard, P. and Redon, F. (1923) *Histoire et colonisation, géographie et administration de l'Algérie: manuel à l'usage des écoles primaires*. Alger: A. Jourdan.

Bessis, Sophie and Belhassen, Souhayn (1992) *Femmes du Maghreb: l'enjeu*. Paris: Lattés.

Chaudhuri, Nupur and Strobel, Margaret (eds) (1992) *Western Women and Imperialism: Complicity and Resistance*. Bloomington and Indianapolis: Indiana University Press.

Clancy-Smith, Julia (1992) 'The "passionate nomad" reconsidered: a European woman in l'Algérie française (Isabelle Eberhardt, 1877–1904)', in Nupur Chaudhuri and Margaret Strobel (eds), *Western Women and Imperialism: Complicity and Resistance*. Bloomington and Indianapolis: Indiana University Press. pp. 61–78.

Garanger, Marc (1982) *Femmes algériennes, 1960*. Paris: Contrejour.

Gartrell, Beverley (1984) 'Colonial wives: villains or victims?', in H. Callan and S. Ardener (eds), *The Incorporated Wife*. London: Croom Helm. pp. 165–85.

GRENAMO (Research group on Maghreb and the Middle East) (1990) *Intelligentsias francisées au Maghreb colonial*. Paris: Université de Jussieu VII.

Guernier, Eugène (1950) *La Berbérie, la France et l'Islam*. Paris: Editions de l'Union Française.

Hammerton, James A. (1979) *Emigrant Gentlewomen*. London: Croom Helm.

Hatem, Mervat (1992) 'Through each other's eyes: the impact on the colonial encounter of the images of Egyptian, Levantine-Egyptian and European women, 1862–1920', in Nupur Chaudhuri and Margaret Strobel (eds), *Western Women and Imperialism: Complicity and Resistance*. Bloomington and Indianapolis: Indiana University Press. pp. 37–60.

Hélie, Anissa (1988) *Les institutrices européennes laïques en Algérie, 1974–1979*. M.A. thesis, University of Aix-en-Provence.

Hélie, Anissa (1990) 'Aurélie Picard-Tidjani', *Parcours: l'Algérie, l'histoire et les hommes*, 7 (2): 184–8.

Hélie-Lucas, Marie-Aimée (1988) 'The role of women during the Algerian struggle and after: nationalism as a concept and a practice towards both the power of the army and the militarization of the people', in Eva Isaksson (ed.), *Women and the Military System*. New York and London: St Martin's Press. pp. 186–208.

Kirkwood, Deborah (1984) 'Settler wives in Southern Rhodesia: a case study', in H. Callan and S. Ardener (eds), *The Incorporated Wife*. London: Croom Helm. pp. 143–64.

Lanly, André (1963) *Le Français d'Afrique du Nord*. Algiers.

Marseille, Jacques (1984) *Empire colonial et capitalisme français: Histoire d'un divorce*. Paris: Albin Michel.

Molyneux, Maxine (1985) 'Mobilization without emancipation? Women's interests, the state and revolution in Nicaragua', *Feminist Review*, 11 (2).

M'rabet, Fadela (1965) *La femme algérienne*. Paris: Maspero.

Prochaska, David (1990) *Making Algeria French: Colonialism in Bone, 1870–1920*. Cambridge and Paris: Cambridge University Press and EHESS.

Ramusack, Barbara N. (1992) 'Cultural missionaries, maternal imperialists, feminist allies: British women activists in India, 1865–1945', in Nupur Chaudhuri and Margaret Strobel (eds), *Western Women and Imperialism: Complicity and Resistance*. Bloomington and Indianapolis: Indiana University Press. pp. 119–36.

Woodhull, Winifred (1991) 'Unveiling Algeria', *Genders*, 10: 112–31.

11

Palestine, Israel and the Zionist Settler Project

Nahla Abdo and Nira Yuval-Davis

In every settler society project, the country is perceived by the settlers, at least to some extent, as a 'new world – available not only for immigration, but also for establishing a 'new and better society' (often called by Christian religious refugees in particular the 'New Jerusalem'). In the specific nature of the Zionist project, this 'new society' was perceived at the same time to be a rehabilitation of an old one – the biblical Judaic state – and the 'New Jerusalem' was going to be built in the land of 'Old Jerusalem'. Theodor Herzl, the 'father' of the Zionist movement, wrote a utopian book which was supposed to describe the desired Jewish state to be established. He called it 'Altneuland' – the Old/New country. The Zionist project, however, was primarily nationalist rather than religious and, even before the development of an Israeli Jewish society, proclaimed essential indigenous status for the Jews in Palestine as the 'Land of Israel'.

In hegemonic Zionist vision, history virtually stopped in the 'Land of Israel' since the Jews were exiled 2,000 years ago. In such a vision, the indigenous population could be seen as part not only of the local exotic 'natural' environment – as the populations of other colonial societies were often perceived – but also of the orientalist vision of biblical times (Shohat, 1991). Zionism has constructed the myth of Palestine as sparsely populated: 'land without people for a people without land.' First uttered in 1901 by Israel Zangwill, a Zionist and contemporary of Herzl (Graham-Brown, 1990), this myth became the predominant ideology of the Zionist settler movement by penetrating much of its cultural fabric (Frenkel and Bichler, 1984).

However, between a vision constructed in Europe and the reality developing on the ground, the difference is vast. As this chapter will demonstrate, the Zionist settler project in Palestine, while unique in its structure, objectives and goals, was not less colonialist than other settler projects (Bober, 1972; Rodinson, 1973; Shafir, 1989; Ram, 1993). Palestine was not sparsely populated and the indigenous Palestinians were resentful of Zionist settlement. Since the crumbling of the Ottoman empire in the late nineteenth century, Arab nationalism in the Mashreq and particularly in Greater Syria – which included Palestine,

Lebanon and Syria – was developing. And while the Zionists in Europe were engaged in vision/ideology construction of the 'new-old world', indigenous Palestinians were struggling for their national independence. On their national agenda, especially after the Balfour Declaration of 1917, was the resistance of the very project of Zionist settlement (Abdo-Zubi, 1989; Hourani, 1946; Antonius, 1939; Chaliand, 1972; Cattan, 1967).

The main thrust of the Zionist settlement project for most of its history has been to dispossess and then to exclude the Palestinians whenever possible from control over the various resources of the country and the state. This chapter examines the nature and character of Zionism as it evolved from a minority political movement into a powerful state in the region. It follows the development of the endeavour, looking at the ways three goals of the Zionist settler movement – the conquest of the land (*Kibbush Ha'adamah*) the conquest of labour (*Kibbush Ha'avoda*), and the conquest of the market (*Totzeret Ha'aretz*) – have been pursued before and after the establishment of the state. The impact of the Zionist settler project on the indigenous population of Palestine will be highlighted. We will also examine the constructions of Israeli citizenship as they have incorporated major exclusionary and inclusionary boundaries – certainly among Jews but more so towards the Palestinians. The chapter concludes with an examination of Jewish and Palestinian feminist politics, emphasizing the *Intifada* and the role of Palestinian women in the national resistance movement. As will be made clear throughout the chapter, the analysis of the Zionist settler project cannot be adequate if it does not incorporate the complex articulations and interrelationships of gender, class and ethnic divisions which underlie it.

The Historical Context for the Emergence of Zionism

Palestine was one of the more developed countries in the Middle East. Although most of the population were *Fallaheen* (peasants), with a significant nomad Bedouin population, it also had a large urban population and towards the end of the nineteenth century was engaged in both international trade and export of agricultural products like oranges and olive oil. Since the crumbling of the Ottoman empire (which had ruled the country since 1571) in the late nineteenth century, Arab nationalism in the Mashreq and particularly in Greater Syria – which included Palestine, Jordan, Lebanon and Syria – was developing, and the struggle for national independence by Palestinians was starting (Hitti, 1951). It was into this historical context that the Zionist settlement project – which aimed at solving the 'Jewish question' and which constructed Jewishness in national rather than religious terms – burst and transformed itself, becoming the primary adversary for the Arab, and especially the Palestinian national movements.

Zionism emerged as one of the responses within the European Jewish community to the major crises of economic and political displacement and of growing anti-Semitism and persecutions in Eastern Europe and of the emergence of biological anti-Semitism towards Jews in Western Europe where processes of Jewish assimilation were halted after the arrival of masses of Jews escaping from Eastern Europe (Bober, 1972; Evron, 1988; Yuval-Davis, 1992). The Zionist movement saw itself as the national liberation movement of the Jews all over the world (unlike the Jewish Bund which fought for Jewish national autonomy within the boundaries of Eastern Europe), and sought to establish a Jewish state in the 'Jewish homeland' in order to 'normalize' the Jewish people and thus solve the problem of anti-Semitism. A minority movement until World War II, considered by Bundists and Marxists to be too utopian and divisive to present any realistic strategy to struggle against anti-Semitism (Yuval-Davis, 1987b), it gained wide international support after the war as a way of solving the displacement of European Jews without opening the borders of western countries for mass Jewish immigration (although the majority of world Jewry has always contin-ued to live outside Palestine/Israel). Supporting the Zionist movement as the representative of the Jewish people also solved the guilty con-science of both western governments and western Jewish communities in the countries which escaped Nazi occupation who felt they did not do enough to help the Jews in Europe before and during World War II. In the prevailing orientalist Eurocentric ideology, the devastating impact of such a solution to the 'Jewish problem' on the Palestinians remained largely invisible (Said and Hitchens, 1988). In addition, the US (and in the late 1940s and early 1950s also the USSR) were able via their support of the Zionist movement and the establishment of the state of Israel to get a foothold in the strategically and economically highly important zone of the Middle East which was, until then, under the exclusive control of Britain and France. The initial imperial support to the Zionist movement – the Balfour Declaration of 1917 – was given by the British (who gained control over Palestine after World War I and their victory over the Ottomans in the form of a mandate by the League of Nations), in the belief that a European settler society in Palestine would be a better ally than an Arab one. At the same time, the Palestinians, bitterly frustrated at being let down by the British who promised them during the war, like the other Arabs, support for national independence after the Allied victory, started their century-long resistance to the Zionist project as the main item on their national agenda.

Although the Zionist movement presented itself as representing the

Jewish people all over the world, it was primarily a movement of Western (Ashkenazi) and especially Eastern European Jews, who constituted the majority of the Zionist settlement in Palestine before 1948 and who continued to dominate the state after it was established in spite of the major demographic changes which took place. Mizrahi Jews have come from Middle Eastern and Muslim countries, and are the descendants of the (Sephardi) Jews who were expelled from Spain at the end of the fifteenth century, as well as of much older Jewish communities which have existed in the Arab world, Africa and Asia for thousands of years. Like many other migrant groups which are encouraged to settle in settler societies when more desirable groups of immigrants are not available, Mizrahi Jews, who constitute today with their descendants the majority of Israeli Jewry, were usually considered second best, to be controlled and used for the promotion of the Zionist project, especially as mass Jewish immigration from the US and the USSR – the two largest world Jewish communities – was not seen in the 1950s to be forthcoming.

As Michal Lis has observed (1986), there were occasions on which Mizrahi Jews were actively excluded from participating in the World Zionist Organization (WZO) in the pre-state period. Although as early as 1911 Yemenite Jews were sought by the Zionist movement as suitable Jewish manpower to successfully compete with and replace the Palestinians in the local labour market, it was only after the establishment of the state of Israel that the immigration of the Mizrahi Jewish communities was actively encouraged by Zionist organizers. Any analysis and evaluation of the Zionist settler project has to consider these internal ethnic/class divisions as well as the Jewish/Palestinian dichotomy. Another major division to be considered has been between those who constructed the Jewish (and the projected Palestinian) state as a primarily secular project(s) or as a religious one(s). Last but not least, gender divisions have been important not only in the ways they affected and were affected by the process of settlement, but also in the construction of Israeli citizenship.

The Settlers and the Colony

The history of the Zionist settler project to date can be roughly divided into three major periods. The first is that of the pre-state settlement which culminated in the establishment of the Israeli state in 1948. Although Zionist settlement started towards the end of the nineteenth century under the crumbling Ottoman empire, it received its legitimacy – and its momentum – only after World War I. In 1917 British military rule was established in Palestine, turning the latter – in 1920 – into a British mandate, a euphemism for the international licence of

Britain's colonial control of Palestine. The Balfour Declaration of 1917 came to express the alliance between the Zionist movement and British imperialism, by legalizing Jewish immigration and settlement in Palestine as the 'Jewish Homeland'.

Such an alliance made it possible for the colonial government to change the legal status of land and property in Palestine, allowing large transfers of indigenous land to the European Jewish settlers (Abdo, 1992). It is against this double oppressive force that Palestinians found themselves in primary contradiction. Various popular revolts ensued during the 1920s and 1930s, culminating in the 1936–39 revolution. By the late 1930s and under mounting economic and political pressures from the Palestinians, the British colonial government, in seeking to maintain its administrative costs, had to opt for curbing its Jewish immigration policies. In the process, this resulted in the emergence of conflict of interest between the two colonial movements.

In the aftermath of World War II and as a result of vigorous political campaigning, the United Nations (UN) officially declared the end of the British mandate and the division of Palestine into two states – Arab and Jewish. The UN partition plan gave the Jews – who at the time numbered 660,000 people or just one-third of the total population – more than 55 per cent of the total area of Palestine including the key ports of Haifa and Tel Aviv. It was rejected by other Zionists, who saw it as 'not conducive to the exclusive Jewish state desired by the movement'. (For Ben Gurion's reasons for acceptance, see Graham-Brown, 1990: 13; for the rejection by other Zionists, see Flapan, 1987; Morris, 1987). Between 1947 and 1948, Israel occupied the territories agreed by the UN for the Jewish state and conquered over half of the designated Palestinian state, overcoming the resistance of the indigenous population and the uncoordinated sparse support they received from neighbouring Arab countries. Following this, Israel annexed about half of the territories designated to the Palestinian state, the Jordanians annexed the West Bank, and the Egyptians administered the Gaza Strip. Most of the Palestinians in the territories under Israeli control were forcefully evicted, while others, under the impact of massacres and other Israeli terrorist techniques, fled out of fear. None of these Palestinians, estimated at about 80 per cent of the indigenous population, were able to return to their homes. They became refugees in the surrounding Arab countries and others were dispersed throughout the Arab world and the west. Those who remained came to constitute a small minority, estimated at about 150,000 Palestinians, in the newly established Israeli state.

The second period in Zionist history took place between 1948 and 1967. This was a period of the consolidation of the Israeli national collectivity and the consequent segmentation and dislocation of the

Palestinian national entity. A high degree of political stability was achieved in Israel in spite of the far-reaching demographic changes, as a result of a carefully controlled process of 'absorption' of the mass (mainly Mizrahi Jewish) immigration, military rule and tight control over the remaining Palestinians who had become Israeli citizens. These processes were taking place in an overall context of a society united under the threat – real or imagined – of the enemy 'who wants to drive the Jews into the sea', but which enjoyed a high degree of economic and political support from overseas Jewish communities and western governments. With the decline of British and French influence in the area – especially after the 1956 Suez war in which the two aging empires together with Israel attempted to control the Egyptian Suez canal – and the rise of Arab socialist and Baa'thist regimes in Egypt, Syria and Iraq, Israel became more and more important to the American strategic plans in the Middle East as part of the Cold War *modus vivendi*.

Things changed during the third period of Zionist history, after the 1967 war when Israel came to occupy the rest of Palestine (the West Bank and Gaza Strip) as well as the Syrian Golan Heights and the Egyptian Sinai desert. During the post-1967 period, Israel for the first time ruled directly over large numbers of Palestinians (which constitute about a third of the population under the control of the Israeli government) and exploited their labour power and captive market. This greatly intensified the capitalist development of the Israeli economy as well as upwardly mobilized certain sections of the Israeli Mizrahi Jewish community, and opened the Israeli political system for the first time to the right-wing Likud government. Although they formally started a few years earlier, it was after 1967 that Palestinians in the diaspora organized their own autonomous national organization, the Palestine Liberation Organization (PLO), and conducted a multi-faceted struggle against Israel and the Occupation. The Palestinian struggle first took the form of armed resistance led by Palestinian refugees from neighbouring countries, followed by a combined international diplomatic campaign and a civil resistance campaign in the Occupied Territories.

The changes in the modes of the Palestinian struggle reflect wider changes in the region, especially the growing influence of the US with the demise of Soviet influence in the region on the one hand and the rise of the Islamist movements after the Iranian revolution on the other. These changes have also created the basis of a common interest between Israel and many Arab regimes (especially Egypt which signed the Camp David peace agreement with Israel in 1978), who all vied for American patronage. It is within this new political reality, which intensified in the aftermath of the Gulf War, that peace negotiations started between Israel and the PLO and the Oslo 'Gaza–Jericho first' agreement was signed in September 1993. This agreement could be seen as a first historical step towards a reconciliation between the Zionist settler society and the native population. However, it was reached under American pressure and under conditions extremely unfavourable to the Palestinians, and it is doubtful whether it would become the basis for an enduring settlement under which the most fundamental legitimate rights of the Palestinians (the right to return to their homeland and the right for independent self-determination) are to be fully or adequately addressed and respected. Nevertheless, there is no doubt that it signals the transition to a new chapter in the history of the area.

The Political Economy of the Zionist Settlement

Politics always took precedence over economics in the Zionist settlement project. It was always assumed that funds would be found to finance the political agenda. How long this policy could continue in future depends to a large extent on international developments, especially on the US agenda.

The dynamics of the Zionist political economy can be summed up in the three slogans of Labour Zionism – *Kibbush Ha'adamah* (the conquest of the land), *Kibbush Ha'avoda* (the conquest of labour), and *Totzeret Ha'aretz* (the conquest of the market) (Bober, 1972: 11).

Kibbush Ha'adamah (The Conquest of the Land)

Although at the beginning of the Zionist movement there was a debate over which territory the 'Jewish state' should occupy, very early on the focus was on Palestine, considered the Jewish homeland according to the cultural/religious Jewish tradition, and the only territory which could attract and mobilize the 'Jewish masses', especially the more traditional ones in Eastern Europe (and later on in the Middle East and Africa). However, it was not clear what the boundaries of the 'land of Israel' were, as religiously the boundaries of the Jewish kingdom(s) changed in different periods and God's promise to Abraham in the Bible basically covered the whole of the Middle East. During the pre-state period, the right-wing revisionists aimed at establishing a Jewish state with boundaries which would encompass the territory called Palestine which was given to Britain to rule as a mandate by the League of Nations after World War I, believing that mass Jewish immigration after the establishment of the state would consolidate its existence. The hegemonic Labour Zionist movement, however, believed that long-term success depended upon consolidating settled Jewish majorities in specific areas 'to determine the facts on the ground. They developed a settlement strategy known as 'Tower and Stockade' in which collective forms of settlements were established in border areas, serving as geo-political and strategic outposts for inland cities and settlements (Davis, 1977).

Unlike other settler movements, the Zionist movement was not a formal part of one imperial government. It therefore did not control, until 1948, any of the public lands in Palestine (which were first under Ottoman and then British control). The lands in which Zionist settlements were being established had to be acquired privately, either individually or collectively. However, the Zionist settler movement was not dependent solely on market conditions – namely, privately owned Palestinian lands from big absentee landlords – nor could it have developed without colonial state coercion. Between 1920 and the mid-1930s, the Zionist movement received full support from the British colonial government in Palestine which played a key role in the materialization of the settler project. The most important role has been in the area of land transfer from the indigenous Palestinians to the European (Jewish) settlers. The Palestinian land-tenure system prior to the British rule was structured in a characteristically pre-capitalist form, thus presenting obstacles to land commoditization and transfer. The Ottoman Land Code of 1857 which aimed at parcellizing the land, albeit with a provision against the dispossession of the peasants, was replaced with new British laws which included the Land Transfer Ordinance of 1920 and laws facilitating the dispossession of the indigenous direct producers (Abdo, 1992).

Legal and illegal coercive measures – including taxation, imprisonment and collective punishment – were used in the process of the one-way transfer of lands from Palestinians to the Zionist settlers. The expropriation between 1920 and 1947 of about 26 per cent of Palestine's cultivated land, and the consequent eviction of a large number of direct producers estimated in 1930 at 48 per cent of the total peasant population, was effected to a great extent by the use of political force (Abdo-Zubi, 1989: 132–40). Until the early 1920s, the settlement in Palestine was largely under the control of private European Jewish capitalists (especially Baron Rothschild). After that, control passed to the Jewish Agency (the executive arm of the WZO) and *Keren Kayemet* (the Jewish National Fund of WZO). Land and labour on land controlled by the Jewish National Fund was declared in its constitution as 'inalienable property of the Jewish people' in which 'it shall be deemed to be a matter of principle in that Jewish labour shall be employed' (CID, 1936). The racist exclusionist policies of the Jewish National Fund were articulated in its constitution: land provided to a settler was to be worked 'by himself or with the aid of his family . . ., if and whenever he may be obliged to hire help, he will hire Jewish workmen only'. (ibid.) In fact, the Jewish National Fund went so far as to impose a penalty on any Jewish owner attempting to employ Arab workers or lease them land.

After the establishment of the state of Israel, such policies could be applied much more widely. In 1948, when Israel became a state, it appointed itself the legal guardian of all the private and public land cultivated and possessed by the Palestinian refugees – including thousands of 'Present Absentees' who had not left the territories under Israeli control but were not at their homes during the 1948 crucial census which was carried out in the midst of the war. Most of these lands either were given to veteran *Kibbutzim* and *Moshavim* or were used to settle the majority of Jewish immigrants, especially Mizrahi Jews who arrived in Israel in the early 1950s.

Further expropriations of Palestinian lands continued during the 1950s and 1960s, through a mixture of legal and administrative manipulations (Jiryis, 1976). Economic considerations provided an important incentive for these confiscations. As Don Peretz observed, 'abandoned property was one of the greatest contributions towards making Israel a viable state' (Peretz, 1977: 116). Land confiscations also took place for demographic reasons in order to try and keep a Jewish majority in all areas of the state, especially in the Galilee with its high concentration of surviving Palestinian villages ('Koenig Memorandum', 1976).

The 1967 war and the consequent occupation of vast Arab territories, including the Golan Heights and the heavily populated Palestinian territories of the West Bank and Gaza Strip, have radically shifted the political agenda of land acquisition yet again. First, arguments about the boundaries of the 'Jewish homeland' which had been dormant since 1948 rose again. Religious–Messianic motivation joined right-wing Zionist voices which called for the annexation of the Occupied Territories (especially as most Jewish holy places are in the West Bank), with the hegemonic Labour Zionists being torn between prioritizing strategic Jewish settlement wherever possible and their desire to keep the Israeli society as exclusively Jewish as possible. East Jerusalem (for nationalist religious reasons) and the Golan Heights (for nationalist security reasons) were formally annexed, while the rest of the Occupied Territories became targets of continuous confiscations and settlements, especially in areas of religious and strategic importance. When the right-wing Likud Party took over the government in 1977, Jewish settlement in the Occupied Territories was accelerated. Massive confiscations of land took place and centres of Palestinian population became more and more cut off from each other, surrounded by a network of Jewish settlements. By the early 1990s it was estimated that 60 per cent of the lands in the West Bank and over 55 per cent in the Gaza Strip were confiscated (Al-Haq, 1990; see also *News from Within*, October 2, 1991: 3). While not all these lands have been successfully Judaized (that is, settled), they nonetheless were considered as Jewish property and their indigenous residents were evacuated.

It was not only international pressure which prevented the full annexation of the Occupied Territories, but also demographic considerations (as will be discussed further later). Annexing all the Occupied Territories with their Palestinian inhabitants would have posed a serious threat to the Jewish character of the Israeli state. This in spite of the fact that during 20 years of occupation and despite the high rates of births among Palestinians, by the mid-1980s the population of the Occupied Territories had hardly changed and even declined compared to earlier decades. The reasons noted include Israel's war measures of mass arrests, imprisonments, expulsions and splitting of Palestinian families.

Political divisions concerning the future of the Occupied Territories became even stronger after the Palestinian popular *Intifada* started in 1987. On the one hand, this resistance brought about a revival of Israeli debates from the pre-state period on population 'transfer' (Masalha, 1992) – that is, 'ethnic cleansing' of the Occupied Territories which would enable an annexation of the land without annexation of the population. On the other hand, with the cost of the Occupation increasing politically, economically and socially, it brought into the centre of the Israeli political agenda for the first time the possibility of withdrawal from the Occupied Territories – and especially the Gaza Strip – and conceding them as a basis for a future autonomous, if not independent, Palestinian political entity (Jaffee Centre for Strategic Studies, 1989). The first step in this direction has been taken with the Oslo 'Gaza–Jericho first' agreement.

Kibbush Ha'avoda (The Conquest of Labour)

The call 'to populate or perish' – so prevalent in other settler societies – has been accompanied in the Zionist project with the warning that the survival and prosperity of the Zionist settlement is a precondition for the survival of the Jewish people as a whole. The 'demographic question' therefore has been crucial all through Zionist history and competed with the 'security' question in its importance (Ehrlich, 1980; Yuval-Davis, 1985).

Labour Zionism, however, believed that Zionism should not only guarantee the continued physical existence of the Jewish people, but also 'normalize' and transform it, by creating Jewish industrial and especially agricultural working classes. Therefore, the more Labour Zionism came to control the Zionist settlement project, the more the Palestinians were both dispossessed and excluded from the new Jewish market.

Kimmerling (1983) has claimed that, as a result of the high density of the population in the territory available for Zionist colonization in comparison with other settler society projects, its 'low frontierity', to use his terminology, has created a need for collective appropriation, settlement and defence of the Zionist settlements. Also, the growth of collective forms of settlements, such as *Kibbutzim*, in addition to their other strategic and ideological importance, can be understood in these contexts as the most efficient forms of social organizations to withstand Palestinian cheap labour competition, especially in relation to domestic labour (Ehrlich, 1980; Shafir, 1989). As a result, women were constantly fighting for their right to move beyond the confines of domestic labour into socially valued 'productive labour' (Bernstein, 1987, 1992) and they were systematically discriminated against in access to both employment and immigration certificates. The function of motherhood then was more in terms of creating the *Sabra* (the 'new Jew') 'cleansed' from the Diaspora mentality and organically connected to the Land, than as supplying future answers to human power demands, which was assumed to come by immigration and, as such, left for the mothers of the Jewish Diaspora to supply (Yuval-Davis, 1985).

As with the *Keren Kayemet* which was established as the exclusive Zionist body in control of land appropriated by the European Jewish settlers, the Histadrut (the General Federation of Jewish Labour) was established in 1920 to promote and, where possible, to impose the employment of Jewish labour. The Histadrut took legal and often illegal measures to ensure the exclusive hiring of Jewish settlers in Palestine. There were incidents where Palestinian labourers who were actually employed in private Jewish firms which did not belong to the Histadrut – particularly in agriculture and construction – were often disrupted, beaten and prevented from entering their working place, by what was described as 'armed guards of the *Histadrut*' (Abdo, 1992). In addition, the Zionist principle of exclusive Jewish labour on land appropriated from the Palestinians remained in effect for many years after the establishment of the state of Israel.

The composition of the Jewish labour market itself, however, changed over the years. As World War II approached, more Jewish settlers came to Palestine in order to escape fascism rather than to take part in the establishment of a visionary society. After the establishment of the state, the picture changed even more radically. During the years 1948–56 most of the immigrants came with their families and communities from Middle Eastern countries, usually with no explicit Zionist ideology, except for generalized religious–messianic sentiment about the revival of a Jewish society in its Land. Their immigration was inspired by the dislocation of the Jews in these societies as a result mainly of the growing Israeli–Arab conflict but also of post-colonialism (Hélie, in this volume) and with the active encouragement of Zionist agents (Abitbul et al., 1986). However, gradually the flow of

Jewish immigration drew to a halt and, except for a small flow of ideological immigration from the west after the 1967 war, mass immigration to Israel stopped until the late 1980s and early 1990s when there was the mass arrival of Jews from Ethiopia and especially from the former USSR.

In order to keep to the principle of an exclusively Jewish labour market and society the Palestinians who came under Israeli rule in 1948 were kept segregated by a military rule which remained operative until 1966. Although originally the overwhelming majority of the remaining Palestinians were *Fallaheen*, the continuous land confiscations forced them (especially the young men) to seek other forms of labour and to undergo a process of proletarianization (Rosenfeld, 1964). For a long time the Palestinian workers were prevented from joining the Histadrut, which remained 'purely' Jewish. In the 1960s they came to constitute a small but significant stratum at the bottom of the labour market of the most exploited cheap labourers. However, given their small percentage in terms of the population, this did not significantly affect the Jewish character of the Israeli labour market as a whole. Also, as Shavit (1992) points out, a high proportion of the Israeli Palestinian economic activity continued to be inwardly directed, constituting an 'enclave economy', and did not seriously compete with Jewish labour.

The principle of segregation was also applied to an extent, if less formally so, to Mizrahi Jews. As the history of their settlement shows, Mizrahi Jews in Israel were tightly controlled. Many of them were dispersed beyond the coastal urban population centres and settled in new 'development towns' or in new rural *Moshavim* (often where old Palestinian villages used to exist). Their educational and political institutions were kept apart from those of the *Kibbutzim*, where they were usually employed as hired labourers rather than allowed to join as members (Rayman, 1981). In general, they played crucial roles as the new Israeli working classes during the 1950s and 1960s in the growing Israeli economy, especially in industry and construction (Swirski, 1989).

The principle of exclusively Jewish labour was eroded after 1967 mainly by the incorporation of a cheap Palestinian labour force from the Occupied Territories. To enhance the already emerging proletarianization process of Palestinians in the Occupied Territories, Israel implemented a string of policies, confiscating vast areas, controlling water resources and placing agricultural production under tight supervision, preventing its export and curbing its ability to compete in Israel's produce market (Hilal, 1976). The effect was to deny the inhabitants of the Occupied Territories any prospect of economic self-sufficiency (Samara, 1988). In less than two years the latter were turned into a pool of cheap labour power for the Israeli labour market. This cheap labour was not only migrant in character, but also working under conditions described by prominent Israeli figures as 'worse than working under the South African apartheid system', (Shahak, 1988).

Yet this process of proletarianization and super-exploitation meant an upward mobility for certain sections of the Mizrahi Jews – as well as some Israeli Palestinians – who benefited from employing the cheap Palestinian labour. This mostly took place in the growing private sector of the Israeli economy in the building and agricultural industries which became dependent on Palestinian labour. This meant that when the 1967 borders partially reclosed after the Gulf War, first as a result of the *Intifada* and then as a result of an explicit decision by the Israeli Labour government, these branches of the Israeli economy experienced an acute crisis despite high unemployment among Jews. Thai and other migrant workers were imported to partially fill the gap.

The segmentation of the Israeli labour market runs according to not only ethnic and national lines but also gender lines, in both the civil and, even more so, the military labour market, with women concentrated mainly in the clerical and service jobs (Izraeli, 1992; Yuval-Davis, 1985). However, women cannot be treated as a homogeneous category – their ethnic and national membership tends to place them in differential positioning in the labour market. Ashkenazi (western Jewish) women have tended to participate in the formal labour market more than Mizrahi Jewish women, with the latter working more often as domestic workers and child carers in the homes of the former, as well as having a larger number of children. With the transformation of the Palestinian *Fallaheen* into commuting (migrant) labourers, the women, with the old men and children, often took the responsibility for looking after the little land plots that did remain in the family.

A process of proletarianization of Israeli Palestinian women, however, began to take place in the 1970s as well. Palestinian women began to join the cheap labour force by taking wage employment in the growing food and clothing industries – industries characterized as the extension of domestic work. As for Palestinian women from the Occupied Territories, employment in Israel was discouraged for national and traditional cultural reasons. Employment in the Occupied Territories, in general, was hampered by the absence of infrastructural bases (Rockwell, 1985), while small-scale subcontractual employment proved to be more oppressive and exploitative (Siniora, 1989). The only viable small-scale employment opportunities were those occupied by urban professional women, primarily in the educational and medical fields.

Jewish and Palestinian women have been used in the 'demographic race' between Israel and the Palestinians. However, Israeli demographic and welfare policies were also affected by contradictory pressures of worry about the quantity and 'quality' of the children (especially as poor Mizrahi families and Ultra-Orthodox Ashkenazi families have constituted the majority of families with more than three children). Other factors were anti-abortion pressures from the religious lobby and anxieties over immigration figures (Ehrlich, 1985; Yuval-Davis, 1987a). The mass immigration of Soviet Jews to Israel since the late 1980s, however, has lifted immediate demographic worries in Israel, which were often in the headlines shortly beforehand in relation to the speedily growing Palestinian population, both inside and outside the 1967 Green Line. It also reinforced the rapidly dwindling secular Ashkenazi component in the Israeli population.

However, the economic burden of 'absorbing' the half-million Soviet Jews in Israel has placed some pressures on its outside resources of funding. This, combined with other pressures put on Israel as a result of the growing international critique of its handling of the Palestinian *Intifada* and the more general changes in global and regional relations of powers, has meant that Israel has come under more external pressures. For the first time, for instance, under the Bush administration the Americans tied guaranteed loans to Israel with its political behaviour. In the future this factor might change some Israeli policy priorities.

Totzeret Ha'aretz (The Conquest of the Market)

Under this slogan two complementary goals were pursued in the Zionist movement – first, to 'conquer' the product market in Palestine and, secondly, to eventually achieve economic independence for the settler state. While the first one was largely achieved, the second one still seems very far away.

The first goal was originally pursued concurrently with the struggle for 'Hebrew Labour' in the first period of Zionist settlement, that is, until the establishment of the state. David Hacohen, a prominent Labour leader, described how difficult it was for him to convince other socialists in London that as part of his 'Jewish socialist struggle' he had, among other things, to 'pour kerosene on Arab tomatoes; to attack Jewish housewives in the market and smash the Arab eggs they had bought' (Bober, 1972: 12). With the growth of the settler movement, both in size and in autonomy, under the control of Labour Zionism, the markets of the two national collectivities in Palestine became more and more separated (Horowitz and Lissak 1977; Saa'd, 1985; Gozansky, 1986).

During the period 1948–67 no Palestinian products competed in the Israeli market. The marketing of Israeli Palestinian agricultural products, when not consumed internally by the community itself, was usually controlled by Jewish agents, mostly from the public sector (such as *Tnuva* & Agresco). Also after 1967, unlike the labour market which was flooded by cheap Palestinian labour power, the Israeli market remained virtually 'free' from Palestinian products from the Occupied Territories. This was partly due to Israel's Labour Party Moshe Dayan's policy of 'Open Bridges' between the West Bank and Jordan, which ensured the continued export of the mainly agricultural products of the West Bank to the Arab world. It was also partly due to Israel's agricultural policies which prohibited the Occupied Territories from producing goods which would compete with the Israeli market (Ryan, 1974; Hilal, 1976). Israel controlled the exports of products from the Occupied Territories to the rest of the world until the late 1980s, when it was forced by the European Community to allow autonomous marketing – one of the more significant diplomatic achievements of the Palestinian resistance movement.

Unlike Palestinian products, goods imported from the rest of the world, especially the west, have come to occupy a very important place in the Israeli market, especially since the end of the 'austerity' period in the early 1950s. As Kleiman (1989) points out, imports exceeded exports in the Israeli market by about 20–25 per cent since the 1950s, in spite of the fact that during this period Israeli exports grew 60 times in real value. The Zionist policy of importing goods from outside – even if such goods were produced more cheaply by the Palestinians – was widely practised during the Zionist settler project in Palestine (Abdo-Zubi, 1989; Gozansky, 1986).

Both the extraordinary growth in Israeli production and the fact that the country could continue to sustain such a heavily imbalanced economy with an increasing standard of living need explanation. Partly, high-growth periods are related to periods of high immigration (or alternatively the incorporation of the Occupied Territories into the Israeli market). Partly, however, it relates to the unique features of Israel as a settler state which had depended not on a single empire but on committed international or more precisely American and European Jewish capital as well as on the dominant empires with increasing alliance and later full dependency on the US empire. As Professor Israel Shahak once commented in a conversation, 'no other state in the world, except the Vatican, is so dependent on outside contributions.' National crises and wars in the history of Israel not only involved more expenditure, but also generated further income, and never occupied, at least until recently, primary concern in Israeli strategy. Israel's heavy dependence on US capital has, despite the state's internal economic problems, enabled it to build a highly sophisticated arms industry and to wage consecutive wars of expansion with relative ease.

Before the establishment of the state, financial, like human, resources were transferred one way from the WZO to the *Yishuv* (The Jewish Settler Society in Palestine pre-1948). During 1949–65, the deficit of (US)$6 billion in the Israeli economy was financed mostly by world Jewry (via the United Jewish Appeal of the WZO) and by the reparation monies paid by the German government to the Israeli government as the representative of the Jewish people. The rest came through long-term capital transfers in the form of bonds, loans and capital investments, largely from the US (Bober, 1972: 94–5).

Gradually, however, the situation has changed, and the economic deficit has come to be financed more and more by loans rather than contributions. This is due both to the demographic and political changes in world Jewry and to the sheer volume of monies required to keep the highly sophisticated Israeli military systems going (Ehrlich, 1987). The interest payments alone for these loans have come to swallow about a third of the added value exports (Kleinman, 1989: 340). Perhaps even more importantly, most of the loans come from the US. Since 1985 the value of direct American aid has been as high as that of the whole of the Israeli economic deficit. This has created an unprecedented dependency of Israel on another state, which had probably not existed in Zionist history since the time of the British mandate. (The other side of the coin is that Israel receives American aid which is much higher than any other country in the world.)

This dependency, as we noted earlier, made it possible for the US to exercise its power and to influence some changes at the political level. But such changes, as the Oslo agreement shows, remain in line with US interests in the region as well as Israel's regional position. Given the American recession as well as the collapse of the Cold War, the primacy of the ideological/political in relation to the economic in Israeli policies is for the first time in doubt. It is quite clear that one of the major reasons for the Oslo agreement is to open the whole of the Middle East as a market to the Israeli economy. It also seems that the contemplated 'economic recovery' of the autonomous Palestinian areas is to occur mainly through the exploitation of the local cheap labour under continuing Israeli domination (if not actual occupation).

State and Citizenship in Israel

It is clear from the Israeli Declaration of Independence that the country was never meant to be a political expression of its civil society, of the people who reside in its territory, or even of all its citizens. It was never meant to be a democracy, but – to use Yoav Peled's terminology (1992) – an ethnorepublic, the state of the Jewish people, wherever they are. This special relationship expresses itself in many different ways – cultural/symbolic, legal and administrative. Its most radical legal expression, however, has been the Israeli Law of Return, according to which all Jews, wherever they come from, are entitled automatically to Israeli citizenship.

It has been argued that this special relationship should not affect adversely the equality before the law of Israel's non-Jewish citizens, because this 'Return' right is primordial and predated the establishment of the state (Peled, 1992: 435). This is, of course, pure semantics, and the Palestinians under the control of the Israeli government, including those who are its citizens, are excluded from full Israeli citizenship (especially if we use Marshall's commonly accepted definition of citizenship (1950) which includes civil, political and social rights). Until 1966 Palestinians were placed under military rule; villages lived in total isolation from each other, segregated from the Jewish population as well as from the rest of the Arab population outside Israel. Confined to their underdeveloped villages, the inhabitants needed special permits from local military commanders to leave them, whether to seek employment or to visit relatives.

In addition to their racial/national segregation, Israeli Palestinians were prohibited from joining Israel's organized labour force, the Histadrut, until 1964. A systematic attempt to eradicate their national identity had begun. Socially and economically suppressed, the Palestinians' very geophysical culture was altered as 444 Palestinian villages were erased from the map between 1945 and 1976 and replaced with Jewish settlements (Nijm and Mouammar, 1984). Almost all new Jewish settlements built on the ruins of Palestinian villages carried a Hebrewized version of the Arabic name of the village. Thus Beisan was turned into Beit Shean, Saffourieh into Zipori, and so on. Similar things happened in the Arab–Israeli school curricula, which were virtually stripped of all Palestinian content (Peres et al., 1970).

Even when the cruder measures of discrimination were abolished in the 1960s, discrimination towards the Israeli Palestinians persisted. Israel's concern with the Jewishness of its citizens resurfaced again in the late 1970s, when the state realized that its immigration policies and encouragement of Jewish births could not offset the high rates of natural increase among its Palestinian citizens. Estimated at 40.7 per thousand against a natural increase of 16.8 annually among the Jewish population (Zureik, 1979: 113), this rate sent alarm signals to Israeli officials. This was indicated in the well-known confidential report written in 1976 and sent to the Israeli Ministry of the Interior, called the 'Koenig Memorandum' (1976). Koenig, the District Commissioner for the Galilee, made policy recommendations which aimed at making Palestinian life unbearable through the intensification of economic discrimination against the Arabs in order to deprive them of social and economic security. One decade after this report, a similar document, known as the 'Markowitz Commission Report' (1986), was published. The latter focuses on the 'illegal' housing construction by Palestinian citizens of the state and the need to curb their demographic growth.

Social divisions in Israel, however, are not limited to the basic divisions between Jews and Palestinians. Different segments of the Israeli population have differential access to the state according to their nationality, ethnicity, religiosity and gender, in ways which are more or less politically contentious (Horowitz and Lissak, 1990).

Although Israel is defined as the Jewish state, the category of 'Jewishness' itself is contentious. The relationship in Jewish history between religion and nationality has been a subject for public debate since the establishment of the state and has not been fully resolved today (Yuval-Davis, 1987a; Libman, 1990; Elazar, 1991).

Zionism has been partly a movement which aimed at reconstructing Jewishness into a nationality and presented itself as a modern alternative to religious Jewishness. However, it could not detach itself completely as it required the religious legitimation both on the claim on the land and as representing the whole of the Jewish people. This is why (in addition to more *ad hoc* government coalition calculations) there has always been a partial incorporation of Jewish religious legislation into Israel's state legislation. A central aspect of this incorporation has been the criteria for membership in the Jewish national collectivity which would entitle a person to automatic Israeli citizenship. According to the Israeli nationality law, a Jew is anybody 'who is born to a Jewish mother or has been converted to Judaism'.

The only version of Judaism which has been legitimized in the Israeli state, however, is Orthodox Judaism. Therefore the Jewish children of those who married and especially divorced, in civil, reform and conservative Jewish courts, and even more so, those who converted to Judaism through them, might not be recognized as Jews in Israel.

This has been an ongoing issue between American Jewry – even those loyal to Israel – and the Israeli state for many years. It received a new twist with the mass immigration of Soviet and Ethiopian Jews to Israel in the last few years. However, given the strong political interest Israel and the US have had in directing Soviet Jews to Israel and given the European (white) character of this immigration, no strict policy has been taken with the many who were suspected not to be 'properly' Jewish. But this was not accepted easily, as indicated in an Israeli newspaper report that the Israeli army refused to bury an Israeli soldier in a rabbinical ceremony among his Jewish comrades in view of suspicion about his Soviet non-Jewish origin (*Kull-al-Arab*, July 22 1993). The treatment of Ethiopian Jews, who have their own version of Judaism, has been generally much harsher; families were separated and only those recognized as 'Jews' were taken to Israel, the others being left stranded in Addis Abeba. Moreover, in Israel, due to this construction of nationality, religious conversion is used in cases when in other states simple acts of naturalization would have been sufficient. As a result, Ethiopian Jews have been forced to undergo acts of symbolic re-circumcision in order to be recognized as 'legitimate' Jews by the Israeli Rabbinate.

The partial non-separation of religion and the state in Israel has also had far-reaching implications for women's citizenship (Aloni, 1976; Yuval-Davis, 1980; Buber-Agasi, 1982). In 1975, International Women's Year, the Israeli Prime Minister established a committee for the examination of the position of women in Israel. Its 241 recommendations encompassed a variety of areas in women's lives, from work to education to political participation. Of these recommendations 170 were not implemented even partially. The one area in which not even one recommendation was accepted was 'the family'. Cultural and religious traditions have joined the social reality of a continuous warfare society in Israel – after the first period of 'pioneering' settlement – as a highly familial society. The committee did not even try to recommend changes of policy in relation to Israeli personal laws, where civil law does not apply and each religious community has a monopoly on its members in terms of marriage and divorce. In the Jewish case, there is a monopoly of Orthodox religious legislation, according to which women are excluded from judging, giving evidence and claiming equal rights to men. Muslim and Christian Palestinian women were equally excluded from all decision-making circles concerning their family or personal status.

After a long struggle during the pre-state period and fierce opposition of the Ultra-Orthodox (Azaryahu, 1977), Israeli women were allowed the right to vote, although their rate of participation is very low in Ultra-Orthodox settlements. Although Golda Meir was a woman prime minister, she had been prevented earlier from becoming the Mayor of Tel-Aviv, because according to Jewish religious law, women are not supposed to be superior to men. A prime minister was defined, for political expediency, as only 'first among equals'. At the present time 10 out of the 120 members of the Israeli Parliament are women. The great majority are middle-class Ashkenazi women and are members of centre and left parties. Mizrahi Jewish women have been virtually absent, and there has never been a Palestinian woman member of the Israeli Parliament.

Mizrahi Jewish representation in the Israeli parliament has shot up dramatically, after many years in which Mizrahi Jews achieved political leadership almost exclusively in local government. One of the main reasons for the rise of the Likud Party to government in 1977 – after continuous control by the Labour Party since the 1930s – has been the aspirations of the Mizrahi Jews to get away from Labour patronage. Although the leadership of the party remained Ashkenazi (with the notable exception of David Levy), about half of its national executive is Mizrahi, while an independent religious Mizrahi Jewish party has arisen as well. In order to regain government control the Labour Party had to follow.

Mizrahi Jewish sense of grievances in Israel has been nurtured not only on grounds of economic and political disadvantage, but also on feeling excluded from the cultural construction of Israeli Jewishness. Mizrahi Jews were revolting against the underrating and suppression of their culture which had been part of their 'absorption' process, whereby modernization was equated with westernization and Jewish nostalgia was focused on the East European mythical past. Things have changed to a great extent during the 1980s with the relative rise to power of Mizrahi Jews, but this process was partly enmeshed with the power struggle of the religious sector to substitute secular Zionist ethos with traditional religious values and the legitimate basis for social and political action in Israel. (On the position of the Israeli Mizrahi Jews see, for example, Smooha, 1978; Ben-Refael, 1982; Shitrit, 1986; Swirski, 1989; Shiran, 1992).

When Ben-Gurion was the Prime Minister of Israel in the 1950s, he expressed the hope that one day the Israeli army would have a Yemenite chief of staff. This sentiment illustrates not only the high priority he gave to the integration of the Mizrahi Jews (among which the Yemenites were considered 'the nicest') in the Israeli national collectivity, but also the central place the Israeli army plays in such integration. The Israeli army is the most important integrative instrument of the Israeli society, as probably befits a permanent warfare society. It is not incidental that at present both the Prime Minister and the President of Israel are retired generals. The army is where most Israeli Jewish males spend at least one month a year until they are 50 and where divisions of class, ethnicity and religious background are least felt. Women are recruited into the army, but mostly only for the first two years of national service and are excluded from the army when they get married and/or pregnant. They are therefore excluded to a large extent from the direct male-bonding process of 'the nation' (although they are incorporated in the process via the strong familial structure of Israeli society). More Mizrahi Jews are excluded from the army than Ashkenazis, which is not only due to the traditional religiosity of many of their women, but also because of low educational levels and other social considerations (Yuval-Davis, 1985).

Most of the Palestinian citizens of the state (except for members of Palestinian minorities such as Druze and Bedouins, many of whom are forced into service, though some volunteer) are excluded altogether from the Israeli army. They are considered unfit on a collective rather than individual basis. 'Not having relatives who have served in the Israeli army' has become a euphemism used in state bureaucratic discourse to exclude Israeli Palestinians from a whole range of welfare benefits – from more than minimal child allowances to housing, student grants, loans and so on. Although Palestinians were permitted to vote, for many years they were not allowed to form their own independent parties (Jyris, 1972). The exclusion of Palestinian citizens, as noted earlier, was almost comprehensive as Palestinians were and remain the focal point in the major contradictions in the Zionist/Israeli settler colonial project.

Despite their exclusion and marginalization, Palestinian citizens have since the 1950s been engaged in different forms of resistance. In the late 1950s the al-Ard (the Land) movement – a national movement advocating the rights of Palestinians to form their own national party on their land – was disbanded, and the leaders of the movement were jailed for long periods of time. In 1967, and while the Israeli state was involved in 'secret' plans to solve the 'demographic cancer' of the Palestinians in the Galilee (as was revealed in the 'Koenig Memorandum') Palestinian masses took to the streets in almost every Arab town and village to protest against their land confiscation and political suppression. Despite the harsh response of the state (tanks were sent in and six people, including three women, were killed), the Day of the Land has become a national celebration and a form of protest since 1967. Palestinians were able to stop the implementation of the 'Koenig Memorandum', but they failed to regain already confiscated lands or other tracks of land the state assumed control over. In the early 1980s they began to form independent political parties and to participate in the Israeli Parliament.

If the Palestinian citizens have at least some civil and political rights as Israeli citizens, the Palestinians in the Occupied Territories have none (Aruri, 1984). They have no rights to vote, no rights of political organization, no rights to unionize, no rights of free movement or to welfare benefits. About one in four men in the Occupied Territories has spent at least some time in prison, people have been tortured, maimed, killed and exiled, lands confiscated and houses destroyed. Resistance to the Occupation has intensified with the years and the Israeli authorities have lost all political legitimacy in ruling the Occupied Territories. The growing frustration with the delay in reaching a peace agreement which would guarantee the Palestinians some form of an autonomous state, combined with the economic destruction of the Occupied Territories and the social breakdown, has furnished the grounds for the rise of the Islamic movement Hamas. Unlike the PLO, Hamas, at least rhetorically, refuses any contact or dealing with the Israeli state. Socially however, Hamas presents a major obstacle to the Palestinian women's movement.

Today, after the signing of the 'agreement in principle' between Israel and the PLO, one cannot but notice the extent to which the Israeli leadership were worried about the spread of Muslim fundamentalism in the region. In their speeches in New York, both to the American public and more so to the Zionist and Jewish lobby and organizations, Prime Minister Rabin and Foreign Minister Peres, have emphasized the importance of signing a deal with the PLO since according to them, this organization is the only force which can check and perhaps stop the spread of Islam, at least in the Occupied Territories. Whether the PLO can cancel out Hamas as a powerful force in the Occupied Territories remains to be seen. However, there is no doubt that the presence of a Palestinian independent or semi-independent political body – no matter how partial and insufficient it is – can provide an alternative leadership and can introduce changes at the infrastructural and institutional levels, which can replace if not cancel out much of the mass influence of Hamas, particularly in the Gaza Strip. However, it seems that, even in a leadership composed of the PLO, women seem to be largely excluded from the new formal polity (Giacaman, 1994). On the other hand, the establishment of even a semi-autonomous Palestinian political entity might provide a legitimate basis for the exclusion of the Palestinians, even those who are presently citizens of Israel, from all membership in the Israeli national collectivity (in the way in which this agreement is already starting to be used for that purpose in Jordan).

Feminist Politics

Given the historical and political reality in Israel/Palestine, it is not surprising that feminist politics on both sides have been crucially affected by the Israeli/Palestinian conflict. During the pre-state period Palestinian women took active part in the general national struggle. Since the early twentieth century Palestinian women's activism has largely been centred around social/family and national issues, aimed at the preservation of a nation undergoing a process of segmentation and threat to its very national existence. Although under the pre-state Zionist settler movement peasant women were, directly and indirectly, engaged in the armed struggle, urban-educated and elite women undertook a public formal channel by waging protests, writing petitions and memoranda to British officials, and internally organizing different charitable bodies (Abdo-Zubi, 1987; Abdo, 1991).

Although women were for a long time a minority among the Zionist settlers, they fulfilled crucial roles in the settlement in carrying out the necessary domestic tasks, by bearing and rearing the 'New Jews', and by acting as 'honorary men', working in the productive labour and the military aspects of the settlement project. In spite of these roles, however, sexual divisions of labour have never been abolished (Bernstein, 1988; Hazleton, 1978).

A basic tension which has existed all along in women's politics has been between tendencies, on the one hand, to totally subsume women's struggles into the 'general national interests' and, on the other, to express the subjective and collective frustrations of women about their positioning both in the family and in the national struggle. The greatest rebellion of Zionist women during the time of the settlement, however, took place when their right to vote was threatened for the sake of 'national unity' with the Ultra-Orthodox (Azaryahu, 1977; Fogiel-Bijaoui, 1992). In general, however, women's politics on both sides followed the national politics (Izraeli, 1992).

A debate which has taken place in Israel following the rise of second-wave feminism in the 1970s has been between those who were organizing around what they saw as purely 'women's issues', such as abortion and domestic violence, and those who (rightly) insisted that such 'women's issues' need to be contextualized within the specific Israeli reality – that, for instance, anti-abortion campaigns have been affected not only by religious attitudes which the Israeli state has incorporated into its policies, but also by the demographic race with the Palestinians as well as collective memories of the Holocaust (Yuval-Davis, 1987a).

The feminist organizations which appeared in Israel in the 1970s were often initiated by women who had been exposed to feminist ideologies and organizations abroad. Feminist ideas have gradually, however, also started to affect more traditional women's circles. Nevertheless, one should not overestimate their influence on the lives of Israeli women in general. Traditional, sometimes religious, family values and the continuous shadow of war in a militarized society have contributed to a hegemonic value system in which women are perceived as strong and active, but whose ultimate goals and life fulfilment is the family, mothering children and catering to their men's needs (Hecht and Yuval-Davis, 1978; Hazleton 1978; Swirski and Safir, 1991). It was only after the 1982 Israeli invasion of Lebanon (which led to the emergence of a small yet vocal peace movement in Israel) and especially after the 1987 Palestinian *Intifada* that more Israeli Jewish women began to form new women's networks. These included Women in Black and Reshet, and they demanded a halt to all forms of oppression, including Israel's withdrawal from the Occupied Territories and the establishment of an independent Palestinian state. Naomi Khazan (1991) has argued that, among other reasons, women have tended to be so active in the peace movement as a result of the limited opportunities open to women in the formal political processes in Israel, as well as the fact that the *Intifada* called for empathy with Palestinian women whose own home front became the battle front to them and to their children.

Most of the women active in the Israeli Jewish feminist movement are middle-class and highly educated Ashkenazi women. While their numbers have been small, they have contributed to the acceptability of this type of political activism. One of the reasons for the failure of the European (Ashkenazi) Jewish women's movement to grow as a powerful force in Israel has been its inability to cross the lines of class and ethnicity which separate them from the majority Mizrahi Jews. As Vicky Shiran has pointed out:

> The Ashkenazi feminists (and white feminists of the west) who have not stood up against their own ethnic group and class and joined the fight against its dominance, are not natural allies in the collective struggle of women from lower ethnic classes, as they do not oppose the existing social order as a whole, but only one dimension of it. (1991: 308)

In the last few years there have been also several attempts by autonomous organizations of Mizrahi Jewish women which have been influenced by black feminist politics. On their agenda has been the struggle against Zionism as an Ashkenazi endeavour rather than an all-Jewish endeavour as it usually presents itself and for Mizrahi feminist struggles to incorporate struggles against the social injustice for all Israeli citizens, including Mizrahi Jews and Palestinian Arabs. It is significant that very recently the Israeli feminist congress has given separate representation to Ashkenazi, Mizrahi and Palestinian feminists.

It is a measure of the complexity of the situation, however, that while Mizrahi feminists are very keen to cooperate with Palestinian feminists, as the two 'underdogs' of Ashkenazi Zionism, the Palestinian feminists have been more wary. For them, internal contradictions among Israeli Jews pale in significance in comparison with the major contradiction between the occupier and the occupied, and they primarily want the Jewish feminists to express solidarity with their anti-occupation and national liberation struggle. Such solidarity, one may add, has been developing. Albeit on a very small scale, left-wing, mainly Ashkenazi, feminist groups like Women in Black – many of whom adhere to non-, if not anti-Zionist politics – have been able to make alliances with Palestinian feminists, in Israel as well as abroad (Khazan, 1991; Abdo, 1993b).

The feminist agenda within the Palestinian women's movement has been, until the *Intifada*, largely subsumed under the larger national agenda of an independent Palestinian state. In the early 1970s the General Union of Palestinian Women emerged as an arm of the PLO.

With Lebanon (which absorbed a very large number of Palestinian refugees) as its base, the organization opened chapters in every Palestinian concentration, both in Arab countries and in the west. Similar activities were present in the Occupied Territories until the early 1980s with the emergence of the *Utor* (grass-roots women's political organizations). Four major *Utor* emerged representing the four major political organizations within the PLO. The *Utor* have differentiated themselves from previous 'traditional' women's organizations by their ability to reach rural areas, refugee camps and other remote places. They established chapters in various rural and refugee centres, launched literacy campaigns, provided some day-care centres and conducted awareness courses and discussions on issues concerning women's health, education and general political national rights.

Yet, it was after the *Intifada* and the massive politicization process it engendered among Palestinian women that the leadership of the *Utor* – themselves middle-class and highly educated urban women – began to realize the extent to which their active womanism had been subsumed to the general male-led national agenda. Since 1990 major debates have erupted within the Palestinian women's movement.

One issue, or rather contradiction, which the Palestinian women's movement – represented in the work of the *Utor* – is currently debating is the relationship between the leadership and the masses. Because of the dependent relationship between the *Utor* and the respective (often conflicting) political factions within the PLO, the *Utor* could not develop a healthy working relationship among themselves, resulting consequently in the fragmentation of the women's movement. Attempts at developing one feminist agenda are currently being undertaken by the various *Utor*. The establishment of the Palestinian Women's Task Force in 1992 under the auspices of the United Nations Development Programme is seen as a potential unifying force for the women's movement (Abdo, 1993a).

Moreover, despite attempts at reaching the rural and refugee areas, the leadership of the *Utor* and almost all decisions remained largely under the control of a small elite residing in the urban centres and not in direct touch with the refugee camps and rural areas. Although in the first two to three years of the *Intifada* these class, urban and rural divisions were subsumed under the heat of the *Intifada* and the strength of national resistance, this could not last much longer (Hamami, 1990). By 1991–92, after the Gulf War, the harsh Israeli clamp-down on the Palestinians, and the US attack on the PLO for siding with the Iraqis, conditions in the Occupied Territories began to deteriorate dramatically. With no political solution in sight, the *Intifada* in general suffered a major setback, and pressure was placed on the leadership of the *Utor* to change their mode of operation.

This question is even more important when taking into consideration the other major debate within the Palestinian women's movement
which concerns the question of what the *Utor* have done to promote
the cause of women's liberation aside from general mobilization
towards the state/nation liberation. A number of national conferences
have been organized to deal with these issues. For example, in 1990 the
Women's Studies Committee at Beisan Centre in Ramalla organized a
national conference with the aim of putting forward strategies to deal
with pressing social/gender issues, such as the imposed veiling of
women, school dropouts among females, early marriages and forms of
domestic violence (Abdo, 1993a).

Generally dissatisfied with the way the *Utor* have been working,
some Palestinian women activists among the middle-class educated
stratum announced their independence from the political *Utor* and
organized themselves as separate non-governmental organizations.
They established women's research centres and began to conduct more
feminist-oriented work. Three such centres have been established in
the West Bank and one in Gaza city. Feminist politics in all these centres is clear from the type of research, training and awareness courses
they conduct. Issues such as domestic violence, polygamy, divorce,
early marriage, inheritance and labour conditions of waged women
have occupied a central place in their activities (Abdo, 1993c).

Israeli Palestinian women have also organized autonomously – in an
organization called Al Fanar (the Lighthouse) – and started to be
active in feminist issues, such as violence and the killing of women on
the grounds of 'family honour' perpetuated by both traditionalists and
new fundamentalists. However, political activism in Israel around these
issues has to be contextualized in the general political reality, as Manar
Hasan has pointed out

> Israeli oppression, accompanied by cultural arrogance and the attempt to
> erase Palestinian national identity, is a permanent factor both within Israel's
> 1948 borders and in the territories which were occupied in 1967. It is impor-
> tant to point out that this oppression is also accompanied by a consistently
> positive attitude towards the traditional patriarchal leadership and towards
> patriarchal social values, and even allows the traditional leaders to
> autonomously enforce traditional practices on their communities, at least in
> the spheres of religion and family law. (1992: 2)

Conclusion

Gender politics and gender relations, like all other political and social
relations in Israel/Palestine, have to be understood as both having
affected and affecting the complex historical dynamics of the Zionist
settler project and the resistance to it.

Unlike other settler projects, the Zionist project was not the outpost of one specific empire and has always had its own autonomous political agenda. This does not mean, however, that it has not benefited, like other settler societies, from a privileged position in its relations with the west, and its dependence on outside resources for survival has probably been greater than that of most settler societies.

This factor and the relatively highly developed nature of the native Palestinian society contribute to the vulnerability of the Zionist settler project. However, the history of the Jews as pariah people (Arendt, 1978), especially in the west, and the collective memories of persecutions and extermination have helped to sever the relationships between the Jews who settled in Palestine, particularly before the 1950s, and their countries of origin and to entrench them in their country of settlement. Moreover, these factors have also helped in the construction of Israel as a 'post-factum homeland' for many Diaspora Jews, even those who have never been to Israel nor have any relatives there. These processes and the old/new place of Palestine as the Land of Israel in Jewish mythology have contributed to the nation-building process of the Israeli people which started to take place during the early part of the twentieth century, and have transformed them into being constructed – by themselves and by many others – as an 'indigenous people'.

In addition, in spite of the very unequal access of different segments of the population to the Israeli state, the very different national, religious and ethnic backgrounds of many of the Jews who are Israeli citizens and in spite of the racist prejudice which many Ashkenazi Jews have been exhibiting towards Mizrahi Jews, the construction of all Jews as being members of the same 'nation' has managed to speed up considerably the process of the transformation of Israeli Jews (as differentiated but also as part of the Jewish people as a whole) into one Andersonian 'Imagined Community' (Anderson, 1983). This is affecting even very recent and very unideological immigrations such as the Ethiopian and Soviet Jews. The Israeli–Arab conflict and the associated fear – at least until the 1980s – that in the case of Arab victory 'the Jews will be thrown into the sea' have played, of course, a major part in this process. However, since the Lebanon war in 1982, if not before, this myth of 'we have no other alternative' started to erode. This created a growing confusion and lack of legitimacy to the Israeli policies in the Occupied Territories at least among some sections of the Jewish population, especially the Ashkenazi middle classes. There are signs that the complexity of the situation and its dynamics have had the effect of weakening collective national bonds, with people withdrawing their primary loyalties more and more from 'the people' into their families and primary relationships (Kimmerling, 1993). On the other hand, among the Palestinians, the *Intifada* has served to promote the nation-building process, and national identities have become relatively more important than before in relation to local and kinship identities (although not necessarily religious identities, especially Muslim). Although among both Israeli Jews and Palestinians there exist major ideological and political forces which deny any legitimate national rights for the other collectivity, during the last 20 years contesting ideologies which assume that any future stable and quasi-just solution to the Palestinian–Israeli conflict would involve a two-state solution have become much stronger.

The Oslo agreement has signalled the beginning of another chapter in the history of the region, although it is much too premature to speculate what would be the effects of this agreement on the future of the Zionist settler project in Palestine in general and on feminist politics in the different communities in particular. The agreement, which was reached in secret and which was cheered by American, Israeli and PLO officials, has major opponents. It is opposed by the Israeli hardline Likud Party and violently resisted by the settlers in the Occupied Territories. Most importantly, since the agreement does not address the Palestinians as a nation and excludes almost 50 per cent – if not more – of the Palestinians who are refugees and descendants of refugees since 1948, Palestinian doubts about it are, at this stage, insurmountable.

If one is to judge from the early signs of where most funding, energies and primary projects and concerns are focused by the PLO leadership, Israel and the international 'funding' community, the emphasis appears to be on building an infrastructural base to accommodate the very basic needs of survival for the masses of refugees and poor in the Gaza Strip, with probably the absorption in the future of no more than 500,000 refugees – the last are basically residents of the West Bank and Gaza who were expelled or left the Territories during the Occupation. Palestinian concern in the immediate and perhaps medium-range future will also be concentrated on establishing some form of stable political regime, amidst current political factionalism within the PLO itself. No objective conditions at present or in the foreseen future suggest or even indicate that the agenda of Palestinian women's liberation can assume a primary concern in the larger PLO nationalist agenda. Recent discussions (Abdo, 1993c) – after the signing of the agreement – with Palestinian women activists from different *Utor* and women's studies centres reveal the extent to which feminists are alarmed and worried about what the future holds for them. Alongside this worry, however, there is also the determination to escalate their feminist activities and elevate their struggle to the state or official level.

References

Abdo, Nahla (1991) 'Women of the Intifada: gender, class and national liberation', *Race and Class*, 32 (4): 19–34.

Abdo, Nahla (1992) 'Racism, Zionism and the Palestinian working class', *Studies in Political Economy*, 37 (Spring): 59–93.

Abdo, Nahla (1993a) 'Middle East politics through feminist lenses: dialoguing the terms of solidarity', *Alternatives*, 18 (1): 29–41.

Abdo, Nahla (1993b) 'Race, gender and politics: the struggle of Arab women in Canada', in Linda Carty (ed.), *And Still We Rise*. Toronto: Women's Press. pp. 71–98.

Abdo, Nahla (1993c) Unpublished report based on research conducted in the West Bank and Gaza Strip during June–August 1993. Research was updated through direct contact and interviews with Palestinian women after the signature of the Oslo agreement.

Abdo-Zubi, Nahla (1987) *Family, Women and Social Change in the Middle East: the Palestinian Case*. Toronto: Canadian Scholars' Press.

Abdo-Zubi, Nahla (1989) 'Colonial capitalism and rural class formation: an analysis of the processes of social, economic and political transformation in Palestine, 1920–1947'. PhD dissertation, University of Toronto.

Abitbul, M., Bar-Asher, S., Barnai, Y. and Tuby, Y. (1986) *The History of the Jews in Islamic Countries*. Jerusalem: Zalman Shazar Centre. (Hebrew.)

Al-Haq (1990) *A Nation Under Siege*. Annual Report on Human Rights in the Occupied Territory. Ramallah, the West Bank.

Aloni, Shulamith (1976) *Women as Humans*. Tel-Aviv: Mabat Publications. (Hebrew.)

Amin, Samir (1976) *The Arab Nation*. London: Zed Books.

Anderson, Benedict (1983) *Imagined Communities*. London: Verso.

Antonius, George (1939) *The Arab Awakening: The Story of the Arab National Movement*. Philadelphia: Lippincott.

Aran, Gideon, (1985) 'The beginning of the road from religious Zionism to Zionist religion', *Studies in Contemporary Jewry*, 2: 402–28.

Arendt, Hannah (1978) *The Jews as Pariah*. New York: Grove Press.

Aruri, Naseer (ed.) (1984) *Occupation: Israel over Palestine*. London: Zed Books.

Azaryahu, Sarah (1977) *The Association of Hebrew Women for Equal Rights in the Land of Israel*. Haifa: Keren Leezrat Haisha. (Hebrew.)

Ben-Refael, Eliezer (1982) *The Emergence of Ethnicity: Cultural Groups and Social Conflict in Israel*. Westport: Greenwood Press.

Bernstein, Debra (1987) *A Woman in the Land of Israel*. Tel-Aviv: Hotzaat Hapoalim. (Hebrew.)

Bernstein, Debra (ed.) (1992) *Pioneers and Homemakers: Jewish Women in Pre-State Israel*. Albany: State University of New York Press.

Bober, Arie (ed. for Matzpen) (1972) *The Other Israel: the Radical Case against Zionism*. New York: Doubleday.

Buber-Agasi, Judith (1982) 'The position of women in Israel', in Ariela Friedman, Ruth Shrift and Dafna Izraeli (eds), *The Double Bind: Women in Israel*. Tel-Aviv: Hakibutz Hameukhad. pp. 210–29. (Hebrew.)

Cattan, Henry (1967) *The Dimensions of the Palestinian Problem*. Beirut: Institute for Palestine Studies.

Chaliand, Gerard (1972) *The Palestinian Resistance*. Harmondsworth: Penguin Books.

CID (1936) No. 2/36 in P0371/200018E-1293.

Davis, Uri (1977) *Israel: Utopia Incorporated*. London: Zed Press.

Ehrlich, Avishai (1985) 'Zionism, demography and women's work', *Khamsin*, no. 7.

Ehrlich, Avishai (1987) 'Israel: conflict, war and social change', in Colin Creighton and Martin Shaw (eds), *The Sociology of War and Peace*. London: Macmillan.

Elazar, Daniel (ed.) (1991) *A People and a Community: the Jewish Political Tradition and Its Contemporary Implications*. Jerusalem: Reuven Mass. (Hebrew.)

Evron, Boaz (1988) *A National Reckoning*. Tel-Aviv: Dvir. (Hebrew.)

Flapan, Simha (1987) *The Birth of Israel: Myths and Realities*. New York: Pantheon Books.

Fogiel-Bijaoui, Sylvie (1992) 'On the way to equality? The struggle for women's suffrage in the Jewish Yishuv, 1917–1926', in D. Bernstein (ed.), *Pioneers and Homemakers: Jewish Women in Pre-State Israel*. Albany: State University of New York Press. pp. 261–82.

Frenkel, Shlomo and Bichler, Shimshon (1984) *The Desperate: the Money Aristocracy in Israel*. Tel-Aviv: Kadima. (Hebrew.)

Giacaman, Rita (1994) As reported in the *Times Union*, May 8.

Gozansky, Tamar (1986) *The Development of Capitalism in Palestine*. Haifa. (Hebrew.)

Graham-Brown, Sarah (1990) *The Palestinian Situation*. Geneva: World Alliance of Young Men's Christian Associations.

Hamami, Rima (1990) 'Women, the Hijab and the Intifadah', *Middle East Report*, nos 164–5 (May–August): 24–8.

Hasan, Manar (1992) 'The fundamentalism in our land', paper, Italian, Israeli and Palestinian Women Conference, Bologna, Italy, September.

Hazleton, Lesley (1978) *Israeli Women: the Reality Beyond the Myth*. Jerusalem: Idanim Publications. (Hebrew.)

Hecht, Dina and Yuval-Davis, Nira (1978) 'Ideology without revolution: Jewish women in Israel', *Khamsin*, no. 6: 87–118.

Hilal, Jamil (1976) 'Class transformation in the West Bank and Gaza', *MERIP Reports*, no. 53.

Hitti, Philip K. (1951) *History of Syria, including Lebanon and Palestine*. New York: Macmillan.

Horowitz, Dan and Lissak, Moshe (1977) *From the Settlement to the State*. Tel-Aviv: Am Oved. (Hebrew.)

Horowitz, Dan and Lissak, Moshe (1990) *Trouble in Utopia: the Overburdened Polity of Israel*. Tel-Aviv: Am Oved. (Hebrew.)

Hourani, Albert (1946) *Syria and Lebanon: a Political Essay*. London.

Izraeli, Dafna (1992) 'The Women Workers' Movement: First Wave Feminism in Pre-State Israel', in D. Bernstein (ed.), *Pioneers and Homemakers: Jewish Women in Pre-State Israel*. Albany: State University of New York Press. pp. 183–210.

Jaffee Centre for Strategic Studies (1989) *The West Bank and Gaza: Israel's Options for Peace*, Report of a JCSS Study Group, Tel-Aviv: Jaffee Centre for Strategic Studies.

Jiryis, Sabri (1972) *Democratic Freedoms in Israel*. Beirut: Institute for Palestine Studies.

Jiryis, Sabri (1976) *The Arabs in Israel*. New York: Monthly Review Press.

Khazan, Naomi (1991) 'Israeli women and peace activism', in Barbara Swirski and Marylin Safir (eds), *Calling the Equality Bluff: Women in Israel*. New York: Pergamon Press. pp. 152–63.

Kimmerling, Baruch (1983) *Zionism and Territory*. Berkeley: University of California Press.

Kimmerling, Baruch (1993) 'Yes, back to the family', in *Politika*, March 1993: 40–51. (Hebrew.)

Kleinman, Ephraim (1989) 'Economic problems of yesterday and tomorrow', in Shmuel

Stempler (ed.), *People and State: Israeli Society*. Tel-Aviv: Ministry of Defence Press. pp. 337–47. (Hebrew.)

'Koenig Memorandum' (1976), translated from *Al-Hamishmar*, in *SWASIA*, 3/41, October 15.

Libman, Charles (ed.) (1990) *Religious and Secular: Conflict and Accommodation between Jews in Israel*. Jerusalem: Keter. (Hebrew.)

Lis, Michal (1986) 'From Morocco to the Land of Israel: the immigrations before the establishment of the state, 1830–1948', in Shimon Shitrit (ed.), *Studies on North African Jewry*. Tel-Aviv: Am Oved. pp. 110–23. (Hebrew.)

'Markowitz Commission Report' (1986) This report was considered secret, but was leaked to the press at a later time. Tamar Kohns, who gathered the report, is in the process of publishing it.

Masalha, Nur (1992) *Expulsion of the Palestinians*. Washington: Institute for Palestine Studies.

Morris, Benny (1987) *The Birth of the Palestinian Refugee Problem*. Cambridge: Cambridge University Press.

News from Within (1991) Alternative Information Centre, Jerusalem, October 2.

Nijm, Bashir and Mouammar, Bishara (1984) *Toward the De-Arabization of Palestine/Israel, 1945–77*. Dubuque: Kendall-Hunt Publishing.

Peled, Yoav (1992) 'Ethnic democracy and the legal construction of citizenship: Arab citizens of the Jewish state', *American Political Science Review*, 86 (2): 432–42.

Peres, Y., Ehrlich, A. and Yuval-Davis, N. (1970) 'National education for the Arab youth in Israel: a comparative analysis of curricula', *The Jewish Journal of Sociology*, 12 (2).

Peretz, Don (1977) 'Social structure of the Palestinian people', *Journal of Palestine Studies*, 8 (1).

Ram, Uri (1993) 'The colonization perspective in Israeli sociology: internal and external comparisons', *Journal of Historical Sociology*, 6 (3): 327–50.

Rayman, Paula (1981) *The Kibbutz Community and the Nation Building*. Princeton: Princeton University Press.

Rockwell, Susan (1985), 'Palestinian women workers in the Israeli-occupied Gaza Strip', *Journal of Palestine Studies*, 14 (2): 114–36.

Rodinson, Maxime (1973) *Israel: a Colonial-Settler State?* New York: Monad

Rosenfeld, Henry (1964) *They were Peasants*. Tel-Aviv: Hotzaat Hakibutz Hameukhad. (Hebrew.)

Ryan, Sheila (1974) 'The Israeli economic policy in the occupied areas: foundations of a new imperialism', *MERIP Reports*, no. 24.

Sa'ad, Ahmad (1985) *Economic Development in Palestine*. Haifa: Al-Ittihad. (Arabic.)

Said, Edward and Hitchins, Christopher (eds) (1988) *Blaming the Victims*. London: Verso.

Samara, Adel (1988) *The Political Economy of the West Bank, 1967–1987*. London: Khamsin.

Shafir, Gershon (1989) *Land, Labour and the Origins of the Israeli Palestinian Conflict, 1882–1914*. Cambridge: Cambridge University Press.

Shahak, Israel (1988) 'Israel, apartheid and the Intifada', *Race and Class*, 30 (1): 1–12.

Shavit, Yossi (1992) 'Arabs in the Israeli economy: a study of the enclave hypothesis', *Israel Social Science Research*, 7 (1–2): 45–66.

Shiran, Vicky (1991) 'Feminist identity vs. oriental identity', in B. Swirski and M.P. Safir (eds), *Calling the Equality Bluff: Women in Israel*. New York: Pergamon Press, pp. 303–11.

Shitrit, Shimon (ed.) (1986) *Anthology: Studies on North African Jewry*. Tel-Aviv: Am Oved. (Hebrew.)

Shohat, Ella (1991) 'Making the silences speak in the Israeli cinema', in B. Swirski and M.P. Safir (eds), *Calling the Equality Bluff: Women in Israel*. New York: Pergamon Press. pp. 31–40.

Siniora, Randa (1989) 'Palestinian labour in a dependent economy: women workers in the West Bank clothing industry', *Cairo Papers in Social Sciences*, 12 (3).

Smooha, Sami (1978) *Israel: Pluralism and Conflict*. London: Routledge & Kegan Paul.

Swirski, Barbara and Safir, Marylin (eds) (1991) *Calling the Equality Bluff: Women in Israel*. New York: Pergamon Press.

Swirski, Shlomo (1989) *Israel: the Oriental Majority*. London: Zed Books. (Originally published in Hebrew, 1981.)

Yuval-Davis, Nira (1980) 'The bearers of the collective: women and religious legislation in Israel', *Feminist Review*, 4: 15–27.

Yuval-Davis, Nira (1985) 'Front and rear: sexual divisions of labour in the Israeli army', *Feminist Studies*, 11 (3): 649–76

Yuval-Davis, Nira (1987a) 'The Jewish collectivity and national reproduction in Israel', *Khamsin*, special issue 'Women in the Middle East', London: Zed Books, pp. 60–93.

Yuval-Davis, Nira (1987b) 'Marxism and Jewish nationalism', *History Workshop Journal*, no. 24: 82–110.

Yuval-Davis, Nira (1992) 'Zionism, Anti-Zionism and the construction of contemporary "Jewishness"', *Review of Middle East Studies*, no. 5: 84–109.

Zureik, Elia (1979) T*he Palestinians in Israel: a Study in Internal Colonization*. London: Routledge & Kegan Paul.

Index